Artillery of the Napoleonic Wars

THE NAPOLEONIC LIBRARY

Other books in the series include:

FROM CORUNNA TO WATERLOO
The Letters and Journals of Two Napoleonic Hussars
1801–1816
Edited by Gareth Glover

ON THE FIELDS OF GLORY
The Battlefields of the 1815 Campaign
Andrew Uffindell and Michael Corum

LIFE IN NAPOLEON'S ARMY
The Memoirs of Captain Elzéar Blaze
Introduction by Philip Haythornthwaite

THE MEMOIRS OF BARON VON MÜFFLING
A Prussian Officer in the Napoleonic Wars
Baron von Müffling

WATERLOO LECTURES
A Study of the Campaign of 1815
Colonel Charles Chesney

WATERLOO LETTERS
A Collection of Accounts From Survivors
of the Campaign of 1815
Edited by Major-General H. T. Siborne

www.frontline-books.com/napoleoniclibrary

ARTILLERY OF THE NAPOLEONIC WARS

FIELD ARTILLERY, 1792–1815

Kevin F. Kiley

FRONTLINE BOOKS

Artillery of the Napoleonic Wars: Field Artillery, 1792–1815

A Greenhill Book

First published in 2004 by Greenhill Books, Lionel Leventhal Limited
www.greenhillbooks.com

This edition published in 2015 by

Frontline Books
an imprint of Pen & Sword Books Ltd,
47 Church Street, Barnsley, S. Yorkshire, S70 2AS
For more information on our books, please visit
www.frontline-books.com, email info@frontline-books.com
or write to us at the above address.

ISBN: 978-1-84832-843-3

CIP data records for this title are available from the British Library

Printed and bound by CPI Group (UK) Ltd, Croydon, CR0 4YY

To my wife and partner Daisy,
who has been "that battery's *vivandière* and real boss,"
and to my son Michael, named for a fallen warrior and true hero,
and who, hopefully, will be the first of the family in many
generations who won't have to follow the road to the rumbling
guns—though there are worse roads to follow.

This is for the two of them, and for all of our absent
comrades-in-arms who have gone across the river.

We sleep safe in our beds because rough men stand ready
in the night to visit violence on those who would do us harm.
—George Orwell

"Virtute et Valore"

Contents

Illustrations

Tables

Acknowledgements

A project, such as a book, on a wide subject, such as artillery from a certain period in history, is impossible to undertake alone. The information is myriad, the sources are widely dispersed and in many languages, and there is too much knowledge for one person to either possess or remember. Additionally, every single relevant subject cannot be covered in a book of this size; but I hope that this attempt will cover at least the major points.

There are also many people to thank for their generous help and selfless giving of time, effort, and expertise. First and foremost, my humble thanks to Lionel Leventhal of Greenhill Books, who graciously allowed me the opportunity to write this first book. Next, I thank my editors, Jonathan North, David Palmer, and Kate Baker: Jonathan approved and nurtured the project, kept me in line and focused, and provided both material and moral support when needed; David provided impetus and had the ability to "crack the whip" when my enthusiasm lagged; and Kate saw the book into print, was very supportive, and was patient with my shortcomings. Without these three this book would never have gone beyond the planning stage. Many and enduring thanks go to Digby Smith, who came up with the idea for the book, and who encouraged me to suggest it as a viable project.

Next, the following friends contributed mightily to the project with material that otherwise would have been ignored: George Nafziger, Don Graves (authority on the War of 1812), Scott Bowden, Steven Smith, Dominique Contant, Greg Gorsuch, Dave Sullivan (of The Company of Military Historians), Alexander Zhmodikov, Yves Martin, Keith Rocco, Tom Holmberg, Bob Burnham (of The Napoleon Series), and Geert van Uythoven. These gentlemen and scholars graciously loaned me many books, pamphlets, regulations, and pictures that were invaluable in the compilation of information and in tying up the many loose ends and solving dead ends that were continuously popping up. Other friends who gave valuable material assistance were Jonathan Cooper, Robert Ouvrard, Robert Mosher, and Mark Urban.

I thank also the many friends and colleagues on three Napoleonic Forums on the ubiquitous Internet, where information flows freely: there are many scholars and knowledgeable historians, much more versed in the history of period than I, especially Max Sewell, Tony Broughton, Alex Stavropolous, James O'Halloran, Howie Muir, Robert Goetz, Donald Brown, Susan Howard, Katherine Luchini, Jan Kowalik, Matt Pavone, Robert Henry, and Marc Moerman. I am also grateful to the staff of Helion Books in Great Britain, who searched and found two volumes that were essential to the completion of this book.

I thank the Marines and sailors of Battery F, 2nd Battalion 12th Marines, whom I had the honor and privilege to command. They were a superb unit, the best I ever saw, continuing in the long and rich tradition of American artillery. There is no greater honor in life than to be a battery commander and a commander of Marines, and I had the privilege to be both twice in my life. I thank all the Marines of the 10th Marine Regiment, past, present, and future, with whom I had the honor to be assigned twice, and with whom I served in combat. The "Death Angels" taught the opposition how to shoot.

I thank Colonel David W. Haughey USMC, Retired, Colonel Mark Davis USMC, Retired, and Lieutenant Colonel Tom King USMC, Retired, who had such a profound influence on me as an artilleryman. They taught me how to become one, and how to command Marines; they also taught me the profession of arms. Many, many thanks: these gentlemen are the essence of what Marine artillery is.

Finally, I give thanks for my family: for my father, Captain Francis M. Kiley, USNR, a veteran of the US Navy in two world wars, a veteran sea dog and "Captain Courageous," who heard the owl and saw the elephant and was a great father; for my mother, Eileen Findley Kiley, who first set me on the course of military history by giving me my first set of toy soldiers and continually encouraging me in my writing; for my eldest brother, Captain Michael J. Kiley USA, USMA Class of 1964, killed in action in the Republic of Vietnam in 1967 while leading his airborne rifle company against the enemy, and who taught me tactics, wargamed with me on the floor battlefields of childhood, taught me his love of our *alma mater*, the United States Military Academy at West Point, and introduced me to the Napoleonic epic with that excellent book, *A Military History and Atlas of the Napoleonic Wars*; for my older brother, Colonel John P. Kiley USMC, Retired, combat Marine and decorated veteran of two wars, who convinced me to become a Marine—one of the best decisions of my life; for my dearest wife and lifelong partner, Daisy, who has stayed the course through good times and bad, through deployments, war, and family moves, and has given excellent advice from time to time to keep me on course—she is the steadying force in my life and all my endeavors; and for my son, Michael John William Kiley, who is the blood of my heart.

Last, and certainly not least, I thank Colonel John R. Elting, and his lovely wife and partner, Ann. Colonel Elting was a dear friend and mentor for over ten years, a military historian and authority on the Grande Armée, a combat veteran and an artilleryman, a gentleman and a scholar, who was the closest thing to a father I had for over thirty years. He taught me how to be critical, how to evaluate source material, how to ask questions, and how not to overwrite. He was the best teacher I ever had. You're greatly missed, old friend, and we'll meet again and talk around the bivouac fire in a far better place. Be thou at peace.

This book was, in the apt words of Napier, "damned hard to write." All of the mistakes in it—and there are undoubtedly more than a few—are mine alone. I quote Clausewitz's words of 1818, "My ambition was to write a book that would not be forgotten in two or three years, and which anyone interested in the subject would certainly take up more than once."

Kevin F. Kiley
Jacksonville, North Carolina
2004

Author's note

The data contained in the tables presented in the text were drawn from a number of sources, including Adye's *Bombardier and Pocket Gunner*, Tousard's *The American Artillerist's Companion*, Smola's *Handbuch für Offizieren*, and Fave's *The Emperor Napoleon's New System of Field Artillery*.

K.F.K.

Points of Interest

- Artillery has a language all its own, developed from the time of the first soldiers who manned a crew-served missile weapon, the "traditional brotherhood of Stone Hurlers, Archers, catapulteers, Rocketeers, and gunners."[1] Generally speaking, the terms used in this volume are in English as they are used today; terms and definitions of the period, however, are in that vernacular. Russian and German artillery terms, when relevant, have been translated. French artillery terms have sometimes retained the original language, to be more colorful. Interestingly, many French artillery terms, such as "sabot," are the same in English.
- Napoleon Bonaparte, French artilleryman and general officer; First Consul and later Emperor of the French has been termed "Napoleon" throughout the text. Properly, though, he is either Napoleon Bonaparte, General Bonaparte, or just Bonaparte, until December 1804, when he was crowned Emperor of the French by his own hand in Notre Dame Cathedral in Paris. Subsequent to that event, he was known simply as Napoleon, or to his soldiers as "*l'Empereur.*"
- French company-sized artillery units have been termed "companies," as they were in the Grande Armée. British equivalents have either been termed "brigades" for foot artillery or "troops" for horse artillery, unless the general term "battery" is used, which was in use at the time in the British Army. Russian, Prussian, and Austrian equivalent units have been termed "batteries," as that was the common nomenclature for them at the time. The United States Army used the term "company" instead of battery during the period.
- Throughout the text, guns have been referred to as "the piece" for single guns and howitzers, and "pieces" for multiple weapons. It is a recurring term in the manuals in English of the period and is still accurate today. The term "gun tube" has been used when referring to the tube by itself, without the carriage, or when mounted on the carriage when the reference is merely to the gun tube itself.
- Finally, in the use of quotations throughout the text and in the appendices, period spelling and capitalization has sometimes been changed to a more modern equivalent for ease of reading and understanding. The old penchant for long sentences broken up by a semicolons instead of using periods has been retained.

NOTE

1. From the induction ceremony for the Order of St Barbara as awarded by the United States Army and Marine Corps, usually, but not always, celebrated on or near St Barbara's feast day on 4 December each year.

Today, across our Fathers' graves,
   The astonished years reveal
The remnant of that desperate host
   Which cleansed our East with steel.

Hail and Farewell! We greet you here,
   With tears that none will scorn-
O Keepers of the House of old,
   Or ever we were born

One service more we dare to ask-
   Pray for us, heroes, pray,
That when Fate lays on us our task
   We do not shame the Day!

                   —Rudyard Kipling, *The Veterans*

The Ravine

It is with artillery that war is made.
　　　　　　　　　　—Napoleon

God fights on the side with the best artillery.
　　　　　　　　　　—Napoleon

2000, 13 October 1806: The Landgrafenberg, Saxony

The long, winding artillery column of guns and ammunition caissons that was the corps artillery of Lannes' V Corps was stuck in a ravine. Having mistaken it for the road leading up to the plateau of the Landgrafenberg, the officers leading the column had turned up this ravine, and now the lead gun was hopelessly stuck between two large rocks, blocking the rest of the column. With no room to turn around, the disgusted officers had left the column in charge of the senior *maréchal des logis* and had gone off in search of supper. If the Emperor found out about this one, the NCOs fumed, there was going to be hell to pay, and that bill would be paid by *messieurs les officiers*.

Being veterans, the NCOs relaxed and lighted their pipes—you rested when you could and there was no time like the present. Being in the ravine and on the friendly side of the Landgrafenburg, there was no way the *sacrés* Prussians would see the dim lights of the pipes in the fading light and gathering darkness. Tired artillery train drivers slid from their exhausted mounts to get a few minutes' rest. Some just relaxed in the saddle, falling asleep on their mounts, as their horses gently nuzzled the ground searching for clumps of grass on the floor of the ravine. Veteran drivers, however, dismounted to feed and water their mounts, and to clean out dusty eyes and nostrils with wet cloths, as well as check their harness and their horses' feet. They would tend to the conscripts later.

Tired, dusty cannoneers promptly fell out to either side of the ravine, taking solace in a piece of issue biscuit or carefully hoarded *eau de vie*. Most, exhausted by this latest of the patented Grande Armée's fast-moving concentrations and horse-killing forced marches, promptly fell asleep, oblivious to those who roamed the column, endlessly inspecting.

Conscientious gun captains and chiefs of sections moved quietly and efficiently along the column, carefully checking guns, trace chains, ammunition ready boxes, horse harnesses for signs of wear, and the batteries' caissons and field forges. Generally, they left the exhausted gunners alone. Every once in a while, however, one was kicked awake or dragged violently upwards by a pack or giberne strap as their equipment—or, worse, their horses—had not been tended to properly. In the gathering darkness the only sounds heard in the ravine were the snores of the sleeping gunners, the coughs and grunts of the resting horses, and the ubiquitous creak of harness leather. The occasional spark from a shod hoof striking the scattered rocks on the floor of the ravine being the only light, aside from the occasional match being struck to light a pipe, men slept and moved in shadow, oblivious to what went on above them.

A lounging, veteran *sergent-major*, leaning against the earthen wall of the ravine and absent-mindedly puffing on his pipe, was suddenly shaken out of his reverie by a bright, shining lantern light on the lip of the ravine above him. Turning violently, the oath starting to break from his lips, the furious NCO was ready to take the offending man's head off, when, not believing what he was seeing, his mouth fell open, his pipe fell to the ground and he silently mouthed, "*Mon Dieu, l'Empereur!*"

The shock of the discovery of Napoleon, standing above them, jaw locked and lips tight in furious anger, surveying the listless artillerymen, went up and down the column like an electric shock. Lounging NCOs suddenly came to life, kicking sleeping gunners awake, pointing to the lip of the ravine. Slack-jawed gunners, veteran and conscript alike, flung themselves instantly to work, some tripping over themselves in their haste to get away from those all-seeing, all-knowing, flashing grey eyes, getting to their posts as their Emperor watched them in silent fury. Sleeping train drivers were knocked awake on their horses, some of them falling off in a clutter of equipment in their surprise and shock. The senior *sergent-major* reported to his Emperor, the Old Sweat standing rigidly at attention, shaking in his fury at *messieurs les officiers*, who by now had found their supper. He sincerely hoped they choked on it.

Furiously angry, but controlling his volcanic temper by his iron will, the Emperor asked a few short, pertinent questions. Receiving short, truthful, and equally blunt answers in return, the Emperor, accompanied by the lantern-wielding *aide-de-camp*, smiling ruefully at the situation, made his way past guns, caissons, and horse teams to the head of the column to inspect the jammed piece. Taking the lantern from the general, Napoleon made a quick, expert survey of the situation and issued a few brief orders, and the gunners, led by the now alert NCOs, followed the Emperor's commonsense instructions and quickly freed the gun blocking the ravine and the column. With a smile of satisfaction, the Emperor turned to the *sergent-major*, his momentary fury long gone, tugged his ear, patted him on the back, and told him to get the column moving and to rejoin his command. He also told him not to worry and that he would deal with *messieurs les officiers* himself.

Orders were shouted, drivers and NCOs mounted up, gunners of the horse artillery company also mounted, and the long column of guns and vehicles lurched forward up the ravine. As each gun and vehicle passed Napoleon and his *aide-de-camp*, the NCO-in-charge briskly saluted. Napoleon, now pleased and satisfied with the work completed efficiently, returned the salute with a swish of his riding crop. It was good once again to be a captain of artillery. Life was so much simpler.

The V Corps artillery again on its way, Napoleon and his companion turned back to their mounts, and the deadly business awaiting them on the Landgrafenberg.

PART I

Beginnings

Artillery, like the other arms, must be
collected in mass if one wishes to attain a decisive result.
—Napoleon

Napoleon was a born gunner. He used [his cannon] with a calm, sure skill, improving his
techniques from campaign to campaign. As expert a lot of artillerists as ever rode together under the
same banner grew up under him. There was Marmont, the imaginative, energetic young would-be
aristocrat, who laid the guns that helped win Castiglione and Marengo but listened too much to his
own ego and to Talleyrand. Another was awkward, honest Druout, son of a baker, the admired and
utterly trusted "sage of the Grande Armee," who studied his Bible every day and often disapproved of his
Emperor's actions but was always faithful. Eble, son of a sergeant, a soldier when he was nine, taciturn
and brusque, called his cannoneers "my children" and knocked them kicking when they misbehaved. He
built the Berezina bridges out of a will colder than the river's ice, saved the Grande Armée, and died
thereby. Lauriston, born in India of a Scots refugee family, a polished gentleman and the artillery
expert among Napoleon's aides-de-camp, commanded the great batteries at Landshut and Wagram.
And there was Senarmont, the mauvais tête whose swiftly served guns ate up the Russian
Imperial Guard and Spanish guerrillas alike.
—John Elting

Their patron was Saint Barbara—she who professed her Christian faith to her pagan father and was murdered for it. Her father was then supposedly struck down with a thunderbolt from heaven as a sign of Divine displeasure. Adopted by long-ago gunners as a protection from premature detonation and death, she is still revered by their lineage.

Down the many long roads to the muttering guns, following the tattered and stained banners of their captains, great or not, cursing, sweating gunners pulled, pushed, and carried their artillery pieces on campaign and served them faithfully in battle. Bronze or iron, muzzle-loading and heavy, named for a fight, a woman, or a favorite song, the pieces were tended by dedicated artillerymen through victory or defeat, defended by them with rammer and handspike as well as double-shotted canister, fending off enemy horsemen and infantry alike, engaging in counterbattery fire if need be. The guns were their standards: losing them to an enemy was a disgrace, and the *bouches à feu* (mouths of fire) had a personality all their own, and were treated as comrades in action.

Starting as a learned, secretive guild, civilian specialists and not soldiers, many times executed when captured, and suspected of working in the "black arts," artillerymen gradually developed their profession into another combat arm, becoming militarized along the way. Smaller than the infantry and cavalry, generally not a deciding factor in battle and never decisive, and many times bridesmaids but never brides, artillerymen expertly handled their guns on every field. Generals and commanders learned through hard experience to mass their cannon in their supporting mission, and most of these captains courageous wanted lighter, more accurate guns with which to fight. But they were long in coming.

Monarchs with a flair for invention, and who also commanded armies in the field, developed better guns and ammunition, but it was not until the mid-eighteenth century that artillery finally started to come into its own as a combat arm. Names of artillerymen, famous and not, are sprinkled down through the development and employment of their guns and their deadly art. Lennart Tortenson, the young Swedish artilleryman fought for the Lion of the North. Gustavus Adolphus, and his expertly served and emplaced guns, shattered the deep Imperial formations on fields far from home. William Phillips led his artillery at Minden in a wild *chevauchée* that was a preview of things to come, and lived by the later French dictum of the horse artillery— "get up close and shoot fast." Henry Knox, onetime Boston bookseller and artillery enthusiast, who became George Washington's chief of artillery and the father of the American artillery arm and was noted by Washington on the field of Monmouth in 1778, founded an arm that coveted the battle honor "No artillery was better served."

However, it was not until a certain Corsican artilleryman with a flair for leadership and winning battles realized the potential of light, hard-hitting artillery that artilleryman were given a free hand, building them into a battle-winning arm whose organization and skill was the best of its day. Frenchmen, Austrians, Prussians and Germans of all states, Russians, Britons, and Americans all built and trained their respective artillery arms so that all were efficient at their trade, and were present on all battlefields of the French Revolutionary and Napoleonic wars. The names of the famous and skilled artillerymen of the period represent an unprecedented mustering of gunners, and their names elicit a drumroll of victories and famous fights the like of which the world had not seen before and has not seen since. The Frenchmen Eble, Senarmont, Drouot, Lariboisière, Songis, Ruty, and Marmont; Britons such as Frazer, Dickson, Ramsay, Ross, and Mercer; the Austrian Smola; the Russians Kutusaiv and Arakcheev; the Prussian von Holtzendorf; and theorists and inventors such as Gribeauval, Lichtenstein, Congreve, and Shrapnel—all of these men, some well-remembered and some unfortunately not, all contributed to their countries' employment of artillery when horse-drawn artillery came of age.

The élan and dash of the horse artilleryman, the plodding solidarity of the foot artilleryman, and the stoic courage of troops of the artillery train, who had to stand calmly under fire, maintaining their mounts under control, without the necessary relief of being able to shoot back at the enemies, all contributed mightily to the success of their respective armies. The crash and thunder of massed batteries firing in anger and spewing iron-shod death permeate the history of the Napoleonic period—desperately served guns being manhandled forward to support clouds of skirmishers; galloping horse artillery batteries straining to keep up with the cavalry they are supporting; gunners fighting with rammers and handspikes in their battery positions against seemingly endless swarming horsemen; large, massed batteries galloping forward under a French artillery general to blow out the center, literally, of their enemy's line. For the first time in military history there are artillery generals who command artillery organizations at the corps and army level, and who command artillery units larger than a single company or battery. No longer emplaced and seldom mobile after the first shot has been fired, they take their just place on the battlefield, mobile dealers of death and destruction, the operational equals of their infantry and cavalry brethren. For the first time in history there are artillery battles, as well as masses of mobile hard-hitting guns that decide the fate of kings and kingdoms.

The personalities of the arm also made their presence felt, be they the artillery chief of an army, or a battery commander, or a corps artillery chief. The brilliant Austrian artillery lieutenant Josef Smola, supporting his defending infantry against a French onslaught at Neerwinden in 1793, took his reinforced cavalry battery to within slingshot range of the French to help hammer out a famous victory. He lost so many of his gunners in the action that officers of the Sztarray Regiment joined in to help serve the guns. The one-legged French Captain Brechtel, commanding his artillery battery supporting the river crossing in the most desperate of battles at the Berezina in 1812 and who had his false leg shot off by a Russian roundshot, continued giving his firing orders, pausing only to stop and calmly ask one of his gunners to get a spare wooden leg from one of the battery wagons.

There was Grouchy's horse artillery, continually bogged down in the muck and mess at Vauchamps while desperately trying to get around Blücher's defeated army and block their retreat; Drouot leading his gunners in a hell-for-leather artillery charge at Lützen in 1813 when he unlimbered as close as possible to the allied line and blew out its center with point-blank canister; the British Captain Ramsay, seemingly cut off by French cavalry at Fuentes d'Oñoro in Spain, ordering his horse artillerymen to charge through the French cavalry, with their guns, saving them in the mass of French horsemen; and the Russian artillery general Kutusaiv, meaning to commit the Russian artillery reserve at Borodino but killed in action before he could put his plan into action.

Finally, and undoubtedly the most important artillery action of the period, there was the wild artillery *chevauchée* at the Battle of Friedland in 1807, where Senarmont led his men in front of the infantry, turning his gunners and their well-served guns into the main attack while he assaulted the Russian center, getting within spitting distance of the solid, seemingly immovable Russian infantry, and in twenty bloody minutes knocking 4,000 of them over, blowing a hole in the Russian line and gutting the Russian center. Artillery tactics were changed for the next fifty years until the advent of rifled cannon: this action alone set the tone for artillery to follow and definitely placed it on an equal footing with the other two main fighting arms on the battlefield, the infantry and cavalry. These are the high deeds of the artillerymen of the period. They set a milestone in military history, and saw their arm grow in strength and prestige and become a force to reckon with on the modern battlefield.

Gunpowder and firearms were introduced onto European battlefields at Crécy in 1346 with a few hand-held iron weapons, and by the Napoleonic period there were hundreds of guns on each side, manned by professional artillerymen who stood by their weapons to the end, mounting up and charging forward like a juggernaut, and manhandling them through muck, mire, and enemy fire. There is an old truism that God made men of all sizes and shapes, and then He invented gunpowder that truly made all men equal. Then God created the artillery. This is their story—the guns, the men, the horses, and the commanders of an arm that eventually became known as the King of Battle.

This study is half-technical in nature. Artillery is a technical, as well as a combat arm. Therefore, technical information constitutes the first part of the book and most of the appendices. However, while tables of data are included, as well as methods of casting and makers of artillery systems, this is not an artillery manual. It is, though, a study of field artillery. The second half of the book is a survey of artillery battles that had impact on the artillery arm and, in turn, of the impact the arm had on warfare in the age of Napoleon, who was himself a highly qualified artilleryman. Siege guns, mortars, and guns used to defend fortresses and sea coasts will not be included in detail, except where it is necessary to enhance the story of the field artillery.

It should be noted that what is now called field artillery was usually referred to as light artillery during the Napoleonic period. This included both foot artillery and horse artillery, the differences between which will be covered in the text. Mountain artillery was also considered light artillery. It should be noted that light artillery, flying artillery, and artillery volante are merely other names for horse artillery. In this study, only the last will be used, as it is the most accurate as well as the most colorful.

Chapter 1
Ultima Ratio Regum

All the nations of Europe have systems copied one from the others, with the same degree of knowledge and understanding, so none of them has any superiority . . .

—Jean du Teil

I don't attach importance to the loss of cannon if the risk of their being taken is compensated for by the chance of success.

—Napoleon

It is necessary that the commanders of troops at least become acquainted with the effects which will follow from the various dispositions or execution of the pieces of ordinance, in order to combine these results in their general deployment.

—Guibert

The creak of harness leather, the rattle of trace chains, the rumble of gun carriage and caisson wheels and the ubiquitous sounds of horses and men trudging along an unmarked rutted road in some godforsaken backwater marked the passing of an artillery battery. The long column would reek of sweat, tobacco, and horse; but the men were used to the smells as they all stank the same and had been on the road to the next fight or bivouac for a long time. Some knew no other life. French, British, Austrian, Prussian, Russian, or American—the sounds were the same, the international language of gunners. Drivers guided, and sometimes fought for control of, their horse teams, each responsible for a pair of horses, be they lead, swing, or wheelers.

Far in the distance, gunfire can be heard. Frantic *aides-de-camp* come pounding down the road. Contact with the enemy has been made and the artillery must move forward at the gallop to reinforce the advance guard. Company commanders yell, motion, or otherwise get their trumpeters' or drummers' attention, and each battery commander takes his place at the head of his battery, now in march column. At the bellowed order "Forward," each gun team lurches ahead and the horses' ears prick up as they hear the familiar sounds of commands echoed by trumpet or drum, and by the urging of their now-alert drivers. Foot artillery gunners double time behind their guns, equipment clattering and bouncing on sore backs and hips. Those lucky enough to have limbers equipped with ammunition boxes for seats can ride limbers and caissons into battle. The mounted horse artillery gallops forward, limbers, guns, and caissons careening down the rutted or paved roads, horses straining in their harnesses, drivers attempting to control the excited animals, ears up, nostrils flared, in their haste to do their masters bidding.

Battery commanders bellow at their trumpeters and swords flash in the sunlight. Trumpets and drums blow or tap out the commanders' wishes, and the long columns of guns and caissons swing into line, veteran horses not needing to be urged or led into the maneuver as they know the drill by heart. Sometimes the train drivers are just along for the ride. Panting foot artillerymen sprint to catch up, and individually mounted horse artillerymen gallop for their positions, gun guides sprinting forward to mark the site for each gun in the battery.

Trumpets and drums again blow and tap out their orders; gun teams swing into their selected firing positions; cannoneers race to their pieces, grabbing hold on each side of the trail to unlimber their pieces and manhandle them into position. Horse artillerymen throw their reins to the horse handlers, and quickly dismount to man their guns. Guns are pushed forward into battery, and laid, and the gunners go through their well-practiced drill, loading their gun tubes while their mounted commander searches for targets, preferably the enemy infantry. They also search for hostile artillery batteries, for a crippled artillery battery is of no use to anyone, and having to engage in counterbattery fire could be a long and tedious job and take their guns away from their main mission—supporting their own infantry and hurting the enemy's foot soldiers as much as possible.

Gun captains signal that their guns are safe and ready with a raised hand, looking at their commander for the "Fire" order. Seeing an enemy infantry concentration coming out of the far woodline, the battery commander barks a fire order, indicating the target and range, carefully watching the gun crews traverse their weapons on the enemy target. Again, the gun captains signal they are ready, and the battery commander bellows "*Feu!*", "Fire!", "*Feuer!*" and the guns belch fire and smoke, and recoil violently as the portfire is touched to the vent, igniting the primer and the powder train. As the gun crews manhandle their piece back into battery and relay the gun tube, the battery commander watches for fall of shot.

The guns were their pride—their flag—and were protected in battle as an infantry or cavalry regiment would protect its flag or standard. Napoleon called his 12-pounders his favorite, his "pretty girls." One French company commander in Spain during the Peninsular War, when urged to abandon his guns during a desperate retreat, proudly proclaimed that the guns of his company "were our flag." Thiebault later remarked, after they had reached safety, that the exertions of Hulot and his artillerymen were "superhuman." Another French artillery officer would remark that his gunners "loved their guns like their sweethearts."[1] They were specialists in the art of gunnery, and of dealing death in large doses, developed over the years since the invention of gunpowder and the missile weapons to use it in the fourteenth century.

*   *   *

Since the first metal tube with a solid missile was used in combat in 1346 at the Battle of Crécy, artillery gradually assumed a larger role on campaign, on the battlefield, and in the plans of generals. Cavalry, especially the heavily armored knights and men-at-arms, had ruled the battlefield then, but the longbow, and the gradual development of black powder and crew-served weapons, as well as pike- and musket-armed infantry, sounded the death knell of that era. Infantry and artillery were evolving into equal partners with the cavalry, but it took longer for artillery to come into prominence. At first very useful for breaching castle and fortress walls, guns gradually became lighter and more mobile, and competent generals who could learn from both victory and defeat began to mass their artillery against targets of importance. The smarter ones directed their gunners to fire at troops and not other cannon, and learned one of the reasons why battles were won.

The first guns were crude, short-ranged, and unreliable. They evolved into larger guns throwing large stones to demolish feudal castle walls, bringing them down with a crash that was heard across Europe: the Turks hearkened and breached the famous walls of Constantinople and the remains of the Byzantine Empire with it. Immobile, slow to load and slower to fire, and difficult to transport, guns then evolved into smaller, more efficient tubes, mounted on wheeled carriages for better mobility. Still, the carriages and the ammunition were cumbersome, and the guns themselves were difficult to maneuver. Gradually, however, gunners brought about improvements to the guns and their performance, both in effectiveness and mobility.

An engraving of a burning ammunition wagon, with a horse team "not God nor man can 'old."

Artillerymen wrote about what they knew, and gunner/scholars penned treatises that were copied and read throughout Europe and found their way to the New World. Müller and LeBlond were known by the crowned princes of Europe, as well as fat booksellers in England's far colonies, who later helped bring an Empire to its knees. Through endless primeval forests in North America, along rivers and in seaports and fortresses, the thunder of the guns reverberated through the English, Spanish, and French colonies in the New World. While cannon were not yet a decisive element in the many battles fought in North America, they did make their presence felt and the new United States, born during the thunder of the guns, was a land rich in iron, strong but brittle, from which cannon could be cast.

The quest for lighter artillery, able to limber up and maneuver with the infantry and cavalry, began with Gustavus Adolphus. He was a military innovator and technician of the highest merit, as well as a first-rate soldier. He was also the first commander to organize his artillery into field batteries.[2] That he was also king of his native Sweden undoubtedly helped in his search for new and lighter artillery. His famous leather gun, though an inefficient artillery piece, was both innovative and a harbinger of things to come.

Lighter, shorter calibers could be moved quickly to the battlefield, as well as maneuvered easily upon it by man or horse. These lighter guns, with higher rates of fire, were able to outshoot the heavier guns as they were easier to load and because more ammunition could be carried for them. The Swedish artilleryman von Siegeroth, who served Gustave, found that shorter gun tubes, if constructed properly, had the same lethal punch as longer ones of the same caliber. Light guns were attached to infantry battalions to enhance their firepower, and gradually the pike—of the famous "pike and shot"—was done away with in favor of the musket with the newly invented bayonet, with which all infantry were now being equipped. Gustave insisted in cooperation among the three arms, infantry, artillery, and cavalry, which gave him an advantage over his tactically more ponderous opponents.[3] The French would rediscover this tactical ingredient after the Seven Years' War and a string of lost battles.

Generals learned to mass their artillery for better effect, the better ones coordinating their artillery with their maneuver battalions and cavalry squadrons. Gustave, and his young, aggressive artillery chief, Lennart Tortenson, smashed Imperial armies at Breitenfeld and Lützen, and established Sweden as a first-rate power on the back of her disciplined farmers with their excellent artillery.

Eventually, artillerymen learned that fighting counter-battery duels with other artillery could be both frustrating and expensive, both in lives and in terms of ammunition expended. They also found it to be largely ineffective. They found that concentrating on the enemy's infantry with massed guns hurt the enemy more, and as long as you were hurting the enemy's infantry and cavalry more than they were hurting yours with their artillery, you were probably getting the upper hand. They also learned, as Frederick did against the Austrians in the Seven Years' War, that properly handled and massed artillery could ruin good infantry in a relatively short space of time. Frederick the Great learned to respect the excellent Austrian artillery and knew that a powerful new force on the battlefield was coming into its own:

> It used to be our custom to form regiments from the largest men possible. This was done for a reason, for in the early wars it was men and not cannon that decided victory, and battalions of tall men advancing with the bayonet scattered the poorly assembled enemy troops-with the first attack. Now artillery has changed everything. A cannon ball knocks down a man six feet tall just as easily as one who is only five feet seven. Artillery decides everything, and infantry no longer do battle with naked steel.[4]

Napoleon later came to the same conclusion:

> The better the infantry is, the more it should be used carefully and supported with good batteries. Good infantry is, without doubt, the sinew of an army; but if it is forced to fight for a long time against a very superior artillery, it will become demoralized and will be destroyed.[5]

Unlike Frederick, however, the Emperor, as an artilleryman, was also very concise in his opinion in the training of artillery officers and the general value they had for the service. Frederick treated his artillerymen, especially his artillery officers, poorly. Part of this was be-

Diagram of the nomenclature of a typical gun tube of the period.

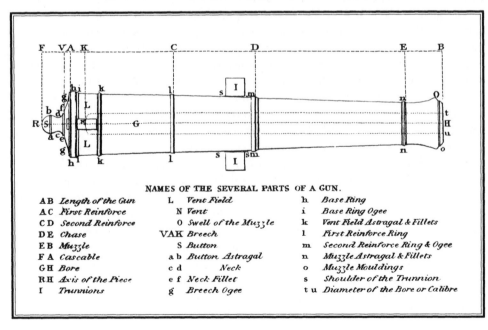

NAMES OF THE SEVERAL PARTS OF A GUN.

A B	*Length of the Gun*	L	*Vent Field*	h	*Base Ring*
A C	*First Reinforce*	N	*Vent*	i	*Base Ring Ogee*
C D	*Second Reinforce*	O	*Swell of the Muzzle*	k	*Vent Field Astragal & Fillets*
D E	*Chase*	VAK	*Breech*	l	*First Reinforce Ring*
E B	*Muzzle*	S	*Button*	m	*Second Reinforce Ring & Ogee*
F A	*Cascable*	a b	*Button Astragal*	n	*Muzzle Astragal & Fillets*
G H	*Bore*	c d	*Neck*	o	*Muzzle Mouldings*
R H	*Axis of the Piece*	e f	*Neck Fillet*	s	*Shoulder of the Trunnion*
I	*Trunnions*	g	*Breech Ogee*	t u	*Diameter of the Bore or Calibre*

cause he did not quite understand the arm, what it was capable of and what its possibilities were. According to H. G. Mirabeau and J. Mauvillon, commentators of the period,

> Live with the Prussian officers and you will see the officers of the infantry, cavalry, and hussars assume a great superiority over those of the artillery. The latter seem to recognize their lowly status, in a manner of speaking. The other officers intermingle and seek each other out regardless of regiment or arm, but it is altogether exceptional for any friendship to be formed between the gunner officers and the officers of the rest of the army.[6]

The Emperor, on the other hand, knew the value of a military education and what good artillery, led and commanded by their artillery officers, was capable of achieving on the battlefield:

> It is necessary to be familiar with artillery . . . I believe every officer ought to serve in the artillery, which is the arm that can produce most of the good generals . . . To be a good general you must know mathematics; it serves to direct your thinking in a thousand circumstances.[7]

It was during the Napoleonic period, with its mass conscript armies, sweeping campaigns, and vicious, frequent battles, that artillery finally came into its own as a separate combat arm and was used with speed and maneuverability on the battlefield to obtain a quick decision. Technical advances in metallurgy aided the new developments, and gun tubes could be made just as strong with half the weight of the older guns. Gunnery was also improved, firing tables for the guns being developed, as well as new sights and gunners' tools for fire control and accuracy. Fused shells took their place alongside the ubiquitous roundshot; grapeshot was gradually replaced by the more deadly canister; and other, more effective types of anti-personnel ammunition were developed and employed.

Artillery became lighter and more mobile, without losing range and accuracy. Cannon were cast and then bored out, instead of being cast around a central core. There were improvements in ammunition and powder, allowing a lighter powder charge to get the same range and effect on target. Professional schools were opened in France and Austria to train artillerymen, greatly improving the base of knowledge and the efficiency and professionalism of the artillery arms. British artillery remained somewhat outside the army, being under the Master General of Ordnance, but was a proud arm, quietly professional; and the British were the only nation to adopt a block trail for their cannon, which in many ways was a great technological improvement over the split trail used by the Continental powers.

More generals came out of the artillery during the period, some staying with their arm, and others going on to command infantry divisions and sometimes corps. The French developed more than artillery doctrine for the fighting of their guns: they also developed a definite command structure for artillery that mirrored the tactical and grand tactical developments with the infantry and cavalry. They undoubtedly had the most highly developed artillery command structure, as well as the most flexible tactical system of the period. The first artillery system generally recognized to have been developed in Europe was the Vallière System of the 1730s. The French artillery arm had been organized as a guild prior to the accession of Louis XIV to the throne, but the massive reforms carried out by Louis and his ministers affected the artillery as it did most every other facet of the French Army, making it the best in Europe.[8]

While the warfare of the period revolved in many instances around the capture of strategic cities and fortresses, the artillery generally was engaged in heavy siege work and not employed as mobile field artillery. However, in France the Swedish lessons of Gustavus Adolphus did not go unheeded. The type or style of warfare dictated the manner in which artillery was used, and what type of artillery was to be employed. In all of the bloody battles of the wars of Louis XIV, the siege was still the dominant military operation of the period. The attack and defense of fortified places, and thus the controlled territory around them, was the object of the exercise. Vauban and his Dutch counterpart Coehorn were the two leading experts in the field of military engineering, and the artillery piece and the shovel were the tools that dominated the siege. Large, heavy-caliber guns were needed to bombard and breach fortress walls, either to pave the way for the infantry assault, or to allow the garrison to surrender with the honors of war.

Some forward-looking officers, however, realized that light, maneuverable pieces of artillery were needed for field operations: artillery needed to keep up with the army on the march and not impede it. So, two distinct artillery systems existed side by side during part of the period—the artillery "*de vielle invention*," which had been in existence for some time, and the new, lighter system "*de nouvelle invention*." The latter system had been brought to France by a Spaniard, Antonio Gonzales, in 1679.[9] The guns were lighter, with larger chambers, the diameter of which exceeded that of the bore of the gun tubes. This type of gun required less powder than one designed in the conventional manner. Additionally, the vent was placed at the top of the breech, igniting the powder from the top instead of the rear of the tube, causing the powder to burn faster. New carriages were designed for the lighter gun tubes, and the gun limber was introduced to pull them. There were some drawbacks to the new system. The guns, being lighter, recoiled more violently, damaging the lighter carriages. There was also greater vertical recoil, which sometimes literally shook the carriages to pieces after prolonged firing. Moreover, the larger, spherical chamber left more residue after firing which was harder to swab out, and the accident rate climbed, especially during rapid fire. These problems finally caused the new, light system to be abandoned by the French in 1720. Still, it was a preview of what Gribeauval would accomplish with his system some 40-odd years later. The cannon "*de nouvelle invention*" was the theoretical ancestor of Gribeauval's excellent system, which was specifically designed to be employed in the mobile warfare the French developed after the Seven Years' War.

Table 1 illustrates the difference in gun-tube weight between the pieces "*de nouvelle invention*" of 1679 and the pieces of the later Vallière system of 1732. A comparison with the Gribeauval-system gun tubes for the three calibers of field pieces of 1765 is also provided for the purposes of comparison. As an aside, it can be mentioned that the comparative weights of the Vallière 12-pounder, the Vallière 8-pounder rebored to a 12-pounder, the Austrian Lichtenstein 12-pounder, and the Prussian 12-pounder at the end of the Seven Years' War were, rounded to the nearest kilogram, 1,566kg, 931kg, 813kg, and 926kg, respectively.[10]

Vallière was the first artillerymen to make any attempt at an army-wide standardization

TABLE 1: COMPARISON OF GUN TUBE WEIGHTS, 1679–1732

La Nouvelle Invention

Caliber (pounds)	Weight (kilograms)	Length (meters)
4	293	1.54
8	489	1.62
12	978	1.98
16	1,076	2.01
24	1,467	2.15

Vallière System

4	563	–
8	1,028	2.85
12	1,566	3.17
16	2,056	3.36
24	2,643	3.53

Gribeauval System

4	290	1.57
8	580	2.00
12	880	2.29

program. While he did standardize calibers at 4-, 8-, and 12-pounders, he did not make any differentiation between field and siege pieces, nor between these and fortress artillery. The guns were all-purpose: they were used for all three functions. They were beautifully made, long, sleek guns, artfully cast and engraved, and a credit to the caster's art, but they were heavy, and there was no standardization on gun carriages nor on ancillary equipment.

There was also no standardization on wheel sizes, only general instructions; the parts from one armory would not fit on a carriage made in another. Sometimes the dimensions of the carriages and vehicles were made to fit the roads where the armory was located. Generally, you went with what you were issued and what came with the gun. Consequently, they were awkward for field use, though accurate, and the army had a very large mobility problem in combat. Guns could not be displaced easily to support troops in trouble or at a decisive time and place on the battlefield. Many times, though the artillerymen were skilled and well-trained, they were both outmaneuvered and outshot.

During the War of the Austrian Succession, the Austrian artillery, still more of a guild than a combat arm or a military organization, was in much the same trouble as the French of the Seven Years' War would be: their guns were not that mobile, which caused problems against the Prussian artillery. After the war, Prince Lichtenstein, who, interestingly, was not an artilleryman but an *Inhaber* of a dragoon regiment, set himself the task of modernizing the Austrian artillery to put it at least on a par with that of Prussia. What Lichtenstein developed, largely using his own considerable fortune (which undoubtedly pleased the perennially financially strapped Austrian government and made him a favorite of the Empress, Maria Theresa), was the first unified system of artillery in Europe. Lichtenstein went much further than did Vallière *père*, and addressed not only the standardization of calibers, but also gun carriages, ammunition wagons, size of wheels, and ammunition. Personnel and professional schooling were also part of Lichtenstein's reforms, and the Austrian artillery was transformed from a quasi-military organization into a highly professional, hard-hitting arm that became the mainstay of the Austrian service.

Lichtenstein decided on 3-, 6-, and 12-pounders as the standard calibers for the Imperial Austrian field artillery, giving them a distinct advantage over the much heavier French guns in the next armed contest, the Seven Years' War. Necessity being the mother of invention, Lichtenstein used the Prussian example, and undoubtedly took his ideas from many sources, including Vallière for the idea of standardization, and the Swedes, along with inventions by the Prussian artillery officer Lieutenant Colonel von Holtzman.[11] This officer was the inventor/developer of the screw quoin with which the Lichtenstein pieces were equipped. Lichtenstein and his cohorts also adopted the same calibers as the Prussians employed.

Not being an artilleryman, Lichtenstein surrounded himself with able subordinates—for example, coaxing the Luxembourg-born Rouvroy away from the Saxon service—as well as employing very capable Austrian officers to design and implement the changes that he deemed necessary and that the Austrian Army undoubtedly needed. Gun tube design was simplified and strengthened, the new Lichtenstein pieces being trim and handsome, and not cluttered with extra decorations and unnecessary ornamentation. They were simple, utilitarian, and handsome guns that were completely functional. Carriages, wheels, and ancillary equipment were standardized, and the number of each was drastically reduced from hitherto. One unique feature of the Lichtenstein 3-pounder field gun and 7-pounder howitzer, as well as of the early 6-pounders, was two tow bars attached to the front of the gun carriage. Through these bars a rod would be emplaced, making it easier for the gun crew to manhandle the gun in the field.

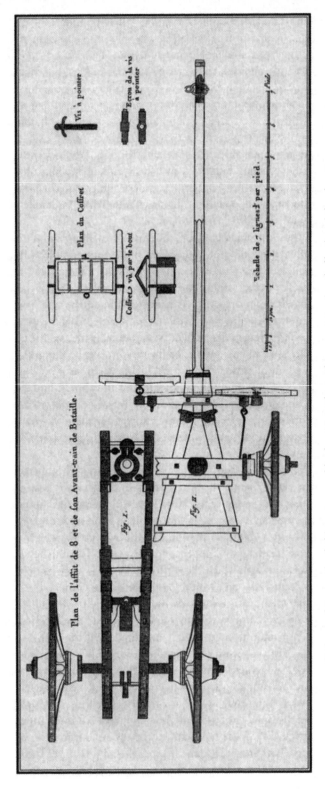

Gribeauval 8-pounder field carriage and limber. Note the trail ammunition box (coffret) and the elevating screw.

Rammers, sponges, and handspikes were placed on the sides of the carriage through a series of handles and hooks, which made storage much easier for the gun crews.

Unfortunately for the Austrians, this system was not updated before or during the French Revolutionary and Napoleonic period. One of the few innovations developed after Lichtenstein's death in 1772 was the introduction of a modified 6-pounder and a 7-pounder howitzer that were fitted with a seat on the long trail that was issued to the newly organized cavalry batteries on which the gun crew was able to ride. In addition to these, caissons were modified with the same type of seat on the top of the vehicle, the crews dubbing these "wurst wagons" for their obvious similarity to a sausage.[12] They must have been interesting to ride on at speed. These modified caissons were later used by the French horse artillery in the 1790s, but were abandoned to mount all of the gunners individually, something the Austrians never did—to their detriment. The Lichtenstein system stayed in service until 1859, while in France the more modern Gribeauval System underwent changes in 1803 and was completely replaced in 1827–29.

The new ordnance developed in the 1780s was used in the *Kavallerie Battieren*, the cavalry batteries, which were not foot artillery and not quite horse artillery, but were mobile and hard-hitting and, when employed by aggressive artillerymen such as Josef Smola, could help achieve decisive results on the battlefield, as did then-Lieutenant Smola at Neerwinden in 1793 when he supported the Austrian right with a reinforced cavalry battery of fourteen guns, smashing a French attack and helping to win the field.

Jean Baptiste de Gribeauval (1715–1789) was an expert artilleryman, a "technical genius," and the father of the most complete artillery system developed up to that time. A qualified French artillery officer, he had made an inspection trip to Prussia before the shooting started in 1756 and observed the same Prussian guns that had impressed Lichtenstein. Gribeauval was a first-rate artilleryman and innovator in his own right, and indeed quite possibly a genius. What he became was "the designer of one of the world's greatest artillery systems." He was "eminently capable of undertaking the task of redesigning [France's] ordnance system," and after his entrance into the French Army and the artillery arm he "rapidly gained a reputation for ordnance construction."[13] This was before Gribeauval was sent to serve with the Austrians and observe and use their new artillery system.

Gribeauval probably started work on his new artillery system before the Seven Years' War, again using the best elements of the Swedish light guns, the Prussian artillery and the Vallière system. Before going to Austria, Gribeauval had already designed new gun carriages for garrison use, and had an established reputation as an extremely talented technician and innovator.[14] He was seconded to Austria in the Seven Years' War in 1758, where he was able to observe and use the excellent guns and material of Lichtenstein's system in training and in combat. He served at the siege of Neiss in 1758, at the defense of Dresden in 1759, and at the siege of Glatz in 1760. He particularly distinguished himself at Schweidnitz in 1761, where he was largely responsible for the successful defense until the defenders ran out of ammunition. The losses inflicted on the Prussians were seven times that of the defenders (7,000 *vice* 1,000), and he earned Frederick the Great's admiration and professional respect (Frederick was present for at least part of the siege), and the offer of a Prussian commission from Frederick himself, which Gribeauval declined. For his services to Austria, he was promoted to the grade of lieutenant general and was awarded the Cross of the Order of Maria Theresa. Upon his return to his homeland, he was made both a lieutenant general and a commander of the Order of Saint Louis.

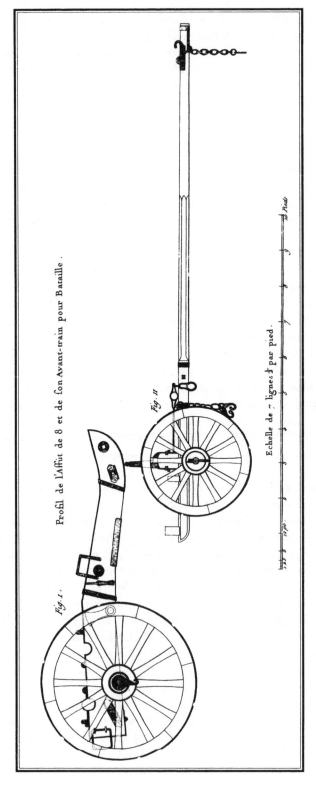

Profil de l'Affût de 8 et de fon Avant-train pour Bataille.

Fig. 1.

Fig. II

Echelle de 7 lignes ⅓ par pied.

Gribeauval 8-pounder field carriage and limber—side views.

Gribeauval undoubtedly continued work on his own artillery system while in Austria, and when he returned to France in 1762 he was promoted and allowed to develop his ideas on artillery. The system he devised served through the Napoleonic period and was partially adopted by the fledgling United States Army in 1809.

Gribeauval completely revamped and reorganized the French artillery. He standardized every piece of equipment, invented or developed new artillery tools and sights, logically reorganized the gunners into companies and regiments, and even changed the uniforms. No artillery system up to that time, including the Lichtenstein system, underwent such a radical improvement in effectiveness and equipment.[15]

Gribeauval also ventured into training for officers and NCOs, professional schools, and employment doctrine. He was instrumental in sponsoring the new artillery doctrine of close and continuous artillery cooperation with infantry, which was one of the cornerstones of the new French tactical system that allowed such a continuous string of sweeping victories through the Wars of the Revolution and, especially, the early Empire period. Never before had one man exerted so much influence on such a large portion of his county's artillery system and war-making potential.

Along with Guibert, Bourcet, the du Teil brothers, de Broglie and others, Gribeauval was a scholar, innovator, technician, and tactician. He retained Vallière's standardized calibers—4-, 8-, and 12-pounders—but designed completely new gun tubes specifically for use as field artillery. These pieces were simple, light, and accurate, as verified during the Strasbourg field tests. They were also without the traditional, and needless, ornamentation that had decorated the breeches of the Vallière pieces. Further, he made a distinction between field and siege artillery. While the same calibers, such as 8- and 12-pounders, were used in both field and siege artillery, they were not the same gun tubes, those for siege and garrison artillery being longer and heavier, and designated "battering pieces."

Setting the length of his field tubes at eighteen calibers (as against fourteen for the Prussian and sixteen for the Austrian), he also used 150 pounds of metal for every pound of shot, making the tubes more durable than the lighter Lichtenstein and Prussian pieces, which had 120 pounds and 100 pounds of metal for every pound of shot, respectively. Every gun tube cast has an active lifespan, based on the amount of rounds shot through the tube. Strengthening the tube in this manner gave the new Gribeauval tubes a longer lifespan per tube. Lichtenstein's were rated at lasting three campaigns before trouble might develop with the serviceability of the tubes; Gribeauval's could last longer with the higher ratio of metal to shot, which was a great advantage as regards the expense of casting new gun tubes, and the reliability under campaign and battle conditions.

Gribeauval also adopted, for the first time in the French artillery, the 6-inch howitzer for field use. The howitzer was not new to the French, who first employed it in 1749, but for use as field artillery it was an innovation. Gribeauval first used a modified copy of the excellent Austrian howitzer, to include the Holtzman (Prussian) screw quoin for elevation, later designing and manufacturing a howitzer of his own design along with the new elevating screw and plate of his own invention.

Gribeauval, moreover, completely redesigned the carriages, ensuring that all were standardized. His work continued for the caissons, limbers, field forges, and *hacquets* for the pontoons. His carriages took into account not only the rearward recoil of the gun, but also the fact that the carriage recoiled down at the same time. Hence, his carriages differed significantly from Lichtenstein's: they were shorter, stronger, and lighter. Additionally, the end of the trail that rested on the ground was completely redesigned, to allow it to be better used with one of Gribeauval's new inventions, the *prolonge*. Instead of the trail being squared off at the end, Gribeauval's new design was shaped with an upward flair so that it would not become stuck in the ground when being towed by a limber with a *prolonge* attached. This is one of the identifying features of a Gribeauval gun carriage, and it was later copied by the other Continenal powers as they adopted the *prolonge*.[16]

The *prolonge* allowed guns to be more easily drawn over rough terrain, including in combat. This was such an innovative piece of equipment that "the invention of the prolonge alone was enough to guarantee Gribeauval a lasting place in the history of warfare."[17] The *prolonge* itself was an ingenious development, and it allowed much more tactical flexibility to the guns, crews, and company/battery commanders (see Appendix I). It allowed the guns to be connected by a long rope to their limbers in action and be able to negotiate difficult terrain such as gullies and rough, uneven ground by horsepower and not merely be being manhandled around the battle-field. It also kept the gun team further from harm's way and available when needed.

Gribeauval organized the artillery arm into permanent companies, giving them a definite structure that was lacking before. Additionally, companies would be assigned to the same "division" of guns so that they would have an investment in keeping them properly maintained: no longer would gunners be shifted from gun to gun during a campaign, not knowing where they would be assigned next. The artillery companies would also have both an administrative and a tactical function. The artillery company was now the tactical "building block" of the artillery arm, as the battalion was for the infantry and the squadron for the cavalry.

Gun tubes had greatly improved since the mid-eighteenth century. Advances in metallurgy had allowed for making lighter guns of the same caliber that could do the same job as the older, much heavier pieces. Lichtenstein had discovered that after the Austrian's rude introduction to the lighter, more mobile Prussian guns that outmaneuvered and outshot the heavier, more cumbersome Austrian pieces in the War of the Austrian Succession of 1740-44.

Gribeauval, who had seen the Prussian guns and had worked with the Austrian ones while serving with the Austrian Army from 1756 to 1762, was undoubtedly influenced by both the Prussian guns and the Austrian artillery system. He was also influenced by Vallière, whose system he hoped to replace. However, the system he developed for his native France was no mere copy of the Lichtenstein system, nor of Prussian or Swedish weapons. A gun of this period was not merely a metal tube with two trunnions to hold it in the carriage and give it the ability to be elevated and depressed for ease of firing. Gun tubes have characteristics which are given to it by its design, weight, and the manner in which it is produced. Moreover, no two guns of the same caliber and design ever shoot the same. (This is still true today, even with the great technological advances of the last two centuries.)

Gribeauval designed his guns to be of eighteen calibers, four calibers longer than the Prussian and two longer than the Austrian tubes, and he moved the trunnions higher up the tube to improve sighting and ballistic performance. He admired the sleek, elegant lines of both the guns of the Lichtenstein system and those of the Vallière system, and his designs were graceful but functional weapons that were undoubtedly also intended to outshoot the Austrian weapons. They were both stronger and lighter than comparable tubes of the same caliber—which also gave them greater accuracy. More significantly, Gribeauval lessened the windage of his new gun tubes to half of that tolerated in the Lichtenstein gun tubes.

Another innovation that marked the Gribeauval System concerned windage. For years, artillerymen had in hand a gauge to measure roundshot as manufactured to ensure that the

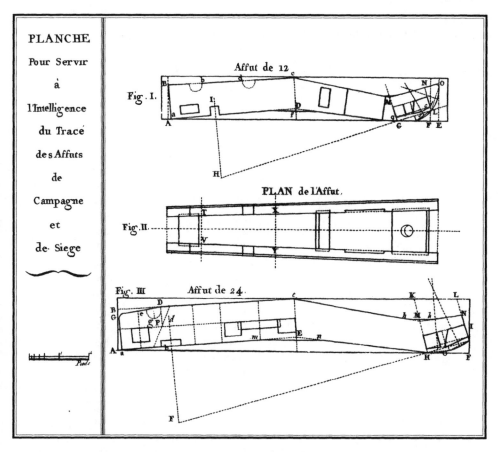

Construction plans for a Gribeauval 12-pounder field carriage and a 24-pounder siege carriage.

round would fit in the tubes of different calibers. Gribeauval went one step further. In addition to the "go" gauge, which marked the high end of the round tolerance, he developed the "no go" gauge, which measured the low end of tolerance, ensuring that the rounds were within the desired windage. This was another measure that assisted accuracy. [18]

Other advantages of the Gribeauval System were a removable and adjustable rear sight for the guns (the Hausse sight), and the inventions of the *bricole* for the gun crews, of the *prolonge* already mentioned, and of a new type of searcher to test for the soundness of the gun tubes. Iron axles were developed for the gun carriages and all of the ancillary artillery vehicles, and all of the new guns were equipped with a newly designed elevating screw, which was greatly superior to the screw quoin used by the Austrians, Russians, and Prussians. [19]

The comparative ranges of artillery from the main Continental belligerents of the period 1792–1815, taken from Adye's *Bombardier and Pocket Gunner*, are shown in Table 2. Generally speaking, the ranges are comparable, though the throw weights are not. One significant difference between the artillery of the various nations was the quality of the gunpowder used. The British was probably the best, followed by the French. Russian powder was thought to be inferior, which led to a disadvantage in artillery range when fighting the French.

Table 3 shows the specifics for the Gribeauval pieces, including, however, the 6-pounder of the AN XI Artillery System, which, though designed largely to replace the Gribeauval guns,

.TABLE 2: ARTILLERY RANGES, 1792–1815

Nation	Caliber	Elevation (degrees)	Charge (English pounds)	First graze (paces)	Extreme range (paces)
France	4-pounder	0	1.5	475	1,500
		1	1.5	757	1,550
		2	1.5	1,100	1,600
	8-pounder (lt)	0	3.0	540	1,800
		1	3.0	925	1,850
		2	3.0	1,270	1,925
	8-pounder (hy)	0	3.0	525	1,800
		1	3.0	900	1,850
		2	3.0	1,250	1,900
	12-pounder (lt)	0	4.5	575	2,250
		1	4.5	1,025	2,400
		2	4.5	1,350	2,450
	12-pounder (hy)	0	4.5	575	2,250
		1	4.5	1,025	2,400
		2	4.5	1,350	2,450
	6-inch howitzer	1	.06 of shell's weight	200	1,200
		5	ditto	950	1,700
		10	ditto	1,500	1,750
		30	ditto	1850	1,870
	8-inch howitzer	1	ditto	230	1,960
		5	ditto	1,000	1,960
		10	ditto	1,700	2,090
		30	ditto	2,100	2,100
Austria	3-pounder	Point blank	0.75	500	1,400
		1st Mark	0.75	700	1,500
		2nd Mark	0.75	900	1,600
	6-pounder	0	1.5	500	1,600
		1	1.5	700	1,700
		2	1.5	900	1,800
	12-pounder (lt)	0	3.0	500	1,800
		1	3.0	700	1,900
		2	3.0	900	1,950
	12-pounder (hy)	0	3.5	550	2,000
		1	3.5	925	2,150
		2	3.5	1,300	2,250
	7-pounder howitzer	1	12oz	125	1,100
		5	12oz	700	1,100
		10	12oz	1,100	1,400
		30	12oz	1,600	1,600

continued . . .

	10-pounder howitzer	1	18oz	180	1,200
		5	18oz	1,200	1,260
		10	18oz	1,500	1,500
		30	18oz	1,800	1,800
Russia	3-pounder	0	1.25	400	1,500
		1	1.25	650	1,700
		2	1.25	1,000	1,900
	6-pounder	0	2.0	430	1,700
		1	2.0	800	1,800
		2	2.0	1,100	1,900
	12-pounder	0	4.0	480	1,900
		1	4.0	800	2,000
		2	4.0	1,200	2,100
Prussia	3-pounder	0	1.25	400	1,400
		1	1.25	600	1,500
		2	1.25	900	1,600
	6-pounder	0	3.0	450	1,700
		1	3.0	820	1,800
		2	3.0	1,250	1,900
	12-pounder	0	4.0	500	1,900
		1	4.0	900	2,000
		2	4.0	1,250	2,100
	7-pounder howitzer	1	1.25	250	1,200
		5	1.25	900	1,400
		10	1.25	1,500	1,600
		30	1.25	1,900	1,900
Saxon	4-pounder	0	1.75	250	1,500
		1	1.75	500	1,600
		2	1.75	1,000	1,700
	8-pounder (hy)	0	3.25	300	1,800
		1	3.25	700	1,900
		2	3.25	1,150	2,000
	12-pounder (Lt)	0	4.0	300	1,900
		1	4.0	800	2,050
		2	4.0	1,200	2,200
	12-pounder (hy)	0	5.0	400	1,900
		1	5.0	850	2,000
		2	5.0	1,300	2,200
	8-pounder howitzer	1	1.5	260	1,200
		5	1.5	700	1,500
		10	1.5	1,200	1,700
		30	1.5	2,100	2,100

limbers, and ancillary vehicles, in fact did not. The need for guns in different theaters outran production of the new pieces, so that, even though the new 6-pounder did replace the 4- and 8-pounders of the Gribeauval System in the main army, in Spain, for example, 4- and 8-pounders were still used. The surplus 4- and 8-pounders were also reissued in 1813 to replace the huge French artillery losses in Russia. It should also be noted that the 4-, 8-, and 12-pounders listed as siege and fortress pieces were not field guns. These were heavier pieces, many of them belonging to the older Vallière system that Gribeauval replaced. They were still excellent guns for both siege and fortress work, even if too heavy and awkward as field pieces. A snapshot of ranges of contemporary British ordnance is shown in Table 4. Some of the data derived from Scharnhorst's live fire tests of the period is presented in Table 5; the comparison with Adye's range tables is interesting and noteworthy.

It is noteworthy also that, when comparing the throw weights of Austrian and French pieces, which were frequently on opposing sides, the word "pound" can be somewhat misleading. The French 4-pound, 6-pound, 8-pound, and 12-pound shot weighed, in kilograms (using a conversion of 2.2 pounds per kilogram, rounded to the nearest tenth of a kilogram), 4.4, 6.6, 8.8, and 13.2 pounds, respectively. It should also be noted that the caliber of the piece was measured differently by the French than by other armies: the French measured it by the diameter of the round, the others by the diameter of the bore of the piece. The Austrian 3-pound, 6-pound, and 12-pound rounds were measured in *Nürnberger Pfunder* (Nuremberg pounds), which had 0.477 kilograms per English pound. This gave the Austrian ammunition the weight, to the nearest tenth of a kilogram, of 3.15, 6.3, and 11.55 pounds, respectively.

TABLE 3: GRIBEAUVAL ARTILLERY PIECES

Weapon	*Round weight (kilograms)*	*Caliber (millimeters)*	*Length (centimeters)*	*Weight (kilograms)*
Field guns				
4-pounder	2	84.0	157	290
6-pounder (AN XI)	3	95.8	180	390
8-pounder	4	106.1	200	580
12-pounder	6	121.3	229	880
6-inch howitzer	11	165.7	76	330
4-pounder Swedish	2	84.0	162	325
Siege guns				
4-pounder (long)	2	84.0	235	560
8-pounder	4	106.1	285	1,060
12-pounder	6	121.3	317	1,550
16-pounder	8	133.7	336	2,000
24-pounder	12	152.7	353	2,740
8-inch howitzer	21	223.3	94	540
Coast defense guns				
12-pounder	6	121.3	317	1,510
16-pounder	8	133.7	336	1,900
24-pounder	12	152.7	353	2,500
36-pounder	18	174.6		3,520

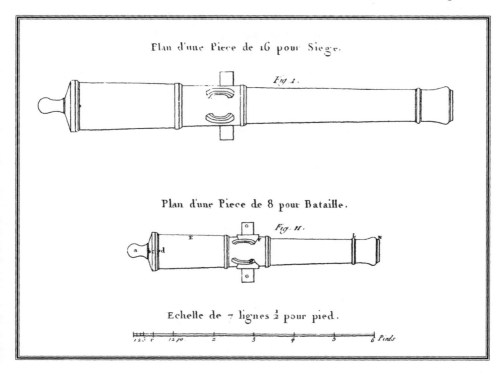

Comparison in size between a Gribeauval 8-pounder field piece and a 16-pounder siege gun.

Except for the 6-pounders of each belligerent—and the French 6-pounder was a newer and much better weapon, based on the newer technology employed to produce it—the Austrian field artillery was significantly inferior in terms of throw weight per class of gun, and this was more keenly felt as the calibers increased in size. This disparity would also be much more critical as artillery was massed—which the Austrians did not do well or effectively until 1809. For example, while a battery of Austrian 6-pounders would throw 37.8 pounds of ammunition, a battery of French 6- pounders would throw 39.6 pounds. However, a battery of 8-pounders would throw 52.8 pounds of shot. Comparing a battery of Austrian 12-pounders with a battery of French 12-pounders, there would be 69.3 pounds of shot thrown from the Austrian tubes, and 79.2 thrown from the French.

Artillery during the period was divided into field artillery, siege artillery, and what the French referred to as *artillerie du place*, or fortress artillery. Field artillery was further divided into three categories—foot, horse, and mountain. The largest caliber field piece that could keep up with an army on the march was a 12-pounder. Common calibers that were used throughout the period were 3-, 4-, 6-, 8-, and 12-pounder cannon. Mountain guns were usually 3- or 4-pounders, the Piedmontese gun being an excellent piece and well thought of by the French. Mountain guns could be broken down into separate loads, and all of these would be carried, along with their ammunition allocation, on pack mules. They could go where the more conventional field artillery could not. Foot artillery and mountain artillery gun crews were expected to walk, though those nations that had developed limbers with attached ammunition chests had the lids fitted out as seats and the gunners could ride; otherwise, the gunners had no option but to "hoof it."

TABLE 4: RANGES FOR CONTEMPORARY BRITISH ARTILLERY

Caliber	Maximum effective range (yards)	Maximum range (yards)	Canister range (yards)
6-pdr	700	1,500	400
9-pdr	900	1,700	450
5.5-inch howitzer	700	1,700	500

Caliber	Elevation (degrees)	Range (yards)	Shell (pounds)	Charge (pounds)
Light 5.5-inch howitzer	0	150	16	1.0
	1	250		
	2	450		
	3	600		
	4	750		
	5	850		
	10	1,200		
	12	1,400		
Heavy 5.5-inch howitzer	0	250	16	2.0
	1	400		
	2	550		
	3	700		
	4	850		
	5	975		
	10	1,500		
	12	1,700		
Light 6-pounder Roundshot	0	200		1.5
	1	600		
	2	800		
	3	1000		
	4	1200		
Spherical Case	1.75			
	2.25			
	3.25			
	4.375			
Heavy 6-pounder and 9-pounder Roundshot	0	300		3.0
	1	700		
	2	1,000		
	3	1,200		
	4	1,400		
Spherical Case	1.75	640–920		
	2.25	930–1,180		
	3.25	1,160–1,390		
	4.375	1,360–1,570		

TABLE 5: RANGE DATA DERIVED FROM SCHARNHORST'S TESTS

Ranges of the 12-pounder with Charges of one-third and one-fourth the weight of the shot (average of 36 rounds fired):

Elevation (degrees)	Charge	First graze (paces)	A Third of the Rounds Reached This Distance
1	¼	702	2,350
1	⅓	814	2,450
4	¼	1,545	2,100
4	⅓	1,675	2,400

Ranges of the 6-pounder with charges of one-third and one-fourth the weight of the shot (average range computed using either 12 or 18 rounds):

Elevation (degrees)	Charge	First graze (paces)	A third of the rounds reached this distance
1	¼	627	1,850
1	⅓	715	1,850
4	¼	375	1,780
4	⅓	1,502	1,950

Range of the 3-pounder with charges of one-third and one-fourth the weight of the shot (average range computed using 24 rounds):

Elevation (degrees)	Charge	First graze (paces)	Extreme range (one-third of rounds reaching this distance)
1	¼	575	1,550
1	⅓	689	1,550
4	¼	1195	1,550
4	⅓	1333	1,650

Horse artillery was a relatively new arm, slowly developed from the middle of the eighteenth century. It was a novel approach to the problem of mobility, and theoretically every gunner was individually mounted on his own horse. Sometimes that did not happen. When the French horse artillery was in its infant stages in the 1790s, a version of the wurst wagon was used, but this finally disappeared with peace and with the finding of suitable remounts. In the Austrian service, the wursts remained until, apparently the 1808 Regulations, when it was specified that pack horses should carry ammunition to make the cavalry batteries more mobile. The Austrian cavalry batteries were not true horse artillery: all of the gunners rode either on wursts or on the seating pads placed on the trails of the light 6-pounders with which the batteries were issued. This slowed down speed and mobility considerably, and these units usually could not keep up with the cavalry, as could true horse artillery.[20]

Gun tube design for artillery was, undoubtedly, of extreme importance. From the very crude and generally ineffective leathern gun of Gustavus Adolphus to the sophisticated guns of the Gribeauval and AN XI system, there was immense progress in casting methods, metallurgy,

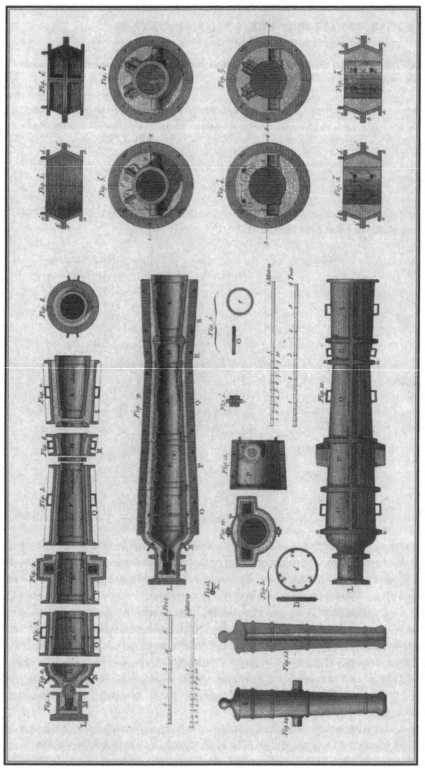

Apparatus used in the casting of ordnance, showing the flasks enclosing the mold. From a drawing in The American Artillerist's Companion of 1809.

and general design.[21] general knowledge of casting and mixing of alloys increased, guns were cast with the bores in place, usually in sand molds. After casting and cooling, guns were then bored out with a vertical boring device. With the advent of the Swiss Maritz and his horizontal boring machine, guns were cast solid, and then bored out to the proper caliber.[22]

There has always been a tradeoff in the artillery arm between range and hitting power versus mobility. Light guns for a long time were very short on hitting power, throwing one- or two-pound projectiles that did little damage. Gustavus Adolphus recognized this—hence his "leather gun," which soon led to better field guns. Standardization was also a problem. The principle of standardization began in France in the 1720s with long arms. When Vallière *père* introduced his new artillery system of 1732, gun tubes and their design and manufacture were standardized, though artillery carriages and vehicles were not. After being rudely surprised by the light and quick-firing Prussian artillery in the War of the Austrian Succession in the 1740s, Austria, under the guidance and sponsorship (largely with his own sizable fortune) of Prince Lichtenstein, pioneered standardization of parts and construction of a complete artillery system, gun tubes, carriages, supporting vehicles and ancillary equipment.

All gun tubes were designed to be sixteen calibers in length. Additionally, weight was cut down so that there was 120 pounds of metal in the gun tube for every pound of shot weight. This standardization was revolutionary, though the old, "antique" and obsolete measure of stone weight for howitzers and mortars was retained in Austrian and Prussian service.[23] Gun carriages were constructed to centrally designed plans which were disseminated to the arsenals, and one size of gun wheel was adopted for all three of the field calibers—though this was somewhat awkward for the light 3-pounder, the wheels actually being too large for the carriage.[24] However, it greatly aided interchangeability, which was one of the hallmarks of the excellent artillery system that bore its originator's name. When the shooting started again in 1756, the Prussians were given a shocking introduction to both the firepower and the maneuverability of the new Austrian artillery system, officially adopted three years before, in 1753: not only was the Austrian artillery now the most efficient branch of the army, but its system was the best in Europe.

Gribeauval was not satisfied with the manner in which the Lichtenstein system employed the principle of interchangeability of parts. While Lichtenstein used only two sizes of wheels for his entire system, Gribeauval had seen the problems with the wheels being too large for the Austrian 3-pounder and designed his system somewhat differently. Thus, he had parts made interchangeable within calibers, not within the entire system. Wheels for the light 4-pounder, for example, could not be used on the 8- or 12-pounder. There was a different limber for the 4-pounder than for the other two calibers, though theirs was the same. Carriages for all three guns were different. Caissons for the 8- and 12-pounders were the same, but that for the 4-pounder was of a different size. While this did call for more wheel designs and different-sized limbers and caissons, the sizes were designed for the particular artillery pieces, by caliber, and the equipment, though not of universal size for the entire system, was better designed and more appropriate to each weapon.

When the Système AN XI gun tubes were designed and manufactured shortly after being approved by the Artillery Committee in 1803, new gun carriages and limbers were designed to go with them. It is highly doubtful that the new limbers saw much service. The new gun carriages, which for the 6-pounder meant no *encastrement*, were not as well designed as the older Gribeauval carriages, and had a tendency to fall apart on campaign. Therefore, the older 8- and 12-pounder carriages were taken out of the arsenals where they were stored and used with the new gun tubes.

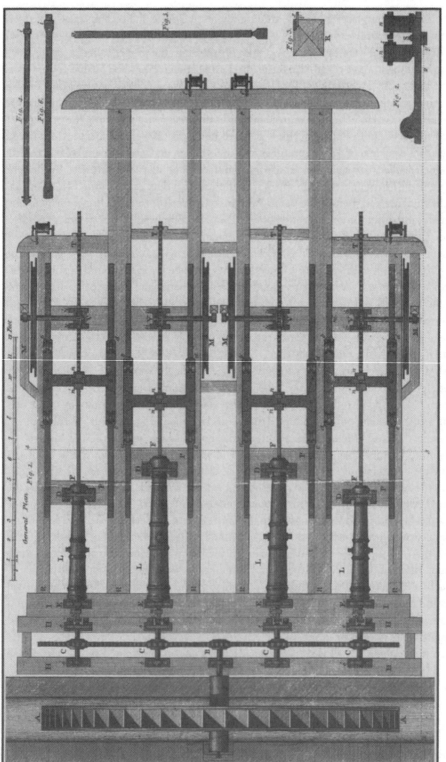

Gun tube boring machine powered from a water mill. From Tousard's The American Artillerist's Companion.

In summary, the Lichtenstein artillery system represented the epitome of mid-eighteenth century technology and the apogee of the older design of field pieces and equipment. Some antique and outmoded appendages, such as the use of stone weight for howitzers and mortars, and the tow bars for the lighter pieces or ordnance, were almost throwbacks to an older way of doing business. Still, it was a major advance, and the method of standardization was a landmark in artillery development. Combat-proven in the Seven Years' War, the Lichtenstein system of guns and equipment was employed by the Austrians throughout the period.

Gribeauval's system was the harbinger of things to come and can be considered the first modern artillery system. Additionally, his reforms were more far-reaching and thorough than Lichtenstein's. Both men took ideas from other places, and the influence of Vallière, the Swedes, and the Prussians is evident in the Lichtenstein system, just as the influence of Vallière, the Prussians, and Lichtenstein is evident in Gribeauval's work. Technological developments do not occur in a vacuum, and there was a considerable cross-fertilization of ideas amongst the European powers: if there was a good idea from another source, it made sense to use it. This both men did for their separate systems, Lichtenstein taking the elevating quoin and standard calibers directly from the Prussians, and Gribeauval adopting a double set of trunnion plates for the 8- and 12-pounder field pieces from the Lichtenstein 12-pounder. In the end, both Lichtenstein and Gribeauval came up with something both unique and utilitarian.

Guns were aimed by pointing the entire piece in the appropriate direction. There were three different types of firing: at random (*à toute volée*), direct shot (*à plein fouet*), and ricochet . Firing at random was "when the object, which is to be battered by a gun which has no elevator, is beyond the point-blank of that gun," it becoming necessary to "fire at random on that object, that is to say, to fire it with the strongest war charge which is regulated for that caliber, and under the greatest angle its carriage will admit." In other words, the gun crew were to "place the axis of the piece in a vertical plane, which should cut the object in the middle by giving the piece an angle of elevation so much the greater as the object stands farther from the piece; so that this angle be not . . . above forty-five degrees." It is noteworthy that "this method, seldom employed except in practice schools for experiments, produces only a useless noise and waste of ammunition." The chances of a hit, unless the target were overly large, was just about nil.

Firing direct shot was the normal practice when firing in the field, especially against troops. Firing direct shot "is to strike the mark in the direction of its trajectory line with the first stroke, without bounding on any other object, and consequently includes also the firing at random, when, by this method, the ball strikes the mark at the first stroke." This would be also be called direct fire. Ricochet firing was used to bound the round along the ground after the first graze, which caused a lot of damage to troops in formation. The round took a somewhat irregular bounce after striking the ground, something akin to a lacrosse ball, which is counterweighted on purpose for a nonregular bounce. Troops in formation could see roundshot coming at them when ricochet fire was employed, and it could be unnerving, especially for green troops. The kinetic energy of the roundshot was amazing. Even when slowing down it could do a lot of damage to the human body. What appeared to be a gently rolling 6-pound ball of cast iron could take a foot and part of a leg completely off if an inexperienced conscript tried to stop it. This meant a visit to the surgeon, whose messmates were now somewhat better educated, and definitely more experienced, in ballistics.

One interesting and somewhat unexpected example of the ability of roundshot to ricochet was experienced by the Württemberg artillery battery commanded by *Major* Faber du Faur while engaged before the walls of Smolensk in 1812:

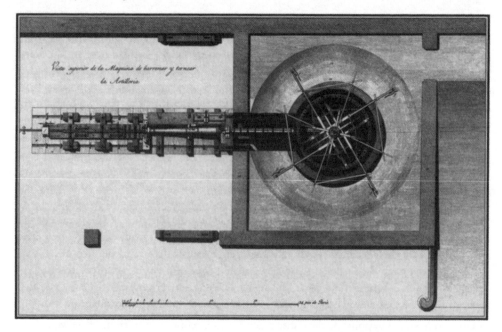

Engraving showing the top of the horizontal boring machine invented by the famous Swiss Jean Maritz in 1739, which revolutionized gun tube manufacturing.

No sooner had our valiant troops established themselves in the suburb on the right bank of the river than they were assailed from all sided by masses of enemy troops. We rushed a few pieces forward to support our men, but these soon came under Russian fire. Before long we found ourselves positioned on ground that, not long ago, had been occupied by the enemy's battalions. The ground was littered with the debris of their equipment, and this served to remind us of the ferocity of the struggle. Cannon balls still bounced towards us, ploughing through the soil and showering us with earth and stones. Even if the missiles went harmlessly by, and we thought the danger over, a number of us were still wounded by cannon balls ricocheting off the walls behind us and once again falling into our ranks.[25]

It must have been like being shelled from two directions at once. The lesson learned was undoubtedly never to pick a battery position in front of fortress or city walls.

Lastly, the term "point-blank" needs to be defined. It was a measure of the distance a round would travel in the air, breaking the line of sight twice. A good definition (from Tousard) would be:

Trajectory line is the curve which the shot describes. The *trajectoire* intersects the sight line (*ligne de mire*) twice; first at a point little distant from the mouth of the piece; the second time at a point far more distant. As the mobile, when quitting the piece, has a direction nearly approaching that of the axis of the piece; their axis is considered as the line of firing (*la ligne de tir*), when we speak of the position of the line of firing relatively to the sight line from the mouth of the piece to its first intersection.

Point blank (but *en blanc*) is the point where the trajectory line intersects the sight line for the second time, and it is denominated primitive point blank (but *en blanc primitif*), when the piece is pointed so that the sight line be horizontal, and loaded with the greatest charge which is regulated for its caliber.

Artificial point blank (but *en blanc artificiel*): When wishing to fire under a great angle, and not being able to direct the sight line to the object which is aimed at, we procure this new point blank; in order to do which, it becomes necessary to raise the sight line at the breech so as to obtain a sight of the object. The height to which the sight line at the breech is raised, and the instrument which serves to procure this elevation, is denominated *la hausse*, elevator, movable sight.

Employment of field artillery is interesting not only in its development, but also in what was finally obtained during the Napoleonic period. From 1807 on, the massing of artillery in batteries of ever-increasing size became much more common, and the numbers of artillery on the battlefield much more dense. Though this naturally followed from larger armies being employed, it was also the result of commanders, especially artillery commanders, realizing that artillery by itself or when supported by infantry and/or cavalry could be a decisive factor on the battlefield—a change brought about by the introduction of lighter, more mobile guns, greater accuracy and fire control, and, finally and most importantly, greater command and control from artillery commanders at the division, corps, and army level.

When light, battalion guns (so-called because they were attached to the infantry battalions as supplementary firepower) were first employed by Gustavus Adolphus in the 1630s, artillery employment was still in its infancy. However, as both warfare and artillery doctrine and practice evolved, competent generals, while still maintaining light guns assigned to their infantry battalions, began to assemble and mass their heavier field artillery pieces to support their main efforts on the battlefield. In size, field pieces seldom exceeded the ubiquitous 12-pounders in any army, other favorite calibers being 3-, 4-, 6-, and 8-pounders depending on which army was involved. Steadily, albeit slowly, commanders began listening to their senior artillerymen, and by 1800 battalion guns began to disappear, though Prussia, Austria, and Russia kept them longer than the French and British. Consequently, on the Continent massed French artillery in the battles of the early Empire tended to be at the decisive time and place, while the usually more numerous Allied artillery was still dissipated throughout the army. There were exceptions. Massed Russian artillery effectively destroyed an attacking French corps at Eylau in early 1807, and a massive Austrian "battery" of 200-odd guns outfought, and outshot, the less nu-

A side view of Maritz's machine, which was powered by horses. The French Navy adopted it before the French Army.

Austrian 6-pounder with limber.

Gribeauval caisson for a 4-pounder.

merous French artillery at Essling (known as Aspern to the victorious Austrians) in 1809, subsequently hurting the almost defenseless French infantry. However, enough French infantry held firm, including the indomitable Old Guard infantry under their amazing commander, Dorsenne, discouraging any subsequent advance by the already defeated Austrian infantry.

NOTES

1. Elting, *Swords Around a Throne*, p. 258.
2. Roquerol, *L'Artillerie au Début des Guerres de la Révolution*, p. 8; and Dodge, *Gustavus Adolphus*, pp. 42-5
3. Dodge, *op. cit.*, p. 42.
4. Tsouras, *The Greenhill Dictionary of Military Quotations*, p. 42.
5. *Ibid.*, p. 43.
6. Duffy, *The Army of Frederick the Great*, page 169.
7. Tsouras, *op. cit.*, p. 43.
8. See John Lynn's excellent *Giant of the Grand Siècle*, pp. 500-12, for the different artillery systems of Louis XIV's army. The evolution of the French artillery from a guild to a militarized branch of the army is plainly explained, taking place over 50 years before the Lichtenstein reforms accomplished the same thing in the Austrian Army. The French Royal Regiment of Artillery (Régiment Royal Artillerie) dates from 1693. In 1710 there were five battalions in the regiment, totaling 236 officers and 3,700 other ranks.
9. Lynn, *op. cit.*, p. 504. The translations for the two systems of artillery that were used is new and old for *nouvelle* and *veille*, respectively. The *nouvelle système* was the lineal grandparent for the later, better Gribeauval System of the 1760s.
10. Naulet, *L'Artillerie Française (1665-1765)*, pp. 323-4.
11. Duffy, *op. cit.*, p. 175. The creative von Holtzman also developed the caisson limber which carried the ammunition box on the limber instead of the *coffret*, or ready box, sitting between the brackets of the carriage (which had been introduced by the Swedes). The Prussians in the first half of the eighteenth century were very active in developing their artillery. General von Linger, who can be considered the founder of the Prussian artillery arm, set the calibers for the guns at 3-, 6-, 12-, and 24-pounders, and *Major* Georg, Friedrich von Tempelhof wrote *Le Bombardier Prussien*, establishing an excellent reputation as an artillery theorist. Unfortunately for the Prussians, Frederick intervened without the requisite technical knowledge, and set them back. The Austrians, with their new system in 1753, definitely set the standard, albeit with great Prussian influence.
12. Tousard, *The American Artillerist's Companion*, p. 39. See also Rothenberg, *Napoleon's Great Adversary*, p. 35. Sources differ as to the Austrian cavalry batteries riding on a wurst as well as the gun carriages. The 1808 Regulations, however, state that the gun crews rode on the gun carriages and had packhorses, not caissons or wursts, to carry the ammunition.
13. DeScheel, *A Treatise of Artillery Containing A New System, or The Alterations made in the French Artillery since 1765*, pp. V-X.
14. *Ibid.*
15. *Ibid.*
16. Alder, *Engineering the Revolution: Arms and Enlightenment in France, 1763-1815*, pp. 153-61 for the construction of gun carriages. See DeScheel, pp. 17-25, for a more technical version, including dimensions.
17. DeScheel, *op. cit.*, p. VIII. Graves, in the introduction to this edition of DeScheel, is citing *Ildefonse Fave: Études sur le passe et l'avenir de l'artillerie* (Paris, 1863), vol. IV, p. 192. Fave was a knowledgeable and prolific author on artillery. It should be noted that the *prolonge* was not the old drag rope, which was less efficient and was not attached to the trail of the piece and the limber for rapid movement,

but used to drag the gun using the crew. The *bricole* was developed by Gribeauval to fulfill that function, which made it easier for the crew.

18. Alder, *op. cit.*, p. 151. Further to ensure accuracy, after the round was within tolerance of the two gauges, it was placed in a metal cylinder of the same caliber as the gun tube to see if there were any casting inaccuracies or imperfections on the surface of the round—for example, "bumps" in the metal—that would impede its progress up and out of the gun tube upon firing.

19. DeScheel, *op. cit.*, pp. VI-VIII. See also Hicks, *French Military Weapons*, p. 142. The new rear sight developed by Gribeauval was fixed onto the breech of the piece, was adjusted by the gunner with a simple screw, and was aligned with the fixed front sight. It remained on the gun tube during fring, which allowed the gun to be relaid much more quickly. The Austrian and Russian sights, in contrast, had to removed before firing and were not as simple and accurate a means of "pointing" the piece. Speed and accuracy of firing are a mainstay of artillery units in combat.

20. Napoleon believed that artillery was more important to cavalry than to infantry, as cavalry had little or no inherent defensive firepower. Hence the usefulness of horse artillery, which he believed cavalry should never be without, whether when attacking, rallying, or in position. Further, he stated that the three combat arms were nothing without each other and should always be employed to support each other, even when in bivouac.

21. The new AN XI gun tubes did away with the usual outer bands on the tubes—the reinforces—which were thought to strengthen the gun tubes, but in reality did not. The AN XI gun tubes had a much cleaner and more modern appearance than the older Gribeauval tubes.

22. Jean Maritz was the inventor of the revolutionary horizontal boring machine, which made gun tubes inherently more accurate. The Maritz family of foundry masters had been in France for quite some time, and operated the French cannon foundries at Douai, Lyon, and Strasbourg. They greatly aided Gribeauval in the development of his new artillery system. See Alder, pp. 40-2.

23. Duffy, *Instrument of War*, p. 284.

24. It should be noted that Lichtenstein's first attempt at a lighter field piece, a new 3-pounder in 1743, was a failure; he and his cohorts learned from their failures as well as others' successes. See Duffy, *Instrument of War*, p. 283.

25. Faber du Faur and North, *With Napoleon in Russia*, Plate 30.

Chapter 2
Scholars

The object of artillery should not consist of killing men on the whole of the enemy's
front, but to overthrow it, to destroy parts of his front . . . then they obtain decisive effects;
they create a gap.

—Guibert

It is by means of the science of movement, the speed and intelligence with which the artillery
chooses its position, that it gains advantages over the enemy's artillery, when it continually trains
its fire on the decisive points and keeps pace with the troops.

—Jean du Teil

2030, 5 March 1762: Vienna, Austria

The artilleryman had just about finished his tour of duty with the Austrian Army. He had served with all of his dedication and skill, as was his mandate from his king, and he had served well. He had seen action, learned more about his chosen profession, and had been promoted for competence, if not brilliance. He had also learned much, and that knowledge he would take back to France with him.

Jean-Baptiste de Gribeauval was an expert artilleryman. He had been that before he was seconded to the Austrian Army to serve against the Prussians. He had seen the Prussian artillery before the war, and had been impressed. He was also very impressed with what the Austrian Lichtenstein had come up with to counter it. The Austrians had the best artillery system in Europe, and Gribeauval now knew what his job was, and to what he would he now devote his career: he was going to develop an system for France that would be the best in the world.

Sitting in his study, he was preparing to write to his patron Choiseul and inform him of some of the artillery developments that the Austrians had introduced. They had admirably standardized their artillery calibers—something that had already been done in France by Vallière—but they had also standardized their gun carriages and other artillery vehicles, as well as their wheel sizes for gun carriages, limbers, and caissons. They had also borrowed von Holtzman's idea for an elevating quoin, which, though somewhat more effective and better than the simple quoin, was not as efficient as it could be. Additionally, the pull bars on their 3-pounders, 6-pounders, and 7-pounder howitzers would have to go: they were too inefficient, and they interfered with loading and swabbing the gun tubes. The Lichtenstein gun tubes were sleek and had beautiful lines, and they were also much lighter than the immense Vallière guns. Lightness, sturdiness, and maneuverability were the hallmarks of Lichtenstein's new guns, and the guns that Gribeauval wanted to design would have to be just as light, or lighter, but the calibers might have to be heavier for better throw weight.

Gribeauval had been working on a new artillery system for quite some time, most of it in his head. He already had developed new carriages for fortress pieces, but French field artillery was too heavy and cumbersome for effective employment. Elevating and sighting mechanisms needed improvement, and there had to be another way to move the pieces in the field quickly over rough terrain when not attached to the limber by the pintle.

As his pen raced across the paper to keep up with his thoughts, visions of rapidly moving light artillery pieces flashed through his mind, equally well served by well-trained gun crews who were permanently organized into companies and regiments, with their officers professionally trained at the best schools France could establish. What Gribeauval wanted was a completely integrated artillery system, to cover artillery from muzzle to trail, so to speak, incorporating excellent gun tubes, carriages, limbers, and all the ancillary equipment necessary, as well as a reorganization France's artillerymen into a modern corps that would be the best in Europe. French artillery would also have to have a howitzer for field use. It was an effective weapon, and it gave artillery companies some flexibility in operations. Finally, artillery employment in combat would have to change, their target in battle to be the enemy's infantry: no longer should they waste time and ammunition in useless counter-battery fire.

Finally, the letter was done, and Gribeauval put down his pen. As he reread what he had written, he noticed a small paragraph that was going to be the *raison d'être* of his new artillery system:

> Our [Austrian] artillery here has a great effect in battle because of its large numbers; it has advantages over that of France, as does the French over it. An enlightened man without passion who understood the [relevant] details and had sufficient credit to cut straight to the truth, would find in these two artilleries the means to compose a single one which would win almost every battle in the field. But ignorance, vanity, and jealousy always intervene: it is the devil's work and cannot be changed as easily as a suit of clothes; it costs too much; and one runs a great danger if one is not sure of success.

He had respect for what Lichtenstein had done, but there were too many weaknesses in the system, and he was not going to throw out the good work that Vallière had done either. For example, the Lichtenstein carriages were not strong enough, and the guns had insufficient throw weight. New ones had to be designed, and he would keep the standardized calibers of the Vallière system. Mobility, hitting power, and standardization, as well as part interchangeability, would have to be the hallmarks of the new guns. That was first and foremost.

He carefully sealed the letter and summoned an orderly to get it to the post and to France as quickly as possible. It was far from being a highly detailed technical manual—which would also have to be written—but it was a thorough outline of what he had learned and what the French Army would have to do to catch up to the Prussians and Austrians in terms of its artillery. He hoped it was enough, and that it impressed his patron Choiseul enough for him to allow Gribeauval a relatively free hand to develop the system that would eventually bear his name. There would be a terrible row with Vallière *fils*, but that was just one more obstacle to be overcome.

* * *

Artillery is one of the two branches of the military service that is both an art and a science, the other being the engineers. Along with the engineers of the period, it was the most technical branch in the army, as well as being a combat arm. Prior to the Napoleonic period, and specifically prior to the introduction of the "new school" of artillery tactics introduced by French artillery General Senarmont at the Battle of Friedland in June 1807, the artillery was considered a supporting arm, there merely to help the infantry and cavalry of the all armies on the battlefield.

Historically, the great changes in artillery employment actually began during the Seven Years' War and in its immediate aftermath. The gradual doctrinal and practical change was first started by the Austrians after the War of the Austrian Succession. Realizing they needed a

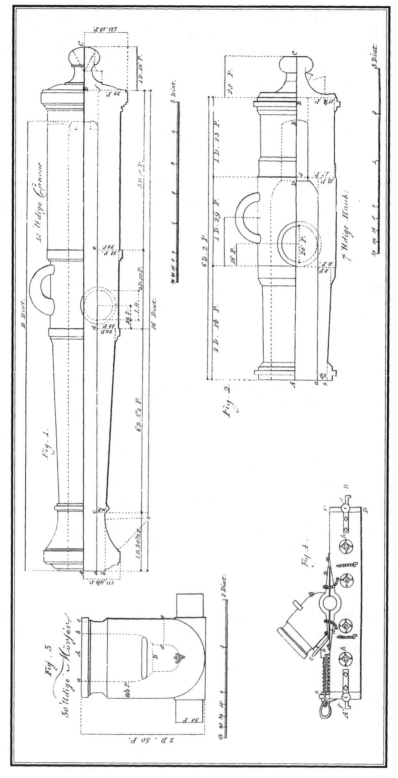

Austrian 12-pounder gun, 7-pounder howitzer, and 30-pounder stone mortar.

battlefield counter to the excellent Prussian infantry, and ruefully acknowledging that the light Prussian artillery had both outmaneuvered and outshot their own, the Austrians, inspired by Lichtenstein, introduced a new artillery system, which started artillerymen on the road to becoming full partners as a combat arm with their infantry and cavalry brethren. Prussia was the other catalyst. Frederick the Great introduced horse artillery in 1759, and constantly expanded his artillery to reinforce and support his infantry, which was becoming increasingly inferior due to very high losses. Interestingly, the Austrians considered Gribeauval a "collaborator" in artillery and engineer matters, which indicates that he may have been more than he appeared.[1]

Between the Seven Years' War and the beginning of the Revolutionary Wars, French military theorists blossomed in order to improve the French Army and the way it fought its wars. Military scholars not only influenced the way the army would fight and train, but also the way it would be organized. Capable military scholars and theorists were not, however, unique to the French Army, although these men produced more than their share: innovators, tacticians, and theorists came to the forefront in other European countries, all of them influencing, to one degree or another, the way their countries' armies would fight. Many of these would directly influence the artillery arms of their respective armies.

As artillery also has to do with mathematics and is classed as a "science," mathematicians of the period also had a great impact on artillery as well.

> Benjamin Robins was in artillery what Sir Isaac Newton was in philosophy, the founder of a new system deduced from experiments and nature. Before the publication of his works (which were printed in London in 1742), the service of artillery was a mere matter of chance, formed on no principles, or at best on such as were erroneous. All the nations of Europe have joined in commendation of Mr. Robins and adopted his axioms. The importance of the materials which are contained in B. Robins' works commanded the attention of the celebrated Euler, who translated them into German; and, not satisfied with having enriched the Prussian artillery with a mere translation, he published them with the addition of a copious and learned commentary, in which he explains the theory of the English author, reduces it to calculation, in many instances improves on it, and renders all the parts of it as luminous as are all his own productions ... Robins works with Euler's commentaries have been translated into French by M. Lombard, royal professor of Auxonne artillery school; from which several of his axioms, propositions and results of experiments, tending to our own instruction, are extracted. By comparing his reflections and experiments on the point blank shot with those of M. Dupuget, officers will be enabled to form correct notions as to the pointing of guns.[2]

Benjamin Robins' greatest contribution was in the area of muzzle velocity calculation. He used a ballistics pendulum to measure the velocity at which a projectile left the gun tube. However, he only experimented with musket balls being fired from period muskets, and it was not until 1775 that Charles Hutton carried out experiments at Woolwich with 6-pounder cannon, using Robins' methods, and measured the velocity of the round leaving the gun tube—the first one so to do . Still, Robins clearly proved that his method was the only accurate way to measure muzzle velocity.[3]

Two other practical developments aided the technological advances in artillery. First, Bernard Forest de Belidor, a mathematics professor, figured out that the same power could be obtained for launching a projectile, and achieving the same range and accuracy, by using a smaller charge of powder. This discovery enabled rounds to be lighter and more rounds to be carried, as less powder was needed. The second development was Jean Maritz's horizontal gun tube boring machine, which allowed cannon to be cast solid, instead of with a core in them, and then bored out completely to the desired caliber. This revolutionized cannon production and also improved the weapons' accuracy. Previously, the partially cast bore had been finished on a vertical boring machine that was not particularly accurate. The cannon tube was lowered onto a bit that revolved, slowly finishing the bore. Maritz's new machine rotated the gun tube, and allowed the bore to be produced in the center of the tube. It was basically a giant lathe, and powered by horses.

The first French artillery school dates from 1720, though unofficially one was founded at Douai in 1679.[4] These were the first professional schools in Europe, and they were copied by the other nations to enable them to train their artillerymen.[5] From that period until the advent of Gribeauval as Inspector General of Artillery, there was a constant argument concerning the balance between the theoretical education of the students in mathematics and the their practical education as future artillery officers. These excellent artillery schools were the first higher-level institutions in Europe where math and science were taught on a regular basis, and throughout their existence in the *ancien regime* the faculty consisted of some of the best mathematicians of their day, such as Camus and LaPlace, with texts written by such as Bezout and Monge. Students were rigorously trained and tested before being sent into the field. By 1720 the standard course of study included classroom work as well as practical application in the field. Students were tested by the mathematics faculty every six months, supervised by senior artillery officers.

In 1732 Jean-Florent de Vallière (1667–1759) introduced what is generally recognized as the first artillery system into France, and Europe. While his system only radically affected gun tubes and their standardization, his emphasis on education and training was noteworthy. He was adamant in his insistence that any officer who was promoted have the skill level required of his rank. Further, this was codified in the *Ordonnance* of 1729: artillery officers had to be "book smart" as well as technically capable.

Further, Vallière was careful of the artilleryman's reputation both inside France and throughout Europe, and demanded that the education requirements for artillery officers be high, setting the standard for the army as the "duty experts" in supporting firepower. The schools' curriculum was to include mechanical drawing in addition to prescribed mathematical theory, all students taking at least a year of each. Each student had to be able accurately to depict artillery equipment on paper as design problems suitable to be used as blueprints.

Gribeauval's continuation on the insistence of an excellent educational background became the hallmark of the French artillery schools up to 1789. Among other things, he insisted that all artillery officers take mathematical analysis, particularly algebraic analysis. He emphasized that training had to be balanced between the academic, or theoretical, and the practical. Once artillery officers had been commissioned, they would spend the first nine weeks with their regiments as enlisted men learning crew drill and the other duties of enlisted French artillerymen. Lastly, he opened an artillery school for French NCOs so that their education would not be neglected: not as extensive as the officer's schooling, it was still a step in the right direction and it was one of the reasons that the French artillery equaled, and in many ways exceeded, the Imperial Austrian in reputation and efficiency before 1792.

The impact on modern artillery development of Gribeauval's reforms, inventions, innovations, and systemization of the French artillery, as well as that of other, lesser-known contributors such as Lichtenstein, Belidor, Vallière, and von Holtzman, is aptly summed up by David Chandler:

> The truly revolutionary improvement in European artillery would date from Gribeauval's great range of comprehensive reforms in the last quarter of the eighteenth century, but considerable preliminary spade-

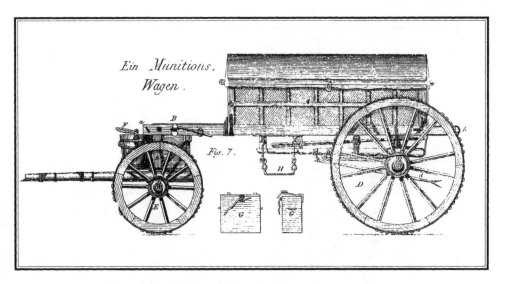

Ein Munitions. Wagen.

Fig. 7.

An Austrian ammunition wagon

work was carried through during the period 1720-1750 by a series of more or less enlightened artillerists and professors, most of them Frenchmen.[6]

Joseph Wenzel Prince Lichtenstein (1696-1772) initiated and developed the Austrian artillery to become the best in Europe by 1756, and his system, which lasted in service until 1859, "has rightful claim as the first unified system of field artillery in the world."[7]

Austrian artillery performance in the War of the Austrian Succession (1740-44) was dismal. The artillery was not a unified system, the guns and carriages, along with the ancillary vehicles, were outdated, too heavy and cumbersome for field service, and the artillerymen were not trained to fight their guns adequately in the field. Lichtenstein decided on his own after the war to devise a new artillery system to make the Imperial Austrian the best in Europe. Luckily for impoverished Austria, Lichtenstein also had the wealth to carry it out. He used his considerable fortune and spent lavishly, but carefully, on his new ideas on and the artillery as a whole. What he developed and championed was the first unified system of artillery in military history.

Lichtenstein conducted a thorough overhaul of the Austrian artillery. His reforms covered gun tube manufacture, and carriage design and manufacture, and he reorganized the entire artillery structure of the Austrian Army. In these tasks, he was ably assisted by a group of talented people, some native Austrians and some not, who were instrumental in applying the new reforms. Ignaz Walther von Waldenau (1713-1760), Andreas Franz Feuerstein (1697-1774), and Anton Feuerstein (later ennobled with the amended name "von Feuersteinberg") were the native Austrian "component" of Lichtenstein's team. Major Adolph Alfson was a Norwegian who found his way into the Austrian service. Joseph Theodor Rouvroy came into the Austrian service from the Saxon Army. He had been born in Luxembourg, but as his father had been a Saxon artillery officer he had followed in his father's footsteps. Apparently, Lichtenstein lured him away from the Saxon service, and he resigned in 1753 to accept a captaincy in the Austrian artillery. A distinguished artilleryman, he was a general by 1763, and he was the commander of the 2nd Artillery Regiment in 1772. He was a *Feldmarshall-Leutnant* by 1775 and commanded the Austrian artillery in the War of the Bavarian Succession. The last of the new team, Berliner Schröder, was a talented Swiss carpenter and mechanic.

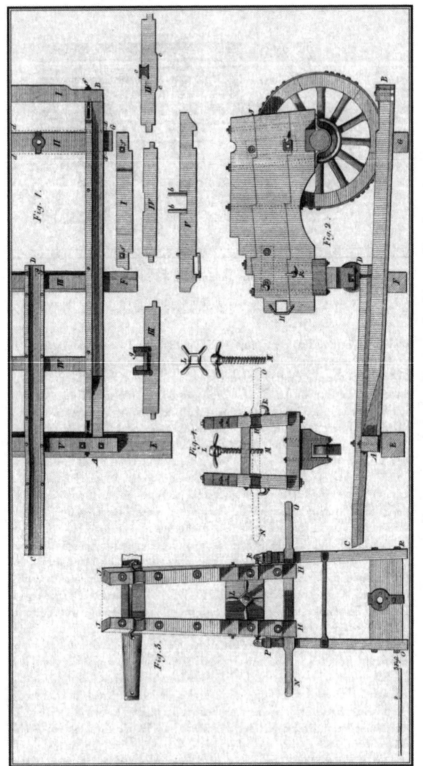

The Gribeauval garrison carriage developed in 1748 and widely copied by other nations.

Lichtenstein took over a service that was still tied to the old guild system (done away with by the French over fifty years previously). Part military and part civilian, the Austrian artillery arm was set in its ways and not ready to listen to a non-artilleryman to tell it what it needed to do to update and modernize. Lichtenstein, however, had the backing of the Empress, Maria Theresa, who was impressed not only with what Lichtenstein wanted to do, but also by his willingness to bankroll the reforms out of his own considerable pocket book.

Lichtenstein and his subordinates set to work with a will. The arm was organized into a Field Artillery Staff (*Feld-Artillerie Stab*), which not only ran the artillery organization, but also was responsible for the technical education of the arm, an ordnance branch (*Feldzeugamt*) which consisted of the artificers who made and repaired equipment—that for the horse teams, the gun tubes themselves, and the ammunition. The *Feld-Artillerie Haupt-Korps* consisted of three artillery brigades, each of eight artillery companies, later increased to ten companies each in 1756. Each company originally consisted of 96 all-ranks, was later increased to 140 in 1759 during the height of the Seven Years' War. Lastly, there was the Netherlands Artillery (*Niederlandische National-Artillerie*), which consisted of eight artillery companies, later increased to twelve during the Seven Years' War. The Netherlands artillery had its own ordnance branch for maintenance and ammunition.

Two other establishment completed the Austrian artillery as reorganized by Lichtenstein. These were the *Handlanger* and the Regiment of Artillery Fusiliers (*Artillerie-Fusiliere*). The *Handlanger* were drafted infantrymen, normally without artillery skills and training, who were employed to help move the guns on campaign and in action and who could assist with minor artillery work on the gun crews. It was an unsatisfactory arrangement, the artillery not being guaranteed to get the same infantrymen attached to them twice in a row, and the infantry regiments would not send their best men. Consequently, the Artillery Fusilier Regiment was formed to take their place on a more permanent basis. The regiment had three battalions of eight companies each. This arrangement proved much more satisfactory, and led to greater efficiency in the field. Lichtenstein's new system (that bears his name) was officially adopted by the Austrians in 1753. It more than proved itself in the next war, the Seven Years' War (1756-63).

Lichtenstein and his confederates did not neglect education, either for the officers or the enlisted men. The Artillery Corps School was established at Budweis, in Bohemia, where most of the artillerymen generally were recruited. NCO schools were established with every artillery brigade. Qualified students could then be passed on to the school at Budweis, the course being either five or seven years in duration, depending on the individual's performance. Graduates who completed the entire course were commissioned as lieutenants. The enlisted men who completed the shorter, five-year course were given the billet of gun captain in the gun companies. The course at Budweis consisted of mathematics, geometry, physics and chemistry, plus military administration, tactics, surveying and fortification. The curriculum maintained a balance between classroom and theoretical work, and practical, or field, exercise. From 1786 the elite *Bombardeur Korps* became a training command, by order of the then Director of Artillery, *Feldzeugmeister* Prince Kinsky. Apparently, the school moved to Vienna in 1790.

A new Austrian artillery Regulation, that of 1757, updated in 1808, was produced by the Lichtenstein team. It was a significant advance over what had gone before. With a few changes, the Regulation stayed in effect for the duration of the French Revolutionary and Napoleonic Wars. What it did not address, however, was doctrine or standard practice for artillery employment above the battery level: that would be left to officers the caliber of Joseph Smola, of which, unfortunately, the Austrians would find themselves somewhat short—"Proper handling [of artillery], such as the provisional battery formed by Lieutenant Smola at Neerwinden, positioned forward to support the line with canister, were exceptional and caused much comment."[8] However, Smola was the exception, not the rule, in the artillery officer ranks, and his aggressive tactics were not copied. They were also few and far between, and most of the Austrian artillery in combat was not uniformly aggressive, usually being kept at long range, which lessened their contribution and lethality, and deployed "by distributing most of its guns in penny-packages" in contrast to the French, who would mass their guns and risk their artillery to gain a decisive advantage.[9]

Lichtenstein chose three calibers for field artillery, 3-, 6-, and 12-pounders, the same as those used by Prussia, plus a seven-pound stone weight howitzer. (Stone weight referred to the size of a stone that had been used in the past for mortar and howitzer ammunition, but it was no longer in general use, being an "antique custom:" the more up-to-date use employed either inches, denoting the bore caliber, or pounds, for the weight of the round, when naming howitzers and mortars.[10] Prussia was also still using the stone weight system.) Another innovation taken by Lichtenstein from the Prussians was the screw quoin developed by von Holtzman. It was shaped like the old, plain quoin, which was nothing more than a wooden wedge that was placed under the breech of the gun tube to elevate or depress it. The new system added a long screw that ran the horizontal length of the quoin. Rotating the screw would move the quoin along a track that was parallel to the gun tube, elevating or depressing it as desired. It was a great improvement over the older, plain wooden wedge, and added some science to elevation of gun tubes. Combining that with Lichtenstein's new gun tubes and carriages, and the emphasis on parts being interchangeable, gave the Austrians a very big advantage when the wars continued in 1756. The Austrians' artillery arm was the most improved and important arm in their army. It also set the standard for the rest of Europe, and was the best in the world during the Seven Years' War and its immediate aftermath.

The new Austrian gun carriages were light, strong, and durable. They were constructed at the armories and depots using centrally designed and approved plans, and were a great improvement on what had been in use for years. Two types of wheels were designed—the large size for guns and the rear wheels of wagons and caissons, and a smaller size for gun limbers and the front wheels of the caissons and other rolling stock. The gun wheel, at a little over 52 inches in diameter from the center to the edge of the outer rim, was probably too large for the light 3-pounder, but it was believed that the principle of interchangeability was more important than maneuverability in the field. Axles were make of wood, however, which became a liability after Gribeauval developed the iron axle in his artillery system, giving the French an immense advantage in construction and durability. For all their powerful appearance, field guns are somewhat fragile pieces of equipment and need constant maintenance and repair, especially during and after a long campaign.

All of the new Austrian field guns initially had a *coffret*, which held the ready-use ammunition and was placed in the trail of the gun carriages and taken out when the guns were brought into battery. Beneath the *coffret*, the carriages were strengthened with iron bands for added support. Later, the *coffrets* would be taken out and placed on the gun limber for transport, being removed by the gunners and taken to the gun line after the battery was emplaced. To make the 12-pounder a better-balanced piece when traveling, two sets of trunnion plates were cut into the cheeks, a rear set for traveling and a front set for firing. Gribeauval later used this innovation—*encastrement*—in both his 8- and 12-pounder field pieces and their gun carriages.

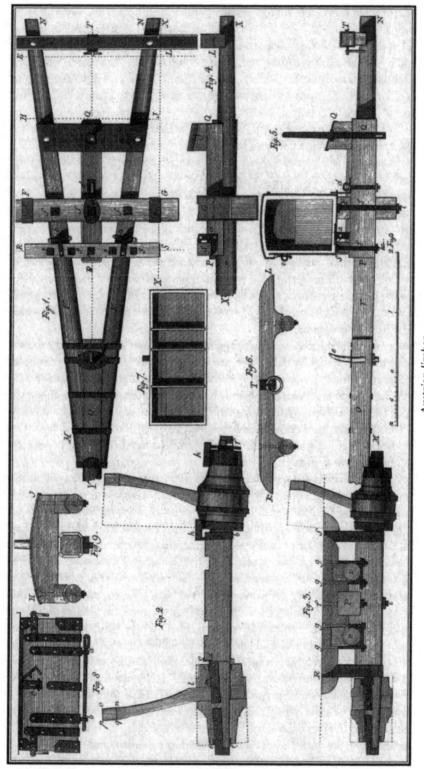

Austrian limber.

Lichtenstein's gun tubes were simple, practical, sturdy, and light. They were cast in bronze, a strong alloy for cannon-making, the "standard Austrian mix" being ten parts tin to one hundred parts copper. Unfortunately, scrap metal was also thrown in during the casting process, which could create flaws in the casting and make the gun tube weak in places, which with the available technology was difficult to detect. As a safeguard, however, every Austrian gun tube was "proven" by test-firing using incrementally larger charges. If the gun tube "survived" the proving process, it was accepted for service.

For the Russians, the greatest innovator for the artillery during the period was Alexei Andreevich Arakcheev (1769–1834), also known as the Grand Vizier of the Russian Empire. He was instrumental in the development of the artillery system of 1805, which made the Russian artillery a player on the battlefields of the Napoleonic period, notably at Eylau in 1807. Arakcheev was Inspector General of Artillery for the Russian Army twice in his career, in 1799 (when Kutusaiv was his adjutant) and again in 1803. He completely reorganized and improved the Russian artillery, developing what became known as the System of 1805. He lightened caissons and gun carriages, though was said to be brutal and not caring of the lives of the men in his charge. He was not a combat soldier: "this brute was not at all a frontline general. He was a paper general." Still, his modernization program was a significant milestone for the Russian Army, allowing it to compete on a somewhat more level playing field than before. Minister of War from 1808 until 1810, he was a trusted confidant of Tsar Alexander and held considerable power in the Russian government.

Possessed of a violent temper, Arakcheev apparently went into a rage on seeing the wreck of the Russian artillery from the Battle of Durrenstein in 1805 and cruelly treated the officers and men. One report has him burying two artillery officers, both lieutenants, up to their necks and left to slowly die. He was also accused of having beheaded another unfortunate Russian officer with his sword in a fit of rage. Whatever the truth of these accusations, he still ranks as one of the noted scholars and organizers of the period, the System of 1805 being his legacy. He was not timid when he wanted something done, and firmly believed that "You don't get things done by talking softly in French."[11]

One of Arakcheev's *aides-de-camp*, Lieutenant Zhirkevich, however, who spent three years with him, described him as honest and direct, proud, self-reliant, and self-assured. He also thought him vindictive and full of animosity. However, he was also kind, thoughtful, and indulgent with those he trusted. The officer noted that he himself had heard nothing good of Arakcheev, but witnessed none of rumors while he served under him. He also stated that the soldiers themselves were much more unhappy under Arakcheev's successor, General Meller, who was considered a kind officer, than during Arakcheev's tenure in the artillery inspectorate. During Arakcheev's tour, only one officer had been reduced, and that was for fraud, which was an offense punishable by being sent to "count trees" in Siberia. Zhirkevich also commented that the reforms instituted during Arakcheev's tenure were his responsibility, even though they were finished after he had left the artillery directorate. Arakcheev was the "firm foundation" of the 1805 artillery reforms which modernized Russia's artillery.[12] Although characterized by his contemporaries as a "paper general," not being a proven combat leader, Arakcheev still contributed mightily to the Russian artillery of the period. More manager than combat soldier, he still ranks with Lichtenstein and Gribeauval, who were proven combat leaders, as an artillery innovator and a "maker of systems."

The new Russian guns had the appearance of both the Prussian and Austrian pieces, and used the same elevating device, the screw quoin, and the same gun carriage reinforcing bands beneath the *coffret* that the Lichtenstein guns had. Russian artillery reforms during the period took place in two stages, one in 1796 and the other from 1802 to 1805. Arakcheev generally was responsible, and gets the credit, for the latter evolution. The first reform period, however, was the responsibility of a man who generally gets little acknowledgment for anything and is most famous for being murdered—Tsar Paul I.

Paul ascended the throne on the death of his mother, Catherine I (the Great). At the end of Catherine's reign the Russian artillery was in disarray, the "artillery pieces were too heavy, and the artilleryman were not well trained. There was no strict standardization of [gun tubes] and carriages."[13] Further, "during peacetime, artillerymen were organized as infantrymen, and were trained to fire from various artillery pieces, but only at the beginning of a campaign were they given the pieces" which they would serve in combat. In addition to this, "artillerymen were not trained to maneuver with their pieces, because most artillery horses were purchased at the start of a war." [14]

Paul's reforms brought order out of chaos. The artillery was completely reorganized in battalions of five companies each, ten foot battalions and one horse artillery battalion. Gun calibers were standardized, resulting in a 6-pounder, two 12-pounders, one of "medium proportion," and one of "smaller proportion." There were no howitzers, but the Russians had an excellent gun-howitzer, commonly called a *"licorne"* ("unicorn"), which had a longer range than a conventional howitzer, but could not elevate as high as a normal howitzer. New four-wheeled caissons were introduced, and "each artillery company became an administrative and tactical unit existing in peacetime," consisting of its regular contingent of officers and men, and the artillery pieces they would take into combat, as well as the ancillary vehicles, caissons, and horses.[15]

To add to this excellent start on artillery reforms, in 1802 further reforms were developed by a special artillery commission. Two years later, the Provisional Artillery Committee was established to start work on updating the Russian garrison artillery. In February 1805, the Committee's mandate was enlarged, authorization being granted to "consider any new artillery projects. All further work an any aspect of the artillery arm was now under the expanded authority of the Commission."[16] What was accomplished was impressive by any standard, and the Russian Army was as a result given an artillery arm that was competitive with that of the other belligerents.

First, the artillery train was completely militarized in 1803. Standardization of the artillery equipment was enforced and all artillery equipment was reduced in weight. The Committee had technical drawings made of the artillery equipment and sent to the depots and arsenals to be used in the construction of all equipment, from gun carriages to caissons. These drawings collectively became known as the Artillery System of 1805. The foot artillery arm was reorganized during 1803–04. Regimental artillery with light guns was now organized into light artillery companies, and light, 3-pounder *licornes* were issued to the *Jäger* regiments, two being attached to every heavy artillery company and issued to the *Jäger* as a campaign opened.

Two areas, however, were not reformed or covered adequately—training and tactics. There was no central artillery school, gunners being trained in their companies. Moreover, no new doctrine was developed for the artillery, and combined-arms training, especially infantry/artillery cooperation, was neglected. The need for this type of training, especially for the artillery officers, would become evident during the Austerlitz campaign.

Thoughtful Russian officers, such as Major General Gogel, Lieutenant D. A. Stolypin of the Guard Horse Artillery, and A. I. Khatov, started to discuss and write on the nature of artillery tactics and employment to improve artillery tactical development. Though many ideas were taken from Guibert and du Teil, their work brought about significant change: the Russian

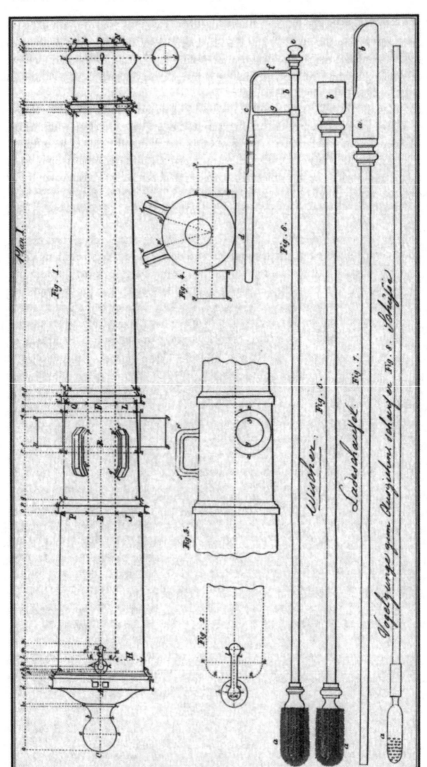

French 18-caliber field piece of the Gribeauval System, with sidearms.

officer corps was beginning the process of educating itself—something Scharnhorst had recommended for the Prussians in 1800 and finally was put into effect after the disasters of 1806. The Russians were starting to think the same way.

The Artillery Committee began its own publication, *The Artillery Journal*, in 1808. It became a forum for officers to publish and talk about new ideas on artillery tactics and employment on the battlefield. Other articles were published in the *Military Journal*. Additionally, General Kutaisov published his *General Rules for Artillery in a Field Battle*, which was a general instruction on the use of artillery in combat (see Appendix XV). While the results were not immediate, there were long-range benefits to the artillery arm, and battlefield performance started to improve when the next war began in earnest in 1812.

In France, after the disasters of the Seven Years' War had proven that the venerated Vallière artillery system was completely unsuitable for field operations, Gribeauval developed the artillery system used by Napoleon and what became the Grande Armée, his system later being called "perhaps the most important innovation in the history of artillery."[17] Gribeauval entered the French Army as an artilleryman in 1732. He had a talent for technical invention, innovation, and achievement, and by the late 1740s he had already developed a new gun carriage for garrison use, one which would revolutionize garrison artillery throughout Europe. Seconded to the excellent Austrian artillery in 1758 during the Seven Years' War, he would gain renown in action with that arm, as well as an offer from Frederick the Great of Prussia of a commission in his army, so impressed was Frederick with Gribeauval as an artilleryman during the siege of Schweidnitz in 1761–62.

Gribeauval knew Prussian artillery from a prewar inspection. He brought back plans of the Prussian light pieces and had one cast, built, and test-fired. He judged it to be too light and not strong enough for extended campaigning. He knew the Lichtenstein system like the back of his hand: he was familiar with its strengths and weaknesses, having served with it and used it in combat for over four years. What he wanted to do when he returned to France (which he did in 1762), was to give France a modern artillery system that surpassed all he had seen, worked and fought with, and fought against.

Gribeauval also had powerful patrons, among them the de Broglie brothers, who, in secret correspondence with Louis XV, would later support Gribeauval's reforms. His immediate superior in Vienna was the French ambassador, the Duc de Choiseul, who would become Minister of War and direct Gribeauval's reforms of the French artillery. Choiseul's successor in Vienna, du Châtelet, was also a Gribeauval supporter. The obsolete Vallière artillery system's days were numbered—though not be without resistance from Vallière *fils*, son of the famous artillerymen and developer of the system that bore his name.

The argument with Vallière *fils* was bitter and long. Gribeauval's new system was initially approved, and then rejected when his patron, Choiseul, was out of favor and a new war minister took his place who supported Vallière. The French artillery community took sides, Gribeauval's adherents being known as the "*Bleus*" and Vallière's as the "*Rouges*" (from the color of the breeches they wanted the French artillerymen to wear). Gribeauval won out, after both systems were tested and retested, and by the mid-1770s his System was the new artillery of France.

Before returning to France, Gribeauval wrote to Choiseul, describing to him what he believed was needed to upgrade France's artillery. However, Gribeauval wanted more than that: he wanted an entirely new artillery system that would encompass the French artillery from "muzzle to butt plate" and include a complete reorganization of the personnel into regiments and permanent companies, and even address their uniforms.

In 1762–63 Gribeauval was asked to prepare a report comparing the Vallière system of France with the Lichtenstein system of Austria. The report had been requested by Dubois, Bureau Chief at the War Office, and that report became the blueprint for the Gribeauval System of artillery–the most comprehensive system up to that time. Not only was the system modern and up-to-date, encompassing standardization of parts, interchangeability of those parts, and a definite division between field guns and siege and fortress pieces, but it also addressed the manner in which the new artillery system would be used in the field. It was the beginning of the artillery doctrine that would be taught in the excellent French artillery schools and that would be proven sound on the battlefields of Europe from 1792 to 1815.

The letter sent to Choiseul from Austria before his return from detached service formed the outline of Gribeauval's new system. In it, he demonstrated clearly the comparison between Vallière and Lichtenstein. Alone among artillerymen, Gribeauval was not only a technical genius, but a developer of artillery doctrine that would see the artillerymen trained under his system enter every European capital as conquerors. Where the Lichtenstein system had been the epitome and last of the older artillery systems, and artillery theory, in Europe, Gribeauval and his new system was the harbinger of a new type of warfare where artillery would finally take its place as an equal on the battlefield with the infantry and cavalry.

The British artilleryman Captain Ralph Willet Adye, author of the famous *Bombardier and Pocket Gunner*, said of the Gribeauval System:

> The French system of artillery was established as far back as the year 1765, and has been rigidly adhered to through a convulsion in the country which overturned everything like order, and which even the government itself has not been able to withstand. We should, therefore, conclude that it has merit, and, though in an enemy, ought to avail ourselves of its advantages. At the formation of their system, they saw the necessity of the most exact correspondence in the most minute particulars, and so rigidly have they adhered to this principle that, though they have several arsenals, where carriages and other military machines are constructed, the different parts of a carriage may be collected from these several arsenals, in the opposite extremities of the country, and will as well unite and form a carriage as if they were all made and fitted in the same workshop. As long as every man who fancies he has made an improvement is permitted to introduce it into our service, this cannot be the case with us.

There were three British artillery innovators: the Congreves, father and son, both named William, the senior developing the new block trail carriage for guns, and the son who developed the famous rocket system for both naval use and for employment on land; and Henry Shrapnel, who developed the fragmentation shell, spherical case shot, for use in both guns and howitzers, that bears his name.

Sir William Congreve (1772–1828), also known as "Congreve the Younger," never held His Majesty's commission. An honorary lieutenant colonel in the Hanoverian service, he nevertheless was an inspired inventor and a "practical genius."[18] Early on he assisted his father, William Congreve, who was the Superintendent of the Royal Military Repository at Woolwich and later the Comptroller of the Royal Laboratory. He also was colonel-commandant of the Royal Artillery in 1803, was promoted lieutenant general in 1808 and was made a baronet in 1812. It was he who invented and developed the new block trail carriage for the British artillery that served for years, and was the most advanced artillery carriage of the period. The block trail system, among other things, gave the guns a much tighter turning radius. Unfortunately, a block trail carriage was not concurrently developed for the British howitzers, which continued to feature the split, or bracket, trail system until the end of the wars. Only after the wars was a block trail carriage developed for British howitzers.

William, exhibiting very early his mechanical and engineering bent, eventually would hold eighteen patents. For the British, he was, along with Henry Shrapnel, the right man at the right time. His three great military contributions were to naval ordnance, the production of gunpowder, and, best remembered, the rocket system that bears his name. What will be covered here is the rocket system.

Rockets had been in existence for many years. However, until the Napoleonic Wars, rockets were not used as military weapons in Europe. Congreve took his cue from the more than effective Indian use of rockets in the colonial wars on the subcontinent, particularly by Hyder Ali and his son Tipoo Sahib. In those cases, the British were on the receiving end of effective rocket fire, and it was very unpleasant as well as a very nasty surprise.

Congreve designed two basic types of rockets, one for naval use and the other for use on land. The naval rockets, which were larger and had a bigger payload than those for land use, were usually launched from two platforms—modified sloops of war, which launched them broadside from specially cut embrasures in the sides of the ship; and ships' boats. Both types were generally effective. Rockets launched against Rapp while defending Danzig played a very large part in forcing the surrender of the city. Streaking over the defenses, the rockets hit the storehouses containing the garrison's food supply, setting them afire and destroying much of the contents. Starving men cannot fight. Conversely, the long and bitter bombardment of American Fort McHenry in Baltimore Harbor in 1814 was an abject failure, the rockets' main contribution being a line in a poem that was to become the National Anthem of the United States, set to the tune of an old British drinking song.

Congreve's guiding dictum for his rockets was that

> . . . the very essence and spirit of the Rocket System is the facility of firing a great number of rounds in a short time, or even instantaneously, with small means, arising from this circumstance, that the Rocket is a species of fixed ammunition which does not require ordnance to project it; and which, where apparatus is required, admits of that apparatus being of the most simple and portable kind.[19]

While they were pioneers in the development of military rockets, the British were not the only belligerent nation to develop operational rockets and units to employ them. The Danes, undoubtedly impressed by the British rockets used against Copenhagen in 1807, developed an effective military rocket based on an "unburned" example that was found nearly intact by 2nd Lieutenant Andreas Schumacher, a Danish Army engineer, after the British bombardment. His attempts to copy the rocket were successful, and a laboratory was built on Hjelm Island in the Kattegat to keep the work secret. Schumacher's work had official support, and by 1811 he had become successful in developing his own system. Schumacher claimed that his rockets were both more portable and more powerful than Congreve's, and they were put into full production at Frederiksvaerk. Later, the Danish Raketkompagniet (Rocket Company) was formed as a permanent part of the Danish Army.

They were employed during the siege of Hamburg in 1813-14, but there is no recorded use of them at any other time during the Napoleonic period. Here, Schumacher cooperated openly with his French allies, the Danes and French conducting live-fire tests of the rockets in January 1814. Rockets were produced by the French and Danes in Hamburg and apparently used during the siege. When Hamburg surrendered after Napoleon's first abdication, the project was dropped, and the remaining rockets were turned over to the allies.

The Austrians developed the largest rocket arm on the Continent, experimentation beginning in 1808. The rockets were produced under the supervision of Chief Fireworks Master Anton Mager, and were, like the Danish rockets, greatly influenced by Congreve's. They were successfully tested in the presence of the Archduke Charles, but nothing much else was done with them until Major Vincent Augustin, an artillery officer, took over the project.

Augustin had been present at Leipzig and had seen the British employment of rockets and was suitably impressed. After peace was declared in April 1814, Augustin was sent to Great Britain and Denmark and used his time to try and learn more of their respective programs. The British were typically closed-mouth, but after a series of high-level negotiations, which included intervention by Prince Metternich, the Danes allowed him access to their program, although he was forbidden from taking any written notes at the meetings. Augustin got back to Austria by March 1815, and by May of that year a rocket laboratory had been built at Wiener-Neustadt, near Vienna. By the end of May, 2,400 rockets had been manufactured, and by the summer of 1815 an Austrian *Raketenbatterie* had been formed, in time to be employed in the 100 Days' campaign at the siege of Huningue.

The Portuguese, Swedes, and Russians made gallant attempts during the period to develop rockets, but these fell on either deaf ears or empty pockets. The Russian Military Study Committee began to look into the potential of the rocket in 1810. Tsar Alexander had seen the British rocket battery in action at Leipzig in 1813, and had offered congratulations in person for their performance in the field. The "father" of Russian military rockets is probably Lieutenant Alexander Zasydko, another artillery officer, who, after the end of the wars, designed what were referred to as "fighting rockets," but as they were developed after the conclusion of the wars, they are outside of our period.

The Portuguese artillery Sergeant-Major Jeronimo Nogueira de Andrade was busy designing a military incendiary rocket in 1796, but it was neither adopted nor fielded, and remained quite literally on the drawing board. The Swedish chemist Jons Jakob Berzillius was quite impressed with the British bombardment of Copenhagen in 1807. In 1810 while in Copenhagen, undoubtedly watching the damage still being repaired, he met with the Danish physicist Hans Christian Orsted, and, together with some Danish Army officers, began discussions about the Congreve rockets, inspecting some of the duds that landed in Copenhagen, retrieving them, and taking some of them back to Sweden. Berzilius did convince the Royal Academy of Military Sciences to study the weapons with the idea of producing them for the Swedish Army, but too many Swedish officers thought the weapon to be outside the purview of honorable warfare, and the project was dropped. However, Master of Ordnance Colonel Paul Schroderstein saw the military potential of the new rockets and started to test them in 1813, ably followed by Captain D. W. Silferstrope in 1829. During this period, Swedish officialdom gave no support to the efforts of these officers, but their work would finally bear fruit in the 1830s.

French rocket development began in 1810 by fits and starts. They had been the first to "benefit" from British rocket fire during the Royal Navy's attacks against the Boulogne flotilla during the Consulate and early Empire. (During this period, Nelson was defeated twice in his attempts to hurt or seriously damage the flotilla by the French Admiral Latouche-Tréville. One such failed attack resulted in at least 500 dead British seamen being washed ashore after the attack.) After a raid on the Île d'Aix in 1809, the French recovered one of the Congreve rockets intact and began their own experiments. The captured rocket was sent to Paris, where a full report of it was made to the Emperor. A board of officers and scientists were ordered by Napoleon to study the possibility of manufacturing military rockets, and the next year two artillery officers, Captain Pierre Bourrée, a naval artilleryman, and Captain Charles Moreton de Chabrillan, an army artilleryman, were manufacturing rockets based on the Congreve model at Vincennes.

The initial experiments were promising, and further testing was undertaken at Toulon from 1810 to 1812. Four rocket factories were established, at the naval arsenals at Lorient, Rochefort, Cherbourg, and Brest, and the intent was to use the new weapons in sieges. The cost, however, was becoming prohibitive, and, when "field-tested" at the Siege of Cadiz, the rockets failed to reach expectations and the project was dropped.[20]

Henry Shrapnel was a serving officer in the British artillery in the Netherlands in 1793 and was wounded at Dunkirk. He became Senior Assistant Inspector of Artillery in 1804, and eventually rose to the rank of major general after the conclusion of the wars. His main contribution to the British Army, and to its artillery in particular, was spherical case shot, later commonly known by the name of its inventor, shrapnel. The round consisted of a hollow shell, filled with musket balls and an explosive, and set off by a fuse after firing. It was designed to explode over the heads of enemy troops, and was an effective round—something of a British "secret weapon" of the period. The French attempted to duplicate its performance, but failed (they did the same thing with rockets, again failing to achieve a satisfactory weapon for field use). The new round was first used with success in India in 1804, having been tested and accepted for military use the year before. Apparently, Wellington first saw it used at Busaco in 1810 and was quite impressed with it. One of its advantages, besides its great reliability, was that, unlike common shell, it could be fired from both guns and howitzers.

The du Teil brothers, Jean (1733–1820) and Jean-Pierre (1722–1794), were two of the foremost authorities on artillery and artillery tactics in France for the period 1763–89. Both were exceptional artillerymen, and both had a lasting impact on Napoleon. They came from a military family with a tradition of long and excellent service to France. Jean-Pierre du Teil, Baron de Beaumont, entered the artillery as a volunteer in 1731 and was promoted to *sous-lieutenant* in 1735. Wounded at the Siege of Tournai in 1745, he was a captain by 1748 and was made a *chevalier* of St Louis in 1753. He served in Germany during the Seven Years' War from 1757 to 1758, but was medically retired in 1760. Nevertheless, he returned to active service in 1761. He was promoted to *chef de brigade* in 1765, designated *chef de brigade* of the Regiment of Artillery of Toul the next year, was promoted to *lieutenant-colonel* in 1768. In 1773 he was the *lieutenant-colonel* of the Regiment of Artillery of Toul, and by 1777 *colonel* of the La Fère Regiment.

Du Teil did not go to North America during the American War of the Revolution, instead being appointed as the Commanding Officer of the Artillery School of Auxonne in 1779. He was promoted in 1784 to *maréchal de camp* at Auxonne, where Napoleon first came to his attention and was an able pupil. It was under the elder du Teil's tutelage that Napoleon was taught, and became expert in, the Gribeauval artillery system.

Du Teil was designated Inspector General of Artillery in 1791 (Gribeauval had died in 1789), and was nominated as Chief of Artillery of the Armée du Rhin in 1792. Too sick to accept and take up the appointment, he was nevertheless nominated as Inspector General of Artillery of the Armée des Alpes the next year. As he opposed the Jacobins, and refused to carry out their more draconian policies, he was accused of treason, arrested, tried and executed at Lyons in 1794.

His younger brother Jean compiled the authoritative *De l'Usage de l'Artillerie Novelle dans le Guerre de Campagne*, which emphasized mobility, firepower, and cooperation on the battlefield with infantry. It had a profound influence on Napoleon, and no doubt on the other artillery generals of the Grande Armée. A *colonel* in 1784, Jean supported the Revolution and served as an artillery commander in the Armées du Rhin, Alpes, and Italie. By 1793 he was a general of division, commanding the artillery at the Siege of Toulon, ably seconded by the then Captain

Bonaparte. He retired in 1794, but was recalled in 1799 as Inspector General and served as commandant of Metz from 1800 to 1813.

The impact of the du Teil's as artillerymen and military scholars cannot be overstated. They both had a profound influence on Napoleon as an officer and artilleryman, and their policies and training ensured that young *Lieutenant* Bonaparte had a firm grounding as both an artillery and a regimental officer. The younger du Teil's treatise stated in clear and distinct terms the French artillery doctrine that would give the Grande Armée, and the artillery generals that commanded and organized its artillery, the blueprint for success.

The following excerpts from du Teil's teachings were the basics of what was taught to students in the excellent artillery schools. (Interestingly, the students did not work from published texts: they took notes from the instructors, which became their text books, from which they studied and were tested.) Du Teil believed in tactical maneuverability, firepower, and cooperation and coordination with infantry to gain success on the battlefield. Only through the use of what would later (in the twentieth and twenty-first centuries) be termed "combined arms tactics" could success—perhaps even overwhelming success—be gained on the battlefield:

> The proper execution of the artillery is based on the art of emplacement and the directing of the fire to cause the greatest possible harm to the enemy, and to give the greatest protection to the troops that it supports. Before the infantry and artillery can protect each other, it is indispensable for the artillery to coordinate its tactics with those of the infantry, or at least with the results of their principal maneuvers, and the greater or lesser effect with it will produce on such or such a maneuver, and to judge their importance, and the need to increase the rate of fire, or to change position.[21]

Du Teil foresaw that artillery could be an overwhelming force on its own on the battlefield, and not a mere supporting arm:

> It is not less significant for the infantry or cavalry officer, who must command a force of all arms, including the artillery, to understand the main differences in the guns, the manner of placing them, and the results generated by their execution ... With this knowledge he will be able to avoid hindering the artillery officer who will be under his command; he will have full confidence in him, because he will be in a position to judge intelligently the dispositions that are made, or to order some others, according to his own ideas, so that by his own skill can provide the protection which the infantry require.[22]

This sounds almost exactly what Victor and Senarmont were able to do at Friedland in 1807— Victor to give Senarmont his head, and Senarmont to use his skill and judgment to the best of his ability to accomplish the tactical mission. This further description of artillery employment is almost a blueprint of Senarmont's attack at Friedland and of Drouot's at Lützen in 1813:

> It is necessary to observe that one can arrive at thirteen or fourteen hundred yards from the enemy without fearing much the effects from their artillery, because it is so distant and also because one is moving. From that distance one would then be able to prolong even close, if one finds some shelter; the majority of artillerists will ride on the horses and taking to the gallop will advance to within 850 yards. At the command to halt, the horses will make a half turn to the right, unlimber the guns, and in a moment the battery will spring into action. I ask if anyone can imagine a more active way to maneuver?"[23]

Du Teil was also emphatic regarding the artillery commander's role before his battery, or batteries, began their movement into position to bring their fire on the enemy:

> When an officer of the artillery intends to take up a position, he must at once go ahead to survey the terrain in regard to the execution of the artillery. He must examine the approaches, and all the details of the terrain that could provide cover to the enemy, or shelter their advance from his guns. He must observe, at the same time, the possibility for establishing new positions facing in any directions, and to seek the means of maneuvering and communication without being seen by the enemy. It is necessary, in

order to fulfill this objective, that the officers possess a refined skill in recognizing terrain, because, with the artillery, more than with any of the other arms, that skill is of the greatest importance."[24]

Mass, concentration of fire, and the husbanding artillery resources were also hallmarks of du Teil's teachings:

> It is necessary to concentrate artillery on the points of attack, which must decide the victory, relieving the batteries which have suffered loss, and replacing them with others, before the enemy can notice or gain an advantage which would boost their morale and discourage our troops.[25]

> The preservation of the ammunition is an object of great importance in the execution of the artillery; without taking proper precautions, are you not leaving too much to chance?[26]

Careful husbanding, care, and handling of ammunition should be

> . . . sufficient to prove how necessary it is to strive to prevent accidents and to preserve the ammunition, the need of which, on the day of battle, can render the greatest consequences since, if it occurs at the height of a main attack, [this] can lead to the loss of the battle.[27]

Finally, du Teil makes a prophetic assessment and prediction about French artillery employment: "Artillery, thus supported and concentrated with skill, will obtain decisive results . . ."

Senarmont, Eble, Druout and the others may have carried out their artillery missions with professionalism, skill, *élan*, and dash, but it was the du Teils who laid the foundation for those successes. They also carefully trained a future Emperor and the commander of the Grande Armee.

Jacques Guibert (1743-1790) is largely touted as the man responsible for the change in tactics that led to French successes on the battlefield during the period. His very influential *Essai Général de Tactique*, written in 1772, was later largely repudiated in his second work, *Défense du Système du Guerre Moderne*, in which he stated that "The vapors of modern philosophy heated up my head and clouded my judgment."[28] However, the first publication was widely read, and the references to artillery were very relevant to what was later done on the battlefield by the French:

> Artillery must be mobile and able to change its positions when necessary during the course of a battle, either to maintain its prolongations, or to concentrate on some decisive point. It needs to seek accuracy above all else, especially at long range. This is more important than speed of fire. As one shortens the range, which makes accuracy greater, one could increase the rate of fire. Artillery should never be used in counterbattery action, except when there are no troops to fire upon. The true targets of the artillery are the enemy's troops and the works with covered them. Its purpose is not merely to cancel out the enemy's artillery but to cooperate with the troops in winning decisive success.[29]

Louis de Tousard (1749-1817) can justly claim to have been one of the founders of the excellent American artillery arm, though Henry Knox alone usually gets all the credit for his service in the War of the Revolution. Tousard first came into contact with the infant United States through service in North America from January 1777 to August 1778. He was one of the superb foreign officers, along with the Baron de Kalb and Baron von Steuben, "recruited" by the very capable American Minister to France, Benjamin Franklin. Badly wounded at the Battle of Rhode Island in 1778, Tousard had an arm amputated and returned to France, where he was promoted to *major* in the French Army and was made a *chevalier* of St Louis. He was promoted to *lieutenant-colonel* in 1784, but was imprisoned by the new revolutionary government in 1792, but was released the next year.

Tousard emigrated to the United States in 1795 and was commissioned as a major in the 2nd US Artillery Regiment. In 1800 he was promoted to lieutenant colonel in the US service

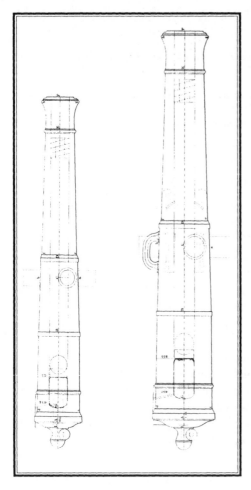

Diagram of the British 6-pounder gun tube of the period (left) and the excellent 9-pounder tube. From A Treatise on Artillery, *by Captain E. M. Boxer, 1853.*

and was made inspector of the US artillery. He had impressed upon George Washington the need and importance of establishing a permanent military academy in the United States for the professional instruction of cadets. From this came into being in 1802 the establishment of the United States Military Academy at West Point as an engineer and artillery school. That same year Tousard retired from the US service, returning home to France. He was reinstated in the French Army, accompanied the expedition to Santo Domingo commanded by Leclerc, Napoleon's able brother-in-law, and returned the same year to enter retirement again. Recalled by the Consulate, he served in America in various administrative and diplomatic posts, returning home in 1816.

However, the most important service Tousard rendered to the young United States Army was his writing of *The American Artillerist's Companion; or Elements of Artillery* which was the first treatise on artillery written specifically for the American service. Consisting of two volumes of text and one of plates, it is a document that draws on most of the important artillery publications and documents of the period (see Appendix XIII) and is a complete handbook on artillery—probably as thorough a treatise as one is likely to come across during the period, rivaling Gassendi's *Aide-Memoir*, upon which it is partially based. His contribution to the American artillery was immense, and his treatise is an up-to-date compendium of artillery material of the period for modern researchers and military historians.

Lastly, the great Prussian reformer Gerhard Johann David Scharnhorst (1755–1813) is not to be forgotten or ignored. A thoughtful and skilled Hanoverian artilleryman, he was an advocate of structured military education for officers and was both a combat veteran and visionary. He labored long and hard to give his adopted country, Prussia, an education system and a competent general staff. He also conducted successful and useful artillery experiments which contributed to the general knowledge. While he was unsuccessful in ensuring that Prussia had an integrated artillery system in 1813 when the country went to war once again against the French and Napoleon, he had ensured that the Prussian Army had improved and had enough artillery to support the troops put into the field and that there was also a new artillery *règlement* to go with them. His early death in mid-1813, from neglect and incompetence, the result of a wound suffered at the defeat at Bautzen, was an incalculable blow to Prussia.[30]

Putting a useful and competent artillery arm into the field was much more than having a collection of guns, men, and horses. It also took a great deal of economic effort and expense, as well as comprehensive and thorough training, part theoretical and part practical. The French were the first to realize this, followed by the Austrians, both of whom had excellent artillery schools and a tradition of fielding excellent artillery. The British had a long tradition of excellence in artillerymen and equipment, and though their artillery arm was much smaller than either the French or the Austrian, the officers and men were well trained both technically and tactically, and, with the advent of the Congreve block trail, they had the best ancillary equipment of all the belligerent powers. Their two gun tubes most often used, the 6- and 9-pounders were excellent weapons, with the most modern elevating screw (that attached to the cascabel), not relying on an elevating platform as did the Gribeauval pieces and being much superior to the screw quoin that was used by Prussia, Austria, and Russia.

Finally, a last word from Guibert on the responsibility of the commander for his artillery:

> The general officer who commands, this man must see all in cold blood and without error, and must be used to the prejudices of the infantry and also those of the artillery, for in the end it is his decision . . . according to the circumstances, to either sacrifice or save the guns. It is for him to calculate on what occasions it is necessary to withdraw the guns, that is to say to go to take up a better position elsewhere, so that the discouraged soldiers do not take the retirement for an escape; on such occasions the guns should be repositioned so that they can continue to damage the enemy; and if at last it is necessary to let the enemy take them, because it costs too much blood, or the time is too precious for the defense; and because after all, in war, there is no shame in doing that which is impossible to avoid.

NOTES

1. Roquerol, *L'Artillerie au Début des Guerres de la Révolution*, p. 15.
2. Tousard, *The American Artillerist's Companion*, p. xiii.
3. See Alder, *Engineering the Revolution*, pp. 104–7.
4. Lynn, *Giant of the Grand Siècle*, p. 270.
5. Alder, *op. cit.*, p. 57.
6 Chandler, *The Art of Warfare in the Age of Marlborough*, p. 188. There is sometimes much chagrin at the level of effectiveness and invention demonstrated by the French in artillery and engineering during the period 1679–1815. The fact of the matter is that the majority of the innovations were either French or introduced by Frenchmen. Belidor, Vallière, Gribeauval and others were instrumental in advancing the *savant* arms to a modern and progressive level. There were other innovators, scientists, and inventors, who were not Frenchmen, such as Robins, Congreve, Shrapnel, and Lichtenstein and his brood, but if you check into the scientific/artillery/engineering lineage and who did what, the fact remains that most were French. Maritz, while Swiss and not French, worked for the French, the French Navy using his horizontal boring machine before Gribeauval adopted it for the Army. Lichtenstein has been touted as the first to standardize artillery, but Vallière was ahead of him in respect of gun tubes, and there had been a light French artillery system during Louis XIV's reign. Additionally, standardization of parts had been steadily developing in France since the 1720s in arms manufacture, which was the responsibility of the artillery (see Alder). There has also been controversy on the ubiquitous Napoleonic forums in the past few years on the development of Gribeauval's artillery system. Comment has been made that Gribeauval merely copied Lichtenstein, which is not an accurate assessment, and one for which no proof has been given. The fact is that there was considerable cross-fertilization of ideas, which Gribeauval himself acknowledged, backed up by Jean du Teil in his field manual. Merely comparing gun tubes and field carriages between the two systems indicates that they are quite different. Further, Gribeauval's development of a new

garrison carriage as early as 1748 and his invention of the new searcher to check for gun tube sound-ness, the adjustable rear sight for gun tubes, the iron axle for gun carriages and other artillery vehicles, as well as the elevating screw, *prolonge*, and *bricole*, demonstrate that his system, while a further development of Lichtenstein's, was no mere copy. For a clarification of the differences be-tween the development of the Lichtenstein and Gribeauval artillery systems, see "Lichtenstein and Gribeauval: 'Artillery Revolution' in Political and Cultural Context" by Ken MacLannan, in *War and History*, vol. 10, Issue 3, 1 July 2003. This article definitively demonstrates that the Gribeauval system was not a copy of Lichtenstein's.

7. DeScheel, p. VI.
8. Rothenberg, *Napoleon's Great Adversary: Archduke Charles and the Austrian Army, 1792–1814*, p. 50.
9. Rothenberg, *op. cit.*, p. 37.
10. Duffy, *Instrument of War*, p. 284.
11. Jenkins, *Arakcheev: Grand Vizier of the Russian Empire*, p. 27.
12. *Ibid.*, p. 101.
13. Alexander and Yurii Zhmodikov, *Tactics of the Russian Army in the Napoleonic Wars*, p. 25.
14. *Ibid.*
15. *Ibid. Licorne* was the French translation of the Russian word for unicorn, which they had dubbed the gun-howitzer.
16. *Ibid.*, p. 62.
17. DeScheel, p. VII, citing Howard Rosen, Le Système Gribeauval et la Guerre Moderne on p. 29 of *Revue Historique des Armées*, 1975.
18. Graves, *The Rockets' Red Glare*. This booklet gives an excellent overview of the Congreve system, both afloat and ashore, with first-class reference material.
19. Congreve, *Details of the Rocket System*, p. 13.
20. For an excellent overview of European rocket development for warfare, see Winter, *The First Golden Age of Rocketry*.
21. Du Teil, *The New Use of Artillery in Field Wars: Necessary Knowledge*, p. 28.
22. *Ibid.*, pp. 14–38. This, and the following five quotations from du Teil's text are merely a sampling of the common- sense guidance for artillery employment which was used or attempted repeatedly by the French artillery in the years 1792–1815. No other nation had the logical doctrine of employment taught in the excellent French artillery schools from the end of the Seven Years' War until 1815. This gave the French an immense doctrinal and tactical advantage over its adversaries for over twenty years.
23. *Ibid.*
24. *Ibid.*
25. *Ibid.*
26. *Ibid.*
27. *Ibid.*
28. Elting, *The Superstrategists*, p. 146.
29. For an excellent analysis of Guibert, du Teil, and other theorists and makers of systems of the period, see Quimby, *The Background of Napoleonic Warfare*, in which this quotation by Guibert, and others, can be found.
30. See White, *The Enlightened Soldier*, for Scharnhorst's attempts at reform in the Prussian Army before 1806.

Chapter 3

"At the Trail of the Piece, Fall In!"

Leave the artillerymen alone. They are an obstinate lot.
—Napoleon

Crack the head of an artillery officer who supplies shells of the wrong caliber...An officer of artillery who runs out of ammunition in the middle of a battle deserves to be shot.
—Napoleon

If there is no one to make gunpowder for cannon, I can fabricate it; gun carriages, I know how to construct. If it is necessary to cast cannon, I can cast them; if it is necessary to teach the details of drill, I can do that.
—Napoleon

1000, 10 November 1785: Le Régiment la Fère, Valence, France

In the old Royal Army, the practice was to train newly assigned lieutenants as enlisted men for nine weeks until they were qualified as artillerymen. What was desired was a balance between the theoretical and the practical. The theoretical part was taken care of by the excellent school system; the practical part was left up to the noncommissioned officers and the senior enlisted men.

Monsieur le sergent, a veteran, grizzled *grognard* who had served with the Auxonne artillery in North America as part of Rochambeau's expeditionary force, watched with grim humor as the new lieutenants of the regiment attempted to go through crew drill on a Gribeauval 4-pounder. Keeping a stern look on his face with great effort—for the "drill" was something to behold, especially for an experienced artilleryman—*monsieur le sergent*, as *messieurs les officiers* on the *ersatz* gun crew were required to call him, tried to keep both his temper and from laughing until tears came to his eyes. Whatever *messieurs les lieutenants* were attempting, it did not belong on the drill field, and definitely not with live ammunition. These newly commissioned *sous-lieutenants* appeared not to know the muzzles from the bores of their pieces, and were continually tripping over themselves, the trail of the piece, or the handspikes being used to traverse the gun. The *sergent* thanked *le Bon Dieu* that they were not conducting a live fire: God knows where the round would have gone with this lively batch of *blanc-becs*!

There was one exception. There was a small, tight-lipped Corsican, who seldom smiled and who took his duties, and this drill, very seriously. When he was in charge of the drill, it became more orderly, and all of the young officers obeyed his sharp, and always correct, commands. This young one knew his gun drill. He also had seen the grimly serious young man use his boot to get his way during crew drill, sending other, larger comrades scampering to their duty, albeit with a scowl and a dirty look; but they obeyed the silent one. The *sergent* pretended to look away in the event something like that happened: it would not do to get him in trouble with their commanding officer, and the other lieutenants were either sufficiently cowed or sufficiently impressed to keep their mouths shut. At least they had sense enough to do that. The Corsican certainly had the way of commanding the other men about him. His commands were crisp, he

Gun crew drill for a 4-pounder.

had the knack of having his orders obeyed, and he never made a mistake. This one would bear watching.

*   *   *

The company was the artillery tactical unit of the Napoleonic period. The building blocks of the artillery company were the gun crews, half-sections, and sections of the company that served the guns. Cannoneers, and the gun crews they made up, lived, breathed, and survived by efficient crew drill. This "cannoneers' hop" was the methodical, seemingly chaotic "ballet" by which the gunners operated the guns and howitzers and allowed them to fire rapidly and accurately in action. No matter the size of the crew, each man had his job and responsibilities, and each was vital to the efficient operation of his particular piece.

Among the different armies, crew drill was basically the same. While the British actually fired the round from opposite sides of the gun and the numbering of the individual cannoneers might differ from army to army, it was essentially the same drill with the same end-game in mind—to load a round rapidly, safely, and accurately into the gun tube and launch the projectile downrange.

A good example of crew drill may be taken from the French manuals of the period. While these do mention that infantrymen were used to supplement the trained artillerymen in the regulations, that did not hold true in action and on campaign for the period. With the exception of instances where artillery units and large batteries suffered heavy casualties, such as at Essling and Wagram in 1809, the French apparently used only trained artillerymen as gun crews on a regular basis. Jean Roche Coignet quite succinctly describes the use of French Guard infantry as cannoneers in two emergencies in 1809:

> There were no gunners left to work our two pieces. General Dorsenne sent forward twelve grenadiers to take their places, and bestowed the cross on them. But all those brave fellows perished beside their guns. No more horses, no more artillerymen, no more shells. The carriages were broken to pieces, and the timbers scattered over the ground like logs of wood. It was impossible to make any more use of them.
>
> The Emperor was informed that the main battery of the Guard would have to be replaced, as the gunners were all killed. "What!" said he. "If I relieve the artillery of my Guard, the enemy will perceive it, and redouble their efforts to break through my center. Call for volunteers at once from the grenadiers to man the guns." Twenty men from each company started off immediately. It was necessary to make a selection, for all wanted to go. No non-commissioned officers were accepted, only grenadiers and corporals. Off they started to man a battery of fifty pieces. As soon as they reached their position, the firing began. The Emperor took snuff, and walked up and down in front of us . . . That night four grenadiers brought in the colonel who had commanded the fifty guns, to which the Emperor sent his "grumblers." This brave officer had been wounded [at] about eleven o'clock. They were carrying him to the rear of his battery. "No," said he, "take me back to my post; that is my place;" and he commanded sitting down.[1]

The crew drill for a French 12-pounder of the Gribeauval System was as follows:

> To serve a piece of this caliber fifteen men are required: eight of the corps of artillerists, and seven of the infantry. The two additional men are designated sixth servants. The accoutrements and implements are the same as for the eight pounders.

On the Right:

> First cannoneer: In marching forward he holds the trail handspike, on the right of the piece, with both hands; in retreating he holds the same handspike with his right hand only. In action he is posted between the trail handspikes; takes care to see that the second cannoneer and all the assistants are at their posts, then gives the word "load;" while they are loading the gun, he directs it by means of the trail handspikes;

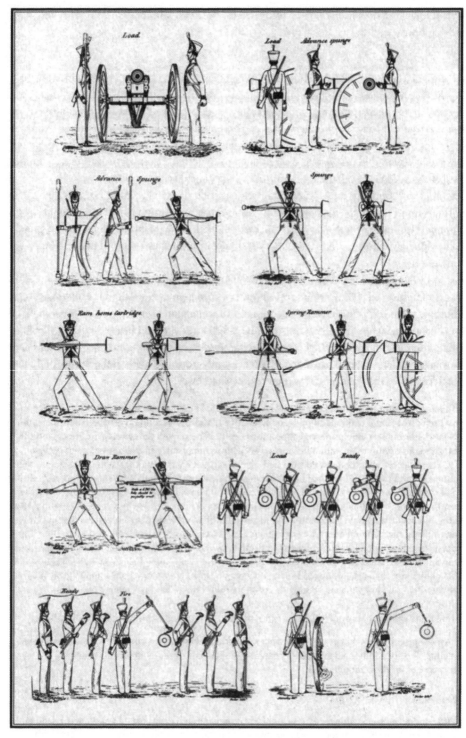

Artillery crew drill, by the numbers. These drawings were produced by Hunley in 1841 as colored plates for the Madras Artillery; in action, the drill would be somewhat less formal.

before the word "fire," he steps to the right or left, as the wind may be, in order to observe where the shot strikes, without being incommoded by the smoke.

First matross: He carries a long bricole; he is charged with the sponge, which he carries in his left hand when marching forward, supporting it on his shoulder, and hooks his bricole to the hook at the head of the cheek; when retreating, he hooks his bricole to the hook at the end of the axletree. In action he is posted in front, out of the line of the wheel; he holds the spunge [sic] horizontally with both hands; at the word "load," he makes a long step with his left foot, and brings his right foot in a line, with his heels eighteen inches asunder; he is then situated parallel to the piece which he spunges; he afterwards rams down the cartridge, and then returns to his former position, without the line of the wheel.

Second matross: He carries a pouch filled with tubes, holding the portfire in his right hand. When marching forward, he places himself behind the cross handspike facing the enemy, and helps to lift and push the carriage: he acts in a contrary direction when retreating. In action he is posted even with the breech; hooks and unhooks the water bucket, and fires the piece when the second matross on the left gives him the signal.

First infantry assistant: He carries a bricole shortened to half its length; in marching forward he hooks at the head of the cheek; in retreating he hooks at the end of the axletree; in action he retires near the limber, where he helps to fill the haversacks of the purveyors, and he is ready to replace occasionally any man that may be wanting.

Second infantry assistant: When the carriage is separated from the limber, he helps the sixth assistant on the left to lift the ammunition box from the carriage, and to place it on the limber. In marching forward, he goes to the cross handspike to the left of the second matross, whom he aids to lift and push the carriage forward; in retreating, he pushes the piece with one hand at the chace, and the other at the dolphins. In action, he retires to the ammunition wagon.

Third infantry assistant: He carries a shortened bricole, which, in marching forward, he hooks at the end of the axletree; and in retreating, at the trail. In action he is at the ammunition wagon.

Third matross: This assistant, always belonging to the corps of artillery, is attached to the guard of the limber, and of the ammunition box. He places himself occasionally at the piece, and helps the two cannoneers at the trail handspikes; he has the charge of advancing and of leading back the limber.

On the Left:

Second cannoneer: In marching forward he holds the trail handspike, on the left of the piece, with both hands; in retreating he holds the same handspike with his left hand; in action, he is posted even with the breech. At the word "load," he stops the vent with his left hand, and with his right gives the proper elevation to the piece by means of the elevating screw, or pointing vice.

First matross: He carries a long bricole, which, in marching forward, he hooks to the hook at the head of the cheek; and in retreating to the washer hooks at the end of the axletree; in action, he is posted without the line of the wheel, and in front. At the word "load," he steps to the mouth of the gun to aid the first matross to sponge; he receives the cartridge from the third matross, puts it into the mouth of the piece, and rams down with the first matross on the right; after which he resumes his post in front.

Second matross: He carries a pouch of tubes at his waist, and the priming wire in his right hand. In marching forward, he places himself at the cross handspike, and assists in lifting and pushing the piece forward and backward. In action, he is at the breech of the piece, on the left of the second cannoneer, who has just pointed it; he clears the vent with his right hand, and with his left puts in the tube; as soon as he has returned to his post, he gives the signal to the second matross on the right to fire.

Third matross: he carries a short bricole, which, in marching forward, he hooks at the head of the carriage; and in retreating, to the washer hook at the extremity of the axletree. He is the purveyor of the piece, and carries a leather pouch containing the cartridge, which he gives to the first matross. When his pouch is empty, he runs to the ammunition box or wagon and fills it again.

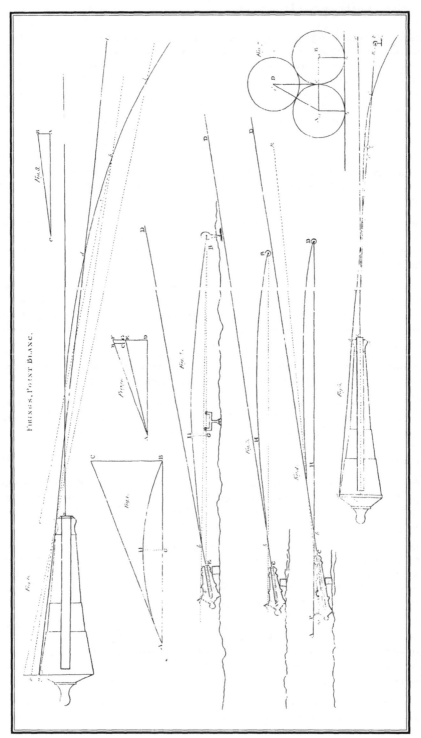

The determination of "point-blank."

First infantry assistant: He carries a long bricole, which, in marching forward, he hooks to the washer hooks, and, in retreating, to the double hooks at the trail. He is, together with the third matross, a purveyor to the piece, and like him carries a leather pouch. He hands the cartridge to the first matross, while his mate is gone to fill his pouch.

Second infantry assistant: He carries a short bricole, and his post is at the ammunition wagon. In marching forward he hooks to the washer hook; in retreating, to the double hooks at the trail.

Third Infantry Assistant: He assists the assistant on the right, to separate the carriage from the limber. In marching forward, he is at the cross handspike, on the right of the second matross, and helps to lift and push the carriage forward; in retreating; he pushes the piece, one hand being at the chace [sic], the other at the dolphins. In action, he is at the ammunition wagon.[2]

The firing process itself was simple enough. The round was brought to the mouth of the tube and loaded, by being placed in the muzzle of the gun tube. Then, it was rammed "home," reaching the base of the tube with a solid "*thunk.*" The powder bag was pierced through the vent by a long wire/metal pick, picker or pricker, which was quickly removed, and a primer of cut reed filled with fine-grain powder was shoved down the vent, entering the cartridge where it had been pierced. The portfire was then placed at the vent, where it ignited the powder, starting the powder train, firing the gun and launching the round downrange. Having no recoil system, which was years in the future—or the entire gun being the recoil system—the gun was thrown violently to the rear when the round was fired. Consequently, the gun crew had to be out of the way (with no one standing behind the trail and the wheels) when the portfire was touched to the vent; serious injury or death could result if they were not. The gun was then relaid, being manhandled back into position by the crew, and swabbed out with a wet sponge, the latter being spun two or three times inside the gun tube to clean it of any powder residue. Then the process began all over again.

The gun was elevated by means of an elevating screw in the case of French and British guns, and by a quoin and screw elevating mechanism in the case of Austrian, Russian, and Prussian guns, and laid after being manhandled into position. To prevent a premature discharge—and a very unpleasant surprise to the two gunners loading and ramming the charge—one of the gunners, wearing a leather thumbstall so that he would not have his digit seared to the bone, placed his thumb over the vent to prevent any premature ignition of the powder as it was being rammed. This was generally termed "thumbing the vent." The entire evolution was quickly done, all duties being executed nearly simultaneously, with no one waiting around for the next man to do his job. Intense, fast, and accurate fire was required, especially for emergencies, and for battery defense if the guns were in danger of being overrun and there was no time to limber up and displace. An interesting footnote should be added: "When the cannoneers and matrosses know and are attentive to their duty, a field piece may be fired . . . without [any of the gun crew] hearing any other noise but the 'fire' and the word 'charge.' "[3]

Guns were generally moved into their initial positions by horse and limber, the gunners unlimbering the piece in the previously chosen gun position. Gun guides from each gun crew preceded the guns and crews into position, staking out and marking the position for each gun, which were generally about twenty yards from the next piece. Guns either were placed in line, or followed the contour of the land, the battery position dictating how they would be emplaced. Limbers were positioned behind the guns, the French generally attaching the *prolonge* as soon as the gun was in position in case of immediate use or emergency. Caissons were generally emplaced to the rear about fifty yards away, or to the flanks, to keep them out of harm's way: an exploding caisson could wreck an emplaced battery, causing high casualties among horses and

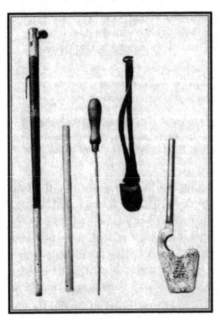

British artillery equipment essential for firing the piece. From left to right: portfire, match, vent picker (or pricker), thumbpiece (or thumbstall), and portfire cutter (attached to the gun carriage).

gun crews. If at all possible, the gun teams were placed under cover to avoid casualties. However, this was a rare occurrence.

The following is the American manual exercise for field guns—specifically, what is done by the gun crew for the particular words of command:

1. "Attention!"

At this order the men must be silent, and observe the greatest attention.

2. "Take off the apron, and take out the tampion!"

The gunner unties the cord of the apron, takes it off, ties it to the fore lashing ring at his side of the carriage, and (only for form sake, as the piece has not been recently fired), stops the vent with the thumb of his left hand, on which there is a thumbstall of thick leather; at the same time the second matross unbuckles the tampion strap, takes the tampion out of the bore of the piece, and buckles it to the fore lashing ring at this side of the carriage; they then resume their first stations and attitudes.

3. "Sponge!"

The first matross throws forward his right foot, turns to the left about on the ball of his left foot, and places his right a large pace in the rear of his left foot; the left side of the right foot is parallel with the axletree of the carriage, and the left foot points towards the said axletree; he brings down the sponge head near the upper part of the swelling of the muzzle of the piece, then brings it down along it on the side next to him to the bottom of it, and guides it into the bore of the piece with his left hand; having, while stepping out, slid his left hand along the upper part of the sponge staff to the bottom of the sponge head, he then takes his left hand from the staff, and with the right pushes the sponge head home to the bottom of the bore, and turns it to the right, three, four, or five times round, as circumstances will permit, and then draws it out; immediately on its being out, he receives the staff of it near the sponge head on the palm of his left hand, and with this hand tosses the sponge head end of the staff over to his right, letting the staff slide down through his right hand until the sponge head touches his hand; as it slides through, he seizes the sponge staff near the rammer head, in the hollow, between the thumb and fingers of his left hand, the fingers on the upper part, ready to enter the rammer head with said hand into the bore.

The second matross, on the order being given to sponge, throws forward his left foot, turns to the right about on the ball of his right foot, and places his left foot a large pace in the rear of his right foot; the right side of his left foot is parallel with the axletree of the carriage, and his left points towards the said axletree; he then holds his hands out towards the third matross to receive ammunition.

The third matross, on the order being given to sponge, takes out of his haversack a fixed round or fixed canister shot (agreeably to previous instructions), and a wad; the wad he puts under his left arm, the fixed round or fixed canister shot he holds between his hands in front of him, with the flannel cartridge of it towards him, and then goes to the right about.

4. "Load-with round shot!"

The second matross receives from the third matross the ammunition, puts it into the piece, receives from him a wad, and puts it also into the piece. The third matross, on delivering the wads, goes to the left about, and is then in his first position.

5. "Ram home-charge!"

The first matross enters the rammer head of the sponge staff into the bore of the piece, slides back his left hand on the sponge staff to his right hand, rams home the strapped shot and wad with three equal strokes; at each stroke, on the rammer head being home to the wad, to give more force to the strokes, he throws his body forward, bends both knees, his right knee nearly to the ground, and throws his left arm off horizontally to the left. He suddenly jerks the sponge staff out of the bore with his right hand, after the last stroke, letting it slide through said hand until the rammer head strikes the hand, then instantly puts his left hand on the upper part of the rammer head; on its being to a poise he takes his left hand from the rammer head, and seizes the staff, breast high, in the hollow between the thumb and forefinger of said hand; at the time of his bringing it to a poise, and seizing it with his left hand, he throws his right foot around to the place it first was in, and turns to the right about on the ball of his left foot, which brings him to his first station and position. The second matross returns to his first station and position at the same time the first matross returns to his, by throwing his left foot round, and turning at the same time to the left about on the ball of his right foot.

When the canister shot is used, two moderate strokes are sufficient to ram home the charge and wad. In close action, with canister shot, the wad is omitted.

6. "Take-aim!"

The sergeant steps to the screw of the piece, puts his right leg between the cheeks of the carriage, takes hold of the handle of the screw with his right hand, with which and the occasional assistance of his left hand, he elevates or depresses the piece; he then takes aim on the superior superfices of the base ring and swelling of the muzzle, putting his two thumbs nearly together on the top of the base ring, and looking between them; and, if the piece is properly disparted, he also looks along the sides of the piece when

French infantry/artillery coordination. From d'Urturbie's 1794 manual.

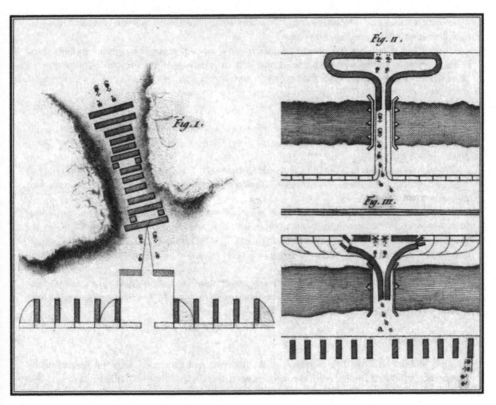

firing point blank shot at a small object. If the piece is elevated so that a sufficient aim cannot be taken on the superfices of the piece, then a plummet is to be used.

The corporal of the trail handspike is to be particularly attentive, when the sergeant is pointing the piece, to move the trail to the right or left on the following signals, given by the sergeant. To move a little to the right, the sergeant gives one tap with the fingers of his left hand on the outside of the left cheek of the carriage, and to move it a little to the left he gives one tap with the fingers of his right hand on the outside of the right cheek of the carriage; giving from one to three taps, according to the distance he wants the trail moved. After the piece is pointed, the sergeant resumes his first position.

7. "Prime!"

The first gunner opens his tube box, takes out a pistol tube, takes his left hand from the vent, puts the tube into the vent, and covers it with his left hand hollowed up.

When the piece is loaded with a paper cartridge and with round or canister shot, the first gunner enters his priming wire into the vent and pierces the paper cartridge, then primes with his powder horn, and presses down the priming powder in the shell of the vent with the side of said horn. The second gunner then fires with a linstock, on which is a lighted slow match; he must be careful to touch the priming powder forward of the vent, otherwise the explosion of the vent will bow out his match.

Some vent shells are made from a little forward of the vent back to the base ring: they ought to be made from a little behind the vent along on the vent-field of the piece.

8. Make-ready!

On this order the following movements are made at the same time: The sergeant steps a large pace with his left foot to the left, brings the heel of his right foot within two inches of his left heel, and stands in the position he was before he moved. The corporal throws back his right foot half a pace past the heel of his left foot, then removes his left foot to the left of his right foot, and stands with his heels two inches apart, in the position of the sergeant. The matrosses at the right and left drag-ropes, wheel back with their drag-ropes in their hands . . . The third matross steps forward obliquely to the left one pace, and brings his right heel up within two inches of his left.

If the second gunner is to fire with a slow match, at this order he stoops down, brings the lighted end of the slow match a little below his left knee, and with the forefinger of his left hand gives the match a gentle tap to clear it of ashes; he is then ready to receive the next order.

9. "Fire!"

"The first gunner takes his left hand from the tube, steps back with his left foot near to his right; stands erect, with his heels two inches apart, keeps his eyes on the tube, and if it should not have the desired effect carefully replaces it.

The second gunner at the same time raises his portfire stock, bends his body forward a little, and fires the piece; previous to the recoil of the piece he steps back, his right to his left foot, and stands erect, with his heels two inches apart.

Immediately after the piece is fired, the following movements are made: the first and second gunner place themselves at the piece in the same postures they were in when the order to prime was given; the matrosses at the drag-ropes straighten their drag-ropes, dress in a line with the axletree of the carriage, and stand in their first positions; and the sergeant, corporal, and third matross take their first stations and positions.

The whole being then in their first stations and proper attitudes, ready for further orders, the officer begins with the order sponge, and puts them from that order through the exercise several times. He then orders,

10. "Change-about!"

The first matross takes the fifth matross's place, after placing his sponge against the axletree of the carriage, the fifth, sixth, and seventh matrosses move to the left, and the eighth matross takes the first gunner's place; the corporal takes the sergeant's place and implements; the second gunner takes the ninth matross's place; the ninth, tenth, and eleventh matrosses move to the left, and the twelfth matross takes the place of the second, and the second takes that of the first matross and the sponge.

These movements are performed nearly all at one time, and take but a few seconds.

The third and fourth matrosses change places afterwards, the first time the fourth brings ammunitions to the third matross.

The officer repeats the exercise, beginning with the order sponge, as often as he thinks proper, and then proceeds to instruct his men in the wheelings and marchings.[4]

Artillery drill was very much a "by the numbers" exercise, and was very precise and demanding. In combat, however, especially when incurring losses in the gun crews, the formality would disappear, though not what each gunner was required to do. Smart battery commanders and NCOs would cross-train their crews to be able to handle any of the duties required to fire their piece. Even when losing men and horses rapidly in combat, gun crews would seldom "miss a beat" firing their pieces, unless the casualties were prohibitive and the crews greatly depleted. Then, they would be supplemented by whatever personnel were available, a deadly and necessary version of "on-the-job training."

The ancillary equipment and accoutrements of artillery gun crews necessary to work the guns included the *bricole*, a leather crossbelt to which was attached a length of rope with a hook on the end. This was used when the gun crew was employed as a "man team" to manhandle the gun forward when the limber was not available. Instructions for artillery leather equipment, especially the *bricole*, were quite specific:

In the service of the three calibers and other field pieces, the artillerists will remember, as general principles, that all the bricoles hang from the left shoulder to the right side: the pouches, haversacks, portfire, and tube cases hang from the right shoulder to the left side over the bricoles. When marching forward, the men on the right hook with the right hand, and, when retreating, with the left. Those on the left, in the first case, hook with the left, and when retreating with the right hand. In the eight- and twelve-pounders and six-inch howitzers, when marching forward, those with long traces hook first; when retreating, the men who carry the shortened traces are within those who carry the long ones.

The strap of the bricole should be made of good and strong leather, and including the iron ring two feet eight inches long. The trace should be of strong well-twisted rope, half an inch in diameter, or one inch and a half in circumference; its length, including what goes round the thimble, should be eight feet, so that the strap and trace together will give a length of then feet eight inches. This is shortened to half its length in passing the trace through the iron hook and hooking the end of the ring.

The pouches should be of dressed leather, experience having shown that leather with hair on is liable to take fire.[5]

The cannoneers' tools, usually referred to as "sidearms," for serving the piece were utilitarian and generally universal among the artillery systems of the different belligerents. They generally consisted of the ladle, rammer and sponge, worm, handle, priming wire, portfire stock, linstock, thumbpiece, also called a thumbstall, and the handspike. The following extract from Tousard's *The American Artillerist's Companion* explains them in detail:

LANTERNE. It is sometimes called cuillier, and in English, ladle. It is made of copper, and resembles a long spoon or ladle, which is fixed to a long pole or handle. Ladles serve to hold the powder for loading guns, and to convey it into the piece of ordnance when cartridges are not used, or the cannoneers have expended them,

The heads, or ladle cylinders, are made of elm wood, and the lanterne is made out of two copper sheets, beaten upon a sized cylinder, rivetted and brazed at their junction (it is best, however, to make them out of a single copper sheet): the first sheet makes the body, and the second, with the square end of the first, the neck of the lanterne.

The end of the first is made circular, with a radius equal to half its height. The copper is nailed in two rows on the heads.

There are five sizes of lanternes for twenty-four, sixteen, twelve, eight, and four pounders, which contain, without the trouble of weighting the powder, 9, 6, 4½, 3, and 2 pounds. There is also another size for the field pieces, which is carried on the left of the caisson.

RAMMER AND SPONGE. The head of the first is a cylinder of elm wood, whose diameter and length are each equal to the diameter of the shot. The second is a cylinder of a size smaller, and of a length somewhat longer than the first; it is covered with lambskin, so as to fit the gun exactly, and is used to clean the piece before and after it is fired. In the English and United States service, both the rammer and sponge heads are fixed to the same handle, either for siege or field service. In the French service those for siege and garrison pieces, (twenty-four and sixteen pounders) are most always separately handled. There are five sizes of the first for 24, 16, and 12 pounders; those for 8 pounders, which serve also for 12, 10 inch and stone mortars; and those for long fours, which also serve for 8 and 6 inch howitzers and 8 inch mortars. Five sizes of the second are similar to the first, and a sixth size is made for the light troops. In general, each field or siege piece is allowed three sponges.

The sponge, with crooked handles, for light four pounders and pieces for light troops, answers both for sponging and ramming in their respective calibers . . . Besides the four sponges which are allowed to each light piece, there are other two sponges, with straight handles, at one end of which a worm screw is fixed.

The extremity of the cylinder is bound with a round copper ferula, fixed with a nail of the same metal.

The sponges, in the French artillery, for the most, instead of lambskin, are covered with bristles, or stiff hair of swine, imported from Russia: those of Alsace are also very good, and are employed when the first cannot be procured. The twisted end of the brass-wire must be uniform, and hold the bristles so that they cannot be pulled off. When the hair is bent, it should be straightened by soaking it in hot water, and then let to dry.

WORM OF A GUN, tire bourre: an instrument, vermiculated or turned around, that serves to extract anything into which it insinuates itself by means of a spiral direction: the branches are folded upon a pattern, made in a frustum of a cone, and its socket has three nail holes.

There are three sizes of worms, siege and garrison; field pieces and light pieces; in the first, the branches are turned in spiral from their beginning; in the two others, between the beginning of the spirals and the bottoms of the fork, a space is left to admit the hook and the strap to carry the handspikes of field pieces.

Worms are also lodged in the sponge heads; they are made of steel, tempered in olive oil, which prevents the necessity of heating them a second time. It is indispensable to have a vice pin to screw them.

HANDLE, hampe: a shaft or long stick, to which all the four preceding implements are fixed. Handles should be made of strong wood, which would not be liable to work itself so as to bend. Although sap or pine wood be very frangible, yet those made out of it are serviceable in garrison or seacoast batteries, because they do not, as those made of other kinds of wood, suffer from the inclemency of the weather; but they are unfit for field service.

All handles should be driven into sockets .532 inch short of their depth. Those for worms and ladles are the same, and their diameter is equal to the rammer and sponge handles.

The handle of the long four pounder ladle, and those for field four pounders, are of the same length, in order that they may be more conveniently carried along side of the caisson. Those of the ladles for field pieces are 7 feet 5.50 inches long.

PRIMING WIRE, degorgeoir, is an iron needle, employed to penetrate the vent or touchhole of a piece of ordnance when it is loaded, in order to discover whether the powder contained therein is thoroughly dry and fir for immediate service; as likewise, and more commonly to search the vent and penetrate the cartridge when the guns are not loaded with loose powder.

There are two sizes and forms: the first for siege and garrison pieces are made without handles, and terminated at one end with a ring, their diameter is .154 inch.

The second, for field pieces, have a wooden handle; their diameter is rather short of .177 inch; between the priming part and that to which the handle is affixed there is a shoulder, the flat end of which closes with one end of the handle, with a thin iron ferula next to the shoulder: the other end of the handle is larger, and turned around.

The ends of the priming wires for field pieces are filed to a blunt diamond point; and, besides these, others are made, the end of which terminates in a gimoet.

PORTFIRE STOCK, port lance: it is different from the linstock, and serves to contain the portfires, which are used, instead of slow matches, to fire artillery. It is made of two pieces of sheet iron, .07 inch thick, and 11.10 inches long, nearly in the form of a pencil case. A ferula is brazed about five inches from the large end, to hold the junction of the two parts, which are also brazed about one inch above the ferula. Two movable ferulas are fixed around it. One is somewhat elastic, as its ends are not brazed together, but only drawn close to each other; it is destined to press the portfire in the case; the other is brazed as a ring. It is thought preferable to hold the portfire across, instead of putting one of its ends in the socket: in this way you let only as much of the portfire out as is necessary. Out of one piece of sheet iron, 26.24 by 18.11 inches, fifteen portfire stocks can be cut.

LINSTOCK, boute feu, is a short staff of wood, about three feet long, one end of which is cut sharp to stick in the ground; the other is split to receive the hanging end of the lighted slowmatch, which is wrapped round it.

There are other linstocks of the same length, having at one end a piece of iron divided into two branches, each of which has a notch to hold a lighted match, and a screw to fasten it there; the other end is shod with iron to stick into the ground.

THUMBPIECE, doigtier, is a kind of small bag, about three inches square, made of strong skin or leather, and stuffed with hair: one of the sides is recovered with a piece of leather, so that the cannoneer may lodge his fingers in it while stopping the vent during the loading of the gun: they are indispensable . . .

FIELD ARTILLERY HANDSPIKES: one for twelve and eight pounders and six inch howitzers, 70.31 inches long, and one 63.39 inches long.

The catching pin is uniformly placed in eight pounders and six inch howitzer handspikes, which are perfectly similar; they are differently placed in the handspikes for twelve pounders; in order to distinguish them, they are painted red.

The catching pin, arretoir, is placed on the butt end of the handspikes; it finds its passage through the rising, which is made in the largest pointing ring; and, when turned, the pin, ceasing to be opposite the rising, catches to the ring, and prevents the handspike from clearing them.

The distance from the outside of the catching pin to the place of the ferrula, at the end of the handspike, is 10.66 inches for twelve pounders; 9.59 for eight pounders, and 7.79 inches for four pounders.

One handle ring is nailed to the small end of the handspike, and filed smooth, so as to make it easy to pass it in the hook, at the side of the carriage.

Pointing handspike for light troops: the catching pin is fixed in the butt end, and with a spring, in such a manner that, while it passes through the maneuver rings, it is entirely contained in a groove in the butt, and, as soon as the handspike gets to its place, springs up, catches against the ring, and keeps the handspike ready.

Instead of a handle ring in iron cramp is placed at the small end in the same direction with the spring; it serves to pass the leather straps which lash them to the side of the carriage.[6]

French gun crews had one other segment of gun drill to perform, at least for the 8- and 12-pounders. Those guns had two sets of trunnion holes on the carriage. Gribeauval designed the pieces to have a traveling and a firing position for the gun tube on the carriage. This "*encastrement*" definitely helped the balance of the piece when both limbered up and in action, but it gave the crew one more headache in serving their pieces.

When the gun was brought into position and the crew was preparing to move it into firing position, they had to move the gun tube from the traveling to the firing position. This was done while the gun was still limbered up, and it was accomplished with the crew using handspikes to manhandle the gun tube from the traveling to the firing trunnion holes. This was achieved by lifting the tube with handspikes, and then placing one handspike under the tube as a "roller" and the gun tube was quite literally "rolled" from one set of trunnions to the other.

Being in the field, and time being of the essence, especially if the units were either engaged or under fire, the use of an artillery gin to lift the gun tube by the dolphins was too time-consuming, indeed, the gin was actually too large and cumbersome for efficient use in the field, especially on an artillery gun line. The process itself was called changing the trunnion plates, and went as follows:

Formerly the carriages had but one trunnion plate, in which the guns always rested both for action and traveling, so that on a march all the weight fell in the rear of the two great wheels, which made the draft more difficult, the carriage more liable to be overset, and tended to the greatest injury of the roads.

The traveling trunnion plate is placed four diameters of the caliber in the rear of the battle trunnion plate. It is only made use of for field twelve and eight pounders, and holds the piece during the march: the breech then rests on the supporting transom, by which means the weight of the cannon is divided between the axletree of the carriage and the axletree of the limber, which very much relieves the former, renders the carriage more manageable, and makes it run more freely than before.

By the manner in which these trunnion plates have been disposed, the piece is made to pass from one to the other with the greatest ease, and in as little time as is necessary to take the trail from its limber.

When it is intended to come to action, the twelve or eight pounders being in the traveling trunnion plate, before taking off the limber the command is given "Change trunnions—for action!" The second matross on the right hooks the lock chain to the highest spoke; the men haul the wheels back to tighten this chain, and by that keep the carriage steady.

The second cannoneer and first matross on the left take out the four handspikes, give one to the first matross and the first cannoneer on the right; each retaining one. During that time the second matrosses take off the cap squares and lay them on the ground; when there is no lock-chain they serve to check the wheels in front: then the first matross on the right and second cannoneer raise the breech with their handspikes, in order to give the first cannoneer the opportunity of passing the round part of his handspike a little obliquely under the first reinforce, as near as possible the flat-head hooks; and that the handspike stopping pins be beside the flasks.

The first matross on the left introduces into the mouth of the piece the butt-end of his handspike; the first matross on the right and cannoneer on the left place the butt-end of their handspikes under the button of the cascabel, and lift up the piece with the assistance of the second. The first cannoneer places his handspike as a roller underneath the first reinforce, and rolls it as far as the center of the flasks. The first matross on the right afterwards crosses with his handspike the one that is in the mouth, and the cannoneer on the left keeps the piece level by passing the big end of his handspike in the right dolphin to a twelve pounder, or the small end of it to an eight pounder. The seconds and third go to the assistance of the firsts, viz. the seconds and the third on the left assist to the cross handspike, and the third on the right to that which is in the chace. The officer, or the first cannoneer, who directs the maneuver, sees everyone at his post in the position for acting; and commands "All-hands!" They all act together with force, precaution, and steadily: those who are in the front, with their handspikes crossed, begin the motion. The cannoneer acts in concert with them by turning his handspike to bring the piece gently to the battle trunnion plate.

The piece being lodged, the two first matrosses heave upon the chace to raise the breech, underneath which the second cannoneer and first matross on the right enter their handspikes to afford the first cannoneer the facility of disengaging his handspike, which served as a roller. The first cannoneer supports the pointing plate when the second turns down the pointing screw, and lays it against the supporting transoms; the second matrosses fix the cap-squares, and place the keys; the handspikes are placed if necessary in the square rings for maneuvering. As soon as the piece is in its proper place, the second matross on the right unlocks the wheel. This maneuver is always performed before unlimbering the piece.

To pass the piece from the battle to the traveling trunnion plate, the position of men, and the distribution of handspikes, is the same as in the preceding command. The officer gives the words, "Advance-limber! Change trunnions to the traveling plate!" The sponge is fixed to the cheek, or laid on the ground, and the cap-squares taken off. The cannoneers disengage the pointing handspikes, and deliver them to the first matross on the right; the carriage is placed on its limber; the second matrosses take off the cap-squares, and lock the wheels with the lock-chain, or, if there be none, wedge them with the cap-squares. The same disposition, as in the other maneuver, is followed to execute the second command, in order to afford the first cannoneer the opportunity of disengaging his handspike from under the piece, the cannoneer on the left enters his handspike under the button, and the second matross under the first rein-force; the second cannoneer inclines the pointing screw, and lowers the pointing plate. The second matross on the right unlocks the wheel; the second matrosses fix and key the cap-squares: the second cannoneer and first matross on the left place the four handspikes in the square ring of the carriage, and the first matross on the right his sponge in the rammer hooks with the assistance of the second.[7]

Aiming the piece by the gun crew consisted of elevating the gun tube by means of the elevating screw, gazing down the line of sight using whatever sights were available and shifting the trails if necessary. The Gribeauval System used the elevating screw and plate upon which the gun tube rested; the Austrians, Russians, and Prussians all used the screw quoin developed by von Holtzman in the 1730s; the excellent British pieces had the elevating screw connected directly to the cascabel button, which was undoubtedly the most efficient elevating system of the period. The French sight was the excellent Gribeauval movable or adjustable *hausse* sight. The Russians developed new, removable sights in their 1805 system which, though inferior to the Gribeauval sights, were a great improvement to what came before. Other nations some-times had a sight mechanism fastened to the breech. However, sometimes all of the belligerents merely used the "line of metal" for sighting the piece. This process of aiming was known as pointing the gun.

As a side note, it is interesting that, during the period, the French used phosphorus to mark the end of the gun tube for night pointing and firing. The adjustable rear sight, in the form of a "T"and a fixed front sight, gave French gunners an immense advantage in terms accuracy over their more numerous opponents. Furthermore, the elevating screw under the platform the breech of the gun tube rested on allowed the gunner to carefully adjust his sights before firing and remained at the same elevation and adjustment after firing the piece, thus increasing the rate of fire if desired:

Fire arms are generally pointed by directing a visual ray along the uppermost surface of the gun, which terminates at the object which is aimed at. This ray is called the sight line, and the action, pointing or levelling the gun.

Formerly the piece was pointed by means of wedges, [but] at present the method of doing it is as follows: the breech of the gun rests upon a moveable wooden plate, the fore part of which is connected by a hinge with the breast transom; the end of this plate is made round, and shaped like the breech; it is raised or depressed by a vice which has an iron male screw, with square threads, and a female one of brass. This screw is placed between the cheeks, about the place where the breech transom was. Its ends are made in the form of trunnions, and are inserted into two iron sockets, fixed by bolts on the inside of the cheeks. The female screw, thus suspended, enables the latter to bear perpendicularly on the plate, so that the head of the screw may enter the concavity which is made underneath the round part of the plate. A brass head is fixed at the top of the screw, which plays in this concavity; and a key, with handles, is applied as a turn screw.

Among the alterations, which appear to belong equally to garrison cannon, battering pieces and field artillery, this new method of pointing, on account of its facility and advantages, seems to hold the first rank.

Formerly a groove, which was called a divisière, was formed at the uppermost part of the plateband of the breech, and a sight button, guidon, fixed on the top of the swelling of the muzzle, de la tulipe, to guide the eye of the cannoneer in pointing the gun; so that the piece was placed upon an horizontal ground, or upon a platform, the sight line, which, from the bottom of the visière, passed to the top of the sight button, was, as the pointing requires, in the same plane with the axis of the piece.

But in all other positions, that is to say, when the carriage wheels are not of an height (as it often happens from the furrows of a ploughed field) the sight line would not be exactly in the same vertical plane with the axis of the piece, though directed to the object, and the cannoneer would then be led into an error by throwing the shot on the side of the most elevated wheel.

To obviate these errors, the regulation of 1732 suppressed the visières and buttons. The cannoneer, for want of this help, was then obliged to take his aim, coup d'oeil, by taking the most prominent parts of the breech girdle and of the tulip, to guide his eye towards the object; which operation, in fact, always places the sight line in the same vertical place with the axis of the piece.

To suppose that the cannoneer could, at one glance, fix on two corresponding points, the most prominent on two great circles, at seven or eight feet distance from each other, would be to suppose what is difficult for a workman to do in his shop even with a rule and level: in battle, where the whole frame of the individual is commonly in an agitation that cannot fail of casting uncertainty in the judgment of this organ, the impossibility is obvious. The precision in the sight is then at least as difficult as the different elevations of the carriage wheels are, strictly speaking, inevitable in a ploughed field. These two methods of pointing are then subject to errors; the first seems nevertheless preferable, because, with the visière and button, it only takes place when the difference of the height of the wheels is much apparent; and this can be avoided, or at least corrected, either by placing the wheel nearly on the same level (which is always possible) or by making use of the coup d'oeil to modify the effect of the divergency of the sight line from the axis of the piece.

From this suppression it arose, that, after several discharges, the cannoneer, who had pointed the gun, could not ascertain whether the error he remarked in the direction, was produced by the aberration of his eye on the two great circles, or by any exterior fault of the piece, or whether any of the two salient points had not been deranged by some shock either in the maneuver or in the transportation; it being obvious that the least impressure, on any of these points, would make the sight line diverge one fourth or one sixth of an inch to the right or left.

Under these impressions and reasonings, which were unanswerable, the regulations of 1765 restored the visières and sight buttons to the pieces; but their reestablishment only determined the direction of the shot when firing point blank, and the question is, when is such firing to be used? Since, among the great number of points which a gun can strike, there is but one point blank: as soon as you are beyond this precise distance, it becomes necessary to elevate the gun, and by this means the swelling of the muzzle conceals the object from the eye of the cannoneer, who is fixed at the groove of the visière at the breech. The visière, therefore, as well as the sight button, are no longer useful, and the cannoneer is left to chance for the elevation and direction of his piece.

Besides the general method of pointing, which we have mentioned, there is another, which has had many partisans. This method consists of directing visual rays along the sides of the piece, so that they are tangents to the trunnions; the aim is then taken by the sides, and these two sight lines are in the same place with the axis, intersecting each other, and the sight line, taken along the upper surface of the gun (if the piece be regularly constructed), in a point from which these lateral sight lines diverge to the right and left of the prolongation of the axis of the same quantity as the upper sight line is below it. This double sight line gives a good direction to the piece as to its elevation, but we have seen, first that when the piece is directed to the mark it strikes below it; second, it has very little influence as to avoiding the divergency either to the right or to the left; third, the operation is longer, and the cannoneer less practiced to it; fourth, the ironing of the carriage sometimes prevents the perception of the object; fifth, the least defect in the configuration or position of the trunnions may occasion some very considerable errors in the pointing.

The regulations of 1765 restored the visières and sight buttons to the pieces, although the error, occasioned by the same cause, that is, by the position of the wheels, must necessarily be more sensible with short pieces, as the divergency of the sight line is greater, especially when by a greater distance of the point blank, it becomes necessary to raise the elevator or hausse to a greater elevation.

We have said that all fire arms were a kind of truncated cone, because they are strengthened at the breech to resist the force of the inflamed powder: the interior cavity of this cone is a cylinder, of which the axis and its prolongation would be the line of firing, ligne de tir, if the shot was perfectly of the same caliber, and if, after quitting the piece, it was to describe a straight line: we have also said, that fire arms are generally pointed by directing a visual ray along the upper surface of the gun, which terminates at the object which is aimed at. Therefore if the projected body described a straight line, of course the sight line would intersect this straight line in a point, and the distance of this intersection from the mouth of the piece might be easily ascertained, knowing the length of the truncated cone and the diameters of its two extremities, by the following rule of proportion: the difference of the two diameters is to the smaller diameter as the length of the truncated cone is to the distance that is sought. By the same consequence, the value of the angle which the sight line makes with the prolongation of the axis would also be found: this angle is so much more considerable as the difference of the two extreme diameters of the truncated cone is greater, and the axis of the said cone shorter. When the same angle is greater in one fire arm than in the other of the same kind, it is usually said that this arm raises the shot, because the line of projection is so much the more above a straight line.

But the projected body cannot describe a straight line, unless it be without gravity, or projected either upwards or downwards, and these cases can never happen.

This body then having weight, and being projected in a line either horizontal or inclined to the horizon, the tendency of its gravity, which acts continually in a vertical direction, will drive it from the straight line, which it tended to describe, from the force of the impulsion, and to cause it to form an angle with the direction of this force. It will then, in its projection, describe a curve, which for a long time was considered as a parabola. If it were possible to project the body in a non-resisting medium (and it would be an absurdity to consider the air as such), it might then, indeed, move in a straight line.

The alteration in the motion of our projectiles is not occasioned solely by their gravity. Being necessarily propelled through the air, the mobile experiences a resistance, which, in the most favorable circumstances (for instance, exclusive of the tenacity and elasticity of the air), is at least proportional to the square of its velocity. With respect to the air's tenacity, it is not sufficiently ascertained whether or not its density increases considerably its resistance; but it is established that the elasticity of the air opposes to the mobile a resistance equal to three times the square of its velocity, when this velocity is sufficiently great to leave a vacuum behind its body; and this happens whenever the velocity is greater than 1330 feet per second in the mean state of the barometer.

In the practice schools, we know, by experience, that with the common charges a shot has a velocity of 1150 feet per second, and with stronger charges would still have a greater velocity: we know also, that, if the shot could preserve its initial velocity for any space of time longer, it would have a much more considerable range, as from other experiments it appears that the initial velocity is at least 1700 feet; from which we may conclude that, during a part of the first second, a vacuum will be formed behind the ball; that the velocity of the mobile diminishes gradually, and the resistance is considerably stronger at the beginning than at the end of its range.

The true line of firing, ligne de tir, is then a curve which is very different from a parabola; but whatever it may be, the prolongation of the axis is a tangent to it at the point of departure, if the mobile be of the same caliber: this curve, mathematically considered, can either be below the sight line, touch it, or cut it. From the construction of most of our fire arms, when properly loaded, the two first cases are impossible: we will, therefore, confine ourselves to the latter, that of the curve of projections being cut by the sight line, since the prolongation of the axis being tangent to it, this curve remains constantly below; whence originated the paradox that an arm can never strike the mark against which it is directed; or, in words to the same effect, that, to strike one mark, the arm should be directed to another.

The curve thus described is below the axis of the piece, so that the axis or its prolongation, as we have already mentioned, is a tangent to this curve; and as the sight line, from the different thicknesses of metal at the breech and muzzle, is determined so as to cut this prolongation, it is evident that this line will also cut the curve of projection in two points.[8]

The primary ammunition in use by all armies was roundshot, sometimes referred to as "ball." It was a solid, cast, spherical iron ball used against fortifications, people and equipment. When the ground was dry and favorable, the effective range of roundshot could be doubled by ricochet fire. At the end of its trajectory, the round would hit the ground and start to bounce or "bound," continuing to roll forward. Both its kinetic energy and force upon impact upon troops was deceptive. The effect of roundshot, especially ricocheting roundshot, on man and horse was devastating. Heads and limbs were taken off, even when the round had slowed down considerably. Whole files and ranks could be gone through by one roundshot. Jean-Roche Coignet left a stark eyewitness account of the Old Guard infantry standing and taking incoming artillery from the Austrians at Essling in 1809 and the deadly effects of the rounds hitting human targets. His graphic description of round shot ploughing through files of his comrades, bearskins being thrown into the air from the casualties, and bits and pieces of the casualties being spattered among the survivors, is one of the most graphic descriptions of artillery casualties of the period. Table 6, based on actual rounds fired, demonstrates the effectiveness of roundshot against both personnel and field fortifications.

For antipersonnel work, either grapeshot or canister was used, canister usually being more widely used and generally more effective against troops. Grapeshot was a round made up of large balls "arranged" around a wooden "tree" and covered with netting or some other such substance to hold the ammunition in place. Canister, of which there were two sizes, was a tin can with an iron lid and base, fitted to the caliber of the particular piece, full of either musket balls, or balls of a slightly larger caliber made of iron, which was the preferred metal. Lead musket balls had been found partially to melt because of the heat of the explosion in the tube when fired, and partially remold into larger masses, significantly reducing the effect of the round. Packed with sawdust, the tin canister exploded on firing, giving the effect of a giant shotgun. At close range, these rounds were deadly and could stop both an infantry assault or a cavalry charge. Two such volleys from Senarmont's large battery at Friedland in 1807 ruined a counterattack by the Russian Guard cavalry, almost literally "blowing them off the field."[9]

Common shell was fired by howitzers. It was a fused round, intended to be exploded over or against formed troops, and was also effective against buildings in either villages or towns, or inside fortifications. Fuses were sometimes unreliable, and were made from wood and slow match. Some, like the better primers, were made from reed. They were ignited when the howitzer was fired. The shell itself was a cast-iron, hollow sphere filled with black powder, which would scatter twenty-five to fifty iron fragments when it detonated over a twenty-yard radius from the explosion. These rounds could also be used as incendiary weapons and could set both buildings and dry vegetation on fire.[10]

Shells were not used in cannon. Howitzers, having a somewhat limited "indirect-fire" capability (though the target still had to be seen[11]), were sometimes grouped into special, task-organized batteries by the French to fire on special targets. This system was put into effect against the Great Redoubt at Borodino in 1812 and again against Hougoumont at Waterloo in 1815. Sometimes the British employed regularly organized howitzer batteries.[12]

As already noted, the British came up with a superior fragmentation shell that could be fired from either howitzers or cannon. Officially known as "spherical case shot," it was more

---

TABLE 6: EFFECTIVENESS OF ROUNDSHOT

Caliber	Range (yards)	Personnel penetrated	Yards penetrated
3-pounder	Point blank	45	1.6
	340	30	19
6-pounder	Point blank	55	2.3
	340	39	
	680	28	
12-pounder	Point blank	63	2.7
	340	48	
	680	36	
24-pounder	Point blank	70	
	340	55	
	680	40	

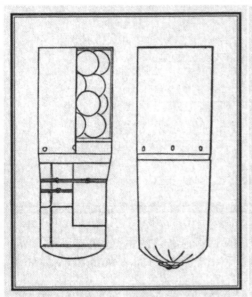

A diagram of a section of "common" shell, clearly showing the fuse, filler (powder or explosive) and the shell casing, which would fragment upon the round exploding.

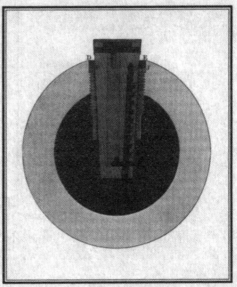

A canister round (also called case shot). This was "fixed" ammunition, as the powder cartridge was attached to the canister.

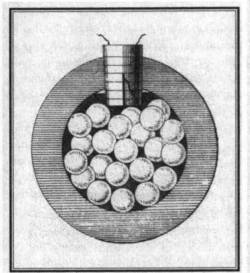

Spherical case shot—later generally referred to as "shrapnel," after its inventor. This shows the fuse, the shell casing, and the lethal fragmentation mixed with the explosive. This projectile was truly the British "secret weapon" of the period, and the most effective long-range antipersonnel round. It could be fired by either howitzer or gun, whereas common shell could be fired only by howitzer.

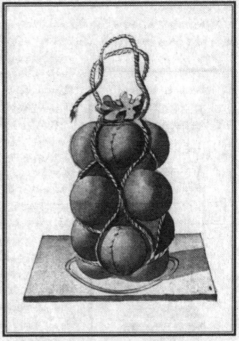

"Quilted" grapeshot. This is the original type of round, from which the term "grapeshot" arose, the round resembling a bunch of grapes by the manner in which it was assembled for firing.

"Tier" grapeshot, assembled with the use of iron plates separating the levels of the individual bullets.

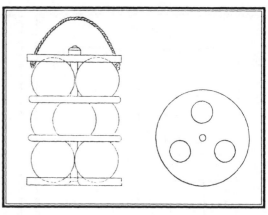

commonly called shrapnel, after its inventor. It was essentially a hollow shell filled with musket balls and explosive and set off by a fuse. It was very effective exploding over the head of troops, especially formed troops in formation. The French artillery attempted to develop one of its own in imitation, but failed, probably because of inferior powder and fuses. Spherical case shot was very effective. It was said that one round could kill an entire horse gun team, even if the round was fired at long range. The round was heartily hated and feared by the French, because it was so effective, and they had nothing like it in their inventory.

Mercer states that when firing against advancing cavalry, he had his battery load first with roundshot, then with one round of canister on top of it. He ordered the troop to fire when the French heavy cavalry was between fifty and sixty yards away, and the effect of the double-shotted guns was "terrible." Nearly the entire front rank of the cavalry fell, and the round shot went the depth of the column in penetrating power. Both men and horses went down in the muck and mire.

Mercer also comments on the steadiness of the gunners waiting for the command to fire. It must have been unnerving, watching an almost irresistible line of heavy cavalry approaching at a deliberate pace, the men silent, the only noise being the hundreds of horses' hooves striking the ground—"the low thunder-like reverberation of the ground beneath the simultaneous tread of so many horses."[13]

Powder had been made up into cartridges for years. The Austrians have been given credit from time to time as the first to develop the powder cartridge, but there is evidence that the British developed their own method during the same period. The actual inventor of the cartridge was most probably the Frenchman, Lieutenant General Brocard, during the 1740s. Later, a complete cartridge mating round and powder, connected to a wooden sabot for balance when loading, and replacing the older wad, was developed, perhaps by Gribeauval, but also perhaps by either the British or the Austrians; the existing evidence inconclusive.

Cartridges were usually made of linen or paper. The cartridge was then, for field pieces generally, made into a complete round composed of the powder cartridge, the round, and a wooden sabot fixed to the bottom of the round to give it

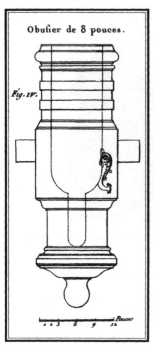

Obufier de 8 pouces.

Fig. IV.

A French howitzer.

stability. This was "fixed'" ammunition, meaning that it came in one package for use. There was also "semifixed" and separate loading. Semifixed ammunition would have a partially made-up round, while separate loading would have the three components, powder cartridge, the round itself (roundshot, canister, etc.), and wadding loaded separately and in order into the piece.

Other types of artillery ammunition included crossbar shot, which looked like a modern dumbbell; jointed crossbar shot, which was two iron balls, each with an iron stem, both of them hooked together with metal eyes cast at the end of the stems; chain shot, which was either two iron balls or iron disks connected with a length of chain; and expanding crossbar shot, which had half an iron ball on each end with an iron stem cast onto the center of the flat side of the half-ball, each of them with a bent eye which fitted over each other, the round expanding on firing. These last four were more fortress, garrison, or naval rounds than field ammunition, but could be issued and used in field pieces if necessary.

There were also illumination shells, the French having an excellent round, usually used during sieges. There were also smoke rounds , as well as the famous "red bullet"—red-hot shot heated in ovens and used for setting wooden structures on fire.

Rockets came in different "models," some of the Congreve types using shrapnel, and others being what would be referred to now as "high explosive." They were effective if used in mass, and were excellent for use against green troops and nervous horses. They did have a tendency to boomerang on their crews after firing. They were sometimes launched by laying them directly on the ground and igniting them. Other types of launchers of the period were tubes set up on tripods, ladder-type launchers used both on land and aboard small boats, and specially designed two-wheeled "rocket cars," which had the launchers built into them and were emplaced by being pointed in the direction of the enemy and with the wagon's tongue laid on the ground.

Originally, fine-grained powder to ignite the powder charge in the chamber was carefully poured down the vent of the piece, priming it to be fired. This was something of a risky proposition due to the hazards of wind and rain, which could either blow the powder away or make it wet before it could be ignited. The solution arrived at was to make a primer in a tube, which originally was either of copper or tin. The primer had a wide mouth at the top to help ignition from the portfire, and the other end was pointed, reinforced by soldering if made of tin, to help it to be inserted into the powder bag in the chamber, even though it had already been pierced by the vent picker.

Metal primers might also have a pan-shaped top that was covered by paper and stopped the primer being inserted too far into the vent. The British and the Austrians both used these, but they were not as effective as the reed primers, and, as noted, did not last as long either in storage or on campaign.

The metal primers were found to be unsatisfactory in that they decayed if exposed to moisture in storage, which ruined the fine priming powder. The French found that reeds cut from swamps and wetlands were superior to the metal priming tubes. They were cut to sufficient length, only those with the correct diameter for the vents of the pieces being used. The insides of the reeds were carefully cleaned of any organic material, small brushes being used for this process, so that only the tough outer "shell" of the reeds remained. The priming powder made into a paste, placed into the reeds and left to set and dry. They were stored in paper in packs of ten each and had a shelf life of about ten years. They were carried by the designated cannoneer in a belly pouch, with the vent picker on the outside of the pouch. His duties on the gun crew were, as previously stated, to clean the vent, puncture the powder bag, and insert the primer.

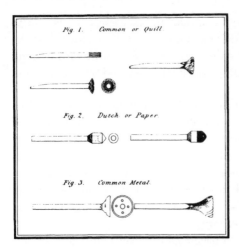

Primers. The most reliable were those made from either goose quill or reed.

The construction and use of primers is more than adequately described as follows:

Priming fuses, fusees d'amorce, have become a very essential part in military fireworks, as well on account of their great consumption as their great usefulness. They answer to prime all sorts of ordnance, and carry the fire with so much promptitude to the powder in the bore of the piece, that too much attention cannot be paid to their fabrication so as to have them well made.

Formerly fuses were made of tin; but it was found that tin was not proper on account of the rust [sic], which, in a short time, spoiled the composition, with which they were filled. At present dry reeds are used, which, having sufficient strength to bear transportation, and not being liable to injure the composition, may be preserved for ten years by taking care not to expose them to moisture.

These reeds, to be fit for making priming fuses, should be cut in December and January, when they are half dry on their own roots. They are found in marshes or ponds in the neighborhood of cities, and the best are taken from bottoms which are not exposed to high winds. A supply of reeds may be preserved for many years by keeping them in dry stores.

The reeds are .27 or .36 inch diameter, and 2.66 to 3.2 inches long; they are cut, with a penknife, square at one end and slanting at the other: to be sure that they are of a proper size, you must measure them by the caliber of the smallest vent of your pieces. The reeds being cut and calibered, they must be cleaned out well, by passing and repassing a small ramrod which rubs off the inside skin and pithy substance, which would otherwise remain there, and prevent the composition from sticking to the sides of the reed.

They are filled with a composition of twelve parts pounded powder, pulverin; eight parts saltpetre; two of sulphur and three of charcoal: all these parts are sifted separately through a silk sieve, then well mixed together, first with the hands, and afterwards with a rolling pin. The whole is made into a kind of paste, with some brandy or spirits of wine: this paste, which should not be too liquid, is put into a glazed earthen pan.

In order to fill the reeds, hold straight two or three of them between the fingers, dip the end which is cut square in the paste, until it comes out at the opposite end; when thoroughly filled, pierce them, from one end to the other, with a fine needle, before the paste is dried, as near the middle of the reed as you can, and put them to dry in the sun, or near a stove.

At the end of several days, when the composition shall have become perfectly dry, pass your needle through again, and, if possible, enlarge the hole, in order to give a greater play, and to transmit the fire with the greater promptitude into the bore of the piece.

As the method above described is long and requires many persons, in order to obtain any considerable quantity, the following method is used, by which one man can fill four or five hundred reeds at a time, almost as quick as one could be filled by the preceding method.

The reeds, being cut of an equal length, are arranged in boxes of oak 4.26 inches square and 4.79 inches high within; the slanting end below, and as many as the box can hold pressed and straight against each other: they are then washed with water, to disengage all the pithy substance, which would prevent the entrance of the composition. The whole being made dry, fill the whole top of the box with one inch thick of composition, and beat the box with a cartouch form, mandrim, to make the composition enter the reeds: repeat the same operation until the reeds are well filled, then take them out of the box to be pierced with a needle as before mentioned. This operation is much quicker, performing in one hour what with the other method would require a much more considerable time. It is true that several defective fuses are found among the number, and that they are not generally made so carefully as when made separately between the fingers.

These tubes are primed with quick-matches as follows: on the end, which is cut slanting with a pen knife, cut two small notches, along which lay two or three quick-matches, about three inches long, which tie with a thread as strongly as you can to it without bursting the reed. This is called putting the cravat to the reed. The end of the reed, where the matches are tied, is cut slanting to facilitate the communication of the fire. The other end is cut square, as well for the purpose of being more easily filled, as to make the composition, which is compressed equally through the whole length, issue straight into the bore of the gun. The quick-match should be fine and well glued. The priming fuses, being thus finished, pack them up in paper by bundles of ten, taking care to envelop the quick-matches lengthways, without compressing them. These small bundles are afterwards packed up by several dozens, which are well tied, and then laid away for use. To fire with these priming fuses, the vent must be well cleared, then the reed put into the vent, and, after having opened the paper which envelops the cravat, the fuse is touched with a match or a portfire.

To avoid the necessity of pricking the gun with the priming wire, which is indispensable when using the reed matches, fusees d'amorce, American, English, and other nations contrive to have them made of tin; their diameter, two tenths of an inch, being just sufficient to enter into the vent of the piece; about six inches long, with a cap above, and cut slanting below in the form of a pen; the point is strengthened with some solder, that it may pierce the cartridge without bending. Through these tubes, as they are called, is drawn a quick match, the cup being filled with mealed powder, moistened with spirits of wine. To prevent the mealed powder from falling out by carriage, a cap of paper or flannel, steeped in spirits of wine, is tied over it.

We have already mentioned the defects of these tubes, which, besides, are attended with another great inconvenience, viz. that their point often becomes blunt, which, in such cases, renders their service long and dangerous.[14]

The fuse was ignited using a portfire, which had a lighted length of slow match attached to it. There was also a linstock, a three-foot length of wood stuck into the ground at the gun position which also had a length of slow match attached, from which portfires were ignited. The linstock could also be used to "touch off" the piece if the portfires were used up.

Artillerymen in any army had to be strong and intelligent, and it helped if they were big men, as in the French service. The French artilleryman considered himself the member of an elite arm, as did those of the Royal Horse Artillery. Undoubtedly, that feeling was shared among the artilleryman of all belligerent nations. Besides the necessary technical knowledge and skill , being an artilleryman required just plain hard work before, during, and after battle.

After firing, especially after hours of combat, the gun tube was filthy and encrusted with the residue of rounds fired. The tubes had to be scrubbed repeatedly to clean them, or they would not be ready for their next action. Vents also had to be cleaned, and checked to see if they had widened after the stress of repeated firings. In that case, they had to be replaced—a task that Gribeauval had made much easier by his development of the replaceable screw vent. Carriages might have to be repaired in the field and wheels or ironwork replaced or repaired. Additionally, ammunition had to be replenished from the *parc* reserves. Horse harnesses might have to be repaired, and horses replaced because of losses or lameness. Lastly, replacements and conscripts would have to be trained, which required more of the endless crew drill.

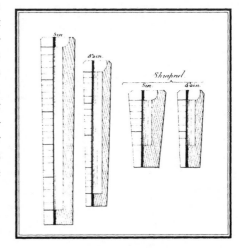

Beech wood fuses for common shell and spherical case shot.

If it is true that God fought on the side with the best artillery, that was due to the caliber of the officers and men of that nation's artillery arm and the way in which they handled their guns.

NOTES

1.   Coignet, *The Notebooks of Captain Coignet*, p. 178.
2.   Tousard, *The American Artillerist's Companion*, vol. II, pp. 122-6. For the Prussian and Austrian crew drill, see the appropriate regulations as listed in the Bibliography. There was no significant difference in crew drill between the armies. In fact, crew drill today is very similar, the major differences being that the round is loaded at the other end of the tube, and a lanyard and firing mechanism are used to fire the piece.
3.   *Ibid.*, p. 121.
4.   *Ibid.*, pp. 135-45.
5.   *Ibid.*, pp. 116-17.
6.   Tousard, vol. I, pp. 390-1.
7.   Tousard, vol. II, pp. 97-100.
8 .   Tousard, vol. II, pp. 199-203.
9.   Esposito and Elting, *A Military History and Atlas of the Napoleonic Wars*, Map 81.
10.   For a good overview, with excellent illustrations, of period ammunition, see Harold Peterson, *Roundshot and Rammers: An Introduction to Muzzle-loading Land Artillery in the United States*
11.   It should be remembered, when studying the field artillery of the period, that all of the guns and howitzers were direct-fire weapons, in that the gunner had to see his target, whether he was firing a gun with a flat trajectory or a howitzer with a more parabolic trajectory which allowed it to fire into ditches, behind walls, etc. Modern fire control methods were unknown during the Napoleonic period.
12.   Of the nine Royal Horse Artillery troops at Waterloo, one was equipped entirely with howitzers, and at least three had been up-gunned from 6- to 9-pounders. The gun teams for these batteries had also been increased from six to eight horses, to give them better mobility.
13.   Mercer, *A Journal of the Waterloo Campaign*, p. 174.
14.   Tousard, vol. I, pp. 382-6. See also Caruana, *British Artillery Ammunition, 1780*, for a section on metal (tin) primers which also has illustrations of the ammunition.

Chapter 4

Boots and Saddles

Where a goat can go, a man can go, and where a man can go, he can drag a gun.
—Colonel William Phillips

Let that general dread my displeasure–he who leaves his pieces behind;
that is contrary to military honor; one ought to leave everything but his cannon.

—Napoleon

Its [horse artillery's] powers consist of its speed and adroitness. Speed means that it is able
to move quickly, over great distances, able to execute quick movements in the face and under fire of the
enemy. Especially while executing the latter, it [horse artillery] is not surpassed by the cavalry, because
these have to ride in close formation in battle during all movement, and save energy and breath;
therefore they can only move at the trot or gallop, except for the shock, speeds that always can be
followed by the horse artillery.

—Lieutenant General Monhaupt

. . . horse artillery is the method of marching the common field artillery with a sufficient
number of horses to enable the men and pieces to reach, much more speedily, such positions as the
general may think it necessary they should occupy.

—Louis de Tousard

0500, 25 October 1808: 45 miles southeast of Pittsburgh, Pennsylvania
Reveille had just sounded, cooking fires had been started, and the NCOs of Captain George
Peter's horse artillery company, the only such active unit in the United States Army, were
rousing the sleeping cannoneers from their blankets, while others checked the horse picket
line. The sounds of an artillery unit waking up were distinctive. Men coughed and cursed as
they went to the sinks for their morning libations, horses whinnied and snickered, they too
being tired from the previous day's march, some impatiently stomping their hooves and snorting their displeasure as they awaited their breakfast. Some greeted with obvious joy their drivers, who wandered sleepily over to check on them after a needed long night's rest. Some of the
gunners still marveled at their horses' ability to sleep standing up by the equine characteristic
of locking their knees. NCO's harsh voices sounded across the bivouac area, as recalcitrant
gunners were reluctant to get out of their warm blankets and face the cool morning air.

Captain Peter was already awake and perfectly dressed and accoutered along with his company first sergeant, a grizzled veteran who never smiled and perennially had a plug of tobacco
in his mouth, though Peter had yet to see him spit. They looked at each other in satisfaction as
the bivouac area slowly came to life. It was a good company, and definitely a show-horse outfit.:
the men were handpicked, as were the horses. Gun teams were matched for color, strength,
and intelligence, especially the wheel pairs. The drivers took good care of them: if they did not,
they felt the first sergeant's dreaded, and sometimes heavy-handed, displeasure. The drivers
were artillerymen, not just drivers and horse handlers who belonged to a separate unit and
assigned to the company. The guns and vehicles were freshly painted and well-maintained, for
Captain Peter was on a mission from the Secretary of War, Henry Dearborn. He was also a
proud officer–proud of his unit, his artillerymen, and of his guns. Somehow the rumbling

guns were things alive and with a mind of their own. That was undoubtedly one of the reasons he was an artilleryman.

The company had been mounted at the direction of the Secretary of War as a horse artillery company to convince Congress, and whomever else in a largely anti-regular army country and government, that the new Regiment of Light Artillery should be entirely accoutered and equipped as horse artillery, not just one company of them. The United States Army was a small outfit, but trouble with England again was becoming continuous, and many of the officers, and certainly the Secretary of War, knew that they needed to be trained and equipped to fight a modern war. The dubious value of the popular militia to fight a war just did not "cut it"—hence the considerable time and effort with Peter's company. It had not been completely individually mounted at first, when the demonstrations took place. Some of the cannoneers had been transported in wagons, but this was soon remedied by the Secretary of War when the company's experiments were concluded.

They had moved from Baltimore to Washington, under the gaze of very critical observers, and had stopped periodically to maneuver and emplace the guns, exercising the crews and firing their pieces. They had moved smartly at a pace of five to six miles an hour, and had impressed everyone with whom they had come in contact. Upon reaching Washington, they had been told that they were all to be mounted, and the light wagons disappeared, the company becoming true horse artillery.

Now they were en route to New Orleans by way of Pittsburgh. They were nattily uniformed, well trained and led, and Peter was proud of them. He nodded to the first sergeant, who moved off to put the fear of God and NCOs into some recalcitrant cannoneer, and Peter nodded to his trumpeter, who then trotted over, wet his lips, wiped his trumpet's mouthpiece and blew assembly. Captain Peter loved the myriad trumpet calls, and he marveled at the horses' ability to memorize them and execute each maneuver by the call without any help from their drivers. It was time to get on the road, and the cannoneers moved briskly to their sections, saddled their mounts, and led them to the main road, where the company was beginning to form up. They did so with the confidence of veterans, though the unit had never seen combat. They were a good outfit and they knew it; they only needed an opportunity to prove themselves.[1]

*   *   *

Horses are magnificent creatures. They are graceful, strong, and intelligent, and have the innate ability to carry a man and his equipment and to pull three times that weight when in draft. They love to run, and they know when they win. They can remember drum rolls and trumpet calls, and they grieve silently, but definitely, for stall and teammates who have died:

> The horse is a remarkable animal, capable of carrying loads across vast distances at an average speed of 3–6 miles an hour. But one swallow of water too many when it has been worked hard—or sometimes one swallow to few—can put them on the sick list.[2]

For centuries, the horse was man's constant companion in wars not of his making. He was used to pull wagons and carts, served as mounts for cavalry and dragoons, carried supplies of all sorts, and, with the advent of artillery, was used to pull the guns. These comrades took the same chances as their human masters, and required certain care to remain serviceable. Strong, long-suffering, and noble, the horse can carry up to a quarter of its weight, and pull three times that burden. Still, they have to be well cared for, as they can be quite fragile. One gulp of water too much, or too little, can kill a horse, and if their masters are not good horsemasters as well as taskmasters, noncombat casualties can take their toll and render an army helpless.

Germany was prime horse country, and some of the best stock came from there. Saxon and Prussian cavalry were famous for being well-mounted. Spain and France were not known for their wealth in horses useful for cavalry mounts, though French and Belgian draft animals were excellent. Poland and Russia had tough, small and well-built horses that were excellent both for artillery, and British horses were among the best in Europe.

Losses in the constant wars were nearly prohibitive. The Grande Armée in all probability lost at least 175,000 horses in Russia in 1812, which crippled their cavalry until the brief respite in 1814–15 allowed them to partially rebuild that arm. Even the German states were having trouble with remounts in the later campaigns, so high were the cumulative losses in horseflesh.

The Revolution closed the French stud farms, the carefully built-up breeding stock being sent to the line units for remounts, something akin to throwing the baby out with the bathwater. Upon his becoming head of state in late 1799, Napoleon reestablished the stud farms to re-plenish the brood mares and blood stock, sending his agents across Europe and overseas to bring back suitable candidates. That process was slow, as it takes more than a few days to grow a new horse, especially in the numbers needed for remounts. In 1813, after the heavy losses in Russia, the artillery and trains took priority for all available horseflesh, definitely hurting the cavalry, but more than enough were scraped up to ensure that the Grande Armée's raw artil-lery arm could move as well as shoot.

Mules were also a factor with artillery trains, especially in Spain, just as they were for trans-port. The mule, sometimes, depending on the army that used it, called "jughead" amid its braying and stubbornness, is nevertheless as good a comrade as the horse. In Spain, the British used mules as much for their artillery as they did for their transport. Alexander Dickinson's manuscript, which is a compendium of his correspondence as he worked his way up to be Wellington's very competent Chief of Artillery, is peppered with a myriad references to mules being used in gun teams.

Native horses were not available in great numbers during the Peninsular War. Both armies either had to bring horses and remounts with them, or use mules. Both armies made use of the mule, both as a draft animal and, on occasion, as a mount. The mule is tough, intelligent, and enduring—a suitable companion to the horse on campaign.

The use, and undoubtedly the usefulness, of mules is illustrated in Table 7, which indicate the number of mules used by both the British and Portuguese in the Peninsula in 1809. It should be noted that, at times, even officers were mounted on mules instead of horses. Gener-ally speaking, the mounted personnel of the King's German Legion were better horsemasters than their British comrades-in-arms. The Royal German Artillery was another, contemporary term for the artillery of the King's German Legion.

There were two great and permanent innovations during this period for artillery, both con-cerning the horse. One was the introduction of a militarized artillery train, those men and horse teams that pulled the guns and artillery vehicles. The other was the reintroduction of horse artillery, this time on a permanent basis for most armies on the Continent as well as Great Britain.

Just as those who first served the guns on a regular basis, when the arm was relatively new, were civilian specialists, so were those who manned the horse teams that pulled the guns to the battlefield. Artillerymen eventually became soldiers, but the drivers did not and remained hired civilians, even into the late eighteenth century. More progressive artillery officers recog-nized the problem, but it took some time to solve it, and some of the solutions were not as satisfactory as they could have been.

TABLE 7: USE OF HORSES AND MULES IN THE PENINSULA, 1809

Return of Horses and Mules of the Royal Artillery under the Command of Brig.-Gen. Howarth, Coimbra, 1 May 1809

	Horses	*Mules*
Captain Lawson's Light 3-pounder Brigade		
6 Guns	4	20
6 Cars	0	12
1 Forge Cart	0	6
4 Ammunition Carts	3	5
Officers	5	2
Non-commissioned Officers and Trumpeters	3	2
Spare	3	2
Captain Lane's First Light 6-pounder Brigade		
6 Guns	34	2
6 Cars	34	2
1 Forge Cart	2	4
1 Cart for Small Stores	0	2
Officers, including an Assistant-surgeon	3	2
Non-commissioned Officers and Trumpeters	5	1
Spare	10	3
Captain Baynes' Second Light 6-pounder Brigade		
6 Guns	36	0
6 Cars	24	12
1 Forge Cart	2	4
1 Cart for Small Stores	0	2
Officers	3	0
Non-commissioned Officers and Trumpeters	4	1
Spare	12	2
General, Field Officers, and Staff		
General Howarth, including Conductor Ambrose and Interpreter	2	5
Colonel Framingham	2	2
Colonel Robe	0	3
Major Dickson	1	1
Captain Terrell	1	0
Lt. Johnstone (Quartermaster)	1	1
Lt. Arbuthnot (Adjutant)	2	0
Lt. Woodyear (Adjutant)	0	2
Surgeon Fitzpatrick, including Medical Instruments and Bedding	3	1
With the Park and Reserve		
7 Ammunition Waggons	16	26
1 Forge Cart	2	4

continued . . .

Captain Sillery	1	0
Mr. Commissary Pickering, his Clerks and Conductor of Stores	11	8
Riders for Non-commissioned Officers	2	7
Total Present	231	147
Left at Lisbon	6	6
Total Strength	237	153

Remarks

The guns are supplied with English horses except the 3-pounder Brigade, which is furnished with large Lisbon mules.

All the other wheel draught is in general from English horses, and the leading draught from the country horses and mules; the latter are too small and weak for this service.

38 horses and mules examined at Coimbra and returned unfit for service would be applicable to carry small-arms ammunition if replaced by English horses. A proportion of those with the Brigade of Captain Baynes will be in a similar state, amounting, perhaps altogether to 60 horses and mules.

Part of the non-commissioned officers of drivers, the clerks and conductors of stores, are supplied from the most inferior horses and mules not fir for draught.

(signed) E. Howarth
Brig. General, Royal Artillery

Return of Horses and Mules of the Royal German Artillery, Commanded by Maj. Hartmann, Coimbra, 1 May 1809

	Horses	*Mules*
Captain von Rettburg's Light 6-pounder Brigade		
6 Guns	36	0
6 cars	28	8
1 Forge Cart	2	4
1 Cart for small Stores	0	2
Officers	4	0
NCOs including 1 farrier	3	0
Spare	7	5
Captain Heises's Long 6-pounder Brigade		
6 Guns	48	0
6 Cars	22	14
1 Cart for spare wheels, etc.	0	6
2 forge Carts	10	2
2 Carts for small Stores	2	2
Officers	3	1
NCOs, including 1 Farrier	1	4
Spare	7	0

continued . . .

Staff

Major Hartmann, including 1 Mule for an orderly	2	1
Lt. Mielmann (Adjt. And Qr. Mr.)	1	0
Assistant-Surgeon Heise, including 1 Mule for carrying the Medicine Chest	1	1

Reserve

Captain Daniel	0	1
1 Clerk and 2 Conductors of Stores	3	0
1 Portuguese Conductor	1	0
1 Sergeant of the Royal Waggon Train	0	1
Total Present	181	52
Left at Lisbon	2	0
At Peniche	1	0
Total Strength	184	52

Remarks

Two horses (being private property) not included, belonging to Major Hartman.

(Signed) E. Howarth
Brig. General, Royal Artillery

Distribution of Mules and Bullocks for Portuguese Artillery—One Brigade

Mules

6 Guns (2 pairs each)	24
6 Ammunition Cars (do.)	24
Officers' Mules	5
Corporal of Drivers and Smith	2
Surgeon	1
7 Ammunition carriages (1 Mule each)	7
1 Baggage Cart (do.)	1
1 Provision Cart (do.)	1
Reserve Mules	7
Total Mules	72

Bullocks

7 Cars (2 pairs each)	28
1 Wheel Carriage	4
1 Forge cart	4
1 Baggage Cart	2
1 Provision Carriage	4
3 Wains	6
Total Bullocks	48

The recurring problem with hired civilian drivers was that they often left the battlefield in a hurry when the going got a little rough, or a few incoming rounds came too close, leaving the artillerymen and their gun in the lurch and to fend for themselves. While this was not always the case, it happened often enough that progressive officers knew that a better system had to be developed. In the 1790s some armies started to militarize their artillery trains. The British were the first in 1794, forming the Royal Corps of Drivers. Next came the French, whose well-organized and trained *Train d'Artillerie* was formed in January 1800. Interestingly, these were not artillerymen *per se*, but classed as train troops whose job was to pull the artillery's guns and vehicles, and to maintain and train the horse teams and harness. Only one army used artillerymen as drivers during this period, and that was the fledgling army of the United States.

All of the European powers addressed the problem in one form or another, introducing artillery train companies and battalions, some more efficient than others, but all having the same idea. Artillerymen on the battlefield could be helpless without their gun teams, especially in defeat and rout, and consequently many guns were lost that could have been saved. Militarizing the train put the drivers in the same category as the artillerymen they supported, and subject to the same discipline and penalties.

The Austrians formed their "field train" in 1782 by order of Joseph II. However, it was still a civilian organization and was not particularly efficient, having all the faults of trying to put civilians both under military jurisdiction and under fire. It supplied gun teams and transport not only for the artillery, but for the administrative and supply trains as well. *Fuhrwesenkorps* units available for employment in 1799 numbered only 695 personnel and 616 horses, hamstringing Austrian operations from the beginning of the campaigns, and the deficiency was never adequately made up. After the campaign or war was over, no *Fuhrwesenkorps* units were kept with the batteries. It was an *ad hoc* organization and, moreover, a stopgap measure. It greatly affected the efficiency of the Austrian artillery arm and hampered army operations as a whole.

Improvements and reform were finally accomplished after Austerlitz. The *Fuhrwesenkorps* was finally militarized in 1806-08, as the French artillery train had been in 1800, and starting in 1808 a cadre of train personnel were left with the batteries with which they would go to war. In 1809, besides the ammunition carried with the guns on their limbers or *coffrets*, there were between 130 and 180 rounds per gun in the artillery park. However, this was not yet an effective organization, and the French and Russians artillery train units were both better trained and more efficient.

The British Army finally tired of civilian artillery transport by 1794; perhaps the dismal campaigns on the Continent had been the last straw. Subsequently, the Corps of Drivers of the Royal Artillery was created in that year to handle the horse teams of the artillery, horse and foot. Another, separate organization, the Field Train Department, hauled the artillery's ammunition, which at best was unhandy.

There were usually either four or six horses per gun team. Sometimes, however, eight were used for horse artillery, as in the Waterloo campaign in 1815. The Corps of Drivers was generally not well thought of. The men did not belong to the artillery *per se*, and the command relationship had to be established by each battery commander with his assigned drivers. A "troop" of drivers consisted of five sections of 90 drivers each, plus the attached artisans to take care of the harness, etc. In 1808 there were eleven troops of drivers. For active service, the troops were divided up and assigned to brigades as needed. Therefore, drivers were usually as good as they were trained, and which battery commander they worked for. They did perform good service, as the horse artillery always maintained a very high reputation for skill, dash, and *élan*, but they were probably a handful.

Sir Alexander Dickson casually mentions in his manuscript the courts-martial that took place from time to time. Usually for the artillery it was a driver. Dickson also referred to the Corps of Drivers as an "Augean stable;" and one British horse artilleryman called them "a nest of infamy". Dickson believed that their officers neglected them, not caring if they were paid and sometimes using their pay for themselves. One of their most nefarious activities was stealing ammunition and selling it to the Portuguese Army.

Never enjoying a particularly high reputation, the artillery drivers were parceled out to the different brigades and troops, the responsibility for them being delegated to the battery commanders. Some served efficiently enough, especially with the horse artillery troops, if Norman Ramsay's famous charge through swarming French cavalry at Fuentes d'Oñoro is any benchmark of their caliber. However, the enlisted men do turn up very frequently in Dickson's correspondence as being disciplined for some infraction or other, sometimes serious and sometimes rather routine. Keeping the units supplied with remounts, especially in Spain, was difficult:

> Horses to drag all this equipment were required in large numbers and were invariably in short supply. Imported animals were preferred when they could be obtained, as local horses and mules were found to be of poor quality. Teams of eight were employed to enable the RHA to deploy and retire their 9-pounders . . . at speed. Many more were required for the ammunition wagons, for other carriages and as mounts for officers.

Napoleon, upon assuming power as First Consul in 1799–1800, found the French Army in very bad shape after years of war and heavy losses and general neglect by the succession of revolutionary governments. One of the first reforms that he initiated was the militarization of the *Train d'Artillerie*. Having always relied on civilian drivers, who were an dubious proposition at best, Napoleon organized battalions of artillery train troops, whose companies would "brigade" themselves with an artillery company, providing the artillery, foot or horse, with horse teams and drivers to move its guns and other vehicles. The experiment proved most satisfactory, the train drivers demonstrating on the battlefields of the Consulate and Empire a stoic courage, having to endure fire without the satisfaction of being able to shoot back, and a skill in horsemanship that was generally above reproach.

The French *Train d'Artillerie* was ordered to be formed by First Consul Bonaparte on 3 January 1800 by a decree of the Consuls. It consisted of twenty-one articles and it laid out the organization, chain of command, uniform, and responsibilities, as well as establishing the councils of administration for the train battalions. Each train battalion was to have five companies. The battalion's elite company, with the best men and horses, was assigned to the horse artillery. Three of the companies went to the foot artillery or to the parks at corps or army level. The fifth company would form the depot which would train recruits and the remounts for the companies assigned to the artillery. Company commanders were *maréchal des logis chefs*. Each company was assigned a trumpeter. Battalions were commanded by captains.

After the campaigns in 1800, the train was reorganized in order to repair noted deficiencies. Eight train battalions of six companies each were organized; battalions were still commanded by captains, but company commanders were now lieutenants. At the battalion level, there was a veterinarian, a master saddler, and a master armorer. The companies had two blacksmiths as well as two harness makers. In wartime, each battalion "doubled itself," sending a cadre from the parent battalion to organize a new one. Both battalions would have the same number, the permanent battalion having its number followed by "*principal*," and the temporary battalion by "*bis*."

Contrary to British practice, the officers, men, and horses for these battalions were carefully selected and well trained. New battalions were organized and formed as needed. By 1810 there were fourteen artillery train battalions, and the first thirteen had "doubled" themselves for the campaigns of 1809, 1812, and 1813. In June 1813, because of a shortage of replacements and heavy casualties, an order went out that all infantrymen or cavalrymen who had been wounded in the hand and were no longer capable of service with those arms were to be transferred to the artillery train. Depots for them were established in Dresden and Magdeburg, and it must have been hard on those troopers handling a pair of horses, as (probably) inexperienced as they were, especially under fire or in bad weather.

The artillery train also hauled the equipment in the different artillery parks at corps and army level. The corps park consisted of spare guns, vehicles, and equipment maintained there to replace *matériel* lost in action. Usually there was one spare gun for every ten assigned to the infantry divisions or the corps artillery. The army artillery park, known as the *Grand Parc*, was divided into a mobile park, which accompanied the army in the field, and the fixed park, which established depots and arsenals in the rear of the army, along its line of communications. It was from the depots and arsenals maintained by artillery park system that ammunition was continuously sent forward to the artillery companies, with the divisions, corps, and army artillery reserve using the artillery train. Every artillery train battalion assigned to the army was under the authority of a general of brigade, as noted in the Decree of 3 January 1800, who carried the imposing title "Inspector General of the Artillery Train."

There is no doubt that the artillery train battalions were an efficient organization, quite possibly the most efficient train organization among the major belligerents, although the arrangement of one train company per company of artillery might seem awkward by today's standards. Train personnel were not artillerymen: they were drivers and horse handlers. Their mission was to drive and take care of the horses that pulled the artillery's guns and vehicles. They were also responsible for the considerable amount of horse harness that equipped the horse teams. They had all of the problems and headaches the cavalry had with their horses. In addition to that, the train troops usually had to be able to "make bricks without straw." Horse pairs and teams had to be carefully matched. Harnesses had to be continually adjusted to take into account the weight lost by the horses on campaign. Teams also had to be carefully trained, the best and strongest (and also, usually, the steadiest) being in the wheel pair, nearest the limber.

The following is an example of some of the hardships that could be incurred by an artillery unit and its accompanying train company. This is from the Russian campaign:

> That night the heavens open again. And all along the Vilna road the rain comes pelting down, forcing Major Boulart to spend the night in one of his artillery wagons. In a freezing wet dawn, somewhere beyond Ewe, he climbs out to see in front of him "a quarter of my horses lying on the ground, some dead or almost, the others shivering." Harnessing up the survivors, he orders men and horses to march—not so much because there's any great hurry, "but to restore their circulation." The 2d Company of the 9th Artillery Regiment, too, is losing its Frisians at an alarming rate. Exposed to this rain as long as it lasted, and after living for several days off barley and other standing crops, Lieutenant N. J. Sauvage sees in the morning "two or three of these beasts in their death throes or laid out lifeless in front of each ammunition wagon. At their side we saw our gunners and soldiers of the Train standing in gloomy silence, tears in their eyes, trying to avert their gaze from this afflicting scene."[3]

Four horse teams were assigned to the 4-, 6-, and 8-pounders, as they were to the battery wagons, field forges, and caissons. The 12-pounders rated a six-horse team, as did one of the 12-pounder caissons. The lead teams also had to be well chosen, and the middle team for the 12-

pounders, called a swing team, had to be even-tempered to be placed between two other teams. All in all it was a hard business, and the runaway artillery team, of which undoubtedly there were many, especially in combat, was almost impossible to stop, unless the horses were shot, run over a cliff, or came up against an obstacle they could neither run over nor run through.

The number of caissons assigned to a French artillery company depended on the caliber of gun the company was using. Each 4-pounder required two caissons, each 6- and 8-pounder was assigned three, and each howitzer and 12-pounder five. Additionally, every company had a field forge, and three wagons which carried "supplies, forage, and spare parts." Artillery companies that were assigned to infantry divisions also were issued four additional caissons to carry musket cartridges to resupply the infantry. Almost every vehicle, be it gun, caisson, or wagon, used a four-horse team to pull it. The exceptions were field forges, 12-pounders, and one 12-pounder caisson, which were issued six-horse teams.

Based on this number of vehicles, a French artillery battery was a very large organization. However, only one caisson per gun was kept with the battery in action. The rest of the caissons were used in a running shuttle service between the firing battery and the artillery parks when in action, and on the march these caissons moved with the park.

In combat, du Teil recommended that

> The ammunition [caissons] which cannot be kept under cover shall form at the same time into two files, with the head of the file on the flanking pieces, keeping a distance of thirty paces between one wagon and the other, to prevent accidents and so that the men of the infantry or cavalry can, if necessary, pass between them easily, either in column or deployed. The first caisson will be close enough to the front trains to be able to provide for their needs. When they are emptied, they will return to the rear of the column, passing on the outside of the flanks, and be replaced by others, and so on; or they will go seek ammunition, if there is any nearby than can be obtained.[4]

The reason for so many caissons assigned per battery was that Napoleon required that there always be a double "*approvisionment*" (standard load) of ammunition per gun with the army— 300 to 350 rounds per gun. The system worked very well, and the Grande Armée never ran out of ammunition. Napoleon wrote the following to Berthier in April of 1809:

> If the Army of Germany has twice the basic load of artillery stores—whether with the divisions or in the army corps parks, or in the general park—it is in god shape. With twice the usual supply of artillery stores there would be enough on hand to fight three great battles like Austerlitz. To drag along more artillery stores, however, is a useless encumbrance. But there is no question that twice the basic issue of artillery stores would be sufficient, if you had a third in the depot four or five marches to the rear of the army. Thus in the actual situation we should have a reserve of cartridges between Ulm, Donauworth, and Ingolstadt, in chests that can be carried in the wagons.[5]

TABLE 8: GRANDE ARMÉE AMMUNITION ALLOCATION, PER GUN

Organization	No of rounds
Division artillery companies plus Division *parcs*	170
Corps *parcs*	85
Army *parc* (mobile section)	85
Forward depot	250
Total	590
	of which 340 "on wheels" (caissons)

French artillery ammunition per gun was assigned as shown in Table 8.

The troops might go hungry, but they could always march or fight. Only once during the course of the Empire's wars did the artillery came close to running out of ammunition. The army trains during the Battle of Leipzig in 1813 were cut off in Eilenberg, north of Leipzig, by the concentric advance of the allies. The French artillery expenditures during the first day of the battle were immense, and resupply was impossible. This went a long way in convincing Napoleon that he had to withdraw. The expenditure was 267 rounds per gun at Leipzig, compared to 100 per gun at Friedland six years earlier.

The Russian artillery train was militarized in 1803, a result of Arakcheev's reforms:

> The artillery teams and harness were also standardized. The team of each heavy cannon consisted of six horses; that of a light or horse cannon had four horses; 3-pounder unicorns were pulled by two horses each; and caissons were pulled by three horses each, except caissons for 3-pounder unicorns, which were pulled by two horses each.[6]

If the terrain was rough or the weather turned nasty, 12-pounder gun teams were usually increased to ten horses. Twenty-pounder *licornes* were always issued ten-horse gun teams.

Russian artillery drivers were not part of a separate train organization as in other armies; they would not be so until 1819. During this period they were assigned to the artillery batteries they drove for as permanent personnel. Sir Robert Wilson gives an excellent description of the Russian gun teams and drivers:

> The draft horses are small, but of great muscular strength, strongly loined, and with high blood. Four draw the light field pieces, and eight the twelve pounders; the latter have sometimes indeed ten horses; but then the roads must be such as are only to be met with in Poland before the frost sets in, or when it breaks up, and which, during the last campaign [1806–07], were in such a state that Bonaparte said he had discovered, by crossing the Vistula, the new element of mud. The power of these animals is however so great, that on taking up positions, they will plunge through the ditches filled with yielding snow, although so deep as to cover their back, and bury the guns altogether; and when the center and right wing retired through the Alle, after the battle of Friedland, at a point discovered on the emergency, they were partly swimming, and afterwards compelled to ascend the banks, which were almost perpendicular. If the horses had possessed less strength or activity, the whole must have fallen into the hands of the enemy; but the Russians seem well aware of the importance of horsing their artillery well, and the Russian government is wise enough to spare no expense that may be necessary for its efficiency and security.
>
> The drivers are stout men: like all other drivers, they require superintendence in times of danger, to prevent their escape with the horses, but on various occasions they have also shown great courage and fidelity; and they have the essential merit of carefully providing subsistence for their horses. Neither gun, tumbril, nor cart belonging to the artillery is ever seen without forage of some kind, and generally collected by the prudence and diligence of the drivers, which might be improper where the issues are assured under regular authority, but which, according to the practices of continental nations, is very commendable and necessary.[7]

The Prussian artillery train is hard to pin down and find information about. Undoubtedly the destruction of much archival material during World War II is responsible for this lack of material. However, what little is known is useful. Of the three Prussian artillery brigades that were formed in 1809, train personnel were assigned to each, later to become assigned to the artillery battery for which they drove and maintained the horses. These were soldiers, not civilians, and their efficiency had greatly increased from the *ad hoc* organization employed in 1806. Frederick the Great had used temporary drivers and horse teams; there was no permanent train organization until the coming of the Great Wars. Horses and drivers were also hired for training purposes, once a year, and this greatly hampered the efficiency of the Prussian artillery.

Horse artillery was first developed and used in combat by the army of Frederick the Great. Formed in 1757, it was unfortunately disbanded at the end of the Seven Years' War. There is a hint here and there that Frederick got his idea from the Austrians, but that remains to be proven. With all of the artillery development going on in Austria at the time, and Lichtenstein being given a relatively free hand, it would not be surprising if Lichtenstein and his talented team of subordinates did come up with the idea first; nevertheless, it was Frederick who first employed the batteries in the field. The following is "An Historical Sketch of the Introduction of Horse or Flying Artillery into the Different Armies of Europe:"

In the campaigns of 1757, 1758, and 1759, against the Russians, it often happened that the Prussian light horse, at the very moment when they imagined themselves sure of success, met with a battery of cannon, though no infantry were present, which led them to suppose that the Russians had horse artillery which were able to follow all the movements of the cavalry. The fact being ascertained, Frederick the Great introduced this artillery into his army in the spring of 1759, when the writer of this sketch, at the head-quarters of Reichnersdorf, near Landschuth, saw him nearly every morning exercise this new corps himself, and direct its maneuvers. At the time, when, in order to resist the league formed against him, his genius multiplied his resources; when the same army, with a celerity and precision till then unknown, and during the same campaign, conveyed itself upon opposite frontiers, to the east and west of his dominions, and triumphed over the superior forces of the league.

He first tried to accelerate and simplify the marches of columns of Artillery when on a route; he then used the same method for the marches when maneuvering in the presence of an enemy; and, at length, applied it to the movements and engagements of advanced guards

The king likewise made a successful trial of his horse artillery, before he left that camp, by covering with it a reconnoitering party, beyond Liebaw, on the retreat of his dragoons, in a manner so effectual that all the attacks of the enemy's horse, though far superior in numbers, completely failed.

The Austrians were the first who imitated this new military establishment. In 1783, under the reign of Joseph II, they maneuvered with horse artillery near Prague; but it was by no means made a principal object. It remained in a state of imperfection that did not admit of the acquisition of all its advantages. The artillerymen were conveyed upon caissons, or stuffed wagons, which were made in the form of old hunting carriages, called wurst wagen. These caissons differ from the common ones only in having the cover stuffed, which affords the facility of placing the gunners upon it in the attitude of a man on horseback. The Archduke Charles, instructed by the success of his enemies, has greatly augmented and improved this arm in the military forces of Austria. The English also have lately introduced horse artillery into their service; but, it is supposed, too sparingly, to derive therefrom its full effect.

Since that time it has been introduced into other armies, yet with considerable difference as to the caliber of the ordnance, and the manner of mounting the artillerymen. The Prussian horse artillery consists of six pounders; the Austrian of light three pounders; the Danish of one pounder; etc. The Prussian artillerymen are on horseback; the Austrian ride on the carriages of the guns, the Hanoverian ride partly on horseback, partly on the gun carriages and wursts, etc.

Into the Neapolitan army Baron Salis introduced two field pieces to a battalion; one piece of cannon to each squadron for the horse or flying artillery, and one howitzer to every two battalions.

But no European power has hitherto derived such important advantages from this new artillery as the French. The adoption of it was for a long time proposed in vain; but in 1791 M. Duportail, then minister of war, authorized the commanding officer of the division of Metz to form two companies of horse artillery; and, finally, in the year 1792, it was adopted generally, and soon carried to great perfection. In order to give it the advantage of a superior fire, the French flying or horse artillery consists of eight pounders, and six inch howitzers; the ammunition is carried in light caissons, and most of the artillerists are on horseback, while others ride on the wursts. By this arrangement, in addition to the known abilities of the French cannoneers, the republican horse artillery soon acquired a decided superiority over that of the Austrians, and other powers, which the imperial horse artillery has maintained, and even surpassed, during a series of victories in the glorious wars of 1805 and 1806.

The success of this experiment in 1791, the extraordinary skill in the choice of the officers and artillerymen, who were employed, and who, in a few weeks, were able to maneuver with the light troops, dispelled every doubt on the subject, and showed how fit the French were for this kind of service.

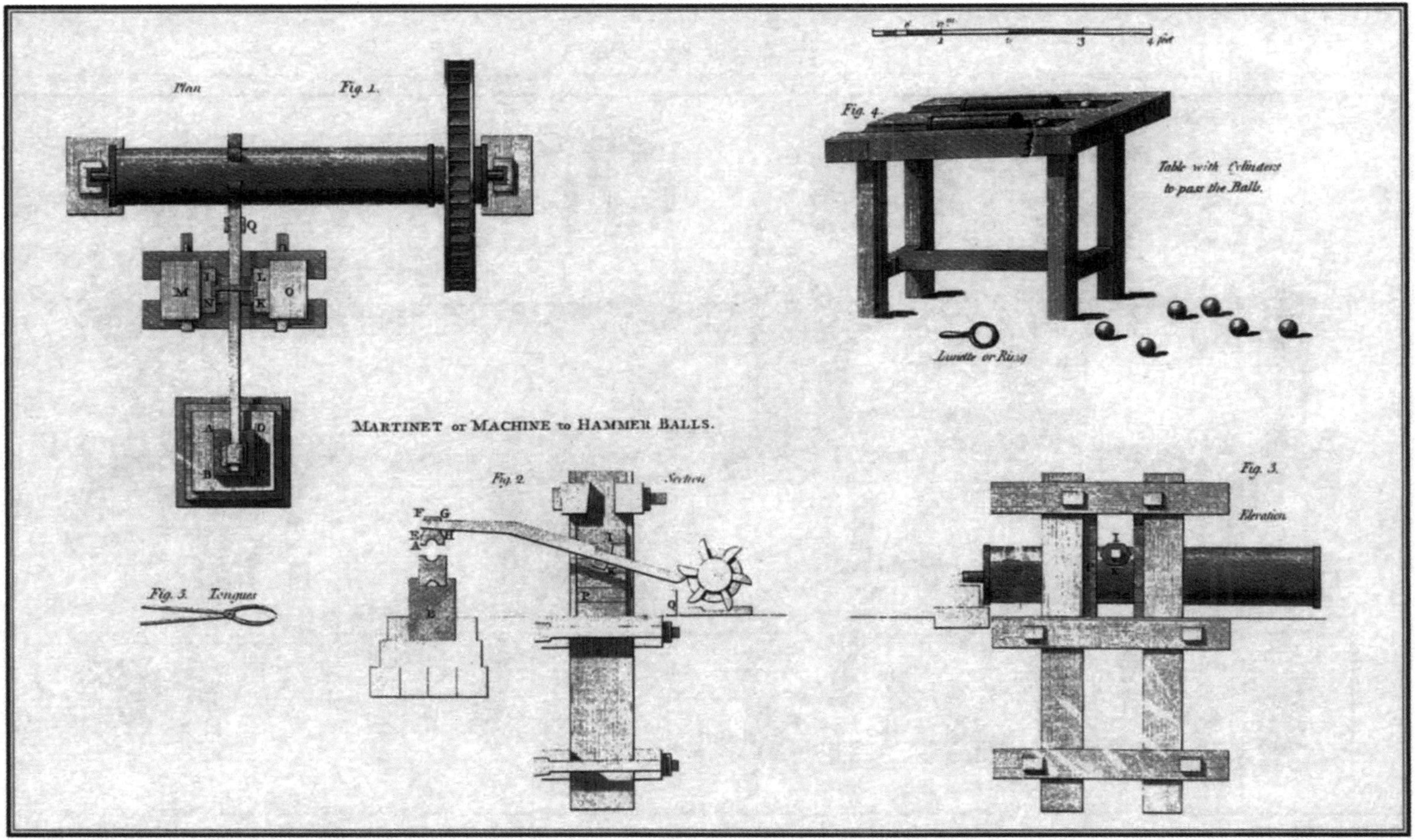
Plan
Fig. 1.
Q
M
I
N
L
K
O
A
D
B
MARTINET or MACHINE to HAMMER BALLS.
Fig. 2.
Section
F
G
E
H
A
I
P
Q
B
Fig. 5.
Tongues
Fig. 4.
1
3
4 feet
Table with Cylinders
to pass the Balls.
Lunette or Ring
Fig. 3.
Elevation

Testing roundshot

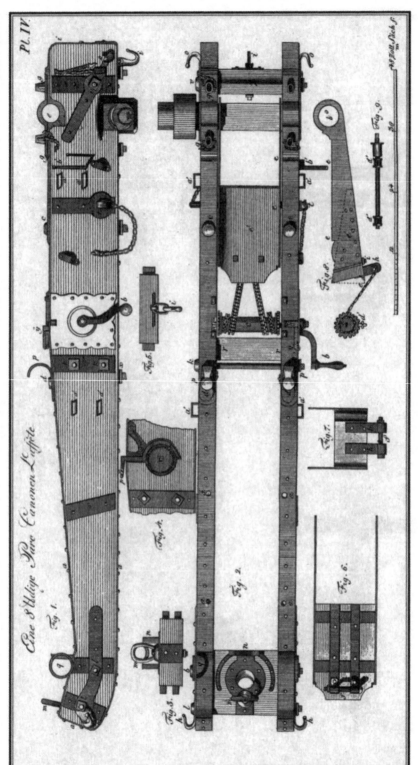

Hanoverian gun carriage.

In 1792, a short time before the declaration of war, M. de Narbonne, who had succeeded M. Duportail in the department of war, formed at his office a committee, composed of very intelligent and well informed officers: thither he summoned the generals of the three great divisions of the army, and the principal generals and field officers of the artillery and engineers. He ordered them to inquire into and decide upon the means of perfecting and extending to the French army the use of the horse artillery.[8]

The use and purpose of horse artillery was succinctly defined by Louis de Tousard in *The Artillerist's Companion* in 1809:

> The principal object of [horse artillery] is to possess such a peculiar organization as to execute with facility not only the most rapid, but, at the same time, the most unexpected movements; to be enabled quickly to bear either upon a point that is attacked, on any part of a seacoast which is threatened with invasion, or on a post which it is requisite to carry by a decisive attempt; to be constantly attendant on the cavalry, if it be required; to confound and embarrass the enemy by every mode of attack and defense, which the theory and practice of the military art, and of artillery, can possibly suggest; and, lastly, to effect these various operations, by the knowledge of displaying, positions, etc. . .[9]

Austria was the only major belligerent that lacked well-developed horse artillery. The Austrians' cavalry batteries were organized in the 1780s, their new light 6-pounder gun and the 7-pounder howitzer being the usual armament of these mobile units. The cannoneers were not individually mounted, but first rode modified caissons, commonly called *Wurst-Wägen*, sitting astride them one behind the other, while others rode the gun carriage astride a specially made seat on the trail. Later, after the implementation of the 1808 update to the artillery regulations, the wursts were done away with and packhorses to haul ammunition were issued each cavalry battery, ostensibly to increase their mobility. The gunners were still not individually mounted as in other armies, and the ride on the padded, elongated gun carriages had to be a minor adventure at any speed faster than a walk. They could not keep up with cavalry, but were much more mobile than the Austrian foot artillery. They needed a cavalry escort to protect the artillery, and the regulations for their use in combat were rather sparse and not specific as to how they were to be employed. They were generally slow, and had to be protected in combat, and although the personnel and equipment were excellent, their employment in combat was not as efficient as that of either the French or British horse artillery arm.

The advantages of having all of the officers, NCOs, and cannoneers mounted in the horse artillery arm was rather obvious, as outlined in the following two excerpts:

> The method of having the horse cannoneers mounted on the wurst was adopted at first; the plan of having the gunners altogether mounted differs little from it, and requires an additional expense of horses, saddles, and equipments for a horseman.
>
> Experience, during this long war, has demonstrated the advantage of mounted cannoneers, and of confining the wursts only to carry ammunition, and such men as may happen to be dismounted; horsemen may always arrive in time with their piece, and need only to remount their horses, when the guns have begun their movement for changing position, and join them afterwards with equal rapidity; on the contrary, the wursts filing off quickly as soon as a maneuver is determined upon, is difficult for the cannoneer to keep up with them; or, if the wursts be obliged to wait until all the men are mounted on them, the delay which would be thus occasioned might prove injurious to the maneuver itself, and entirely defeat its object, independent of the difficulties of the ground to be traced, and the accidents that may happen in case the wurst should overset. To those officers only, who have now a sufficient practice of horse artillery, it belongs to determine which is the best to be adopted. What operates more strongly in favor of the cannoneer being mounted is the celerity with which all maneuvers are performed by the French artillery compared to the Austrians, who use only wursts; but it is said they are about to abandon this method, and adopt that of the French, of the superiority of which they are well aware.
>
> The superiority of the French horse artillery . . . would doubtless be still more conspicuous if the troops of cavalry . . . with whom they perform the maneuvers, knew how to cover its batteries, and to

unmask them only at the proper time; for, if the enemy be aware of the approach of a division of flying artillery, he can prepare, at a distance, the means of avoiding its fire, or of defeating its object and rendering it abortive by changing the maneuver against which it was directed.

The great advantage of the horse artillery, with the cannoneers mounted on horses, consists in having men, accustomed to horses, who may arrive fresh and lively at the moment of action, whereas the foot cannoneer arrives almost exhausted . . .

Horse artillery should never, or at least very rarely, act as a corps of light horse; their duty is both to serve and to defend their pieces: instead of the habits and morals of light horse and free corps, they should adopt the steady courage, and the old plain simplicity of the foot cannoneer: therefore they should never precede their cannon, except some of them as eclaireurs, and need not arrive before the pieces to which they are attached.

A horse can easily draw fifteen hundredweight on an horizontal ground, and on difficult ground this weight can be reduced [by] one fourth: a horse may draw seven hundred and fifty pounds, and, at the same time, carry one hundred and fifty pounds (the weight of a man), with the diminution of one fourth in the above supposition.

Let us observe, upon the whole, that, to execute the same movement, the foot artillery requires eight horses less than the horse artillery. At first it might appear necessary to submit this disposition to experiment, but when we recollect the above observation that the cannoneer need not arrive before his piece, and that both ways the piece moves with the same rapidity, the equality of the two services is obvious, and needs no further trial.

In order to be prepared for the urgency, a few hundred saddles should be had in readiness, and the cannoneers be accustomed to ride from the right. They should also be provided with pantaloons and half boots.

Four pounders appear to us sufficient for the horse artillery, especially in a country which is exposed to be attacked only by troops coming from distant countries, who are not supposed to bring with them a much heavier metal; consequently this caliber ought to be generally adopted for the horse artillery of the United States, without excluding altogether the six and nine pounders from that service, as circumstances may render them necessary. Horse artillery being destined to reach and occupy important positions with the utmost rapidity, and to crush troops unexpectedly, this light caliber is well calculated for this service, and adds much to the celerity with which it ought to execute its movements. In case the greater range of the larger calibers be made an objection, we will remove it by asking, Is not eight or twelve hundred yards the distance a gun may fire at with some degree of accuracy? The four pounders range that far, and overset lines, men, etc. If it [is] necessary to break open abattis, entrenchments, etc., these immovable butts will certainly give sufficient time for the eight and twelve pounders to arrive.[10]

Wilhelm Faber du Faur, a Württemberg artillery officer attached to Ney's III Corps in Russia in 1812, vividly described an action in which French cavalry, commanded by Murat, inhibited the effectiveness of its supporting horse artillery:

The use of a "wurst" caisson by horse artillery. This is an illustration from The American Artillerist's *Companion.*

In the afternoon of the 14th [of August], Ney and Murat arrived before Krasnoi, a small village some twenty miles from Smolensk. A Russian infantry regiment had barricaded itself in the village but was forced out by Ledru's division. It fell back and joined some five or six thousand Russians positioned on the Smolensk road and supported by artillery and cavalry. It was Neverovskii's division. These troops had been surprised and now found themselves on a plain stretching for miles, amongst the ripening cornfields. The Russians were now entirely exposed to the charges of our cavalry. Only a small stream separated the two opposing sides, and problems encountered by our cavalry as it tried to cross this stream gave Neverovskii time to ready himself and form his infantry into one huge square. No sooner had he done this than he saw his cavalry charged and flee in disorder and his artillery taken, whilst his infantry were forced to withstand the massed attack of the cavalry. He set his square in motion despite being assailed by Murat's cavalry—he would owe his survival as much to the tenacity of his own troops as to Murat's poorly directed attacks and impatience. As soon as the guns of our 2nd horse artillery battery opened up with a devastating discharge of canister, Murat, brandishing his saber, charged across our muzzles and we would have to cease fire as the massed cavalry prevented our firing again. The Russians would then reform, their ranks leaving no trace of any loss, and would continue their retreat.

And so it went on from position to position. The Russians eventually reached a wooded defile and, with their flanks covered, they managed to slip away towards the safety of Smolensk having lost 2,000 men.[11]

France came into the horse artillery game somewhat late. Asked why he did not organize horse artillery immediately into his new system of artillery, Gribeauval replied, "You witness the difficulties and enemies which my endeavors to destroy ancient prejudices have raised against me; at a future period we may execute your plan; digest and improve upon it; for the present it would be asking too much." Finally organized in 1792, allegedly by Lafayette, the French horse artillery quickly developed their own tactics and dressed the part, wearing a modified light cavalry uniform, albeit in the artillery colors of dark blue and red.

They quickly proved their worth, and were mounted both on wursts and individually. They served with ever-increasing skill, dash, and *élan*, and were soon made a part of the regular French artillery establishment. They were also in very high demand by the various French army commanders. They became a true elite arm of the service, and were assigned generally to the cavalry divisions of the Grande Armée. Some of the best French artillery commanders, such as Eble and Desvaux de St Maurice, who was killed in action at Waterloo, came out of the horse artillery.

British horse artillery was a true *arme d'élite*, the gunners individually mounted or mounted on their limbers, upon which the ammunition box doubled as a seat. Normally they used the light 6-pounder gun, but for the Waterloo campaign in 1815 they were all issued the heavier 9-pounder. It was a small, highly select arm that produced such battery commanders as Hew Ross, who served with the Light Division throughout the Peninsular War and was probably the most skilled of all. There was Norman Ramsay, famous for his escapade at Fuentes d'Oñoro in 1811, where, almost caught and surrounded by French light cavalry, he ordered a charge that took him and his men at and through the astonished French troopers to reach the British lines in safety. Finally, the famous author and battery commander Cavalie Mercer, who first saw action at Waterloo, did more than his assigned duty and had the presence of mind to write about it. His memoirs of the Waterloo campaign are a vivid, first-hand account of what it was like to be an artilleryman on a Napoleonic battlefield.

The United States Army of the period had great teething problems. The powers-that-be, generally speaking, were against having a regular military establishment in any numbers. After the advent of the Jefferson administration in 1801, followed by that of Jefferson's *protégé* James Madison eight years later, there was a definite prejudice at the national level against having any regular military establishment at all, be they soldier, sailor, or Marine. Consequently, the United

States lagged far behind its European contemporaries in maintaining a combat-ready army of any type. The two administrations preferred to rely on the dubious quality of the state militias.

Secretary of War Henry Dearborn had one artillery company mounted in 1808–09. It was commanded by Captain Peter, who was a good and experienced officer. After initial success with the battery, all the cannoneers were issued horses so that the entire battery was mounted and not carried in any type of wagon, which it had been initially. It was a show-horse outfit with special uniforms—natty in appearance, but more than made up for by the troops' efficiency. Unfortunately, with the advent of the Madison administration and a more than usual penny-pinching attitude, the battery was dismounted by order the new Secretary of War, and the horses sold as an economy measure. Captain Peter resigned in disgust, though he later did volunteer for service in the War of 1812.

Then, the unprepared US Army did not have one mounted battery in the Light Artillery Regiment. Most of the artillerymen would serve as infantry during the war and would distinguish themselves, especially along the frontier with Canada. Those who did serve in gun companies also distinguished themselves in nearly every action in which they participated, especially Chippawa, Lundy's Lane, and New Orleans, being favorably compared to the artillery of the Grande Armée by the British. Tousard summarized the service of horse artillery as follows:

General Dumourier demonstrated all the importance of this artillery in an invasive war, at the end of the campaign of 1792, in Belgium; and there have since occurred other very remarkable instances of success, which have been owing to the horse artillery both in offensive and defensive operations.

At the battle of Castiglione, after the raising of the siege of Mantua, the Emperor, having ordered General St Martin to collect and place to advantage several divisions of the flying artillery, broke the line of the Austrians, and decided the fate of Italy.

At the battle of Waterloo, four thousand men of the army of Flanders, maneuvering with horse artillery (and this testimony is adduced by officers of the combined army), sustained the attack of an army of thirty thousand men, supported by a train of artillery at least treble that of the French.

The horse artillery contributed much to the gaining of the battle of Etlingen, in which general Moreau, although inferior in cavalry, supported his left wing against all the cavalry of the Archduke. A similar maneuver procured [for] general Hoche similar success upon the Rhine, at the affair of Neuvied, where the horse artillery, advancing rapidly in front, and firing briskly, silenced the fire of an entrenched line, which was flanked by strong redoubts: general Debelle, who commanded it, is one of the officers who formed the first horse artillery companies at Metz.

The Archduke, availing himself of these experiments, had greatly augmented and improved this species of artillery in the Austrian army. He attached some divisions of horse artillery to different corps of light troops, from which he derived the greatest advantages in the rencontres and engagements of advanced posts before the decisive battle of Stockach.

The following is extracted from a letter of the general chief of the staff of the army of the Rhine to the minister of war, dated headquarters of Steyer, Nivose the 5th, Year 9th.

"Horse artillery distinguished itself by the regularity of its firing. Six pieces, supported by two of the enemy's squadrons, made a terrible destruction of our infantry on the heights of Haigertoff; the second company of the seventh, and the fourth of the eighth regiments of horse artillery, with six pieces, however, checked the enemy; in less than half an hour they dismounted four of their pieces, burst three of their caissons, and forced them to retreat, with the loss of their cannon. Two of our pieces were then drawn up to the top of the heights: two of the enemy's squadrons, which had rallied under cover of a wood, made a charge upon and carried them; our horse cannoneers, unappalled, immediately mounted their horses, charged the hussars with the greatest intrepidity, recovered and brought back their pieces in triumph. In this charge, citizen Jajul, marechal des logis, lost his right arm by the stroke of a saber. In general it is impossible to praise sufficiently the advantages of that arm, either in action or in its organization, the details of which are attended to with the most astonishing perfection. It is but justice to pay this tribute of praise to general Eble, who commands it, and who may justly be looked upon as one of the best officers in Europe for this service."

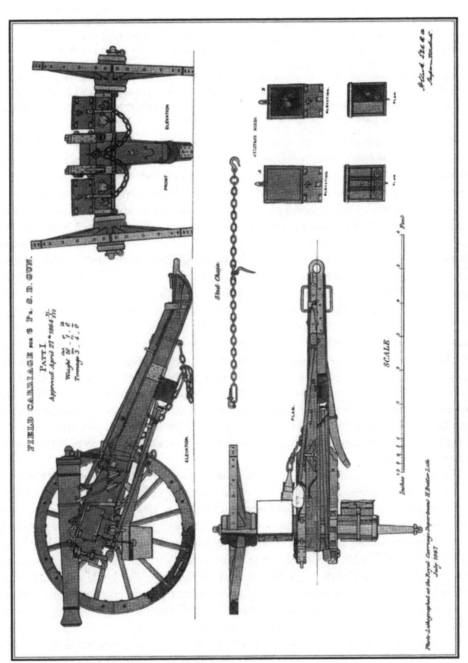

The British 6-pounder gun, complete with sidearms.

At the battle of Rostock, in 1778, Frederick had brought with a detachment, which he led himself, one of these flying batteries: this modern invention of cannon served by mounted cannoneers, the quick motions of which vie with the celerity of cavalry, which they follow everywhere, and support in all their evolutions, may justly be called the greatest improvement in the art of destroying men, and, on this occasion, evinced all the advantages which could be expected from such artillery, when served by cannoneers as skillfully trained as the Prussians. This battery consisted of six guns and one howitzer: it was employed so as to sweep with grape and canister shot all the ground which was occupied by the enemy's cavalry. At a signal the squadron of horse, which masked the maneuver, with the rapidity of lightning, displayed to the right and left; at the same moment the battery opened its fire, and five or six precipitate discharges had such an effect that the enemy's horse, which was collected by squadrons, and occupied all the field of battle, immediately dispersed, throwing themselves pele mele, part on the left, part in the rear, and all, in an instant, were out of the reach of the Prussian shot.[12]

Horse artillery was a vital weapon, another "arrow in the quiver," so to speak, for the commanders to have on hand and to wield. According to Monhaupt, "horse artillery is able to keep up with the cavalry for distances of several thousand paces, even for miles." That gave a resourceful commander several options on the battlefield. Horse artillery could keep up with even the fastest-moving cavalry, even in the attack, and either assist in the attack, especially against infantry, or be used to cover cavalry withdrawing, reforming, or when retreating. An outstanding example of covering a withdrawal was by the British horse artillery at Fuentes d'Oñoro in 1811, when it was employed with both infantry and cavalry. Artillery commanders had to be able to time their withdrawals almost perfectly, or disaster could result, as Norman Ramsay almost found out to his great chagrin. His quick-witted action saved the day, but only just.

French recognition of the value of horse artillery in adverse weather conditions was evident at Dresden in 1813. A wet and soggy battlefield, so muddy that cavalry could not get into a gallop, required artillery to be as mobile as possible. Napoleon recognized this, artilleryman that he was, and scraped every spare horse he could find and assigned them to the French horse artillery. After the fighting on the second day began, the French attacks on the Allied left flank were brilliantly supported by still mobile and deadly horse artillery. As the Allies collapsed under the unrelenting French offensive, their infantry formed squares. Muskets useless because of wet powder, they held firm until the French horse artillery slid into range and position. The mere threat of what they were going to do at very close range forced the Austrian infantry to surrender.

There were times, though, when the elements were too much. At Vauchamps in 1814, after Blücher began his retreat in almost perfect order but under pressure from Drouot's artillery and Nansouty's Guard cavalry, the constant pounding wore down Blücher's Prussians and Russians, turning the once orderly units into a growing indisciplined, and somewhat panicked, mass. Grouchy took two divisions of cavalry (St Germain and Bourdesoulle) with their horse artillery north of Blücher's route of retreat. The cavalry got in front of the Prussians and Russians, but the horse artillery got bogged down in the rough clay mud, which had to be almost like concrete on the gun and limber wheels. Consequently, after desperate fighting, Blücher broke clear, though with heavy losses. Had the French horse artillery kept up with Grouchy, Blücher might very well have been destroyed.

Colonel Séruzier, who commanded the twelve artillery companies attached to Montbrun's cavalry corps in 1812 (seventy-six 6-pounders and 24-pounder howitzers), stated that

My horse artillery and the divisions of light cavalry escorting them fought serious combats with the Russians. We were having to bombard each other for two or three hours at a time, before the enemy were so kind as to leave us a position where we could pass the night. At each withdrawal he blocked the roads and destroyed the bridges. I was every bit as busy rebuilding them. Each evening I saw my men drop from

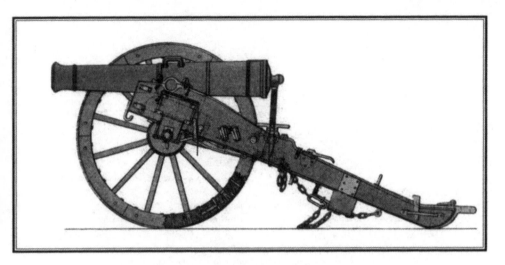

The British 9-pounder gun on its excellent block carriage—undoubtedly the best-designed gun carriage of the period.

weakness and exhaustion. I went into the water up to my waist and planted the first piquet. Despite their exhaustion, my behavior gave my men back a little energy. They got up, forced me to retire, and without saying a word got busy repairing the passage.

In conclusion, the horse was just as important, if not more so, to the artilleryman as to the cavalryman. Napoleon, after the heavy losses in Russia, ensured his artillery were given adequate remounts before the cavalry received them. Horse artillery was a relatively new and elite arm that enhanced the battlefield response time of artillery units, and allowed cavalry to have attached artillery that could move and fight with it. All horse artillerymen considered themselves members of an elite arm, dressed to demonstrate the point, and generally proved it by their performance. Much later, the horse artillery batteries of the United States Army would continue that tradition through the violent cauldron of their Civil War.

NOTES

1. Information on Captain Peter and his horse artillery company is contained in Elting (ed.), *Military Uniforms in America, Vol. II: Years of Growth, 1796–1851*, p. 4.
2. Elting, *Swords Around a Throne*, pp. 227–8.
3. Britten-Austin, *1812: The March on Moscow*, pp. 67–8.
4. Du Teil, *The New Use of Artillery in Field Wars: Necessary Knowledge*, p. 34.
5. *Napoleon's Correspondence*, XVIII, no. 15043, pp. 456–7, Napoleon to Berthier, 10 April 1809, as cited in Luvaas, *Napoleon on the Art of War*, p. 117.
6. Zhmodikov and Zhmodikov, *Tactics of the Russian Army in the Napoleonic Wars*, vol. I, p. 63.
7. Wilson, *Campaigns in Poland 1806 and 1807*, p. 20–5.
8. Tousard, *The American Artillerist's Companion*, Vol. II, pp. 38–40.
9. *Ibid.*, p. 35.
10. *Ibid.*, pp. 56–8.
11. Faber du Faur and North, *With Napoleon in Russia*, Plate 25.
12. Tousard, *op. cit.*, pp. 33–5.

Chapter 5
Tête de l'Armée

Cannon his name,
Cannon his voice, he came.

—George Meredith, *Napoleon*

There had been kings who had made artillery their hobby;
Napoleon was an artilleryman who made a hobby of breaking and making kings.

—John Elting

In my youth we used to march and countermarch all the Summer without
gaining or losing a square league, and then we went into winter quarters. And now
comes an ignorant, hot-headed young man who flies about from Boulogne to Ulm, and from
Ulm to the middle of Moravia, and fights battles in December. The whole system of his
tactics is monstrously incorrect.

—An old German officer

In most battles the Guard artillery is the deciding factor,
since, having it always at hand, I can take it wherever it is needed.

—Napoleon, 1813

It is easy to conceive that the General of the
army and Commandant of artillery should act in concert.

—Louis de Tousard

0200, 20 June 1809: 40 miles west of Ingolstadt, Bavaria

The green Berline carriage rumbled like a juggernaut through the Bavarian countryside towards Ingolstadt. A large, specially modified vehicle, fitted with large, strongly built artillery wheels, it was escorted by grimly silent light horsemen uniformed in light green. The horses were lathered and showing the strain of the pace, and the carriage and escort finally pulled up in a clatter of hooves and trace chains in the next small village, where it was known that a French relay station had been set up.

Slowing down gradually on the cobblestoned street, the entourage still made enough noise to wake the dead, and the bone-tired troopers were near enough to the village cemetery for some of them to take a wistful look at the garden of stone in the moonlight. Villagers who were awakened by the awful clatter peered out of their shuttered windows to see the cause of their interrupted night's sleep. One angry villager was about to shout down to them when he saw who it was that stepped down from the Berline. Another such spectator was the local Burgomaster, who lived across from the temporary relay station.

Opening his shutters and gazing into the street, he saw a very familiar scene. The team horses were being efficiently exchanged with a relief team, the only light being provided by the half moonlight and a few large lanterns. Still, it was light enough to see clearly. The troopers of the escort were watering and feeding their mounts, taking a little time to sip warm wine that had hastily been brought from the nearby inn. Even though it was hard to tell colors in the false light, the Burgomaster could see the escort was uniformed in faded, dust-covered light green, instead of the remembered dark green and scarlet. This puzzled the Burgomaster, especially when one of the NCOs started to berate a trooper for not being able to control his mount in fluent, idiomatic German. The officer who had dismounted from the carriage was wearing a nondescript grey overcoat and a small hat, though he was wearing riding boots. He was talking to another officer, who was more impressively dressed in dark blue trimmed with gold and had just dismounted beside the carriage. While they were talking, an older officer stepped down from the carriage, and the two men turned to engage him in conversation.

Suddenly the routine was interrupted by a courier clattering down the cobblestoned street, coming from the direction of Ingolstadt. Reining in his sweating horse, the junior officer dismounted, saluted the trio of senior officers, and gave the officer in the grey overcoat some type of dispatch. Tearing it open and glancing at it, he motioned to one of the escort who had a lantern to come closer, briefly read the contents, and barked quick, succinct orders, in French, to the rest of the party and escort.

Frenzied activity followed the officer's last syllable. The replacement team was run into place and hitched quickly into place, and the escort swung into their saddles and formed up. Watching the two senior officers get back into the carriage and slam the door as the third mounted his horse, the officer in charge merely motioned his hand forward and the entire column lurched forward carrying the Emperor Napoleon deep into the German night on his way to once again face the enemies of his Empire—this time the formidable Archduke Charles and his *Kaiserlichen*.

Shaking his weary head, the Burgomaster could only feel vaguely sorry for the Austrians, who had once again invaded his country two weeks before. The terrible vengeance of the Grande Armée, led by the Emperor of Battles, was once again being unleashed on the enemies of the Empire. The Burgomaster had seen it before, and it was not pretty.

*   *   *

Across Europe they strode like a Colossus. Ragged, undisciplined volunteers, johnny-raw frightened conscripts and sullen regulars, led sometimes by unwashed *sans-culottes généraux*, commissioned former *sergants-major*, and the vicious, sometimes helpful Representatives on Mission against the armies of the kings. Under execrable conditions, their officers, under threat of a "Republican Shave," imprisonment, or the seemingly overwhelming numbers of enemy men and guns, whipped them into shape to defeat the enemies of the Republic who had placed *La Patrie* in danger. The survivors of these campaigns, which used up men wholesale, always moved forward by force of character, or the character of their commanding officers. These were the men that shaped the armies of the Republic, their tactics, organization, and training. Their remnants were iron men, honed by defeat and hardship, and they led the "wolf breed" of the Revolution through years of bitter struggle and hard-won victories. Somewhere along the grim road, they became professional soldiers and knew no other life. From their ranks came an individualistic, practiced, and hard group of men that were the artillery generals of the French armies.

Napoleon was the only head of state who took the field as commander-in-chief of his armies, and as commander of the Grande Armée. The Allied sovereigns at times also took the field. Alexander was present at Austerlitz, and thought himself in command. Frederick William III was the nominal commander-in-chief of the Prussian Army, was present at Auerstadt in 1806, and displayed admirable courage on the battlefield, but he did not assume command until after his field commander, the Duke of Brunswick, had been mortally wounded:

The Grande Armee was the trenchant instrument with which Napoleon reshaped both Europe and the art of war. Swift-marching, furious in the attack, grimly enduring, high-hearted, stubborn in disaster, it still ranks among the few greatest of the great. It also was many men of many different nations—many heroes, not a few cowards, and the multitude who were neither but did their duty as they saw it . . . The Grande Armee was Napoleon's unique creation. He worked steadily at improving its organization, tactics, and weapons . . . Just as it was his creation, so it was his home. He was another solider there among soldiers, a father among his children. He could talk to them—collectively or man-to-man—in their own speech (not excluding a few popular expletives) and was an expert at the blague (blarney) or a quick fight talk. The Grande Armee gave him strange nicknames: "Le Tondu" (The Shorn One), "Father Violet," and "John of the Sword." Together, they put fear into the souls of Europe's kings and foreign generations—a terrible reality and an enduring legend.[1]

Napoleon was also the only period commander-in-chief who was an artilleryman. Scharnhorst, who was chief of staff to Brunswick in 1806, chief of staff to Lestocq in early 1807, and later chief of the Prussian General Staff, was also originally an artilleryman, but he was not an army commander, nor the commander of his adopted nation's armed forces. Being an artilleryman, Napoleon took more than a normal interest in his army's artillery; he was a moving force behind its development. Some of his artillerist generals, such as the du Teils were his teachers, and some, such as Gassendi, were senior to him. Others, such as Marmont, "grew up under him" and were also comrades of long standing.

Napoleon was also the consummate artilleryman, and "at heart, Napoleon was a gunner . . . Probably he never was, in his inner life, far from that at any time." Proof of this was his finding Lannes' artillery the night before Jena and sending it on its way. It would be interesting to find out what he said to the artillery officers who left the column stuck in the ravine and in the lurch while they went "off looking for supper."[2]

Part of the artillery Napoleon inherited both as a commanding general and later as head of state was

> . . . full of the most ridiculous fiddle-faddle. They never consider the good of the Service . . . The junior officers in the ministry sprinkle holy water [make empty promises] and our country suffers . . . I have received only forty horse artillerymen, who have not seen combat and are without horses. Send me therefore six companies, and do not trust the execution of that measure to the officers of the [artillery section], since it takes them ten days to expedite an order, and they probably would be stupid enough to draw them from Holland, with the result that they would not arrive until October.[3]

Upon becoming First Consul, one of the first things Napoleon did was to reorganize the artillery staff and establish a large artillery staff at army level that was responsible to him and him alone.

The French had five types of troops that were considered to be artillerymen. These were the horse and foot artillery (*artillerie à cheval* and *artillerie à pied*), *pontonniers*, artificers (*ouvriers*), and armorers (*armuriers*). Along with these troops, the artillery train (*Train d'Artillerie*) was established in 1800 to haul the guns and artillery vehicles (see Chapter IV). There were eight regiments of foot artillery, which formed the greatest part of the artillery strength of the Grande Armée. Each regiment was composed of twenty companies. Napoleon organized a ninth regiment of foot artillery, and increased the companies in each regiment to 27 or 28 companies per regiment. A company of foot artillery was composed of five officers, six NCOs, one drummer, and 81 enlisted men. There were six regiments of horse artillery, each of eight companies by 1814. Each regiment was given a depot company in 1807. A horse artillery company was composed of four officers, five NCOs, two trumpeters and 65 enlisted men. Each horse artilleryman was armed with a sabre and two pistols. While most were assigned to the cavalry divisions, Napoleon also tried to assign as much horse artillery to the different corps of the Grande Armée as possible, usually one per corps. Having all personnel individually mounted gave the horse artillery an immense advantage over the foot artillery in mobility, and they could be used in more fluid situations or react to emergencies much more quickly.

Gun crews by regulation were to be partly made up of assigned infantrymen, although there is no evidence that this was a permanent arrangement. It happened in an emergency, as at Essling and Wagram in 1809, artillery losses being so heavy that the Old Guard infantry was asked for volunteers to man the guns. Coignet mentions that, at Wagram, everybody volunteered to get into action. Gun crews numbered fifteen for the 12-pounder, thirteen for the 8-pounder, eight for the 4-pounder, and thirteen for the 6-inch howitzer. The crew for the new 5.5-inch howitzer remained the same when it was introduced with the new AN XI guns, and the 6-pounder had a crew of thirteen, the same as for the 8-pounder it replaced.

Pontonneers (*pontonniers*) belonged to the artillery and not to the engineers during this period. They were commanded by artillerymen, such as Eble, and not only were able to "throw" a pontoon bridge across a water obstacle, but also were capable of building trestle bridges. They

Scale drawing of the French 6-inch howitzer and carriage of the Gribeauval System, produced for Tousard's The American Artillerist's Companion. *While the United States Army adopted the Gribeauval System in 1809, it was an incomplete adoption in that the Gribeauval gun tubes may or may not have been used in quantity, although the gun carriages, side arms, and ancillary vehicles undoubtedly were.*

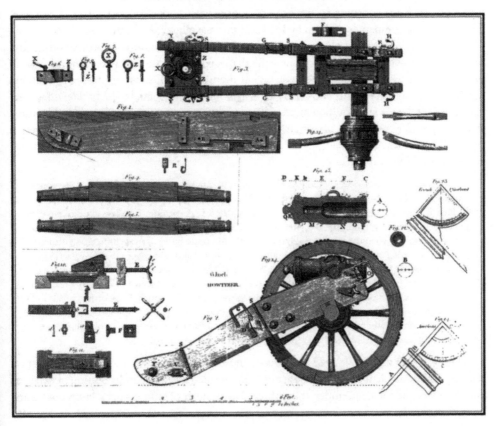

were initially formed and organized at Strasbourg in 1792, and were originally an undisciplined group of Rhine River boat and bargemen. A second battalion of pontonneers was organized on the Rhine during 1796–97 and a third in Italy in 1800. The 2nd and 3rd Battalions were amalgamated in 1801. From then until the end of the Empire, there were between six and fourteen companies of pontonneers, not including the Imperial Guard.

One company of pontonneers was assigned to each *corps d'armée*, to the Cavalry Reserve, to the army *Grand Parc*, and to the Guard (which eventually had its own). A pontonneer company could "throw" (construct or emplace) a bridge of between 60 and 80 pontoons over a waterway in about seven hours, the length of this bridge being from 350 to 500 feet. Pontoons were carried on long two-wheeled wagons called *hacquets*, which were fitted to the usual artillery limber in the front to make it a four-wheeled wagon. Other wagons carried the ancillary equipment, such as planks, anchors, etc., needed to finish a bridge.

The pontonneers' finest hour was undoubtedly at the Berezina in 1812, when their herculean efforts built two trestle bridges under extreme conditions, allowing the Grande Armée to escape from Russia. The pontonneers suffered ninety percent casualties in that gallant performance. Equally as impressive was the massive effort for the second Danube crossing in 1809, where they built a 179-yard-long pontoon bridge and swung it out from under cover and had it in place in five minutes for the troops to rush across.

The *ouvriers d'artillery* were the artificers—skilled workmen who built and repaired the artillery's vehicles and gun carriages. They were assigned to the arsenals and the parks, though some of them got into action. In 1801 there were fifteen companies of them, and in 1810 eighteen. The *armuriers d'artillerie*, or armorers, were the personnel who worked on and repaired weapons. There were five companies of them by 1810 and they usually served in the arsenals and parks.

The Grande Armée had no permanently organized units of mountain artillery, though it was certainly used when required. Foot artillery was trained to be able to employ any type of gun, and these were the companies assigned as mountain artillery when needed. Mountain artillery comprised light guns and carriages, usually specially designed to be broken down into mule loads. All guns and equipment, as well as ammunition, were carried by mules. Captured Austrian pieces were used as mountain artillery, mounted on specially designed carriages, as well as Piedmontese 3-pounders. Some tools, such as a folding handspike, were also designed for use with mountain guns:

> These light three pounders were mounted on two kinds of carriages; those taken from the Piedmontese had wheel carriages; the French made use of them, but constructed none of this first kind: the other were of French construction, and had chevrette carriages. The wheel carriage, however, appears the most preferable, because the piece stands higher, its service is more easy, and is not so liable to overset as the chevrette carriage, when the piece is fired; the weight is the same, but is of more difficult construction. Both can be carried on mules, each weighing about one hundred and twenty pounds. The wheel carriage has an iron pointing plate, which is fixed with a hinge at the head of the carriage, and, by means of a bolt which traverses both the flasks at the other end, can be placed at three degrees of elevation. This, with a very short pointing screw, gives the facility of leveling the piece either much above or much below the horizon, which in mountains is very important. The button of the piece is hollowed; the end of the pointing vice is forkated [sic] in two branches, each of which have a hole to receive a bolt, which, passing also through the button, prevents the jerking of the piece when it is fired.[4]

There was also a portable field forge that could be packed on mules in boxes for transport with the mountain artillery. The number of mules needed for a 3-pounder section of two guns was eighteen, and for a 4-pounder, thirty-three. The number of gunners per section was six and sixteen, respectively.

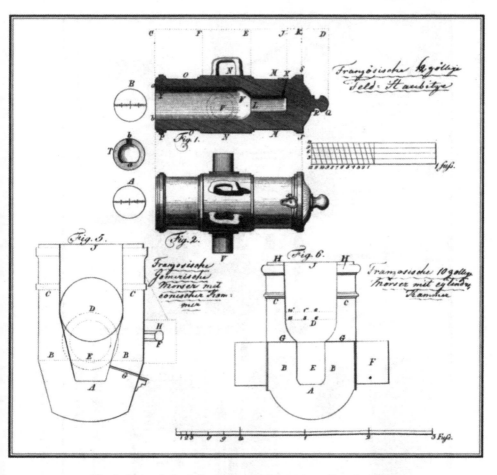

The Gribeauval 6-inch howitzer, and (bottom) two French mortars.

DuTeil, in his treatise, stated that, based on experience in fighting in Corsica,

> In extreme situations, where the ordinary carriages are not practical, one will instead supply the guns with sleds, which will fulfill the dual capacity for moving on the bad roads, such as are seen when traveling in the Alps, and also facilitate the emplacement of the cannon, for the fire from these sleds will be executed better than that done from the regular carriages.[5]

Also, it had to be understood that, in mountain warfare,

> It is, therefore, just as necessary in mountain warfare, as in that of the plain, that the artillery be well-conditioned, such as we have adopted. One can rest assured that no obstacles will be able to hinder the rapid operations of the entire army, as was the case formerly . . . Whatever the objective of the army's conduct in the mountains, one cannot doubt that the artillery is an indispensable necessity. Can this war not be considered similar to a battle for a strong position, for who are better in the attack or the defense of positions, for reducing obstacles, and for the forcing of passages, than the artillery?[6]

Mountain artillery was used successfully in Italy, in the Tyrol, and in Spain. For the Marengo campaign, artillery needed to be taken over the Alps. Regular field artillery was taken, and the carriages to get the guns over the mountains and through the snow proved to be unsatisfactory.

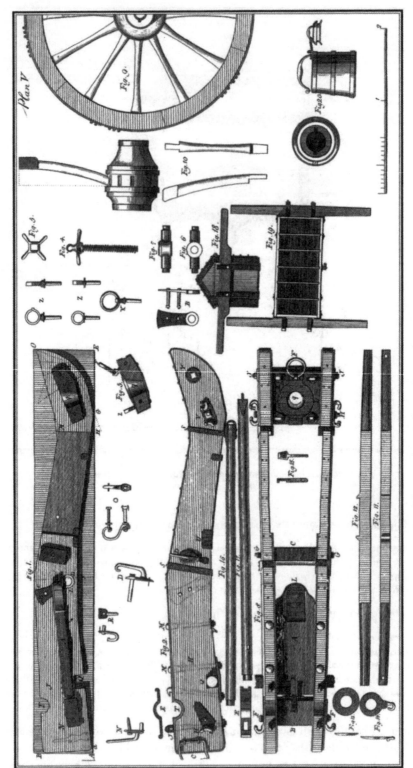

Schematic for a Gribeauval 4-pounder gun carriage.

What the French artillerymen did, therefore, was to hollow out tree trunks for the gun tubes and drag them over the mountains.

French artillery employment and doctrine were based on infantry/artillery cooperation. This was taught in the excellent French artillery schools and was emphasized by the du Teil brothers and Gribeauval. Napoleon would also remark on how the French were to employ their artillery, and it peppers his correspondence:

A system of regular war requires a large quantity of artillery. Everywhere a regiment goes you need artillery. You must have as much artillery as your enemy, based upon four guns per 1,000 infantry and cavalry. The better the infantry, the greater the need to be careful of it and support it with good batteries. The greatest part of the artillery should be with the infantry and cavalry divisions, the smallest portion in reserve. Each gun should have 300 rounds, not counting the small chest. That is the normal expenditure for two battles.

It is necessary to be familiar with artillery . . . I believe that every officer ought to serve in the artillery, which is the arm that can produce most of the good generals . . . To be a good general you must know mathematics; it serves to direct your thinking in a thousand circumstances.

The artillery staff must serve with greater activity on the battlefield. It is up to the artillery commander and staff officers to place the guns in position and to withdraw them, to anticipate the expenditure of ammunition, to correct poor sites that the company officers select, and finally to have artillery perform the duty that it has always done with such distinction.

It is the duty of artillery general to understand all for the operations of the army, insofar as he is forced to provide the different divisions with arms and ammunition. His contacts with the individual battery commander in each division enable him to know everything that is going on.

As for the artillery, I think that the first inspector will have given the necessary instructions so that the duty for that is followed with the greatest activity. My intention is that in each regiment of mounted artillery notice will be taken of those gunners sighting the piece who hit the most targets, that you take similar note of the men working with mortars and howitzers who have lobbed the most shells into the circle, and those who will have fired the most shells.

From September 2nd to the 7th, each of these regiments will send its ten best gunners to La Fère, where they will be trained in large artillery drills consisting of firing siege guns, field artillery on their carriages, howitzer and mortar batteries, hot shot, and every other kind of fire, in order to determine which of these eight regiments will supply the best man who aims a gun.

—Napoleon to Berthier, 25 March 1803[7]

French artillery doctrine can be neatly summed up in this passage from Tousard:

In defensive positions, place the large calibers in situations from which you can discover the enemy at a great distance, and from which the most extensive parts of its front are to be seen.

In attack, place these large calibers in the weakest part of your order of battle, consequently the most distant from the enemy; on the same side with the with the false attacks; on such heights which can, in securing them from insult, afford you the means of seconding the flanks of the real attack, and, if possible, batter de revers, the points which are attacked . . .

You should know the effect which you are to produce; the troops which you have to support; the points of attack, and take your positions so as not to impede your troops, nor occupy such where infantry could be more usefully employed than artillery. Avoid bringing your cannon too near and exposing them too much. Avail yourself of the disposition of the ground to cover your front, and especially your flanks; and, unless you are sure of a decisive effect, never trust your cannon from the protection of the troops.

Your crossfires should embrace the whole of the enemy's position, and the ground he must march over to attack you. Let your fire be concentrated, that is to say, offer to the enemy only scattered subdivisions to fire at, whereas from your several positions you may batter the same object.

These same objects, in the defensive, are the Debouches, or openings of the enemy; the heads of such of its columns which threaten you; the ground in front of your weakest parts.

In the offensive; the whole front of the enemy's army on which you should fire, in order to check and perplex him; and the parts which you intend to attack and destroy.

Force the enemy to make use of direct fire, before their crossfires might annoy your attacking troops; and, when forced to cease firing on the points which your troops attack, batter such of the enemy's as are collateral to them.

Fire on an extent which covers the amplitude with the divergency of your shots.

Make your shot range the greatest dimension of a troop. Consequently, batter a line obliquely, or en echarpe, and a column with direct fire, but never trust your pieces from the protection of your troops.

Place your cannon so as to be beaten neither en echarpe, in flank, nor in the rear, unless you can shelter yourself, or have the certainty of producing the expected effect before you can be entirely disabled, and put hors de combat.

Before adopting a situation, consider the nature of the site, to avoid the miry, stony, and broken ground.

Secure to yourself easy means of advancing or retreating.

Choose positions not too much elevated. The maximum which is the most advantageous, is thirty or forty yards on six hundred, and sixteen on two hundred.

Avoid taking your situation behind your troops; your fire makes them uneasy, and presents two objects instead of one to the enemy's fire.

Give at least thirty-six yards for each piece of your battery, unless the enemy may batter you en echarpe, under a very favorable angle; for they fire on a front, and not at a single piece.

Prefer positions from which you may batter the enemy for a longer time.

Never fire gun against gun, unless the enemy is under shelter, and his cannon exposed; moreover, unless your troops, being more annoyed by their fire than their troops are with yours, should be rendered incapable of performing their maneuvers.

Embrace with your fire the whole field of battle, or such part of it where the greatest number of their troops are collected, and do not fire on a contracted point.

Accelerate your firing so much the more as you may do it with more justness.

Make use of the grapeshot at shorter distances than such as are prescribed by the tables, if the field of battle is unequal, soft, covered, plunging, or plunged.

Spare your ammunition for a critical moment. Infantry, at quick time, march two hundred yards in three minutes; cavalry, at gallop, in half a minute.

Never abandon your cannon but when the enemy enters the battery. The last discharges are the most destructive: they may perhaps be the means of your preservation, but for certain those of your glory.

While the tumult of the Revolution did not affect the artillery officer corps as much as it had in the infantry and cavalry, 81 percent of the artillery officers on the Army List in 1789 emigrated. This left a burden on the remaining officers, such as Napoleon, and the NCOs, which was eventually filled to some extent. Newly commissioned officers also filled the void: Marmont, for example, expertly served and smoothly emplaced guns to support Desaix and Kellermann at Marengo in 1800, smashing the Austrian pursuit and helping turn defeat into victory.

Tactics employed by the artillery units in the Wars of the Revolution reflected what had been taught in the schools before the wars. Although not always successful, and many times outnumbered in guns and equipment by the Austrians, the French artillerymen learned their trade and supported their infantry brethren on the battlefields of the Republic. The horse artillerymen brought a new variable into the artillery/infantry equation, and Séruzier remarked that "they were renowned for their courage, and no less for their contentious spirit. They pushed esprit de corps far beyond the point of virtue and believed themselves infinitely superior to their comrades in the foot artillery." Horse artillery were assigned to the cavalry as, according to Kilmaine, "it is the only way to make up for our scarcity of cavalry." They fought alongside the clouds of light troops that screened attacks, closely supported attacking infantry in line or column, and in the advance guard of the army. They furnished the needed artillery fire with the support that sometimes kept a faltering attack moving. At the Battle of Wattignies in October 1793, a French concentration of five artillery companies, three horse and two foot, totaling thirty guns, paved the way for the decisive infantry assault: the three horse artillery companies accompanied the French infantry, while the two foot companies conducted counterbattery fire against the opposing Austrian artillery. The doctrine taught and written about before the wars was starting to bear fruit.

When the French phased out the divisions of all arms by 1800, artillery was still assigned to infantry and cavalry divisions. Artillery was initially employed to support the skirmishers in attacks, as well as being formed in multiple company batteries along the front of the army to support the infantry's main and secondary attacks. One of the problems in the Revolutionary campaigns was that the French were many times outnumbered in artillery by the excellent Austrian artillery, and were many times outshot, as at Neerwinden in 1793.

Napoleon's coming to power in 1799 gradually changed all that. The artillery arm was enlarged, and more guns were manufactured and issued to the gun companies. The Grande Armée of 1805, the best Napoleon ever led, was short of horse transport (which is an indication that Napoleon's actual intention was to invade England), and the artillery was short of horses when it moved east to face the Austrian invasion of Bavaria. Not all the guns and ancillary equipment could be taken until the horse shortage could be solved. Davout had to leave some of his guns and artillery equipment at Mannheim during the French offensive, to be retrieved later.

After the Austerlitz campaign and subsequent peace treaty, Napoleon reorganized his artillery in a more logical manner. New guns of the Système AN XI, of which the 6-pounder, a new 12-pounder, and a 5.5-inch howitzer were being produced, and now were issued as soon as they were manufactured. What Napoleon wanted to do was issue every infantry division in the Grande Armée with two artillery companies. He also wanted one of them to be a horse artillery company if there were enough to go around. One horse artillery company would be assigned to every light cavalry division, and the heavy cavalry divisions would get two each, and all divisional artillery companies would be equipped with 6-pounders and 5.5-inch howitzers. An army artillery reserve would be formed, where most of the 12-pounders would be held. Additionally, corps artillery reserve companies would be held by the corps commanders. The 4- and 8-pounder Gribeauval guns would either be placed in the arsenals for storage as they were replaced by the new ordnance, or assigned to armies in secondary theaters, such as Italy and Spain.

In December 1814, General Ruty conducted a study that favored the older 8-pounder Gribeauval gun tube over the newer and widely employed 6-pounder of the Système AN XI. His main points were that the older piece was better and more accurate, that there had been no field testing comparing the two pieces, and that the weight saved by using the lighter piece failed to give it a decisive advantage over the older 8-pounder. See Table 9.

Ruty also found that the companies of each gun type were almost identical in size, and that the number of horses needed to haul both guns and their ancillary equipment was also nearly identical. He also came to the conclusion that

> The 8 caliber has, in all respects, an undeniable advantage over the 6-caliber. The use of the former, in preference to the latter, could not be put in doubt if we disregarded all economic considerations in the use of the resources. If, on the other hand, we proposed to coordinate with these last considerations, rather than with the first ones, the determination of the field calibers, the advocates of the old system would appose [sic] to the 6 caliber, the 4 caliber which, for the economy of the resources, obtains more advantages in relation to the 8 caliber. Yet, if the question was considered from only one of these points of view, it would be discussed in an incomplete and wrong way. In order to grasp the real point of view of the question, we must determine, in a more precise manner, the various purposes the cannon can serve in field warfare and then, examine if, for a definite sum of resources, the combination of the 8 and 4 calibers serves better these purposes than the intermediate 6 caliber.

Finally, Ruty stated that

If the reasoning itself did not suffice to establish the advantages of the 8 caliber or the 6 caliber in the formation of the batteries . . . it would rely on the memories of the past to convey its undeniable advantages . . . Twenty years of brilliant success had sanctified it. Nobody can feel more inclined than an artillery officer to grant the personnel a share of merit it has to claim in these successes; yet it is for the same officer to judge to what extent the nature of the weapon has played a part in obtaining these successes. It seems impossible to deny that the material and positive superiority of a caliber more significant than the usually weaker caliber, had a lot to do with the superiority of our horse artillery batteries generally accepted at the time of the war currently being discussed. This opinion was so widespread that the gunners brought themselves reluctantly to renounce a weapon that so many reasons of pride and trust made it precious to them. They seized with eagerness the opportunity to take it back, wherever the 8 caliber was still accepted in the composition of field companies, in competition with the 6 caliber, which has been introduced in our armies only successively.[8]

The addition of the new 6-pounder into the French artillery simplified many issues, such as ammunition resupply and the number of calibers used by the field armies. However, the Système AN XI was not fully implemented, only the 6-pounder and 5.5-inch howitzer being issued in large numbers. Furthermore, as has been noted, the new carriage for the 6-pounder was unsuitable and fell apart after hard campaigning, so the 6-pounder had to be remounted on the older Gribeauval carriages taken from the armories.

On campaign, French artillery was organized by company, the companies being assigned to a separate corps under a corps artillery chief who was usually a general officer. Companies of the same regiment did not necessarily serve together, or even in the same corps, though sometimes it was specified that they should. There was no battalion-level organization in the artillery regiments.

Corps artillery was organized with a corps reserve, and with every infantry division receiving one company of foot artillery. Those companies were also issued with four extra caissons to carry ammunition resupply for the infantry. There were also companies assigned to the army artillery reserve, that mission generally being taken over after 1809 by the larger Guard artillery. A typical artillery order of battle for a corps in the Grande Armée is represented by that of Davout's III Corps at the Battle of Auerstadt on 14 October 1806 (Table 10).[9]

The total authorized strength of the French artillery arm in 1809 at the height of the Empire was as described in the following extract:

The French imperial corps of artillery, at this time, is composed of eight regiments of foot artillery, and six regiments of horse artillery. The full complement of the first is two thousand five hundred and eighty-two men, including the officers, and the total of the foot artillery is twenty thousand six hundred and fifty-six men. The full complement of a regiment of horse artillery is five hundred and twenty-four men, and the total is three thousand two hundred and twenty-nine men.

TABLE 9: GRIBEAUVAL SYSTEM 4- AND 8-POUNDER GUNS COMPARED WITH SYSTÈME AN XI 6-POUNDER

Caliber	Caisson load (rounds)	Caisson weight (pounds)	Caissons/tube	Trail chest (rounds)	Total (rounds)
8	92	1,200	2	15	199
6	140	1,360	1½	21	231
4	150	1,000	1	18	168

TABLE 10: DAVOUT'S III CORPS, BATTLE OF AUERSTADT, 14 OCTOBER 1806

Corps Chief of Artillery: *Général de Brigade* Hanicque

1st Division: *Général de Division* Morand; Chief
  of Artillery: *Major* Vasseras

11th Company, 7th Regiment	Five 8-pounders, one 6-inch howitzer, and one additional gun of unknown caliber
1st Co, 5th Horse Artillery Regiment	Six 4-pounders
1st Det, 6th Det, 1st Bn, Arty Train	

2nd Division: *Général de Division* Friant; Chief
  of Artillery: *Chef de Bataillon* Villeneuve

2nd Company, 7th Regiment	Five 8-pounders and one 6-inch howitzer
2nd Company, 5th Horse Artillery Regiment (Det.)	Two 4-pounders
3rd Det, 1st Bn, Arty Train	

3rd Division: *Général de Division* Gudin; Chief
  of Artillery: *Chef d'Escadron* Pelegrin

3rd Company, 7th Regiment	Five 8-pounders and one 6-inch howitzer
2nd Company, 5th Horse Arty Regiment (Det.)	Two 4-pounders
4th Det, 5th Det, 1st Bn, Arty train	

Corps Artillery Reserve: *Colonel* Geoffrey
2nd Company, 7th Regiment
3rd Company, 7th Regiment
15th Company, 7th Regiment
2d Det., 1st Bn, Artillery Train
1st, 3rd, 5th, and 6th Dets, 3d Prov. Bn,
  Artillery Train

Fifteen companies of artificers, ninety-two men including four officers, thirteen hundred eighty. Eight battalions of the train, the great complement of which is four hundred and seventy-seven men, and the total, including the officers, thirty-eight hundred and sixteen.

When the battalions of the train are put on the war establishment, they are increased to the same number of battalions, of six companies, each of ninety-nine men, sixty of whom are conscripts.

There are also two battalions of pontonneers of six hundred and ten men; officers, soldiers and artificers, total twelve hundred and twenty men.

Fourteen companies of veteran cannoneers, fifty men each, seven hundred men, and one hundred and twenty-eight garde-côte companies of one hundred and twenty-one men each, which give a complement of fifteen thousand four hundred and eighty-eight men.

The whole of the French artillery is thus forty-six thousand four hundred and eighty-nine men, including the officers. In this number are not included the sappers and miners, which were formerly attached to the artillery, and which now form part of the corps of engineers, the total of which is five thousand four hundred and forty-five men, exclusive of four hundred and twenty-eight officers, who compose the imperial corps of engineers.[10]

Regimental guns were phased out of the French service in 1800. Napoleon partially revived them in 1809, and again for the invasion of Russia in 1812. Generally, regimental gun companies were to be of two guns each. However, when Napoleon wanted them reformed in 1810, they were supposed to have four 4-pounders, as well as two officers and 95 enlisted men per company, bit it proved difficult to procure the required ancillary equipment (caissons, field forges, limbers, horse harness, etc.). There was also a shortage of guns, some companies being issued Austrian 3-pounders and even old Piedmontese guns, which were completely unsuitable. Therefore, Napoleon ordered that the old two-gun company organization of two officers and 68 enlisted be reinstated. On campaign in Russia they proved to be more of a hindrance than a help. According to General Merle, a very competent division commander in Oudinot's II Corps in 1812,

> That artillery has poor drivers and poor horses. It daily blocks the roads, impedes the march of the regular artillery, and deprives the ranks of seventy to eighty bayonets which would do the enemy much more damage than these poorly served cannons which cannot march.

Napoleon saw it differently:

> Every day convinces me of the great damage that has been done to our armies by removing the regimental guns. I desire therefore that in the organization, each regiment will have two 3-pounders; but, during the time that we should have only guns and ammunition for 4-pounders, you will give them 4-pounders. The gunners, horses, and men of the train will be supplied by the regiments.

In this case, Merle was right and his Emperor was wrong. The regimental artillery did not serve well, and most, if not all, was lost in Russia.

The most interesting artillery unit during the period was that was used by the Dromedary Regiment in Egypt. The attached artillery company consisted of two 4-pounders, two caissons, and ten dromedaries, each of which carried two men. The total company strength was 24 all-ranks, and it was formed on 25 November 1800.[11]

Napoleon's note and instructions for Marshal Davout, in May 1811, partially in preparation for the massive buildup for Russia in 1812, are of interest here:

> I have ordered that your artillery be completed for five divisions and composed as follows:
>   — Two reserve batteries, served by the fort artillery, each comprising two long-range howitzers and six 12-pounders;
>   — Five batteries of horse artillery (one per division), each of two howitzers and four 6-pounders;
>   — Five batteries of foot artillery, each of two howitzers and six 6-pounders; and finally
>   — Two batteries of horse artillery for the cuirassiers.
>   This makes twenty-eight howitzers, twelve 12-pounders, and fifty-eight 6-pounders, a total of ninety-eight guns. Added to the sixty-four guns of the corps trains, this makes a total of 162 guns. By this means your five divisions will be organized. The number of wagons will therefore be 992. You must have only two train battalions.[12]

Napoleon's interest and emphasis on formal education, which was mandatory for both artillery and engineer officers, occupied much of his time. He not only established military and civilian formal schools, but he also supervised the curriculum, food, attire, and general activities of the students and faculties. The following order is typical of the time and correspondence, as well as inspections, spent on his military schools:

> The total length of the course of the school being fixed at two years, we must divide the course into four parts, each comprising six months of study. Students in the first class will learn:
>   1. The infantry maneuvers of the platoon and battalion.

2. The maneuvers of field and siege artillery as well as those of mortars and howitzers

3. Technical maneuvers . . . the composition of explosives

4. The principles of the attack of fortifications

5. The entire portion of the aide-memoire pertaining to firing, and finally

6. Everything necessary to the gunner and the engineer in the field.

Students will be led to the target range; they will lob bombs into the target barrel, fire blank cartridges, etc., and construct every kind of battery. They will continue their [initial] course of construction.

In the third class, students would pursue their studies in hydraulic architecture, civil and military. They would busy themselves with the most complicated part of construction and learn everything necessary to direct and superintend the construction of a fort. They would take cognizance of the details of foundries, mines, etc.

The fourth class would be dedicated to perfecting the students in the different subjects that they have been studying. They would go over all the details of arsenals, mines, galleries, etc.—in brief, everything that would complete their instruction as engineers and gunners would belong to the curriculum of this class . . .

In general, in the establishment of a school for engineers and artillery, one should consider the knowledge of the maneuvers of all the guns and the tactics of infantry as the principal object. When a student is admitted to the School of the Battalion, he would be forced to perform the manual of arms and the maneuvers of the battalion at least three times every ten days.

It is important for the maneuvers of artillery to keep in mind that nothing is more uncertain that the art of firing. This portion of the military art is classified among the physio-mathematical sciences, yet its results are dubious; those of practice are certain. Students having completed one course in mechanics know nearly everything that they must understand and apply.

It is appropriate therefore to strive above everything else, and not as one of the foremost foundations of the instruction, to see that each student executes the manual of arms and all of the maneuvers of artillery better than a veteran soldier, that he is skilled in large practice and has perfect knowledge of the employment of artillery. No one can be considered a good student if, upon graduation, he cannot go immediately to a battery or a siege. It is proper that upon joining his unit he should instruct a class of recruits in the maneuvers of artillery and infantry and in the mechanical maneuvers. How often do you not see officers unable to place a gun carriage, direct a mechanical maneuver, fashion explosives, and forced to take lessons from old sergeants?

When a student can aim a gun better than the soldier, no one will question either his right to advancement or the other advantages of his education. Old sergeants will not be jealous of these young officers when they never have to teach them anything.

—*Notes on a Plan of Regulations for the Artillery*
and Engineer School, 27 June 1801[13]

Each French artillery regiment in the old Royal Army was an artillery school. The seven artillery regiments went by names, and were not numbered until the Revolution did away with the names of all regiments of all arms, as they were a vestige of Royal prerogative. The old regiments are listed in Table 11.

The French military school system of the old Royal Army was disbanded by the Revolutionaries in 1793 (it was the same with the Royal Stud Farms, which were closed and had their horses sent to the field armies). Some enlightened ones fi-

TABLE 11: FRENCH ROYAL ARMY REGIMENTS[14]

Regiment	Numerical designation in 1793
La Fère	1st
Metz	2nd
Besançon	3rd
Grenoble	4th
Strasbourg	5th
Auxonne	6th
Toul	7th
Rennes	8th[14]

nally realized that you could not train artillery and engineer officers without some degree of formal schooling, so in 1794 the École Polytechnique (originally called the Central School of Public Works) was opened. However, not all of its graduates went into the service, many opting for civilian employment instead.

Napoleon set to work immediately to remedy the situation as First Consul. The Châlons artillery school was revived, as was the École de Mezières, though the latter was moved to Metz and was later combined with Châlons in 1802 to become the excellent École d'Application de l'Artillerie et du Génie. St Cyr evolved from a combination of the Prytanée Militaire and the military school at Fontaineblue during the period, and the top ten percent of its graduates went into the artillery by 1811.

Napoleon had been very well educated, first at the newly established military school at Brienne, and then at the prestigious École Royale Militaire, where he finished the two-year course in one year and was commissioned a *sous-lieutenant* at sixteen. He was further very well self-educated, reading all the pertinent military literature that was available (which was considerable), especially Jean du Teil's *De l'Usage de l'Artillerie Nouvelle dans la Guerre de Campagne*. He wanted his officers to be so educated, as he did by developing his public school system for the civilian population.

Finally, two anecdotes from the ubiquitous *Major* Boulart, who was a witness to Senarmont's *chevauchée* at Friedland in 1807 and was a well-trained and skilled officer who took great pride in his Guard artillerymen, are given below. Both of these incidents took place during the buildup for and invasion of Russia in 1812.

> Major Jean François Boulart, a man who in odd moments likes to play the flute, has brought one of the Guard's three artillery columns all the way from its depot at La Fère, outside Paris. In their tall, plaqueless bearskins and dark-blue, red-trimmed uniforms, he says, his gunners were "a magnificent object of general admiration. On 5 June the Emperor had come and reviewed my artillery. He wasn't a man to make compliments, but he found it handsome. He had the goodness to spend a lot of time in my company."

And:

> For quite a while my gaze followed the three Guard batteries under a well-nourished fire and covered with a hail of roundshot whose falls one could only see by the dust they were raising. I thought they were lost, or at least half so. Happily, the Russians aimed badly, or too high.

The artillery of the Imperial Guard, which grew into the Grande Armée's artillery reserve, had inconspicuous beginnings. It originated with the light artillery detachment of Napoleon's Guides; part, if not all, came back from Egypt and was incorporated into the new Consular Guard before Marengo in June 1800, where a small company served (and lost heavily). By 1802 Songis was the commander of the Guard artillery, which was composed of two artillery companies and a train company.

In 1804, when the Consular Guard became the Imperial Guard, there were only two companies of horse artillery and two artillery train companies. Two years later, the horse artillery had grown into a regiment of six companies, accompanied by six companies of the train battalion. One of the artillery companies was Italian. They were the pick of the line, and were well trained and equipped. By 1808, Napoleon had ordered *Colonel* Drouot to organize a Guard foot artillery regiment. Three companies were first organized, and served excellently at Wagram. Additionally, three companies of "conscript artillery" were formed, later becoming Young Guard artillery. When the foot artillery regiment was formed, the Guard horse artillery regiment was reduced to two squadrons of two companies each.

After the war with Austria in 1809, Drouot finished organizing his regiment of foot artillery, giving it a band and *sapeurs*, and finally issuing it with bearskins in place of the shakos the men had previously worn. By 1813, the Guard had six companies of horse artillery, and six of foot artillery, both classed as Old Guard; one company of horse artillery; and fifteen companies of foot artillery classed as Young Guard. The artillery train had become a regiment of twelve companies, and there was a company of *ouvriers* and *pontonniers*, and a Young Guard artillery train regiment was formed as an adjunct for the Young Guard artillery companies.

When the Guard artillery was being overhauled and rebuilt after heavy losses in Russia, some of the troops were drawn into it from the excellent and well-trained Artillerie de la Marine, who also served as infantry, forming four large regiments assigned to Marmont's VI Corps. They were issued dark blue overcoats like those of the Imperial Guard, and fought so stoutly at Lützen that the Allies thought them to be Guard infantry.

The Guard artillery served as the army artillery reserve from 1809 until the end of the Empire. As such, it formed the major part of Lauriston's huge 102-gun battery at Wagram in 1809, suffering such heavy losses that it had to be reinforced with Guard infantrymen. Coignet stated that when the Guard infantry was asked for volunteers, everyone wanted to go. It participated in Drouot's artillery attack at Lützen in 1813, as well as the decisive element at Hanau the same year. It also formed the artillery mass that blew out the Prussian center at Ligny in 1815, as it had the Allied center at Lützen, again paving the way for the decisive assault by the Guard infantry. The Guard artillery gave the Emperor a reserve of highly trained, well-equipped, and very motivated artillerymen who could perform any artillery mission assigned to them.

The Guard artillery held annual gunnery (shooting) contests at La Fère. Guns and equipment were always kept in the highest state of readiness, and even in the first battles of 1813, with many inexperienced gunners in the ranks, they fought excellently, generally outperforming their Allied opponents.

One interesting situation developed in the Guard artillery between the officers who had been "school trained" and long-service officers who had ended up in the artillery or had been promoted up through the ranks and had never been to a formal school. They were experienced officers, but they were now were being considered as "unqualified" because of a lack of schooling. They were long in experience, however, and the common-sense decision was finally rendered that they could keep their status and station.

The ammunition load and projectile capacity for the French pieces of the Gribeauval System were as shown in Table 12. One type of canister contained 42 large lead bullets according to Gassendi, and the other between 60 and 100, depending on the caliber of the gun. At the highest elevation, the range limits for the 12-, 8-, and 4-pounders were 1,200, 1,500, and 1,800 meters. The maximum range with roundshot for the same three calibers was 800–900meters for the 12-pounder, and 800 and 700 for the 8- and 4-pounder. Canister range was

TABLE 12: AMMUNITION LOAD AND CAPACITIES, GRIBEAUVAL SYSTEM

Caliber	Coffret (trail chest)	Caisson (roundshot)	Caisson (canister)
12	9	48	20
8	15	62	20
4	18	100	50
6-inch howitzer	4	49 (shell)	11

600, 550, and 400 meters for the 12-, 8-, and 4-pounder. The 6-inch howitzer used a fused shell that could be exploded between 700 and 1,200 meters. Its bursting radius was 20 meters. The fuse, like the primer, was a hollow reed, "about 8 cm long filled with strands of match impregnated with a compound of powder, saltpeter, sulphur, and pitch." The fuse had a burn time of between 3 and 4 seconds, the flight distance of the round being about 600–800 meters. It should be noted that the new 5.5-inch howitzer that replaced the 6-inch model was sometimes termed the 24-pounder howitzer.

One officer of the Guard artillery, *Major* Boulart, left an interesting memoir of his service in the Grande Armée. One story he related took place after the bloodbath at Essling in May 1809. He had been hotly engaged against the Austrian artillery, dueling outnumbered, and had suffered some loss. After the battle he met Napoleon, who stopped to question him about his unit's performance, the losses he had suffered, and how he was going to replace what he had lost. He informed the Emperor precisely what shape his unit was in, and that he had one gun that needed a vent replaced and would have to go to the armory for repair. Napoleon, seemingly displeased, demanded to know why this problem had not been taken care of earlier, and, not waiting for Boulart to reply, told the unhappy officer that he would inspect him the next day and that he expected him to have all of his pieces in serviceable order and present for action.

Boulart went to his superior, told him of his apparently insurmountable problem, and was given permission to procure one of the captured Austrian pieces of the same caliber for the purposes of the inspection and to keep it until his original piece was returned, repaired, from the arsenal in Vienna. Boulart did so, and when Napoleon showed up the next day at the appointed time and place, he asked Boulart if he was prepared for inspection. Boulart told him he was, how he had brought his battery up to strength, and waited the Emperor's pleasure. Napoleon smiled at him, told how pleased he was, and informed him that he did not need to be inspected. Undoubtedly, he wanted the good *Major* Boulart to have his full complement of artillery and found the correct way to motivate him, Napoleon's personal inspections being somewhat dreaded in the Grande Armée.

French artillery tactics and employment stemmed from the doctrine taught in the excellent artillery school system developed after 1763. Artillerymen were taught to cooperate closely and support infantry. That being so, and the army in 1792 being organized in permanent divisions in the field, each with its own attached artillery, the principles of combined-arms tactics between the infantry and artillery was employed, experimented with, and developed. Artillery companies were used to support both troops in formation as well as in open and skirmish order. Attacks delivered in column or line, with large bodies of skirmishers deployed in front, were also supported by artillery, sometimes as far forward as the skirmish line itself and not just on the flanks of the units. Whenever possible, artillerymen massed their fire, employing at least two batteries to gain either local fire superiority or to destroy opposing infantry.

Counterbattery fire was discouraged: it took too long and used up much of the ammunition allocation. On many occasions it was ineffective, and it took artillery away from supporting their own infantry and cavalry. The rule of thumb used by artillerymen was that if the enemy's artillery was hurting your infantry more than you were hurting theirs, then there was a need to engage the enemy's artillery. Light guns were best, as they had a higher rate of fire than the heavier 12-pounders (sustained rates of two rounds per minute versus one per minute). Battery commanders would mass their fire on one enemy gun at a time, killing or wounding the crew or disabling the gun, then move onto the next one. That was much more efficient than targeting an entire enemy battery with one French battery. If multiple batteries were to be used, they would do the same thing but on a larger scale—concentrate one battery per gun of the enemy, and so on until the enemy artillery was knocked out.

French artillerymen usually chose positions on low hills or other eminences in the terrain with good fields of fire and little or no dead ground to the front and flanks (though howitzers might emplace in dead ground which offered sufficient cover and concealment). Artillery seldom took position directly behind friendly troops, for two reasons: first, the troops did not like it, as a round could fall short and cause friendly casualties; and secondly, the reaction of those troops to their own artillery might be detrimental to the offending artillerymen's state of mind and personal safety.

Artillery was usually employed massed. Napoleon massed a considerable 30-gun battery at Lodi in 1796 to support the closed-column rush across the bridge. A 25-gun battery was employed on the Landgrafenberg at Jena in 1806 to support Lannes against the more numerous Prussian guns. In that same battle, French horse artillery was used to support French infantry in column, in line, and in open order, along with light cavalry, to defeat Grawert's division, as well as Ruchel's later in the day as it arrived on the battlefield when the rest of Honenlohe's army was falling apart.

Increasingly after 1807, massed artillery was brought forward rapidly into canister range in order to "blow away great sections of the enemy's line" and thus to seek a quick decision. This tactic was pioneered by Senarmont at Friedland in 1807, and was used to good effect at Ucles, Ocana, and Somosierra in Spain, as well as by the great 102-gun battery commanded by :Lauriston at Wagram in 1809, which not only covered a tactical corps change of front but preceded Macdonald's famous attack that shattered the Austrian line. The best example of this tactic, however, was undoubtedly Drouot's artillery attack at Lützen, in which his 80-gun battery completely blew the center out of the Allied line, paving the way for the decisive assault of the Guard. Further examples occurred at Hanau, at Ligny, and at Waterloo, as well as at Raab in 1809.

Waterloo is interesting, as the aggressive employment of French artillery did not take place. The French infantry reverted to the old tactic of large skirmisher swarms sweeping up to the enemy line, and starting to shoot it to pieces. Enough French cavalry remained intact to support this movement, forcing the Allied infantry to stay in squares—perfect targets for the French artillery, which was manhandled into 100–250 meter range to support the infantry and demolished the squares with point-blank fire. If this had been employed earlier in the day, Napoleon could very well have won the day. (As it was, the Prussians were coming in on the right flank and the numbers were overwhelming.)

On the defensive, French guns were "fought to the last extremity," gunners making combat with handspikes and rammer staffs (which could inflict serious injury if they connected with a vital part such as the skull), as the Guard artillery did at Hanau, helping fight off Allied cavalry until the Guard cavalry counterattacked. When the enemy was in columns, he was engaged head on; if in a linear formation, French commanders attempted if at all possible to get onto his flanks for enfilade fire.

The French used their guns to gain every possible advantage. While it was abhorrent for an artilleryman to lose his guns to the enemy, French artillery commanders would risk this in order to gain a decisive advantage on the battlefield. Poniatowski used his guns in his skirmish line; Foy, a horse artilleryman, had as his dictum, "Get up close and shoot fast." Interestingly, the elite British horse artillery considered their French counterparts to be more daring than they were themselves.

When necessary, howitzers were massed for special missions, as at Borodino, where they lobbed shells into the Russian field works, and at Waterloo, where they were massed against Hougoumont on the British right flank. They were also massed at Dresden against a fortified village on the French left flank. Sometimes, howitzers were emplaced in low points in the ground so that only the heads of the gun crews were visible. One Russian artillery commander was faced with this situation, but could not fire at them, as their *licornes* were unable to elevate to a sufficient degree to fire into the depression.

There were no written French artillery regulations. The Guard finally had an unofficial set of rules published in 1812, but the French artillerymen were taught their doctrine in their schools, and were constantly trained in its application. They also learned by experience, especially in the early days of the Revolutionary Wars, when they were usually outnumbered by the Allied artillery—especially the excellent Austrian artillery. What they learned they applied, and they fielded the best overall artillery arm during the wars.

French command and control was excellent. French corps artillery chiefs were, with few exceptions, general officers; one reason undoubtedly was to prevent their being intimidated by the infantry and cavalry generals or by their own corps commanders. In the chain of command, it was quite different being a senior field grade officer attempting to advise or convince a general or marshal than being a fellow general officer with an established reputation. One of the problems with common-sense artillery employment in other armies was that their artillery chiefs, except at the army level, were usually not general officers, and were not listened to because of their relatively low rank and low level of expertise.

The corps artillery chiefs also had their own staffs, and the army artillery staff backed them up. It was no disadvantage that their commander-in-chief, Napoleon, was also an artilleryman—and their Emperor to boot. For this reason, Senarmont could convince his corps commander at Friedland, Victor, to let him use the corps' entire complement of artillery for an unsupported attack on the Russian center.

Battery operations and employment were simple and straightforward. First, guides from each gun crew staked out their gun's position, which the horse team would gallop into. As the horses came to a halt, the crew would first change the gun tube from the traveling to the firing mode (if an 8- or a 12-pounder; 4- and 6-pounders did not require this added duty), and then unlimber and lay the piece. The guns were normally about 20 meters apart, but that was always dependent on the ground. The limber would usually stay close, and the *prolonge* would be attached from the trail of the piece to the limber. Caissons, one per gun, would be positioned about 50 meters to the rear, usually under cover to protect the horse teams. Ammunition *coffrets* would be taken from the trail of the piece and placed on the limbers, opened, and one round brought to the muzzle of the piece and loaded on command. The gun would be laid, aimed, and primed, and then the gun captain would await the company commander's "Fire" order.

Artillery was a hard business, requiring big, intelligent men. They not only served their guns in combat but had to clean and maintain them afterwards. Moving a gun through rough or weatherbeaten terrain could be heartbreaking. Additionally, for all their firepower and apparent strength, the guns and vehicles were rather fragile and needed constant repair and maintenance. Artillerymen, being elite troops, received "haute pay"—the "sou of the grenade."

Allied and client-state artillery grew in importance from 1807. Dutch horse artillery had an excellent reputation and served well in Spain, notably at Talavera in 1809. Strength differed from year to year, the Dutch becoming excellent at shuffling their units around in constant reorganizations, "undoubtedly to conceal their actual weakness from Napoleon."[15] Their horse artillery went from four companies in 1807 (one being assigned to the Royal Guard) to two in 1809, and the Dutch foot artillery was a four-battalion regiment that year.

The Army of the Grand Duchy of Warsaw had excellent artillery, both horse and foot, and included a company of *pontonniers*, an artillery train battalion, and a company of artificers. Its equipment was a mixture of captured Prussian and Austrian. In 1810, by the royal decree of 30 March of that year, the artillery consisted of a Foot Artillery Regiment of 16 companies, four of which were field artillery, and a Horse Artillery Regiment of four companies. The foot artillery companies each had five officers, six NCOs, six artificers, two drummers, one *enfant de troupe*, and 108 enlisted men, the horse artillery companies five officers, ten NCOs, two trumpeters, eight artificers, two *enfants de troupe*, and 144 enlisted. Field artillery companies manned a division of guns consisting of four 6-pounders and two 6-inch howitzers; horse companies served the same type and number of guns. There was only one company of foot artillery serving 12-pounders, and six with no attached howitzers. In June 1811, a supplementary artillery battalion was formed, with eight companies.

Eugène's Kingdom of Italy, of which he was Viceroy, and the army commander-in-chief, had a large artillery arm. Six companies of horse artillery and twenty-six foot artillery companies, plus a company or two of *pontonniers* and the requisite artillery train troops, made up the strength. Because of a chronic shortage of horses, oxen were sometimes used by the train units instead of horse teams. The Royal Guard, a miniature version of the French Imperial Guard and similarly organized and uniformed (except that the Italian national color of dark green replaced the French blue), had a small, expert artillery contingent. It consisted of one company of horse artillery and one company of foot artillery, and a train "detachment" to pull them.

The Danes had a small but efficient artillery arm, consisting of both foot and horse, sometimes referred to as "riding batteries". However, the two horse artillery batteries were equipped with a largely useless 3-pounder gun that was too light for effective service, and in 1813, Davout issued them more useful French and captured Allied pieces. The Danish rocket company, commanded by Captain Schumacher, had a strength of 85 all-ranks—four officers, eight NCOs, one trumpeter and 72 privates. They were on active service, engaging the Royal Navy from Langeland Island, and the company was eventually increased to 114 all-ranks, an designated the *Raket Corpset* (Rocket Corps). There is no evidence that Schumacher's Rocket Company was part of the "Auxiliary Corps" that supported Davout in northern Germany in 1813–14.

The Confederation of the Rhine, Napoleon's most important military ally, consisted of a multitude of minor German states, the most important, and generally the most enthusiastic, being Baden, Hesse-Darmstadt, Saxony, and Bavaria. All of these states possessed solid artillery arms which rendered good service during the course of the wars, their most important contribution probably being in the 1809 war against Austria.

Baden had one artillery battalion of three companies, one of them, the 1st Company, being horse artillery and the other two foot artillery, plus the requisite train troops. The 3rd Company served in Spain, giving excellent service. Its misfortune at the Battle of Talavery in 1809 got Senarmont in trouble for taking the time to write to the Grand Duke telling him of their good and loyal service. Baden's artillery contingent had always enjoyed a good professional reputation, usually contrary to the rest of the army. The Badeners were "highly prized" by the French, and thought to be on a par with the French artillery. They were well-trained, and their artillery material and guns were of excellent quality.

Bavaria had the largest contingent of any Confederation state, and its artillery regiment had four battalions of five companies each. There was an artillery train battalion, which was milita-

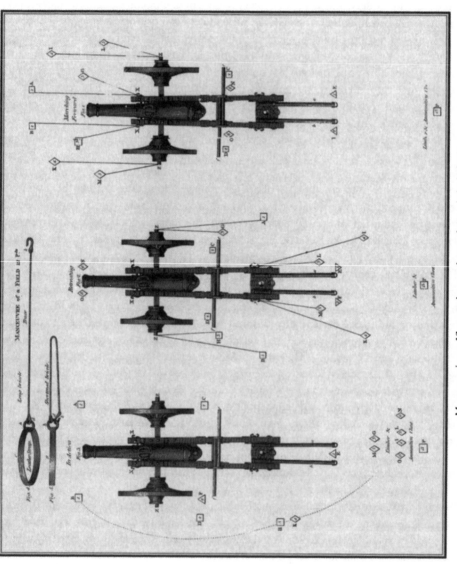

Maneuvering a 12-pounder; and two views of the bricole.

rized in 1806. The Bavarians prior to 1813 gave excellent service: they were part of Lauriston's large 102-gun battery at the Battle of Wagram in 1809 and did particularly well in Russia with St Cyr on the northern flank.

In 1809, the Bavarians had a regiment of twenty companies, thirteen of which were assigned to the field army, which became the VII Corps under French Marshal Lefebvre. The batteries were of three types—line, light, and reserve. The line and light batteries were assigned the same ordnance, four 6-pounders and two howitzers. The gunners in the line batteries walked, and those in the light batteries either rode the limbers or were mounted. The reserve batteries manned four 12-pounders and two howitzers, and they were assigned to the corps reserve artillery along with one of the light batteries. The train battalion (*Fuhrwesenbataillon*) had been militarized in 1806 and were an efficient organization, proud to now be soldiers and carrying arms and wearing the Bavarian *Raupenhelm*.

Hesse-Darmstadt fielded "excellent troops, raised from a population with a tradition of worldwide mercenary service."[16] They manned one battery of foot artillery, five 6-pounders and one 7-pounder howitzer. They also had a recently militarized train company of 108 personnel that was still short of equipment, such as harness and saddles, and some of the personnel were either poor riders, or no riders at all. Still, the artillery contingent served well. In 1812, they "marched with the Young Guard,"[17] and brought all their guns home.

The Saxon artillery school was founded in 1766 with a small staff which included a director from the artillery staff, four officer instructors, and four NCO assistants. It was relatively efficient in the period of the Seven Years' War, but little or no progress was made in the artillery arm from that time through 1809. Becoming inefficient because of a lack of training and shortages in equipment, the Saxon artillery was reorganized in 1810 into a foot artillery regiment of three brigades, with a total of 16 foot companies, and a horse artillery brigade of two companies, plus sufficient train troops to get the four brigades into the field. This was a far cry from what had been available in 1809. The Saxons fielded no horse artillery, and horses were in such short supply that battery officers also served on foot. Units trained together but once a year, and the batteries were organized only following orders for mobilization. Just four batteries were sent to the field for service with the IX Corps under Bernadotte, each made up of four 8-pounders and two 8-pounder howitzers. The artillery of 1809 was the weakest arm in the Saxon Army.

The Saxons also had a company of artillery artificers to take care of, and repair, their equipment. New guns, lighter and with a better performance than the older pieces, were also developed. A new 12-pounder, a 6-pounder, and an 8-pounder howitzer were used to great effect, though the older weapons were kept at the depot. For the 1812 campaign in Russia, the Saxons fielded four foot, six regimental artillery, and three horse artillery companies. These performed excellently along the southern flank of the Grande Armée under Reynier.

The reorganization of 1810 provided for a foot company of four officers, twelve NCOs, sixteen artificers, two drummers, and 98 enlisted men. The horse artillery brigade consisted of ten officers, eighteen NCOs, two surgeons, four trumpeters, two farriers, and 204 enlisted men.

Württemberg fielded probably the best and most efficient army in the Confederation. In 1809 the state had three companies of artillery, two horse and one foot, one of the horse companies having Guard status, for a total of 22 pieces of artillery. The horse artillery manned four 6-pounders and two 7-pounder howitzers for each company, and the foot artillery company had eight 6-pounders and two howitzers. There were eighteen caissons with the companies and a further twelve in the park.

The French looked upon the Württembergers as military equals, Ney remarking in 1812 that his Württemberg horse artillery was as good as his French companies, and probably better—high praise indeed. The Württembergers were described as a "tough, dashing arm," and they could think for themselves in a pinch. However, in 1812 their field forges could not keep up with the generally hard marches, and so the artilleryman improvised their own from "Russian farm wagons and the forges and tools of local blacksmiths;" clearly, they could make bricks without straw.

The Württemberg artillery was always "well-trained and equipped." These were the last of the Confederation contingents to leave the Grande Armée in 1813, and there was no nonsense about them—no betrayal, no underhanded maneuvering. One Württemberg cavalry brigade under Nordmann had refused to charge at Leipzig, and, as a result, their sovereign, Friedrich, cashiered Nordmann and disbanded the two cavalry regiments.[18] Friedrich called the Württembergers home during the retreat from Leipzig, as he was being threatened by the Allies. Passing Fulda, the contingent turned north, leaving the Grande Armée reluctantly, parting from the French "like good comrades."[19]

NOTES

1. Elting (ed.), *Military Uniforms in America, Vol. II: Years of Growth, 1796–1851*, pp. xi, 65.
2. *Ibid.*, pp. 264–5.
3. As quoted in Elting, *op. cit.*, p. 250.
4. Tousard, *The American Artillerist's Companion*, pp. 169–76.
5. Du Teil, *The New Use of Artillery in Field Wars: Necessary Knowledge*, p. 54.
6. *Ibid.*, p. 55.
7. There is much common-sense instruction on artillery, as well as other military matters, in *Napoleon's Correspondence*. Other useful volumes that contain much of what Napoleon wrote are Luvaas, *Napoleon on the Art of War*; J. C. Herold *The Mind of Napoleon*; John Eldred Howard, *Letters and Documents of Napoleon*; Tsouras, *The Greenhill Dictionary of Military Quotations*; and David Chandler (ed.), *Napoleon's Maxims*. Most of what is quoted here can be found in these volumes in English to help in research and as a quick reference.
8. The material on General Ruty and the Système AN XI was graciously furnished by Scott Bowden.
9. This information was furnished by Robert Burnham of the *Napoleon Series*, and is gratefully acknowledged.
10. Tousard, *op. cit.*, vol. II, p. 75.
11. This extraordinary information was furnished by Peter Schuchhardt.
12. *Napoleon's Correspondence*, XXII, No 17708, pp. 149–50, 10 May 1811, as cited in Luvaas, pp. 57–8.
13. *Ibid.*, VII No 5621, pp. 183–5, as cited in Luvaas, *op. cit.*, pp. 59–60.
14. The 8th Artillery Regiment is in some sources cited as having been formed from the colonial artillery, which is the most likely candidate.
15. Elting, *Swords Around a Throne*, p. 389.
16. *Ibid.*, p. 401.
17. *Ibid.*
18. Nordmann was also the officer who ran down Lützow's Free Corps in 1813 and destroyed it after Lützow had violated the summer armistice.
19. Information on the Confederation of the Rhine was taken from Elting's excellent *Swords Around a Throne*, and from his *Napoleonic Uniforms*, vols I–IV; from Commandant Sauzey's work on the armies of the Confederation contained in many of the older "La Sabretache" books; and from Gill's definitive work *With Eagles to Glory*, on the Confederation in 1809.

Chapter 6

Coalitions

> Then shook the hills with thunder riven,
> Then rushed the steed, to battle driven,
> And louder than the bolts of Heaven,
> Far flashed the red artillery.
> —Thomas Campbell, *Hohenlinden*, 1803

> O, you mortal engines, whose rude throats
> The immortal Jove's dread clamors
> Counterfeit . . .
> —Shakespeare, *Othello*

> It is better to have a known enemy than a forced ally.
> —Napoleon

1600, 1 February 1814, La Rothière, France

The Prussian Marshal Blücher, the Russian General Barclay de Tolly, and the Bavarian General Wrede all undoubtedly thought they had Napoleon's measure and could finish him off, though the weather was lousy and darkness was starting to close in on the desperate fighting. Their exhausted Prussians, Russians and Bavarians had finally succeeded in capturing the town of La Rothière from the equally exhausted and outnumbered French. They did not know that Napoleon was preparing to take it back. Wrede should have known better, as he had vainly attempted to stop Napoleon's exit from Germany at Hanau in November, and had seen a goodly portion of his Austro-Bavarian army thrown into the River Kinzig. He had also seen his attached Cossacks ruined by the Guard's train troops under General Radet and chased and scattered by the Gendarmerie d'Élite of the Imperial Guard. Hopefully, that would not happen here.

On the other side of the field, talking to Ney and his staff officers in front of Ney's leading division, Napoleon told the assembled officers what he wanted done to retake the village of La Rothière. Drouot, whose massed Guard artillery had played a very large part in ruining Wrede in November, was massing his Guard artillery for one last effort, and as the meeting broke up, Napoleon signaled for his escort to bring up his horse. As the exhausted Guard *Chasseurs à Cheval* brought up the horses at the walk, Napoleon mentioned that he wanted to check one more time on Drouot's guns. The lieutenant commanding the picket of Guard cavalry nodded slowly, wearily saluting his Emperor, then quickly snapped orders to his troopers, suddenly alert to his mission and the needs of his Emperor. Napoleon quickly mounted, and he and the escort galloped off to visit the gunners.

The men on the gunline stood to their guns, ready for action. They had fired fast and often today, and Drouot and their officers told them they had to give one last effort. The *sacrés* Prussians had taken La Rothière, and the Emperor wanted it back. The veterans among them checked equipment and ammunition, and the conscripts looked around them, shocked that they were still alive. They didn't notice the man on the gray horse, wearing the nondescript gray overcoat and hat, trot up behind them with his small escort. Dismounting to walk the gunline,

Napoleon said nothing to the preoccupied gunners, acknowledging the nods of the veterans, especially the ones whom he knew.

Suddenly, the Allied artillery began to bang away at the French gunline, ranging shots at first, and then more serious business. At the gun the Emperor was walking behind, one of the gunners had his head taken off by a roundshot. The conscripts in the gun crew were wide-eyed with shock, spattered with the blood and brains of their unfortunate comrade. They ignored the commands of the veteran gun captain, and the gun fell silent among its noisy comrades. Seeing this, Napoleon quickly dismounted, threw the reins to one of his escort and launched into the gun crew with a will. Applying his boot liberally to two of the shocked youngsters where it would most readily get their attention, Napoleon and the veteran gun captain, a *caporal*, got the conscripts back to their fumble-fingered duty. The youngsters who were more than shocked to see their Emperor laying about him like a man possessed, finally heard the bellowed commands of the gun captain above the thunder and mess. Two of their number had been knocked across the trail by the enraged *caporal*; two others nursed injured dignity by rubbing their behinds. The rest of the young gunners went to work with a will, serving the piece alongside their Emperor.

Seeing that the gun was once again in action, and the gun crew running more or less as they should, Napoleon turned control over to the grizzled veteran, the two men looking and smiling at each other. He tweaked the ear of the gun captain, mumbling "*C'est bon*" to him as he went back to his mount and the business of beating the Allies. As he and his escort galloped off to inspect the rest of the gunline and to observe the coming assault, the conscripts on the guilty gun crew looked sheepishly at each other and smiled, one of them getting a final kick in the rump by the disgruntled gun captain, soon to be promoted *sergeant* by a grateful Emperor.

*　　*　　*

The Prussian artillery of the period was probably, along with the engineers, the most neglected arm in the Prussian army, and arguably the worst artillery of the major warring powers. Frederick the Great, though using his artillery to advantage at times during his wars, never really understood the employment, training, or usefulness of a fully developed artillery arm, and his successors were even less able to define it than he was: "the artillery and engineers, arms that Frederick never had quite comprehended, were in bad condition, their officers poorly trained and considered something less than gentlemen."[1]

Throughout the period, Prussia had no unified artillery system. It was not until 1816 that the System of 1812 was fully implemented.[2] Prussian artillery doctrine was also somewhat archaic, and, of the higher-level artillery officers, only von Holtzendorf actually distinguished himself. The artillery chief during and after the Reform period was Prince August, who was not an artilleryman, though undoubtedly a wise choice as he was a Hohenzollern and able to exert some influence to help his adopted arm of service. During the war, though, he reverted to being an infantry commander. Napoleon's opinion of Frederick as an artilleryman is quite enlightening:

> Frederick, great man though he was, did not understand artillery. The best generals are those who come from the corps. It is believed that knowing how to place a battery is nothing, but it is all-important. Put the artillery into action behind the first line and you at once unmask 60 or 80 pieces on a target. Thus victory is decided.

Further, Frederick considered both the artillery and engineers as "grubby bourgeois arts, demanding hard and unglamorous toil, constant patience and the precise calculation of physical forces—all of which was alien to the temper of the old European military nobility;" and "he never showed himself more arbitrary, obtuse or ill-informed than when he was dealing with his gunner . . ." This attitude carried into the next regime after Frederick's death in 1786. Of all the major European powers engaged in the wars from 1792 to 1815, Prussia had the least effective artillery arm. Their first artillery school was not started until 1791, and, with one outstanding exception, Prussia produced no artillery senior officers of any note.

In 1806 the Prussians still employed battalion artillery and had no central army artillery reserve. They also had recently adopted the divisional system, though it was the division of all arms, a concept the French had stopped using in 1800. For the short Jena campaign, the Prussian Army had no central artillery direction, and no doctrine establishing procedures of artillery working with infantry on the battlefield, with the exception that artillery was attached two per infantry battalion. Not that Prussia was without skilled artillerymen. In 1759 Frederick established the first horse artillery of any European power. Finding this more than useful, the other European powers had copied the process by 1789, though the Austrian cavalry batteries were not true horse artillery by any stretch of the imagination.

In the 1740s the talented Lieutenant Colonel Ernst von Holtzman, who was assigned to the 2nd Artillery Battalion, developed a limber with a permanent ammunition chest built on it. He also was responsible for developing a new elevating system that was copied by both the Austrians and Russians. For years gun elevation had been accomplished by the use of a wooden quoin, which was a simple, wedge-shaped piece of wood that was pushed or hammered under the breech of the gun tube to elevate it. Holtzman developed that idea into a screw quoin: this maintained the principle of the basic quoin, but the actual work of elevating the gun tube was done by a screw mechanism in the quoin that made it move along a track under the gun tube, parallel to it, thereby making elevation both easier and much more accurate. Holtzman also designed a screw sight for new, light, 12-pounder guns that had been introduced into the Prussian service by Lieutenant Colonel von Dieskau.

Frederick's interference with gun tube design greatly hurt the Prussian artillery. He insisted that 6- and 12-pounders be redesigned to have chambered breeches in the manner of howitzers and mortars. This made loading more difficult and slower, and it also greatly increased the chances of a misfire. Frederick also had ignored the great advances made by the Austrians between the War of the Austrian Succession and the beginning of the Seven Years' War with their new artillery system. Where once the Prussians had a definite advantage over the Austrians, that advantage had been overcome with the advent of the Lichtenstein artillery system, which not only introduced newer, lighter artillery pieces to the Austrian Army, but also benefitted the organization and training of what was essentially a new artillery arm that was now the best in Europe.[3]

Frederick was also a proponent of artillery being employed in a counterbattery role, an opinion he finally started to change by the end of his reign. By that time Gribeauval and the excellent French artillery school system had been teaching French artillerymen to concentrate their fire on the enemy infantry, as well as emphasizing infantry/artillery coordination on the battlefield as the way to achieve decisive results. The Prussians were being left behind by a significant margin.

In 1787 Prussia had four artillery regiments, each with a strength of 53 officers, 2,320 enlisted men, ten surgeons, eleven drummers (the 3rd and 4th Regiments only had ten), and eight musicians. The horse artillery was assigned to the 1st Artillery Regiment, of which there were only three batteries, their total being sixteen officers, three surgeons, and 588 enlisted men. There were 972 gunners assigned to the infantry regiments to man the regimental light guns. Two years later there was a major reorganization of the four regiments. The first three regiments were given 33 foot artillery companies and two horse artillery companies apiece. The 4th Regiment was assigned the four Guard batteries and the light batteries that would be parceled out to the fusilier battalions, as well as the guns for the park and two mortar batteries.

There was another reorganization in 1792, each regiment being now being equipped with two battalions of five companies each, plus an independent artillery battalion and seven horse artillery batteries. Two more horse artillery batteries were added in 1797. These were amalgamated with the existing horse artillery batteries into a horse artillery battalion of five companies, each company of horse artillery consisting of five officers, one trumpeter, one surgeon, 48 enlisted train drivers, and 174 enlisted men. The horse artillery was steadily increased, so that by 1801 a horse artillery regiment was organized. In 1804 it had ten companies of horse artillery.

This was the basic field artillery organization that went into the field for the Jena campaign in 1806. The Prussians, and their reluctant Saxon allies, had plenty of artillery; in fact, they outnumbered the French in artillery in the field. The problem was that there were too many guns with the infantry battalions, and there was no central direction at the division and army level. Consequently, the Prussian artillery was outmaneuvered and outfought by the outnumbered French artillery. In the aftermath of the twin disasters at Jena and Auerstadt, most of the Prussian artillery was taken: 200 were lost at Jena, and Davout, outnumbered more than two to one and executing a double envelopment of the Prussian Army, overran and captured 115 guns. In the subsequent ruthless pursuit many more were lost. Artillery units ceased to exist, and cannon-studded fortresses surrendered without firing a shot to small units of determined Frenchmen.

With Jena and Auerstadt lost, so were the first three Prussian artillery regiments: "The 1st, 2nd, and 3rd Artillery Regiments were completely destroyed." The only Prussian units not destroyed or captured were with Blücher in Lübeck on 7 November. Murat's comment, "The combat ends for lack of combatants," was grimly accurate: the French had taken 140,000 prisoners, 250 flags, and 800 field guns. The Prussian artillery, except for the units stationed in East Prussia, was destroyed along with the army. A large portion of the surviving Prussian guns were lost at Friedland the following June.

The Prussian reformers rebuilt the Prussian artillery arm around the survivors of 1806; disgraced Prussian units of all arms were not reactivated The 4th Artillery Regiment, which had performed well in East Prussia in 1807, was redesignated the 1st Artillery Regiment. As a start in the reorganization, Prince August was appointed to head the Prussian artillery arm, as the brigade general of the Prussian artillery corps. Though he was not an artilleryman, his prestige in belonging to the ruling House of Hohenzollern gave the artillery a needed boost. Prince August also set to work with a will to reestablish the Prussian artillery and to make it into an arm that would be effective on the battlefield. He also saw to it that the Prussians had a new artillery regulation, the excellent 1812 *Règlement*.

The *Règlement* was an up-to-date, modern artillery manual that spelled out in excruciating detail what gunners, batteries, and commanders were expected to do with their artillery. Gun drill was made uniform for the entire army. The *Règlement* was well illustrated, with easy-to-follow diagrams. It did, correctly, name the battery as the tactical unit for the artillery, just as the battalion and squadron were the tactical organizations for the infantry and cavalry. It was how the commanders of the day reckoned their artillery strength. What the *Règlement* did not do was to address tactics at higher levels, such as at brigade and corps. This was a major weakness, and it hindered the performance of the Prussian artillery during the campaigns of 1813–15 at the higher tactical and operational echelons.

Prince August reorganized the survivors into three artillery brigades, named East Prussia, Brandenburg, and Silesia. The Cabinet order of 21 February 1809 decreed that the artillery be formed into brigades of the same composition. Each would consist of three horse artillery companies, eleven foot artillery companies, and one company of *Handwerker* (artisans). The different types of artillery companies were horse artillery, 6-pounder foot companies, 12-pounder foot companies, and 7-pounder howitzer companies. The 6-pounder batteries each had five officers, one surgeon, two artisans, fifteen train troops, and 136 enlisted men; a horse artillery battery had the same except 147 enlisted; and the 12-pounder foot batteries had the same except 201 enlisted. Finally the howitzer batteries had five officers, one surgeon, fourteen train troops, and 167 enlisted men.

Every battery, except for the howitzer batteries, were to have six guns and two howitzers. Both the horse artillery batteries and the 6-pounder foot batteries were equipped with six 6-pounders and two 7-pounder howitzers, while the 12-pounder batteries were issued six 12-pounders and two 10-pounder howitzers. Each 6-pounder was drawn by six horses and each 12-pounder by eight. The Prussian limbers, except those with the 12-pounders, had the ammunition box on the limber and not on the trail of the gun, so personnel could ride on the limber. This was an advantage over the French foot artillery who could not, as their limbers did not have ammunition boxes. Each Prussian battery probably had a field forge attached to it, but there was not as much ammunition assigned to the guns as in the French service. Each battery had fewer caissons assigned than their French equivalents. For example, a Prussian horse artillery battery had only six caissons assigned, four for standard artillery ammunition and two for howitzer ammunition.

The pick of the Prussian artillerymen, "formed with officers and men who had served with great distinction during the 1806 campaign," were designated as Guard units. There were two companies: one horse artillery company and one foot artillery company.[4] Those Prussian artillery units that went into Russia in 1812 with the French managed to save most of their guns and equipment. They were assigned to the northern flank under Macdonald and thus escaped the horrors of the retreat of the main army.

The Prussians mobilized against France after the Russian disaster, and the Army underwent a somewhat rapid expansion. By the time of the armistice after the French victories of Lützen and Bautzen, the Prussians had managed to assemble 34 artillery batteries for field service. In August, at the time of the Battle of Dresden, they had 45 batteries in the field—twelve horse artillery batteries, twenty-six 6-pounder batteries, six 12-pounder batteries, and one 7-pounder howitzer battery.

The Prussian Army did not serve together in the 1813 and 1814 campaigns, but it had improved immeasurably over its predecessor of 1806. It had adopted the corps organization, and a rudimentary General Staff had been organized and trained by Scharnhorst. Brigades, which were the equivalent of French divisions, made up the different corps, and each brigade and corps had its assigned artillery under a corps artillery chief, usually a senior field grade officer, a colonel or lieutenant colonel. The artillery chief at army level was usually a general, but there was no army level artillery reserve, which was a handicap. That left nothing for the army commander to use, in terms of artillery, on order to exploit an advantage, or commit at the decisive time or place. Additionally, having the brigade and corps artillery chiefs merely senior field grade officers left no one to advise the respective commanders on the best ways to employ their artillery assets. This was especially critical at the corps level, as the corps artillery chief was not equal in rank to the brigade commanders comprising the corps, and many times they were not listened to or were overruled by the senior officers of the corps. This was one of the main differences between Prussian and French artillery employment and higher-level organization.

When fighting the French, the Prussian artillery, though well-trained and generally well led at the battery level, was not as sophisticated as the French in either command and control or tactics above the brigade/division level. This was readily apparent at Ligny in 1815, when Napoleon fought one of the best battles of his career against a slightly stronger Prussian army commanded by Blücher, with Gneisenau as his Chief of Staff. The Prussian guns were badly handled, and, worse, the army artillery chief, Karl Friedrich von Holtzendorf, was seriously wounded, losing a hand, and was sent to the rear. His place was taken at army level by the senior corps artillery chief, a mere lieutenant colonel, which effectively negated any coordinated artillery direction with the senior staff and commanders as the man was too junior in rank to accomplish his mission.

The French artillery clearly dominated the field at Ligny. The Guard artillery was massed against the Prussian center at 2000, and blew a hole in the Prussian lines, paving the way for an attack by the Imperial Guard and Gérard's IV Corps which split the Prussian Army in two and won the battle for the French.

The Prussian artillery was under a handicap during the entire period of the Revolutionary and Napoleonic Wars. Very few of its senior officers after 1806 understood the new nature of artillery employment as defined by the French. The most distinguished Prussian senior artilleryman was probably Karl Friedrich von Holtzendorf. Assigned as Bülow's artillery chief and commander of the corps reserve artillery in 1813, he distinguished himself at the Battle of Gross-Beeren on 23 August 1813, facing Reynier's VII Corps, part of Oudinot's French army ranged against Bernadotte in front of Berlin. Von Holtzendorf, seeing an opportunity to inflict serious hurt on the Saxon artillery, moved his reserve artillery forward, after a singular confrontation with the Russian artillery commander attached to his reserve artillery. After the two had spent "a few awkward seconds" in a futile staring contest (the Russian artillery officer, who outranked von Holtzendorf, but was subordinate to him by billet, hesitated to follow von Holtzendorf's orders), von Holtzendorf led his two Prussian batteries forward into action anyway. The Prussians galloped into position, unlimbered, and opened fire without the support of the Russians. For whatever reason, the Russian, a Colonel Dietrichs, finally ordered his two batteries forward, giving the Allies numerical parity with the Saxons.

There were 46 Allied guns against 44 Saxon pieces when sixteen more Allied guns showed up and opened fire. Even though a Prussian horse artillery battery was knocked out in the now uneven fight, von Holtzendorf kept feeding guns into his now large battery until he had 82 guns, which finally overpowered Reynier's artillery. This was the decisive action of the battle, as now, without artillery support and outnumbered as well, Reynier's troops could not hold and were forced to retreat.[5]

This significant little action demonstrated that, even though they emerged victorious, the Prussians had weaknesses in their system. The senior Prussian artillery officer did not possess the requisite rank to obtain instant obedience from his subordinates. Colonel Dietrich's hesitation to commit his artillery on von Holtzendorf's orders could have had a decisive and detrimental effect on the battle. Additionally, the Prussian and Russian habit of engaging in counterbattery fire first before concentrating on the enemy infantry was an expensive and time-consuming evolution that, had Reynier's artillery been more numerous, could have spelled defeat for the Allies.

Prussian artillery doctrine was out of date and still retained some of the older, obsolete ideas of Frederick the Great. Infantry/artillery cooperation was still in its infancy in the Prussian service, and, though that would change after the wars, it was still a handicap during the Napoleonic period.

The Austrian Army—more properly the Kaiserlich und Königliche Armee—possessed one of the best artillery arms in Europe in 1792. It had once been Europe's preeminent artillery arm, but it had not kept pace with new developments and had not improved its material or doctrine since the Seven Years' War, with the exception of adding cavalry batteries in the 1780s, which introduced a new, modified 6-pounder gun and 7-pounder howitzer carriage, together with methods of moving and employing this mobile artillery. The Austrian artillery was well-equipped and its personnel very well trained and skilled. The reforms of Prince Lichtenstein in the 1740s and 1750s had raised the arm to be the best in Europe by 1763, though it did begin to stagnate afterwards, losing its preeminence to the French by 1789 with the full implementation of the newer and more efficient Gribeauval System.

In 1792 the Austrians had three artillery regiments, but these were administrative units, and not tactical formations. The Austrian Army had no artillery tactical formations in peacetime. Later, a fourth regiment was added. In 1807 the four artillery regiments were given territorial designations: the 1st Regiment was entitled the Bohemian Regiment, the 2nd the Lower Austrian Regiment, the 3rd the Moravian Regiment, and the 4th, activated later than the other three, the Inner Austrian Regiment. The Artillery Fusiliers had been deactivated in 1772, but in 1790 they were reactivated, again to be disbanded in 1802. The Handlanger-Corps was reactivated in June 1808, cadred by artillerymen and filled out with infantrymen. They would again assist gun crews in nonspecialist jobs on the gunline.

As in other armies, the battery was the basic tactical unit of the artillery. The men of the artillery regiments, upon mobilization, were assigned to man the battalion guns assigned to the infantry regiments. Two other artillery formations, the Bombardeur Corps and the Regiment of Artillery Fusiliers, were employed to man the heavier guns that were in the army artillery reserve. Augmented by odds and ends from fortress artillery units, this, with one exception, was the artillery organization for combat in the Austrian Army. That exception was the Kavallerie Batterien, which was formed in the 1780s and issued a light 6-pounder gun and a 7-pounder howitzer, both with elongated trails (that must have made them somewhat awkward to use in action) and with a pad on the trails for the gunners to ride on when displacing or travelling. However, this was not true horse artillery, merely more mobile artillery field artillery. None of the cannoneers was individually mounted, most riding on the padded gun trails and the remainder initially riding on padded caissons (wurst wagons), though later changing to riding the guns only, the ammunition being carried by led packhorses as specified in the 1808 Regulations.[6] The rest of the Austrian artillery arm was foot artillery. They had no organic horse teams and drivers, these being provided by the *Fuhrwesenkorps*, which was not militarized until 1808. Then, only a cadre remained with the batteries, though that was a great improvement over the previous arrangements.

Personnel were excellent and well trained. Many, if not most, were Bohemians, as were the officers. The battery commanders were skilled, if old for their grades, but by 1809 the Austrian artillery was performing superbly in larger batteries such as that formed by *Oberst* Smola at

Essling (Aspern to the Austrians), where they outshot and overwhelmed the French artillery and caused heavy casualties among French infantry and cavalry.

Change, however, came slowly. By 1805 there was another artillery regiment, and overall end strength had increased, although efficiency had not. Each artillery regiment now had sixteen companies, but permanent horse teams and drivers were still a thing of the future. Troops who had not worked together before were sent into combat half-ready.

Most of the light pieces were still with the infantry—something the French had abandoned long ago. Artillery was taken away from the cavalry brigades, though the majority of the infantry brigades were assigned a battery of 3-pounders. Since there were no permanent organizations at the higher operational levels, there was also no permanent artillery organization. Batteries that had not worked together before were now expected to coordinate their efforts with each other and the infantry they were assigned to. Though "competent commanders had massed their artillery for years,"[7] this standard practice, known to every army, was alien to, or had been forgotten by, the Austrian Army of 1805. A reserve artillery organization had been established, and this was given additional caissons to haul ammunition, but there were no artillery officers senior enough on the staff to get the artilleryman's point of view on employment across to the senior Austrian commanders. Having such generals as the Archdukes Ferdinand and John did not help the myriad difficulties in the Army, the artillery being part of the larger, graver problem.

After the campaign of 1805 and its attendant disasters, reform was finally started and pushed through, and the Archduke Charles, Francis's only competent sibling and the only archduke who was an able commander and troop leader, was given full reign to reorganize and improve the Hapsburg army. Even the *Hofkriegsrat* was reorganized to an extent, now having military departments, one of them being the *General-Artillerie-Direktion* directly under Charles's control. Battalion guns were finally abolished. An *Artillerie Handlanger Corps* was again created, as it had been in the days of Maria Theresa and Prince Lichtenstein, to assist the artillerymen in fleshing out gun crews in the field, replacing detailed infantrymen.

The units and strengths of the Austrian artillery were as shown in Table 13. There were four artillery regiments, of sixteen companies each. The field artillery was organized into 3-pounder infantry brigade batteries of eight pieces each. All 6-pounders went to the artillery reserve, and these, with the addition of two howitzers, were made into support batteries. There were also 6-pounders, 12-pounder, and even some 18-pounders organized into position batteries, each of which was generally assigned two howitzers.

The cavalry batteries had their own problems. The recent cavalry regulations of 1806 did contain a complete section on the use and employment of horse artillery. However, the cavalry batteries were not fully mounted, most of each guns crew still riding on the gun's trail, which prohibited the batteries from keeping up with the cavalry they were supposed to support.

TABLE 13: UNITS AND STRENGTHS OF THE AUSTRIAN ARTILLERY

Unit	No of companies	Strength, all ranks
Artillery Regiment	16	2,811
Bombardeur Corps	5	1,075
Artillerie Handlanger	8	1,179

TABLE 14: EQUIPMENT OF AUSTRIAN BATTERIES

Unit	Guns	Howitzers	Personnel
3-pdr brigade battery	8	0	64
6-pdr brigade battery	8	0	80
6-pdr support battery	4	2	66
12-pdr position battery	4	2	66
6-pdr cavalry battery	4	2	32

TABLE 15: AUSTRIAN BATTERIES: ALLOCATION PER GUN

Gun	Round shot	Canister (large)	Canister (small)	Shell	Caissons
3-pdr	90	2	12	0	8/btry
6-pdr	94	0	26	0	8-12/btry
12-pdr	123	12	40	0	3/btry
6-pdr cavalry	94	0	26	0	24 pack
7-pdr howitzer	0	12	0	72	horses/btry

TABLE 16: AUSTRIAN BATTERIES: GUN CREWS AND HORSE TEAMS

Caliber	Gun crew	Horse team
12-pdr	12	6
6-pdr	10	4
3-pdr	8	2
7-pdr howitzer	7	2

While the new packhorses probably added to overall mobility, they still had to conform to the pace of the overloaded gun teams. Additionally, the Austrians did not train the cavalry batteries to support cavalry offensively; indeed, some authorities maintain that the cavalry was intended to support the cavalry batteries. The cavalry batteries were normally used as "mobile field artillery," since all of the other Austrian artillery, whatever the designation and role, was foot artillery.[8]

Austrian batteries were equipped as shown in Table 14; the allocation per gun was as shown in Table 15; and the gun crews and horse teams assigned were as shown in Table 16.

Major Augustin's *Raketenbatterie* was completed and ready for field service by mid-1815, with 2,400 rockets as well as four companies of artificers to support it. Eighteen ammunition carts were supplied to carry the rockets into the field on campaign. *Major* Augustin never actually commanded the battery, but he was made commandant of the *Kriegs-Raketen Anstalt* (War Rocket Establishment) and did watch the rockets in action at the siege of Huningue in the summer of 1815. The rocket establishment was kept on after the wars, and grew in importance as part of the artillery. With the exception of the British, the Austrians had the most effective rocket units during the Napoleonic period.[9]

Senior artillery officers were assigned to the new Corps Headquarters to act as the corps commander's advisor on artillery. However, none of them were general officers, and most could not make their opinions felt to their seniors, which included the corps Chief of Staff. Smola was the obvious exception to that rule, as witness his performance at Essling. However, "there developed a real gap between the 'scientific' artillery specialists and field generals which tended to interfere with efficiency." The individual battery commanders, described by Charles as "often old and frail, and having been slowly advanced up the ladder,"[10] still tended to regard the individual piece as a discrete fire element, while generals often lacked feeling for the proper use of artillery. As a result, the Archduke's instructions that artillery should always act as part of a combined arms team as often were neglected. In short, the Archduke was ignored to the detriment of the Army.

Austrian artillery employment was usually conservative, sometimes to the point of their great disadvantage. Austrian artillery was generally employed in two ways. Guns and crews were "issued" to line units for direct support, and the rest were kept in reserve under army control. Most of the light pieces found their way to the infantry battalions, and any sort of concentration was lost. While sometimes battalion guns would be gathered together to form small batteries of four to six guns in the infantry regiments, that was hardly massing artillery.

There was a great improvement in the Austrians' artillery organization and employment in 1809. However, it did not match that of the French in that regard, nor in terms of its central control. The light 3-pounders were formed into batteries of eight guns for use with the infantry brigades. The 6-pounders and their attached howitzers were now classified as "support batteries," and they and the cavalry batteries were assigned to the corps as reserve artillery at that level. There were also "position batteries," formed by both 12- and 6-pounders. Sometimes, 18-pounders were used in position batteries, but these were generally too heavy to be used as field artillery.

Charles wanted the artillery to cooperate with both infantry and cavalry units, as did that of the French. Austrian corps commanders were neither familiar nor skilled enough to orchestrate what Charles wanted to put into practice. Additionally, corps artillery chiefs, such as *Oberst* Smola, were not sufficiently senior enough always to get their opinion across to their highbred corps commanders, and therefore their influence was not always as it should have been. Nevertheless, the Austrian artillerymen served efficiently and gallantly in the first half of the campaign in the operations around Ratisbon, and the French considered them a worthy adversary. The Austrian artillery had 742 field guns in 108 batteries available for service at the beginning of the campaign.

The Austrian artillery's most impressive performance came on the second day of the Battle of Aspern/Essling in May. Smola wrangled permission to assemble a huge battery of almost 200 guns after the Austrian infantry assaults failed in the center. He outgunned the outnumbered French and mercilessly pounded them for over two hours, overpowering their artillery and severely hammering their infantry, the Old Guard having to be committed in the French center to endure the bombardment after part of the "hard-used II Corps flinched."[11] Subsequent to that, heavy losses in horses and transport hampered the Austrian artillery for the rest of the campaign, and they never regained their old efficiency for the remainder of the war.

The Russians had for decades been proponents of a large artillery arm. However, until the reforms initiated by Arakcheev and the adoption of the System of 1805, the Russian artillery arm was somewhat antiquated. Sir Robert Wilson's description of 1806–07 is very enlightening:

The Russian artillery is of the most powerful description. No other army moves with so many guns, and with no other army is it in a better state of equipment, or is more gallantly served.

The piece is well formed, and the carriage solid, without being heavy. The harness and rope-tackling is of the best quality for service, and all the appurtenances of the gun complete and well arranged . . .

The artillerymen are of the best description, and the non-commissioned officers equal, but the artillery officers of inferior rank have not the same title to estimation as in the other European services, for their education is not formed with the same care, and their service does not receive the same encouragement. To them is the toil and the responsibility, but the honor is by no means assured them. Some favorite officer, completely ignorant of the science and practice of the artillery, is frequently in the day of action appointed for the day to the command of their batteries, and the credit is in the dispatches given to him for a service which depended on long previous systematic arrangements and laborious attention, with which he never was acquainted: an injustice mortifying to the corps, injurious to the individual artillery officer, and gravely detrimental to the general interests.[2]

Russian gun carriages and artillery vehicles were painted apple green, with black ironwork.

Russian armies were "artillery-heavy." There were as many guns assigned to a Russian division as to a French corps, as many to a Russian brigade as there were to a French division. Their fire could be effective and deadly—witness the destruction of Augereau's corps in the snow at Eylau in early 1807. The Russians classified their field artillery as light, horse, and position. Foot artillery battalions had two heavy and two light companies.

A heavy artillery company consisted of fourteen guns, made up of four light 12-pounders, four heavy 12-pounders, four 18-pounder licornes, and two 2-pounder licornes.; a light artillery company consisted of twelve guns, comprising four light 6-pounders, four medium 6-pounders, and four 10-pounder licornes; and horse artillery companies generally consisted each of six light 6-pounders and six 10-pounder licornes.

In 1806-07 there was one heavy company assigned to each brigade and two heavy companies to each division. The 2-pounder licornes were attached as battalion artillery, two per battalion, and the remainder were massed in their own batteries. The light companies were assigned one per brigade and division, but the guns were assigned two per battalion, so the light artillery companies were broken up and not under their own commanders.

After the implementation of the System of 1805, Russian artillery continued to improve. Markevich's diopter sight was employed to improve gunnery, but was found to be inferior to French sighting systems, the main drawback being that it could not take into account the changes in sighting when guns were emplaced on uneven ground. The Russian gunner's quadrant was also inferior to that in other countries' equipment, as it had to be used by inserting it into the muzzle of the piece. Markevich did invent a new gunner's quadrant which could be used on a flat piece of metal attached to the side of the gun tube; similarly, Lieutenant Colonel Kabanov developed a new sight that was attached to the gun tube and "was hung on a pin inserted into a special bracket screwed on the top of the breech." The sight was weighted so that no matter the angle of the gun, it was always in a vertical position, ready for use. There were two advantages to Kabanov's sight—it's use was not hampered by a strong wind, and it had to be taken off the gun for each shot. Invented in 1809 and adopted by 1811, it was still not issued to all batteries by 1812.[13]

Russian artillery officers were somewhat hesitant in their overall employment of artillery. Losing a gun in any army was seen as a disgrace. However, the French were very willing to risk that if it gave them a significant advantage on the battlefield, as witness Senarmont's artillery assault at Friedland in 1807. The Russians, however, were very hard on battery commanders who lost a gun, some of them being executed for that offense and disgrace. This served to squash initiative on the part of junior officers, and also encouraged them to limber up and displace if they believed their guns to be endangered, whether or not this left the units they were supporting in trouble.

There was also a predilection for engaging in counterbattery fire, whatever the occasion. Counterbattery fire could be time-consuming and heavy on ammunition usage, and both the British and French refrained from it unless it was absolutely necessary. Moreover, units engaging in counterbattery fire also did not fire at the enemy maneuver elements, especially infantry, which could be dangerous, as they were the component that took and held ground.

Beginning in 1807-08, the Russians began to change their artillery doctrine. No longer would counterbattery fire be the priority. Enemy formations, especially the infantry, would now be the prime targets on the battlefield. Horse artillery would be held in reserve, used to reinforce or to exploit a success. Long-range fire was, it was felt, inaccurate and wasted ammunition: infantry commanders who wanted artillery batteries to engage in long-range artillery duels were officially discouraged. Artillery emplacement was to be carefully considered. Batteries were to be emplaced on high ground, with hard ground to the front to heighten the effect of ricochet fire. Positions that provided advantages to enemy skirmishers were to be avoided, as skirmishers were particularly dangerous to artillery. Firing at skirmishers with artillery was likened to "chasing a swarm of bees with a club."[14]

Massing of fires, cooperation between multiple batteries, and obtaining favorable positions for an artillery crossfire were advantages and tactics that were stressed by the Russian artillery officers. General Sievers published the situations when counterbattery fire could and should be employed:

1. When an enemy battery prevented friendly infantry or cavalry from occupying a desired position;
2. When an enemy battery prevented passage through a defile;
3. When one intended to attack an enemy battery, then artillery had to fire on the enemy battery to divert its attention from the attacking friendly troops; and
4. When making a breach in an enemy fortification.
    In all other cases, artillery was to fire at enemy lines and columns, trying to enfilade them or to fire obliquely.

Artillery was seen as a support weapon for the infantry and cavalry. There was no doctrine developed to use artillery as an offensive arm; that particular development remained a French innovation and tactic. The Russians had used artillery brigades in 1806-07 in the field, each division having an attached artillery brigade. When the fighting was over and the army went back to its peacetime cantonments, the artillery reverted to its assigned battalions and regiments. Before the campaign of 1812 opened, however, this changed. The artillery brigade with its attendant guns, caissons, ancillary vehicles, drivers and gunners became a permanent unit. They all were uniformly organized with one heavy and two light artillery companies, and the brigade commander was normally the commander of the heavy artillery company.

Regimental light pieces attached to the infantry battalions became the subject for debate after Tilist. Major General Gogel listed the arguments for and against regimental artillery.

For:
1. Infantry regiments competed in keeping their artillery pieces in good condition.
2. They took care of them as well, as they did their colors.
3. They fought more bravely when supported by their artillery.

Against:
1. Terrain favorable to infantry is not always favorable to artillery.
2. Artillery pieces placed along the front of infantry could hinder the movement of the troops.
3. Infantry regiments were not able to train artillerists to the same degree of skill as artillery brigades.

4. Regimental commanders considered their pieces good if the paint on the carriages was in good condition.
5. The men were picked for their height rather than their skill in working the pieces.
6. Rapid fire was seen as better than accuracy.
7. The attachment of a regiment to its artillery pieces seemed to be not very strong, while the contempt for the pieces of other regiments was well known.
8. Infantry officers ordered the regimental artillery to fire at too great a range and withdrew it before it would become effective because they were afraid they might lose the guns.

The argument floated back and forth, much like it did when Napoleon opted to reintroduce regimental artillery into the French infantry regiments in 1809. The Russians finally did away with it after the 1812 campaign, and after Kutusov died in early 1813, Russian regimental artillery disappeared.

The Russian artillery steadily grew and improved from 1808-12. In March 1812, "there were five companies of Guard Artillery, 49 companies of heavy artillery, 54 companies of light artillery, 22 horse artillery companies, two pioneer regiments and 24 pontoon companies."[15]

The artillery of the Russian Guard consisted in December 1803 of one battalion of five batteries—two light 6-pounder batteries, two 12-pounder batteries, and one horse artillery battery. In March 1805, the horse artillery battery became the Life Guard Horse Artillery; in October 1811, the battalion became the Guard Artillery Brigade.

When emplacing their batteries, the Russians usually put the licornes on the batteries' flanks. Thus, in both light and heavy batteries, there would be two licornes as flank pieces, two on each flank. The center pieces would be four medium 12-pounders on the left side and four light 12-pounders on the right . In the light artillery battery, the licornes would be emplaced as flank pieces in the same manner as in the heavy battery, the center of the battery being the eight 6-pounders.

Battery commanders usually fired by piece, that is, one gun at a time, usually starting with a flank piece. They also fired in salvo, or by volley.

In action, only one caisson per gun was kept with the battery. The other assigned caissons were either kept under cover or were shuttling ammunition forward from the parks and reserve. There was a problem with battery commanders leaving their positions stating that they had run out of ammunition. Barclay de Tolly finally fixed this problem in 1813 in his General Instruction on the Order of Troops on the March, in Camps, and in Battle, stating that battery commanders were forbidden to abandon their assigned positions unless they were specifically ordered to do so. If they ran out of ammunition and had not been relieved, they were to hold their position until either ordered to displace to the rear or were resupplied.

The greatest problem facing the Russian artillery throughout the period—and one which the Prussian and Austrian artillery also suffered, the Prussians more so than the Austrians—was in command and control on the battlefield. Division and corps artillery chiefs were usually not general officers. They were, in general, junior to the commander they supported, and at times could not force their advice across to the infantryman in charge. At both Barclay's and Kutaisov's urging, an army artillery reserve was formed in 1812, which was a great improvement over earlier artillery organization. However, Kutaisov was killed in action leading an infantry counterattack during the intense fighting around the Russian field fortifications, leaving the reserve artillery without an effective commander. Its employment was not effective, much of it stayed in the Russian rear in permanent reserve, with the gunners sitting on their thumbs while the expertly served French artillery dominated the field.

British field artillery, both horse and foot, was an expert arm, with a proud tradition of service around the world. Small and well trained at Woolwich (commonly referred to by artillerymen as "The Shop"), the artillery arm was organized in battalions of foot artillery and squadrons of horse artillery, that arm being somewhat new to the service, having been organized as recently as 1793. The horse artillery arm was never large. In 1801 seven troops had been formed and trained; and by 1806 there were only twelve on the rolls. The Royal Artillery itself, or the Royal Regiment of Artillery if you prefer, was organized administratively in battalions of ten companies each. There were eight battalions in 1803, nine in 1806 and ten in 1808.

In the field, the foot artillery was organized for tactical employment in brigades, which were of battery strength, that term not yet being used by the British artillery for company-sized artillery units. Horse artillery batteries were known as "troops." A subunit of the brigade or troop of two guns was known as a "division", and that of a single gun a "subdivision."

Lastly, the Royal Artillery was answerable to the Master General of the Ordnance, not to the Army Headquarters at Horse Guards. Something of the army, and then something quite not, its officers, well trained and highly skilled, were promoted by seniority and did not purchase their commissions.

A typical British artillery company in 1799 had five officers, eight NCOs, three drummers, and 105 other ranks. By 1808 and the beginning of the Peninsular War, the artillery company had been increased to five officers, eight NCOs, three drummers and 125 other ranks. Sometimes, but never officially, the foot artillery arm was referred to as the Royal Foot Artillery. It is so in the Dickson Manuscripts. A horse artillery troop was made up of five officers, eight NCOs, one trumpeter, and 146 enlisted men, which included the assigned drivers, and seven artisans:

> The armament of a field brigade of Royal Artillery, such as Captain Maxwell's, was most often 9-pounders—five of them plus one 5.5-inch howitzer. A troop of RHA at the beginning of the Peninsular War might be equipped with either two 9-pounders or two heavy 6-pounders, together with three light 6-pounders and one heavy 5.5-inch howitzer; it would have some six ammunition wagons and four other carriages. Before Waterloo, however, in order to match the weight of the French artillery, many troops of the RHA were reequipped with 9-pounders. The guns were fitted into the newly developed General Congreve block trailer, which allowed them to be maneuvered more easily and, consequently, laid with greater accuracy than was formerly possible.
>
> The effective point blank range of a 9-pounder with a 3-lb charge was 300 yards. A two degree elevation of the gun extended the range to 1,000 yards; a further degree to 1,400 yards. The accuracy was something like plus or minus 10%. Surprisingly rapid rates of fire could be achieved by means of the efficient gun drill of the day—as high as one round at ten second intervals if so desired, for instance when firing at advancing infantry at point blank range.
>
> Three types of ammunition were in use: solid round shot, canister shot (each canister carrying forty-one 5-ounce bullets), and spherical case shot containing a large number of bullets together with a bursting fuse. The amount of each type carried in the field was generally based on the proportion 70% roundshot, to 11.5% canister shot and 18.5% spherical case.[16]

The excellent King's German Legion (KGL), recruited from the disbanded Hanoverian Army, also provided artillery companies to the British Army—two horse companies and three foot companies. Well-trained and motivated, they made up some of the artillery shortages in the Peninsula. Of the five British artillery companies with the field army in 1809, two were from the KGL. Initially, the word of command was in German and the Hanoverian drill regulations were followed. However, by 1808 British drill regulations had been adopted and the word of command changed to English, especially if the KGL were working in conjunction with regular British units. It should be noted that though the KGL was a "German" unit generally in the makeup of its personnel, it was a part of the British Army and therefore a British unit. It should also be noted that although the overwhelming majority of its personnel initially were

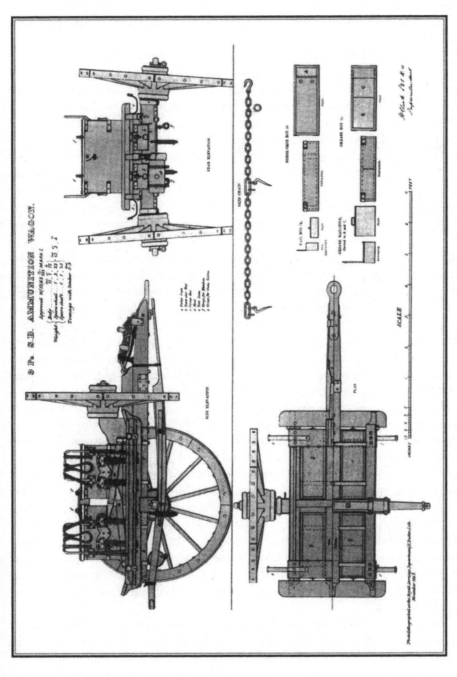

The British "limbered ammunition wagon," or caisson, of the period—an outstanding example of a more modern design, later copied by the French in the Valée System of 1827 (as were the gun carriages).

Hanoverians, the Legion was also allowed to enlist other Germans, Poles, Hungarians, Danes, and Russians, though no French, Italians, or Spaniards were taken. They were never allowed to enlist British subjects. A typical KGL artillery company was composed of six officers and 219 other ranks. They used British artillery equipment and were uniformed and equipped as the Royal Artillery.

The guns used by the British were generally the 6-pounder, 9-pounder, and 5.5-inch howitzer. There was an excellent 12-pounder, but it was little used in the field, as it was considered too heavy. Brigades and troops usually were assigned six pieces, normally five guns and one howitzer. Howitzer batteries were not unknown, however. Sometimes all gun batteries without the usual one howitzer per battery were also used. All of these were excellent weapons, and had been developed by Thomas Blomefield, the Inspector General of Artillery in the 1790s.

The British had two advantages over the artillery of any other nation, both of them innovative and a harbinger of things to come. First, Congreve had developed the block trail for guns (but not for howitzers, which continued to use the split, or bracket, trailed gun carriage). The trail was a single piece of carved wood instead of two "cheeks" that were connected by transoms. This made the gun carriage much sturdier and completely did away with the Austrian and French practice of having two sets of trunnion plates for the gun tube (traveling and firing), resulting in a much better balanced gun as the tube was now placed further forward than it had been in the past. It made for a shorter piece, with a much smaller turning radius of gun and limber. In all, the concept was one of the greatest improvements in overall gun design since the standardization of parts by both the Lichtenstein and Gribeauval artillery systems. When the French finally phased out the Gribeauval System in 1827, their new gun carriages were block-trail types based on, and influenced by, the British gun carriages of the Congreve pattern. The standard British limber was also much better designed than Continental patterns, and allowed for the gunners to ride on the attached ammunition box, which was especially helpful for foot artillery (Prussian and Russian limbers also had that capability, however). The Congreve gun carriage also had two ready ammunition boxes placed on the axle on either side of the gun, negating the need for a *coffret* and fulfilling the same function.

The use on land of Congreve rockets was not only interesting, but innovative. Two units used them, the Royal Marine Artillery and the Royal Horse Artillery Rocket Troops. The Royal Marine Artillery was generally used in North America during the War of 1812 and served at Bladensburg, Hampton, Virginia, Ocracoke Inlet, LaColle Mill, Quebec, Oswego, and Lundy's Lane. Another RHA troop served at New Orleans. American troops, especially the militia, were initially frightened by the horrific noise of the rockets, which were quite unlike conventional artillery, but they later learned largely to ignore it as the fire was inaccurate and tended to boomerang on its crews; experienced troops learned to live with it. However, the American militia at Bladensburg in 1814 were stampeded by rocket fire: "A few rockets, passing close over the heads of the American militia battalions . . . started them running, and they bolted off and could not be stopped."[17]

The Royal Horse Artillery organized their rocket batteries into troops just as they did for their gun companies. Such a troop had five officers, fifteen NCOs, 90 gunners, 60 drivers, eight artificers, three heavy rocket cars, three light rocket cars, six ammunition tumbrils, one field force, 42 *bouches à feu* (rocket launchers), and 164 horses for officers, vehicles, and troopers, and rocket ammunition.

The troop was organized into three divisions, each of two subdivisions. Each of the latter consisted of five sections of three men, each with two drivers. Each section was equipped with

Right: General of Division Baron Joseph Corda, Ney's artillery commander at Friedland in 1807, commanded the artillery that helped to silence the Russian batteries on the other (east) bank of the River Alle during the battle which had earlier ruined Ney's first attack on the Russian left flank.

Below: General of Division Antoine Drouot, an exceptional artillery commander—so deeply intelligent, indeed, that he was known as the "Sage of the Grande Armée." He organized the Regiment of Foot Artillery of the Guard and led it in action at Wagram in 1809. He read his Bible every day.

Right: Joseph Freiherr von Smola, the brilliant artilleryman who organized and commanded the huge Austrian battery (almost 200 guns) at Essling in May 1809. His exploits at Neerwinden in 1793 with his reinforced cavalry battery helped to stop the main French attack. Unfortunately for the Austrians, his boldness and élan were the exception, not the rule, in the Austrian service.

Left: General of Division Comte de Lariboisière, an expert organizer who commanded the artillery of the Grande Armée in Russia. He, along with Eble, died at the end of the retreat. His son, a carabinier officer, was killed in action at Borodino in September 1812.

Right: General of Division Jacques Alexander Bernard Law Lauriston, one of Napoleon's généraux aides-de-camp, and the artillery expert among this select body of general officers. He organized and led into action the large artillery battery (102 guns) at Wagram, of which Drouot's regiment was part.

Left: Marshal Auguste Frédéric Louis Viesse Marmont, Napoleon's oldest friend and a skilled artilleryman. He commanded the artillery that supported Desaix's counterattack at Marengo and defeated the victorious Austrians. A competent corps and army commander, he later betrayed Napoleon in 1814, the latter finally saying of him, "The ingrate—he will be much unhappier than I."

Above: The French artillery foundry at Douai in 1770. This was also the location of the first French artillery school. All of the major functions of casting artillery gun tubes are pictured here, and an artillery gin for lifting gun tubes by the dolphins is shown at the lower left.

Below: Napoleon pointing an artillery piece at the Battle of Montereau in 1814. Napoleon also liberally applied his boot to the appropriate piece of anatomy of some reluctant young gunners to motivate them when appropriate during this last, bitter campaign.

Above: Three methods of transporting artillery—by horse team and limber (top), debarking from water transport (centre), and by 'man team' up an incline (bottom).

Above: A simple but accurate depiction of a Gribeauval artillery piece and a gunner, sketched by a Belgian artilleryman in a letter to his father. The sidearms are laid neatly at the side of the piece on the ground, and the gunner is using a portfire to discharge the piece. Note the depiction of the round leaving the tube.

Left: French troops, led and commanded by the famous Rampon, "swearing on their field piece" to defend the Montebello redoubt.

Left, upper: Detail from the famous painting of Napoleon's "whiff of grapeshot" against the Paris mob. This is an outstanding depiction of the gun crew of Gribeauval field pieces from the rear, "pointing" (aiming) the piece, as well as preparing to fire.

Left, lower: Artillery at the famous storming of the Bridge of Arcola in 1796.

Above: Loading French gun tubes in hollowed-out tree trunks for the crossing of the Alps by Napoleon's Army of the Reserve in 1800. The specially designed carriages intended for the crossing did not work, and this field expedient method did.

Below: An Austrian artillery gun crew of 1800.

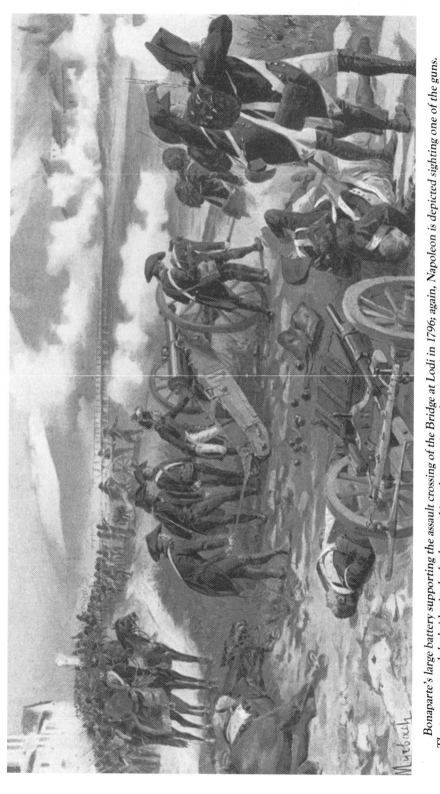

Bonaparte's large battery supporting the assault crossing of the Bridge at Lodi in 1796; again, Napoleon is depicted sighting one of the guns. The troops crossed the bridge in the background in column against infantry and artillery fire. When the attack stalled, infantry jumped from the bridge onto sandbars in the river, to give the rush close fire support, supplementing the artillery fire from the bank. The head of an assault column was a dangerous place to earn a living.

Moving a piece by the gun crew (or detachment, as used in the British service) from the front by drag ropes. The handspike in the trail is being used by one of the gunners to keep the piece aligned.

Moving a piece from the front by horse team in harness. This type of movement was depicted in the manuals. Gribeauval's invention of the bricole and prolonge changed this manner of movement, since they were much more efficient.

The round being rammed. Note the other end of the rammer, which is the sponge.

Drouot's large battery of Guard artillery being charged by Allied cavalry at Hanau in late 1813, after Leipzig as the French were retreating from Germany. The French artillerymen decimated the Allied horsemen as they attacked the battery, and the remnant did get in amongst the gunners, who defended their guns with musket, bayonet, rammer, and handspike. The Grenadiers à Cheval counterattacked and routed what was left of the Allied horse.

Division squares in Egypt, 1798. Artillery was emplaced at the corners of the squares. Horse artillery are in the foreground, foot artillery in the background. Division squares, with baggage in the center, would again be used—in Russia in 1812.

Above: French artillery in Russia in 1812. Note the caisson and spare horse at left center. The gun depicted in the center of the picture might belong to a horse artillery battery.

Below: Napoleon at Friedland, June 1807: a good view of a French artillery piece and its "wheelers" from the rear.

French artillerymen and grenadiers pulling the guns over the Alps, May 1800.

Left: A Russian artillery officer in field uniform, 1812.

Below: A depiction of the Austrian 6-pounder cavalry gun. The elongated trail was equipped with a seat for most of the gun crew.

one rocket launcher, so that a subdivision had five on the line at any one time, the troop being able to field thirty rocket launchers in action at full strength. Each division could also be equipped with two rocket cars, one of them light and the other heavy, that the division could also employ as launchers.

Rocket troops were employed at the Battle of Leipzig in 1813, where the troop commander, Captain John Bogue, was killed in action. The rockets were usefully employed and their fire routed a French infantry brigade. Lieutenant Fox Strangways, Bogue's second-in-command at Leipzig, was personally decorated on the field by the Tsar, who had witnessed the effective fire put down by the rocket troop. Another rocket troop, commanded by Captain E. C. Whinyates, was in Belgium in 1815 and was present at both Quatre Bras and Waterloo. One had also been sent to the Peninsula to reinforce Wellington's artillery there. Wellington reportedly was "eager to have them," but he wanted the troop's horses for his conventional artillery and did not care for the rockets, or their performance. He believed that rockets were good for setting fire to built-up areas, and that did not interest him. He ordered the troop, when it arrived, to turn in their rockets and ancillary equipment for guns. He was informed that his action would "break the troops commander's heart." Wellington, being Wellington, snapped back, "Damn his heart; let my order be obeyed."[18]

Artillery employment was usually by battery, across the front of the army as it was emplaced, horse artillery being held in reserve to be used as needed. While large massed batteries on the French model were not used, the British artillery of the period, especially in the Peninsula and at Waterloo, did excellent service and was highly regarded by their French opponents, as it would be by the Americans in the War of 1812. The only real problem for the British artillery (aside from their rowdy corps of drivers) was that there was not much of it:

> Only a short note is required as to Wellington's use of artillery. In his early years of command he was almost as weak in this arm as in cavalry. There was not one British battery per division available in 1809. But the Portuguese artillery being numerous, and ere long very efficient, was largely used to supplement the British after 1810. Yet even when it had become proportioned to the number of his whole army, the Duke did not use it in the style of Bonaparte. He never worked with enormous masses of guns maneuvering in [the] front line, and supporting an attack, such as the Emperor used. Only at Bussaco, Vittoria, and Waterloo do we find anything like a concentration of many batteries to play an important part in the line of battle. Usually the Duke preferred to work with small units—individual batteries—placed in well-chosen spots, and often kept concealed till the critical moment. They were dotted along the front of the position rather than massed, and in most cases must be regarded as valuable support for the infantry that was to win the battle, rather than as an arm intended to work for its independent aims and to take a special part in the war. Of several of Napoleon's victories we may say that they were artillerymen's battles; nothing of the kind can be predicated of any of Wellington's triumphs, though the guns were always well placed, and most usefully employed, as witness Bussaco, Fuentes d'Oñoro, and Waterloo.[19]

British artillery deployment to the Peninsula in 1808–09 was almost nonexistent. At the end of 1809 there were only five British artillery batteries with the field army, and two of those were from the King's German Legion. Two horse artillery batteries had landed and were in-country, but were not with the field army. (For a complete list of the British artillery batteries in the Peninsula by year, see the Appendices).

By 1812, more artillery had been dispatched from Great Britain, and Wellington was able to attach one or two artillery brigades to every division in the army. The one exception was the Light Division, which wanted to keep Major Hew Ross's troop, which had given such valuable service in the past. Wellington was also able to assemble a small army artillery reserve under his own control. His artillery strength increased over the next two years, though he never was able

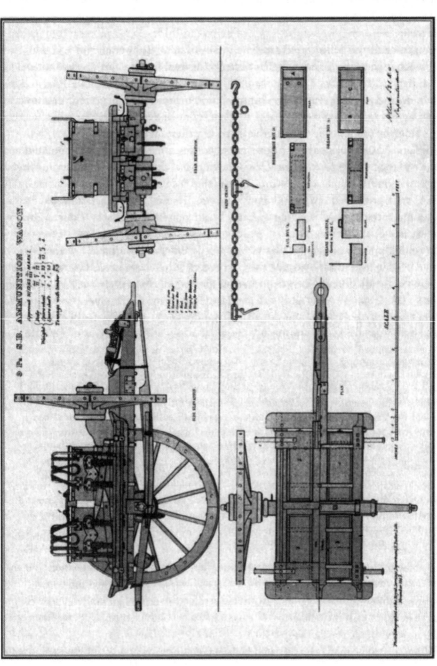

British horse harness of the Napoleonic period and after. The two horses pictured made up the "wheel" pair–that closest to the gun and limber. The left, or "near," horse was ridden, the right, or "off," horse was not, the driver controlling both horses. The other two horses in a six-horse team were the lead and swing pairs. When there were only four horses in a gun team, only the lead and wheelers were present.

to assemble the mass of artillery that was available to Napoleon. Perhaps that is the difference in employment of artillery between an infantryman and a gunner.

To make up this critical shortage, the British trained and fielded an excellent Portuguese artillery arm that more than made up for the shortage. Originally made up only of garrison artillery, the Portuguese unit took readily to the conversion to field artillery and went to work with a will. Composed of four artillery regiments—1st (Lisbon), 2nd (Lagos), 3rd (Estemoz), and 4th (Porto)—the four regiments had been disbanded by the French upon their occupation of Portugal in 1808. However, they were re-raised and reorganized late in 1808, and went through a period of much confusion as they tried to get their hands on any type of artillery equipment and uniforms that were available. They were short of everything from personnel to field guns, but order eventually came out of chaos with the intervention of the British, who supplied arms, equipment, and ammunition, along with an expert cadre to organize and train the Portuguese for field service.

The staff and two of the three artillery brigades in Alexander Dickson's artillery division in June 1809 at Abrantes, Portugal, comprised the following. The staff consisted of an adjutant, a surgeon, an assistant surgeon, and a park sergeant and a park corporal; the 1st Brigade had three officers, fifteen NCOs (including one farrier), two drummers, 84 gunners, and 39 drivers; and the 2nd Brigade consisted of four officers, ten NCOs (including one farrier), two drummers, 83 gunners, and 38 drivers. In an order—more along the line of an SOP (Standard Operating Procedure)—from Captain May to his Portuguese artillery division dated 5 June 1809, it was stated that

> It is absolutely necessary that every soldier accustoms himself to cleanliness, which is good for his health, and to uniformity in dress, which ought to imbue him with feelings of pride, and place him upon a level above ordinary folk.
>
> While on active service much cannot be expected, but in quarters the following points are indispensable, and must be attended to.
>
> 1. Cloaks will not be worn except in bad weather, or at night. NCOs and men who disobey this order will be punished by being stripped of their shirts, and will have to walk up and down in front of their quarters for the rest of the day.
> 2. To ensure uniformity, no clothing is allowed to be worn (unless permission is granted) except the regulation uniform sent from Lisbon. NCOs and men contravening this order will have to wear their coats turned inside out, in front of their quarters during the day.
> 3. If NCOs and men do not shave, they will be shaved in view of everybody on parade.
> 4. Men who turn out with clothes, buttons, or boots not properly cleaned, will be punished by having to wear their coats inside out. For a second offense they will be marched up and down in front of their quarters for the rest of the day with a piece of paper on their back on which the particulars of the punishment are written.
>
> As people are in the habit of being smartly dressed on holidays and fete days, soldiers should consider every day as a holiday—in the matter of dress.
>
> The Commandant looks for hearty cooperation from the NCOs and men, and activity from the officers.
>
> There will be a Parade every morning at 11 o'clock until further orders to see that the points above mentioned are duly attended to.

The British General Beresford was seconded to the Portuguese service, being named Marshal of the Portuguese Army, and was responsible for its complete overhaul, reorganization and training to become a first-rate fighting force. Its artillery was sent forward to the field army by battery as it became available for field service. The Portuguese artillery was considered as good as its British counterpart, and it filled the very large void in the artillery strength of Wellington's forces. Most of the ordnance was supplied by the British. The Portuguese also had a battalion of train personnel from October 1812. There were four companies in the battalion, and these troops not only were horse-team drivers, but also could function as artillerymen, manning the guns when needed:

> The rule of the combination of British and Portuguese units which prevailed in the infantry, though not in the cavalry, was to be found in the artillery also. In 1810, when Wellington drafted a Portuguese brigade of foot into each of his divisions, he also attached to several of them batteries of Portuguese artillery. So small was his allowance of British gunners, that in 1811, when he had created his two last infantry divisions, he would not have been able to provide one field battery for each of his eight units, unless he had drawn largely for help on his allies. At the time of Fuentes de Oñoro and Albuera there were in the field only three British horse artillery batteries (attached to the cavalry and the Light Division) and five British field batteries attached to infantry divisions. The 3rd and 7th Divisions had only Portuguese guns allotted to them. But by utilizing the very efficient artillery of the allied nation, to the extent of eight units, Wellington was able to put thirteen field batteries in line, which enabled him to provide the 2nd, 3rd, 5th, 6th, and Hamilton's Portuguese divisions with two batteries apiece, [and] the 1st, 4th, and 7th with one each. The two nations were worked as successfully in unison in the artillery as in the infantry organization.[20]

Lastly, regarding British command and control of their artillery it must be stated that, while the senior artillerymen with Wellington's army in the Peninsula were only senior field-grade officers, the artillery functioned excellently in the field. Sir Alexander Dickson worked his way up through the Portuguese artillery to become Wellington's artillery chief, and he had an excellent working relationship with Sir Augustus Frazer, the senior horse artillery officer. Both fitted well into Wellington's unique command system, and the artillery worked well with the other arms in combat. As a command and control team it was a success, and probably the best of all in this category amongst the Allied armies as a whole.

The regular Spanish Army was repeatedly defeated by the different French armies in the Peninsula. Their artillery was based on the French Gribeauval System, which made it easy for the French to integrate the equipment with its own when captured. By 1812 the Spanish regular artillery had five foot regiments, first four and then six horse artillery squadrons, and five companies of artificers. Until 1813, Spanish train units were civilians, which once again repeatedly proved to be unsatisfactory, especially when they were shot at. In April 1813 five, and later six, train companies were formed for service with the field armies. They did not attain the level of skill of the Portuguese, or of the British artillery units.

In summary, the British and Austrian artillery arms were undoubtedly the best of the main Allied opponents to Napoleon, the British probably getting the nod as the most efficient regarding training, skill, motivation, and dash. Their equipment, especially gun carriages and limbers, was undoubtedly superior to any other, including that of the French. The Austrians had excellent guns and equipment, but, with the exception of Smola, failed to produce the aggressive, imaginative officers required to make their artillery the arm it could have been. They were well trained and competent, but uninspired, and their command and control at division level and higher left much to be desired. Additionally, their lack of a true horse artillery hamstrung operations and left their cavalry unsupported in the field; in fact, the cavalry had to support the rather slow-moving *Kavalerie Artillerie* to prevent it from getting overrun in action by cavalry and the much more mobile and aggressive French horse artillery.

Russia came into the wars with an artillery force that was outdated in terms of both equipment and doctrine. The Russians caught up in equipment and organization by 1808, but their command and control, despite the efforts of Barclay de Tolly and Kutaisov, were still a major problem to be overcome. Russian artillery officers' professional education was lacking, and there was no formal schooling process during the period. While the Russian artillery arm was large and had impressive successes, such as at Eylau, it was technically and tactically inferior to the French, British, and Austrian, which undoubtedly hurt Russian arms. They undoubtedly had an excellent artillery train, probably as good as the French, and undeniably superior to the British and Austrian equivalent.

The Prussians possessed the least effective artillery arm amongst the major belligerents; it was, in fact, "frequently neglected." Lagging behind initially because of Frederick the Great's interference and a lack of trust in the "*savant*" arms, the Prussians possessed no unified artillery system until 1816. Their artillery was overwhelmed and largely destroyed in 1806. It was painfully rebuilt in the years 1808–13, but produced only one senior artilleryman of note, von Holtzendorf. Higher-level command and control at division and corps were inefficient, and they used no artillery reserve at army level. Individual batteries performed well, though they were short of everything from uniforms to horse harness, much of which was supplied by the British. In fact, without generous British subsidies in 1813 and 1814, the Prussians could never have kept a large army in the field.

NOTES

1. Elting, *Swords Around a Throne*, p. 516.
2. Information provided by Steven Smith.
3. Information on the Prussians was taken from Duffy, *The Army of Frederick the Great*; Nafziger, *The Prussian Army of the Napoleonic Wars (1792–1815). Volume III: Cavalry, Artillery, Technical Troops, and Train*; Pietsch, *Formations und Uniformierungsgeschichte des Preussischen Heeres 1808 bis 1914. Band II*; and Jany, *Die Preussische Armee von 1763 bis 1807*, vols III and IV.
4. For organizational information on the Prussian artillery in both 1806 and 1813, see Nafziger, vol. III; and Jany, vol. III, pp. 501–5, and vol. IV, pp. 29, 93–4. There is also an excellent organization chart contained in Pietsch.
5. Leggiere, *Napoleon and Berlin*, pp. 168–9.
6. Tousard, *The American Artillerist's Companion*, vol. II, p. 39.
7. Esposito and Elting, Map 82.
8. See both Rothenberg, *Napoleon's Great Adversary*, and Anton Dolleczek, *Geschichte der Österreichischen Artillerie*. Josef Smola, *Handbuch für Offizieren*, is full of Austrian technical data. The 1808 Regulation has an interesting diagram outlining the cavalry batteries' particular organization, clearly showing the use of ammunition packhorses. The information for the four Austrian data tables in this chapter was extracted from Günther Rothenberg's *Napoleon's Great Adversary: Archduke Charles and the Austrian Army, 1792–1815*, pp. 148 and 150., and originated in Major Semek's "Die Artillerie im Jahre 1809," Mitteilung des k.u.k. Kriegsarchivs, 3rd Ser., III (1904), pp. 74 and 84. The total strength for the four Austrian artillery regiments was 11,276, organized in 64 artillery companies, as that listed in the tables illustrates only one regiment, not the aggregate strength of all four.
9. Winter, pap. 86–7.
10. Rothenberg, p. 150.
11. Esposito and Elting, *A Military History adn Atlas of the Napoleonic Wars*, Map 102.
12. Wilson, *The Campaigns in Poland in 1806 and 1807*, pp. 20–1.
13. Zhmodikov and Zhmodikov, *Tactics of the Russian Army in the Napoleonic Wars*, vol. 2, p. 57. The two volumes of this work constitute the best reference in English for Russian artillery organization and

tactics. They have been used heavily here as a source. The Russian artillery arm was founded in 1700, somwhat later than those of other powers, but as early as 1713, during the Great Northern War, it reputedly had 13,000 guns of all calibers (see Chandler, *The Art of Warfare in the Age of Marlborough*, p. 148). Apparently, fear—both of their sovereign Peter the Great and of the Swedes—was a great motivator for the Russians.

14. This comment was made by an observant artillery officer during the American Civil War. See Bruce Catton's excellent *Glory Road*, the second book of his trilogy on the Union Army of the Potomac.

15. Zhmodikov and Zhmodikov, *op. cit.*, p. 65.

16. Webber, *With the Guns in the Peninsula*, pp. 37–8.

17. Elting (ed.), *Military Uniforms in America*, vol. II, p. 4.

18. See Graves, *The Rockets' Red Glare*, as well as Winter, *The First Golden Age of Rocketry*. Both are quite thorough in their treatment of Congreve and his rocket system. Additionally, Congreve's own *Details of the Rocket System* is invaluable.

19. Charles W. Oman, *Wellington's Army*, p. 113.

20. *Ibid.*, pp. 176–7.

PART II

Cannonade

*Blessed be those happy ages that were strangers to the dreadful fury of these
devilish instruments of artillery, whose inventor I am satisfied is now in hell, receiving the
reward of his cursed invention, which is the cause that very often a cowardly base hand takes
away the life of the bravest gentleman.*

—Miguel de Cervantes

The Napoleonic Wars were the age of the artillery battle. Increasingly after 1805, artillery organization, employment, and command and control was consistently improved among the major belligerents. The number of guns assigned to the armies also greatly increased, and the artillery organization at division and corps level increased in efficiency. Kutusaiv in Russia, along with others—notably Barclay de Tolly and Ermelov—clamored for an army artillery reserve commanded by, and under the operational control of, an artillery general that could be committed on the order of the army commander and at the decisive time and place by artillerymen on the battlefield.

Colonel Josef Smola, still the young, aggressive Austrian artillery lieutenant of 1793 at heart, and who would mass almost 200 guns against the French at Essling in 1809 and dominate the field, smashing the outnumbered and outgunned French artillery, was undoubtedly the best artillery tactician the Austrians possessed. If his aggressive and imaginative tactics, so ably demonstrated at Neerwinden in 1793, had been copied by other Austrian artillerymen, there is no limit to what they might have achieved. That was opportunity lost, and opportunity lost is opportunity gone forever.

British artillery, both horse and foot, small in numbers but augmented by the excellent Portuguese artillery, would be used expertly in the Peninsula by Sir Arthur Wellesley, who would become, because of his ability to "beat the French," the Duke of Wellington. Having excellent guns and the best-designed artillery carriages of the period, British artillery usually numbered too few guns on any field to dominate it, even when reinforced by the Portuguese and the sometimes dubious Spanish. However, what they did achieve under the expert guidance and leadership of Alexander Dickson and Augustus Frazer was consistent, solid, and a fine example of what well-trained and well-led artillery could accomplish.

However, artillery organization, command and control, and a new brand of aggressive, offensive tactics reached its epitome during the period with the French and the solid artillery arm of the Grande Armée. Its material, and its gunpowder, might be inferior to that of the British, but its organization, tactics, and leadership was superior to that of any other European army. Artillery generals commanded it at the army level, and each corps had an artillery chief who was a general officer. Additionally—and unique to any army of the period—artillery general officers were infantry division, corps, and army commanders from time to time. Foy, the old horse artilleryman, whose dictum of getting close to the enemy and shooting fast was the common trait of that hard-hitting arm, was an infantry division commander. Lauriston, the artillery specialist among Napoleon's generals' *aides-de-camp*, and who had defended Ragusa in 1806 against the Russians and native tribesmen, was a corps commander in 1813, as was

Marmont, whose expertly handled guns played a large part in making Castiglione and Marengo into victories. Marmont also commanded independently in the Illyrian provinces and in Spain, though his activities on the latter country ended in defeat and a crippling wound.

Then, especially after 1808, there were the increasing numbers and professionalism of the artillery of the Imperial Guard that became the army artillery reserve and that was committed under its own generals by order of the Emperor. As Senarmont had expertly done at Friedland , the French now specialized in artillery maneuver, the artillery sometimes becoming the main attack in battles. If not, such as at Ocana in Spain (and with Senarmont again commanding the artillery there), the French artillery proved to be decisive in the outcome of the battle. Time and again throughout the period, French artillery commanders led large batteries to the decisive time and place either directly to support the main effort or itself lead the main attack. This happened at Wagram in 1809: Lauriston took a 102-gun battery first to fill a gap left by the maneuver of Massena's IV Corps, and then to pave the way for MacDonald's supporting attack against the Austrian line. At Lützen in 1813, Druout led a 72-gun wild *chevauchée* up into slingshot range of the Allied line, then blowing out their center with point-blank canister, the massed Young Guard attacking behind the bombardment into the wreckage. At Hanau later that year, Druout again led his artillerymen against the Austro-Bavarians under Wrede, pulverized their center, and beat off a cavalry counterattack against his gun line, fighting alongside his gunners who were defending their "pretty girls" against the Allied horsemen with handspike, rammer, and bayonet until the *grenadiers à cheval* rode to their rescue. At Ligny in 1815, massed French artillery took the Prussian center apart, again blowing a hole in the defense that preceded an attack by the infantry of the Guard and Gerard's corps. Finally, at Waterloo two days later, French artillerymen manhandled their guns at the battle's ending to within 100–250 yards of the Allied line, blowing holes in Wellington's ranks and demolishing Allied infantry squares with point-blank cannon fire.

The gunners of all the armies were generally a tough, skilled lot, who took the loss of their guns as a cavalry or infantry unit would take the loss of standard or eagle. They fought their guns, many times to the last, against all-comers, and some, such as the Württemberg horse artillery of Faber du Faur in Russia, were paid high compliments for their skill and dash. Ney remarked that the Württemberg horse artillery was as good as, if not better than, his French horse artillery companies. In reality, there was little to choose between the gunners and batteries of the nations. All served with professional skill and devotion, ably supporting their comrades in the infantry and cavalry, and "promoting" their arm as an equal partner on the battlefields of Europe and North America.

The gunners of all nations upheld the honor and spirit of their arm. Undoubtedly, Saint Barbara smiled down upon them all.

Chapter 7

Senarmont

"A gunner ought to be a sober, wakeful, lusty, hardy, patient, prudent, and quick-
spirited man; he ought also to have a good eyesight, a good judgment, a perfect knowledge
to select a convenient place in the day of service, to plant his ordnance where he may do
most hurt to the enemies, and be least annoyed by them."
—Niccolo Fontana Tartaglia

"Get up close and shoot fast."
—Foy

"Never interrupt your enemy when he is making a mistake."
—Napoleon

"What cannoneer begot this lusty blood?"
—Shakespeare, *King John*, ii, 2, 1596

1700, 14 June 1807: Behind the village of Posthenen, East Prussia
The artillery companies were limbered up behind the small village that masked them from
Russian observation. Luckily, there were also out of range. The Russians always brought an
inordinate amount of weaponry with them; look what they did to Augereau at Eylau in February. They were not that accurate, but they threw more than usual weight of metal at a target.

NCOs casually moved down the sleepy, exhausted columns, the Grande Armée's marches
not being the most pleasurable experience a soldier had to face—especially the forced ones.
Harness was checked, and equipment given a careful once-over, some of the NCOs stopping to
pat a favorite horse, gently lifting the animal's fetlocks to check tender hooves and horseshoes.
Horses cropped at the remains of the spring grass, their swishing tails brushing away the flies
while worn-out drivers of the train companies dismounted to clean the animals' eyes and nostrils of the bothersome dust. Dust in summer, mud in winter, and little enough in between.
Vive le paix, and a bit more.

Both men and horses ignored the vulgar uproar off to their right near the Forest of Sortlack,
getting what rest they could, the horses again demonstrating their unusual ability of locking
their knees and sleeping standing up. Gunners of the horse artillery companies went to reclaim
their animals from the designated horse holder, and check their weapons and equipment.

On that slight rise to their front, two of their company commanders stood puffing their
pipes while their bored trumpeters held their horses. They watched the dark masses of Ney's VI
Corps spill out of the woods on their right, like an immense blue wave. The two officers stood
wide-eyed in amazement as Russian cavalry seemed to appear out of nowhere and jumped
Ney's infantry before they could deploy or form square and drove them back into the shelter of
the woods. Russian artillery rounds from massed batteries across the river were falling on Ney's
shaken infantry. They could hardly miss that big a target at that range, causing considerable
loss, and ploughing red furrows through the packed ranks of the hapless infantrymen. They

could now see, though, at least two of Ney's regiments forming square to defend themselves against the Russian horsemen. French cavalry was riding to the rescue, but the damage had been done. The Emperor would not be pleased. It would take some time for "Red Michael" to get his infantry reformed and the main attack jump-started.

The two officers' attention was suddenly drawn by a shout from one of their trumpeters. Pounding up the slope towards them was one of General Senarmont's *aides-de-camp*. They wondered what their chief of artillery wanted of them. At the *aide*'s hail, the two officers quickly swung into the saddle, and followed him to the artillery assembly and into a whirlwind of activity. The other company commanders were hastily summoning their officers and senior NCOs. Junior NCOs, corporals, and brigadiers were forming the companies for rapid movement, cuffing and kicking awake dozing train drivers and sleeping cannoneers who couldn't stay awake in the early summer warmth. More than one train driver, contentedly sleeping on his mount, fell of in a clatter of equipment after being smacked by an NCO running down the columns of guns and caissons.

Behind the gun companies, Senarmont was conferring with his corps commander, General Victor, and a sweat-stained, grime-covered senior officer who was forcefully pointing towards the enemy to their front. One of the company commanders swore viciously under his breath. That senior officer was Marshal Lannes. *Sacré merde!* That wry-necked bastard loved to fight. Well, the officers' mess would be short a few members this day.

Suddenly, Senarmont saluted, roughly turned his horse and trotted to the front of the massed artillery companies. Politely asking one of the horse artillery company commanders for the loan of a trumpeter, which was granted immediately, Senarmont placed himself, and the terrified trumpeter, at the front of the formation and nodded to the wide-eyed youngster. The frightened and astonished trumpeter, resplendent in a new red-braided dolman and red breeches, complete with colpack, quickly wiped the instrument's mouthpiece, raised the trumpet to his shaking lips, and sounded "Charge!" as Senarmont raised himself in his stirrups, turned smartly in the saddle towards his artillerymen, bellowed "*En avant!*" and sank spur.

*   *   *

The year 1807 was to usher in a new era in field artillery operations. Because of two savage encounters between the French and Russians in eastern Europe, the way battles were fought, and the importance of artillery in those battles, would change the nature of warfare. The first of those encounters was at Eylau in the dead of winter in East Prussia. A massive concentration of Russian artillery completely wrecked one French army corps and severely hurt another. The second, at Friedland in the early days of summer, heralded an entirely new tactical era for artillery that would last until the first rifled cannon made their presence felt on the battlefields of North America in the 1860s.

Eylau was a drawn-out, very bloody "slug fest." Road systems were primitive or nonexistent, and the rainy season in the fall turned what roads there were into long troughs of mud. The battlefield itself was dotted with many small villages, excellent for defense, and they could be a hindrance to an attacking army in the best weather. In the cold of East Prussia, at least one, Preussisch-Eylau itself, was fought over by the Russians and French on the evening of 7 February, the brawl finally won by the troops of Soult's redoubtable IV Corps—and at least they, or some of them, had a place to stay that brutal night.

The terrain in the vicinity of Eylau was "generally open and rolling, broken in summer by multitudes of small lakes, marshes, and creeks—all of which were now frozen solid and invisible beneath one to three feet of snow."[1] The morning of 8 February was very cold and overcast, and there was a storm brewing. For dominating terrain in the area, there was a ridge north of the village of Serpallen, and east of Eylau itself there was a knoll where the church and its attendant cemetery were located.

Napoleon was outnumbered by Benningsen's Russian army, having approximately 44,000 men immediately available against about 60,000. However, Ney was approaching from the north with 10,000 of his VI Corps, and Davout's arrival with 15,000 of the III Corps was imminent. Ney was chasing the Prusso-Russian Corps of the Prussian General Lestocq, whose intervention sometime after 1400 on the Russian left flank undoubtedly saved the battle for Benningsen and was perhaps the salvation of Benningsen's entire army.

The other salvation of the Russians was the numerous and well-handled Russian artillery. In the center of the Russian line were three large Russian batteries of artillery totaling 170 guns. There was a very large battery of 70 guns directly opposite the village of Eylau. To its right, there was another of at least 60 guns, and to the left a smaller one of 40 guns. The rest of the Russian artillery was dispersed throughout the army, though there were 60 guns in reserve, giving the Russians a total of 460 such weapons on the field:

> Independently of the artillery, which was deployed along the line and kept with the reserve, the 1st battery of 40 heavy pieces and 20 light pieces was at first stationed on the right flank of the army, next to the Konigsberg highway; but when the town was occupied by the enemy it was moved 700 paces further away from it; the 2nd battery of 70 heavy pieces was positioned almost in the center of the army, about a mile from the city, and the 3rd battery of 40 heavy pieces stood between the center and Sausgarten. All three batteries were bolstered by troops of our first line, like bastions protruding from fortifications.[2]

These and the other Russian artillery on the field opened fire at daylight, the French artillery immediately replying, the cannonade developing into a counterbattery fight, though Soult's corps was badly hurt merely by the weight of the Russian bombardment:

> Soon after daybreak the Russian cannon opened, and played very heavily, but rather at hazard, as the French columns were principally concealed by the favoring swells of their ground and the town and suburbs of Preuss Eylau. The French cannon quickly replied with vigor and effect, as every man of the Russian army was exposed from head to heel.[3]

Kutusaiv, probably the outstanding Russian artillery general of the period, was present at Eylau, but his exact location during the fighting is unknown. Some authorities state he was with the horse artillery in the reserve, which "drawn up in two dense columns and had 50 pieces of horse-drawn artillery." However, that could merely be conjecture: he could have been with one of the large batteries that destroyed Augereau. A good, general picture of how the Russians assigned their artillery is given in Table 17, which shows the artillery brigades assigned to the infantry divisions for the 1806-07 campaigns, and which was in effect for the Battle of Eylau in February 1807.

Count Alexander Ivanovich Kutusaiv (1784-1812) was the son of *Graf* (Count) Ivan Pavlovich Kutusaiv and was "promised" to the army while still an infant in the cradle. He enlisted in the Horse Life Guards in 1793 and was a captain by 1796. He became adjutant to Arakcheev in 1799 and was promoted to colonel. Still a colonel in 1805, he was a major general the next year, distinguished himself at Eylau and served excellently through 1806-07, being present at Guttstadt, Heilsberg, and Friedland. For his service at Eylau he was decorated with the Order of St George 3rd Class, and the next year was awarded the Order of St Vladimir 3rd Class. In 1810-11 he was assigned to travel throughout Europe studying architecture, fortification, and

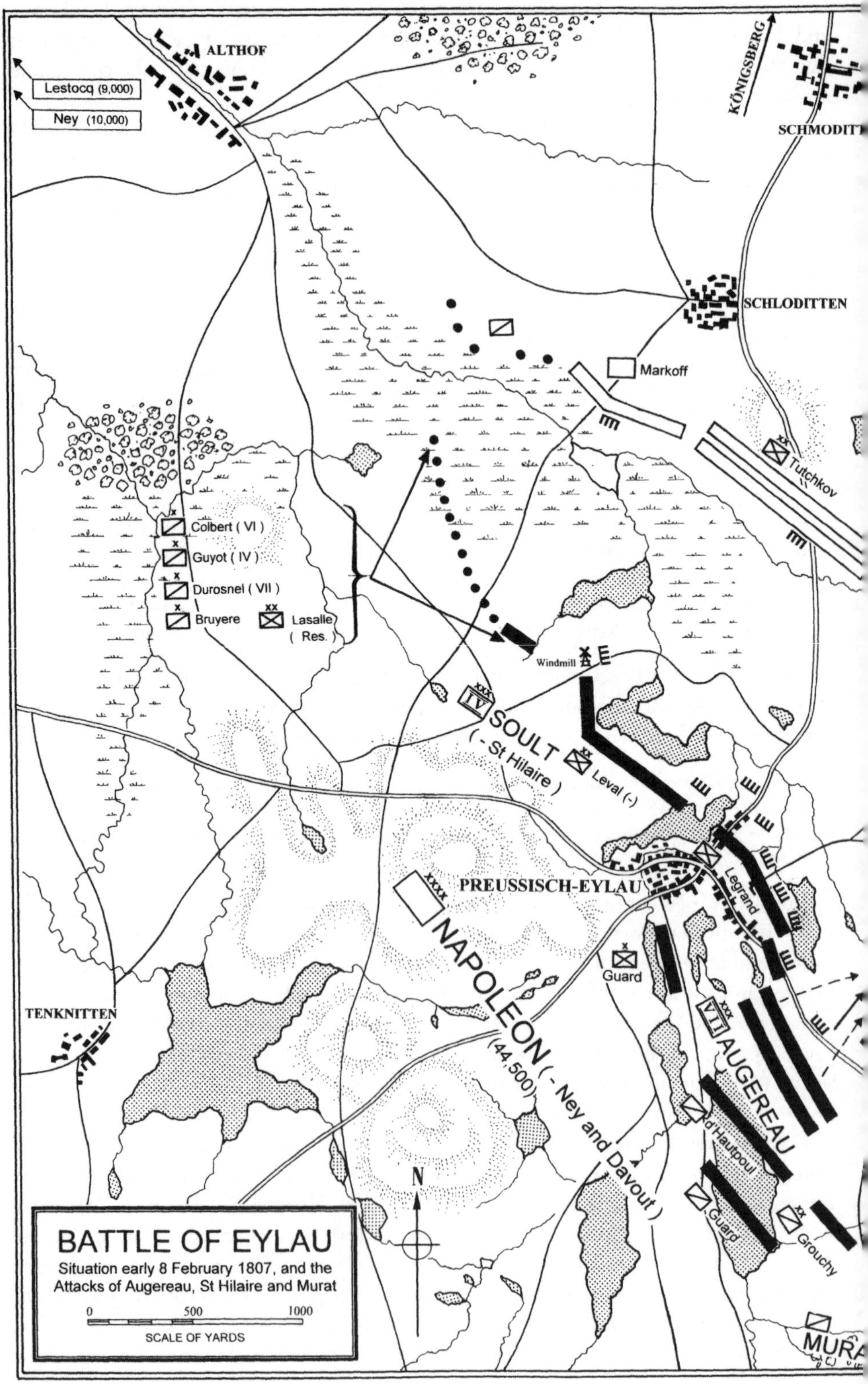

ALTHOF

Lestocq (9,000)

Ney   (10,000)

KÖNIGSBERG

SCHMODITT

SCHLODITTEN

Markoff

Tutchkov

Colbert (VI)

Guyot (IV)

Durosnel (VII)

Bruyere   Lasalle
                   (Res.)

Windmill

IV SOULT
(- St Hilaire)

Leval (-)

PREUSSISCH-EYLAU

NAPOLEON

Guard

(- Ney and Davout)

Legrand

VII AUGEREAU

d'Hautpoul

Guard

Grouchy

TENKNITTEN

MURA

N

BATTLE OF EYLAU

Situation early 8 February 1807, and the
Attacks of Augereau, St Hilaire and Murat

0   500   1000

SCALE OF YARDS

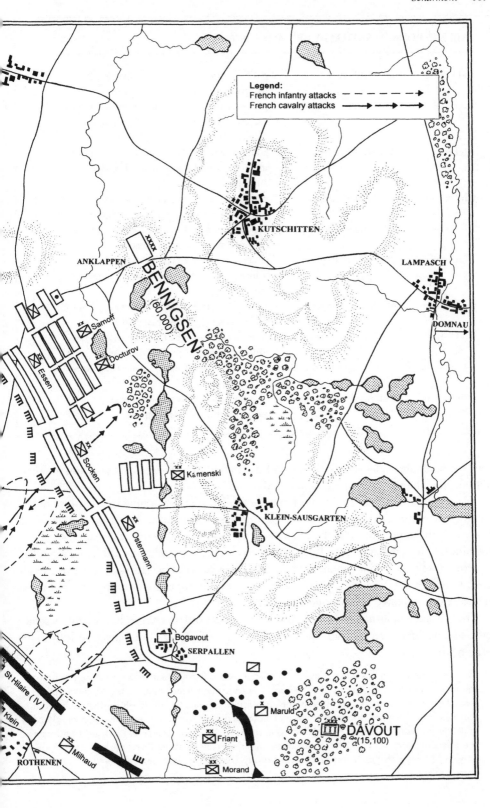

Legend:
French infantry attacks
French cavalry attacks

KUTSCHITTEN

ANKLAPPEN

LAMPASCH

BENNIGSEN
60,000

DOMNAU

Samoff

Docturov

Essen

Socken

Kamenski

Ostermann

KLEIN-SAUSGARTEN

Bogavout

SERPALLEN

St Hilaire (IV)

Maruld

Klein

DAVOUT
(15,100)

Friant

Milhaud

ROTHENEN

Morand

TABLE 17: RUSSIAN ARTILLERY BRIGADES, 1806–07[4]

2nd Division	2nd Artillery Brigade:	2 position batteries, 2 battalion batteries, 1 horse artillery battery, 1 pioneer company
3rd Division	3nd Artillery Brigade:	2 position batteries, 2 battalion batteries, 1 horse artillery battery, 1 *pontonnier* and 1 pioneer company
4th Division	4th Artillery Brigade:	2 position batteries, 2 battalion batteries, 1 horse artillery battery, 1 pontoon and 1 pioneer company
6th Division	6th Artillery Brigade:	2 position batteries, 2 battalion batteries, 1 horse artillery battery, 1 pioneer company
5th Division	5th Artillery Brigade:	1 position battery, 2 battalion batteries, 1 horse artillery battery, 1 pioneer company
7th Division	7th Artillery Brigade:	2 position batteries, 2 battalion batteries, 1 horse artillery company, 1 pontoon and 1 pioneer company
8th Division	8th Artillery Brigade:	2 position batteries, 2 battalion batteries, 1 horse artillery battery, 1 pioneer company
9th Division	9th Artillery Brigade:	2 position batteries, 3 battalion batteries, 1 horse artillery company, 1 pioneer company
10th Division	10th Artillery Brigade:	1 position battery, 3 battalion batteries, 1 horse artillery battery
14th Division	14th Artillery Brigade:	1 position battery, 2 battalion batteries, 1 pontoon and 1 pioneer company

artillery, no doubt under orders, in the old Russian tradition, to keep a close eye on the probable enemies the Russians would fight in 1812.

Kutusaiv was the author of a study of rules for artillery on the battlefield, and in 1812 he was the artillery commander of the First Army of the West. A general at the very young age of 22, he served efficiently, and gallantly commanded the rearguard at Smolensk, again distinguishing himself. He commanded the Russian artillery reserve at Borodino in 1812, and was killed in action leading a Russian counterattack at the Raevski redoubt. His body was never recovered. His death deprived the Russian reserve artillery of a commander of its own, and it was therefore not employed as envisioned during the battle.

The use and employment of a centrally commanded artillery reserve, by an artillery senior officer (and preferably a general), had been the subject of a letter from Barclay de Tolly to the Tsar in 1810:

Two considerations on this subject [of artillery assignment]: a.) it is necessary that the infantry divisions are not encumbered with an excessive quantity of heavy artillery which opposes the rapidity of movements by its transportation difficulties; b) the heavy artillery should be judiciously distributed between the infantry divisions and the excess assigned to the artillery reserve of each army. These reserves, placed under the immediate authority of the [army] commander-in-chief, can be employed with great advantage at the decisive moment of a battle. In accordance with these considerations I have the honor to propose (to your highness), that each corps be assigned two reserve artillery batteries, composed of heavy and horse artillery.[5]

Unfortunately for the Russians, Kutusaiv's death at Borodino in 1812 left the question of the artillery reserve's usefulness unanswered.

The Russian artillery fire, at least initially, was described as wild and inaccurate, though the preponderance of Russian artillery on the field to a large extent made up for this. The sheer volume of the Russian cannonade severely hurt Soult's IV Corps, even though it was partially under cover at Eylau. While this was going on, Davout was slowly building up his advance against the Russian left flank into a decisive flank attack. Friant's division, effectively covered by Marulaz's cavalry brigade, drove the Russians out of their positions in and around the village of Serpallen, defeating a Russian counterattack. His artillery, however, was badly beaten up by the heavier Russian concentration that covered the Russian withdrawal.

As Davout's other divisions—Morand's and Gudin's—came up, they continued what Friant had begun, pressing back the Russian line, until by 1600 it was bent back on its center at a 90-degree angle. This was about the time that Lestocq's fortunate intervention in the battle took place. As Davout's attack started and gained momentum, Napoleon launched his main effort. Augereau's VII Corps was to attack the Russian center with his two divisions; the French artillery was to maintain its bombardment in support of the attack. Augereau was very sick, and had to be strapped to the saddle to maintain himself. His marshal's hat was tied to his head by a large kerchief, and, ready or not, he led his corps from under cover on Soult's right to a deployed attack formation, both of his divisions in line, for his penetration of the Russian center.

From the start, Augereau's corps attacked in the teeth of "murderous" artillery fire. Though there was a 30-minute preparatory bombardment by the French artillery, the targets were generally the Russian infantry, who, in contrast to the French (who attempted to keep most of their troops under cover), were aligned and massed in full view of the enemy and made excellent targets. (The Russians would do the same thing at Borodino in 1812.) The guns inflicted very heavy losses on the two infantry divisions of Heudelet and Desjardins as they struggled through the snow to reach the Russian line. Almost immediately, a heavy snowstorm broke over the battlefield, completely obscuring Augereau's attack from the French lines, though the Russians could still see them advancing. Because of the snowstorm and heavy bombardment, and no doubt helped by Augereau being ill, the corps attack drifted to its left, both divisions now being pounded in enfilade by the three large Russian batteries. Still, the redoubtable French infantry continued to advance, only to meet another burst from hell.

The French artillery kept firing during the snowstorm, and were unaware that the French infantry divisions were drifting to the left, which brought them under fire from the massed French batteries. Caught between two fires, still trying to advance, and with casualties piling up around them, the French infantrymen had to face yet one more avalanche on that bloody field. The Russian cavalry burst forward against Augereau's thinned ranks, herding the survivors ahead of them. Some were captured; others broke and ran; many died in the snow. Some units did fight their way out of the rout and mess, but with heavy, sometimes crippling losses, many exceeded 50 percent casualties. The result was that Augereau's corps was wrecked, Augereau and both of his division commanders were casualties, and the French assault was defeated. The Russian artillery certainly earned its pay that morning. In thirty minutes, Augereau's corps suffered 929 dead, 4,271 wounded, and untold numbers of missing and prisoners. Compans, Soult's Chief of Staff, had rallied about 3,000 of them by nightfall and had them in line between two divisions of the IV Corps.

Napoleon, finally seeing the wreck of Augereau's corps, calmly turned to Murat and ordered him forward into the void. Murat led 10,700 cavalrymen on one of the greatest charges in military history. The French cavalry came pounding out of the snow and cold in a column of divisions, Grouchy's dragoon division leading; d'Hautpoul's cuirassiers and Klein and Milhaud's dragoons followed. It must have seemed as if hell itself had opened up and unleashed its demons.

Grouchy charged the cavalry pursuing Augereau's survivors and drove it off. The cuirassiers attacked to his right, and cut through and overran both lines of Russian infantry. As a shocked Benningsen committed his reserve to stop the French cavalry, some Russian infantry that had been overrun "toughly reformed," and began firing into the rear of the leading French cavalry divisions. Unseen, the French Guard cavalry exploded onto the battlefield, again overrunning the unfortunate Russian infantry. Now free of the Russian fire, the French cavalry that had just wrecked Benningsen's center turned for home, French trumpeters blowing the recall. D'Hautpoul was knocked out of his saddle, mortally wounded leading his troopers, and Lepic, the commander of the *Grenadiers à Cheval*, was almost captured. Some troopers were cut off and killed or captured, but the great mass of French cavalry found its way home, horses blown and comrades missing. However, for the loss of 1,500 officers and men, they had restored a bad situation and Benningsen's center now had a huge hole in it.

The rest of the battle was conducted mainly by Davout, whose flanking attack, now becoming the main French effort, swept forward, taking ground and killing Russians until it looked as if he would fold the Russian right flank back on top of its center. The right-flank units of Friant's division were just clearing the village of Kutschitten when the Prussians and Russians of Lestocq's Prussian corps, about 7,600 men, hit Davout's extreme right flank and enveloped it. The villages of Kutschitten and Anklappen were lost, but Davout's troops and their veteran commanders rallied and counterattacked, gaining back some of the ground before darkness fell, ending the bloodbath. Russian artilleryman A. P. Ermelov succinctly stated:

> I did not know what was the intention to send me there, who I would find there, and under whose command I would be [placed]. Having taken one more company of horse artillery, I arrived in a large field at the end of our left flank, where some very weak remnants of our troops barely held out against a superior enemy, who moved to the right, placed his batteries on the hills and occupied a manor house almost in the rear of our troops. I set the latter on fire and drove out [the enemy] infantry that inflicted casualties on my troops with their shots. I started a cannonade against [enemy] batteries and held that position for almost two hours. Then the corps of General Lestocq approached, with our Kaluzhskii and Vyborgskii Regiments at the head of the column, marching to the very end of the enemy flank. The fire against me became less intensive, and I saw that most pieces directed [their fire] against General Lestocq. I sent our limbers and all our horses, including my own, to the rear, told my men that they were not to think about retreating, and manhandled my pieces forward every time they were hidden by the smoke. I . . . directed all my attention to the road, which was at the base of the hills and along which the enemy attempted to march, since it was not possible to march another way because of the deep snow. Every time I forced them back with a great loss with canister fire of the thirty pieces. Up to the end of the battle, they had not passed my battery, and there was no time to look for another way around, because General Lestocq, having met moderate [enemy] forces, overthrew them [and] outflanked the enemy batteries on the hills, the enemy abandoned them to him [and] turned to flight, and the dark of night fell on the field of battle. Our commander-in-chief [Benningsen], wishing to see the actions of General Lestocq, was on the left flank, and having found all of the horses and limbers of my companies and no guns, was surprised. When informed of the reason he was very satisfied.

The battle was a hard-fought draw. The French losses were between 20,000 and 25,000. The Russians captured five eagles and took 1,200 prisoners. Russian losses have never been accurately assessed, although there were 11,000 Russian dead on the field. The French took 2,500 prisoners, most of whom were wounded. They also reported that they had captured sixteen flags and 23 guns.

This battle is noteworthy for the well-handled Russian artillery, especially its employment in mass. The use of an artillery reserve is noteworthy, and the number of guns employed was almost overwhelming. Augereau was defeated by artillery, including some of his own. In 30 minutes, his VII Corps, except for the corps cavalry and artillery, had ceased to exist. This was not lost on the Corps Artillery Chief, Alexandre Senarmont.

The war begun by Prussia against the French Empire in the fall of 1806 had flowed into Poland, mud, and misery for the remnants of her army that survived in East Prussia following its near-destruction at the Battles of Jena and Auerstadt. The French pursuit was ruthless. Prussian fortresses surrendered to handfuls of French cavalry; columns of demoralized troops were rounded up by the French and sent to the rear. The Russians belatedly came to the aid of their Prussian allies, whose units in East Prussia attached themselves to the their army. What followed was a bitter and difficult winter campaign in the miserable snow-covered wastes of eastern Poland and East Prussia. This campaign culminated in the vicious pounding match at Preussich-Eylau in early February 1807. Both armies suffered crippling losses. The French claimed victory as they held the field, but the victory had not been as at either Austerlitz or Jena, and the indecisive results had not justified the very heavy losses. Both armies went into winter quarters to retrain and refit.

The Grande Armée of 1806 that had gone into Prussia "was more professional and less enthusiastic" than that of 1805, and "one soldier out of three had had less than a year's service." After Eylau, units were brought to eastern Europe from Italy, and replacements trained at the camp at Pontivy by General Delaborde were taught "combined infantry/artillery tactics . . . [and] field operations with frequent changes of bivouacs" and "small maneuvers . . . cavalrymen were taught mounted marksmanship."[6] With these replacements, some of them entire units, Napoleon once again demonstrated his terrible genius for organization and training, returning the Grande Armée to fighting efficiency. Commanders, given the tools they needed, ensured that their units were ready both for the Emperor's grueling inspections and for the coming contest in the spring.

Spring did come, though many thought it would not, and with it the two opposing armies took the field. Benningsen obliged Napoleon with his desire for a decisive battle by shoving his head into a tactical sack at the little village of Friedland on the River Alle. Crossing the river with the bulk of his army to engage and destroy what he perceived to be the isolated corps of Marshal Lannes, Benningsen thought he could quickly defeat Lannes and recross the Alle, taking up his pontoons, without becoming decisively engaged.

Knowing that Napoleon was within supporting distance with at least three corps, Lannes sent aides galloping off with messages for help, and waged an expert delaying action to fix Benningsen in place. With never more than 26,000 men, Lannes forced Benningsen to commit progressively more troops across the Alle to defeat him. Always showing a bold front, he expertly maneuvered his available troops to give the impression he had more numbers than he actually had, committing troops repeatedly to defeat Benningsen's attempts to drive him off or destroy him, especially in the tactically vital Forest of Sortlack on the French right flank. Meanwhile, Napoleon was hotfooting it to the rescue.

Lannes could not believe that Benningsen had put himself in such a position—the river at his back, his pontoon bridges badly placed, all in Friedland in the bend of the river, and now outnumbered—but he held off the Russians until Napoleon had massed 80,000 troops on the battlefield and was ready. Benningsen was trapped and had to fight it out, no matter what his original intentions were or might have been.

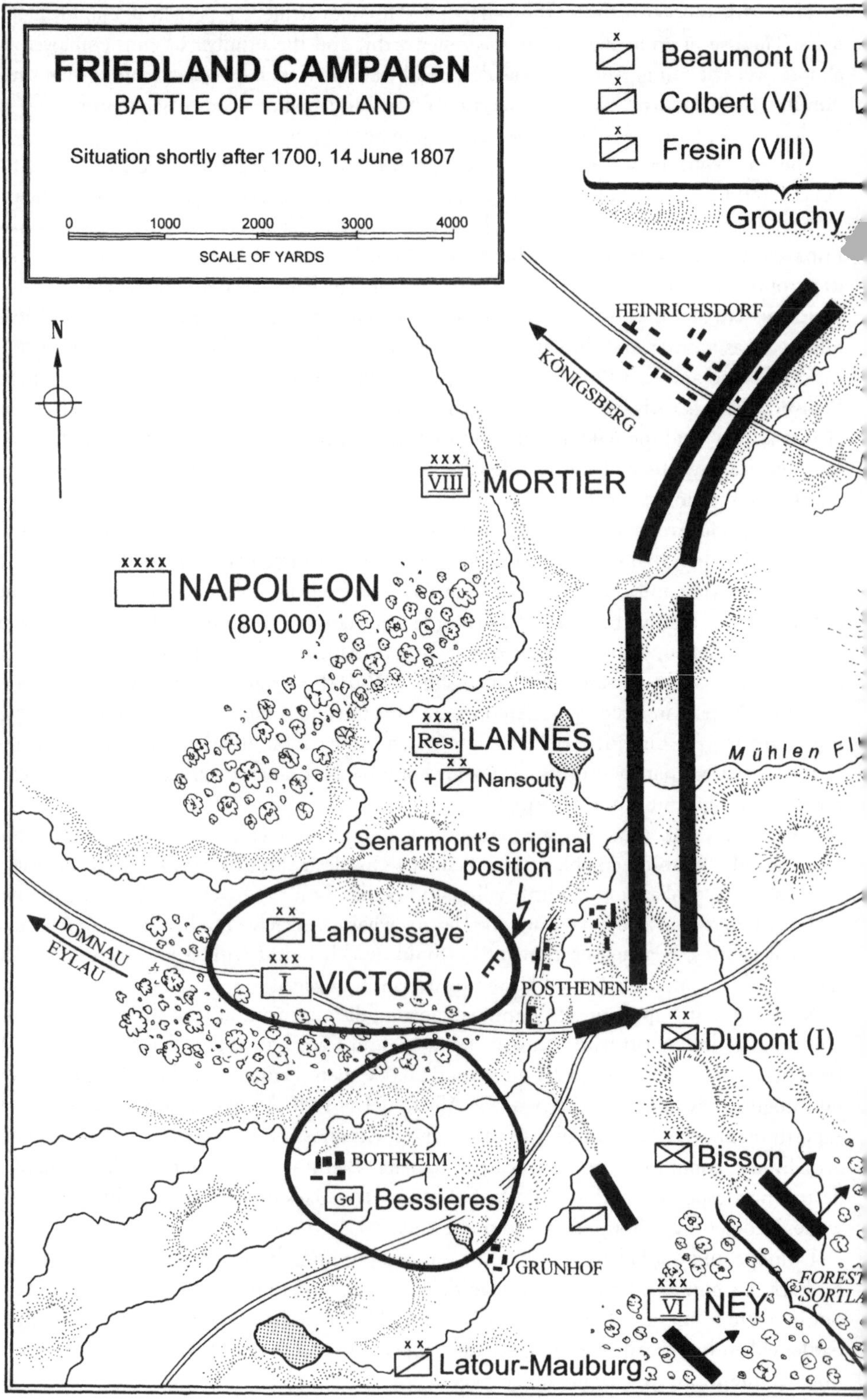

FRIEDLAND CAMPAIGN
BATTLE OF FRIEDLAND

Situation shortly after 1700, 14 June 1807

0   1000   2000   3000   4000
SCALE OF YARDS

N

Beaumont (I)

Colbert (VI)

Fresin (VIII)

Grouchy

HEINRICHSDORF

KÖNIGSBERG

XXX
VIII MORTIER

XXXX
NAPOLEON
(80,000)

XXX
Res. LANNES
X X
(+ Nansouty)

Mühlen Fl

Senarmont's original
position

DOMNAU
EYLAU

X X
Lahoussaye

XXX
I VICTOR (-)

POSTHENEN

X X
Dupont (I)

X X
Bisson

BOTHKEIM

Gd Bessieres

GRÜNHOF

XXX
VI NEY

FOREST
SORTL

X X
Latour-Mauburg

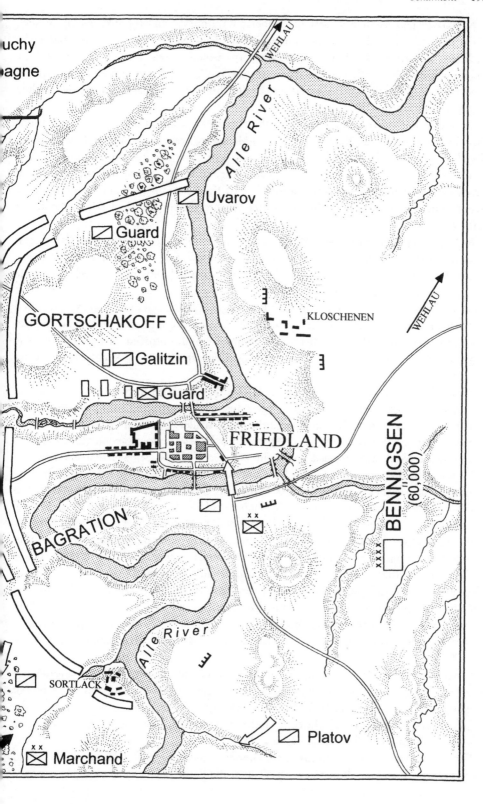

Napoleon's plan was to hold with his deliberately outnumbered left flank, employing Ney's VI Corps to deliver the decisive attack on the enemy's right. Ney's preparations were hidden by the Forest of Sortlack, which was used as the corps assembly area. Victor's I Corps held the center, with Mortier's VIII and the Guard in reserve. As Murat was at Heilsberg, Grouchy acted as Chief of Cavalry, particularly distinguishing himself on the far left flank, and holding off superior numbers of Russians.

On order, Ney's corps debouched from the Forest of Sortlack, the two infantry divisions forming abreast in closed columns, with Latour-Maugourg's cavalry division in direct support. Ney cleared the woods, but failed to deploy and kept on going, keeping his original deep formations. This tempting target was taken advantage of by the massed Russian batteries on the other side of the Alle. Russian cavalry charged the heads of the French columns, and, except for three regiments that rallied and formed square, the corps hotfooted it for the shelter of the woods.

As Ney's attack fell apart, one of Victor's infantry divisions in the center—Dupont's—began advancing without orders against the Russian center, attempting to bring order out of chaos. Seeing this, Senarmont, Victor's Chief of Artillery, supported Dupont with twelve guns. He then secured permission from his corps commander to support Dupont's advance with the whole of the corps artillery—thirty-six guns. Permission granted, Senarmont quickly organized his companies into two large, fifteen-gun batteries, keeping six in reserve. Placing his two batteries on either side of Dupont's division, Senarmont rapidly outpaced the panting, sweating infantry and attacked the Russian center on his own, reportedly causing Napoleon to exclaim, "*Senarmont déserte.*"[7]

Alexander-Antoine Hureau Senarmont (1769-1810) was born in Strasbourg. His father, Alexandre-François Hureau de Senarmont was a general of artillery, later commanding the French artillery at Valmy. The son entered the Metz Artillery School in 1784 being commissioned into the 2nd Regiment at Besançon the next year. By 1792 he was a captain with the Armées du Centre and Nord, and was *aide-de-camp* to his father in 1792, also being present at Valmy.

He served at the Siege of Anvers in 1792 and the Siege of Lille in 1793, and was the commander of the *pontonniers* of the Armée de Sambre in 1794, the same year being promoted to *chef de bataillon*. He was with the Armée de Sambre et Meuse from 1794 until 1797, and in the Armée du Rhin by 1799. In 1800 he was Chief of Staff to Marmont and the Chief of Artillery of the Army of the Reserve, and was he present at Marengo. With the Grande Armée from 1805 to 1807, and present at Austerlitz, he was promoted to *Général de Brigade* in 1806. He was the VII Corps Artillery Chief in 1806, and replaced Faultirer as the I Corps artillery chief in 1807. Present at Friedland, he introduced a new school of artillery tactics which made the artillery into a maneuver arm, and not just a supporting arm. Artillery now moved and held ground, and from then on was used to seize the tactical initiative in battle and pave the way for infantry assaults. He again distinguished himself as an innovative artillery commander at Ocana in 1809.

Senarmont was made a commandant of the Légion d'Honneur in 1807, and a general of division in 1808. He distinguished himself at Somosierra in 1808 and was Victor's Chief of Artillery in I Corps in Spain. In 1809 he was briefly the commander of the artillery of the Army of Spain, then being made the commander of the rrtillery at the Siege of Cadiz, where he was killed in action by a shell on 26 October 1810.

Senarmont was a true *mauvais tête* in the Grande Armée. A superb artilleryman, he would go on to distinguish himself in Spain, especially at the Battle of Ocana in 1809. He was once caught in a Spanish defile by guerillas, who, sensing a quick and easy kill, swarmed in on his artillery column. Quickly ordering his gunners to action, front, flanks, and rear, Senarmont directed a notable defense of his column, meeting the guerillas' impetuous rush with point-blank canister that made their attack a red ruin and drove them off.

Senarmont's massed artillery companies clattered past Dupont's weary infantrymen, the foot artillery gunners running to keep up. Trumpets clarioned and drums rolled, and the artillery, led by their general, broke into a charge. When they reached an optimum range to target—the Russian center—trumpets again sounded, and one the companies wheeled into a firing position and began to unlimber. Company commanders' sabers flashed in the June sun as they directed their guns into position, each gun captain looking for his gun guide. Company commanders were shouting their "fire" orders as the drums and trumpets sounded "Action front!"

Responding automatically to the drum and trumpet calls, well-trained artillery horse teams swung into formation without direction from their drivers. Panting, sweating gunners caught up with the gun teams, horses snoring and breathing heavily in their sweatsoaked harnesses. Slippery, calloused hands grabbed handspikes, trace chain, and gun trails, and the heavy carriages were lifted from their limbers by grunting, swearing gunners. Trails were swung round and the guns were manhandled into battery by sweat and muscle, their places already marked by the gun guides. Trail ready boxes were lifted and placed on the ground, the lids open to reveal their deadly cargo. More trumpet calls, the rush and snort of horse teams—and the two fifteen-gun batteries advanced by successive bounds towards the enemy line. To the rear, the six reserve guns remained limbered up, their teams and crews waiting for the order to support their comrades. Their company commander had to be the most frustrated man on the battlefield.

Russian artillery was beginning to find the range. Men and horses were beginning to get hit. Horses, terrified, screamed and went down in a mess of blood, harness, and severed body parts, the gunners and drivers hustling to cut the wounded or dead animals free to allow the rest of the team the ability to move when ordered. Men were cut down without a sound, or screamed like their four-footed comrades as hot metal cut into flesh. Plunging and ricocheting roundshot decapitated gunners, the wounded staying at their posts until relieved or passing out from loss of blood.

Completely ignoring the Russian artillery, Senarmont ordered his companies to concentrate their fire on the Russian infantry to their front. Not satisfied with the range to target, Senarmont ordered his wide-eyed, frightened trumpeter to blow another call. Alert chiefs of section ceased fire, followed by their comrades at other guns, while gun teams raced up to retrieve their weapons and limber up, mount, displace forward. At 150 yards from the enemy position, the terrain narrowed so that both batteries had to combine into one. Another trumpet call, echoed by all the other trumpeters in the companies—"Action front!"—and then the gunners again had to halt, dismount, unlimber, race to catch up, all the while enduring the *sacré* Russian counterbattery fire that could not, however, stop the momentum not the rapid change in range of Senarmont's juggernaut. More men and horses were hit and went down, blood splattering guns, limbers, and harnesses, but the gunners calmly and expertly reopened fire.

Through the noise and mess of that shot- and smoke-filled inferno, Senarmont set an admirable example of coolness to his gun crews, imitated by the company commanders and battery officers. Still not satisfied with the range to target, he again ordered the companies forward to get within slingshot range. To save depleted horse teams, the gunners fastened their *bricoles* to their guns, turning themselves into "man teams," and went forward by alternate bounds to 120 yards from the enemy.[8] Finally satisfied with the range, Senarmont ordered a halt, the guns were once again swung into position, and the gunners quickly reopened fire. Rapid fire started to take the Russian center apart, and at this range the gunners simply could not miss: out of effective range of the Russian muskets, they blew the center out of the Russian line, round after accurate round going down range into the massed enemy infantry. In twenty minutes the Russian center was ruined, 4,000 mangled corpses marking the position. Benningsen's center had ceased to exist. The battle was already over, though Benningsen did not know it.

Back in the Forest of Sortlack, Ney cursed and pounded his two divisions back into formation, leading them back to the assault on the Russian left flank "fairly frothing at the mouth in his fury."[9] His corps artillery finally went into action against the Russian batteries across the river, giving a much-needed respite to Senarmont's weary command. Other French artillery joined in, and rapidly built up fire superiority over the less expertly handled Russian guns, finally silencing them.

Latour-Maubourg again advanced in support of Ney, fighting and routing the cavalry with which the Russians were attempting to stop them. Dupont's weary infantrymen caught up with Senarmont in front of Friedland as the Russian Imperial Guard launched a counterattack. Leading his division against the infantry of the Imperial Guard, Dupont's *lapins rudes* defeated them in a savage bayonet fight, and the Russians bolted for Friedland and the perceived safety of the bridges.

The cavalry of the Russian Guard made an attempt to silence Senarmont's battery. Advancing against his left flank, they had an opportunity to overrun the companies and roll up the entire gun line, finally silencing it, but, seeing the impending threat, the quick-witted Senarmont immediately ordered the companies to the alert with trumpets sounding "Action Flank!" Trumpeters and drummers echoed the command down the gunline. Alert company officers and gun captains bellowed at the exhausted gunners, some pointing in the direction of the new threat. Sweat-soaked and grime-covered artillerymen redoubled their efforts, trails swinging to the right, bringing the ominous, smoking muzzles to the left to face the Tsar's picked cavalrymen. Ammunition handlers ran forward with canister rounds, handing them to anxious gunners, who placed the deadly antipersonnel rounds in the muzzles, where they were promptly rammed, gun captains' hands flying into the air to signify "Ready" on hearing the satisfying "*thunk*" when the round was properly seated.

In the distance, Russian trumpets blew and the Guard cavalrymen cheered as they burst into the charge, going at the artillerymen at the dead run. Company commanders waited to almost the last possible moment to get the greatest effect on target, and almost as one they bellowed, "*Feu!*" Portfires touched vents, and the guns exploded in fire and smoke with a deafening roar, violently recoiling back, the deadly canisters exploding almost literally in the faces on the onrushing cavalrymen with the effect of giant shotguns. Excited crews manhandled the guns back into position, frantically going though the intricate gun drill to reload with canister for another volley. Tubes were relaid by outwardly calm gun captains. The smoking monsters were swabbed out, as the ammunition handlers passed their rounds forward to the muzzles of the hungry guns. Once again, as the rounds were rammed, sweaty thumbs over the vents to prevent accidental discharges, gun captains listened for the rounds to be seated, raising their hands when ready. Again, battery commanders, mouths dry with apprehension and caked powder, bellowed "*Feu!*" and the line of guns belched forth the deadly canisters.

Portfires again dropped on the guns' breeches, and the guns crashed out, recoiling back one more time. Once more, the deadly ballet of crew drill took over, as the guns were manhandled back into position, relaid and reloaded. Through the smoke and mess, "Cease firing" was sounded by the trumpeters along the line, dutifully echoed by the company drummers. As the smoke cleared, the gunners saw the red ruin they had caused: the Tsar's picked cavalrymen had been blown off the battlefield.

This was the decisive action of the battle. The Russian center had been destroyed: Ney's second assault had been successful, pocketing the Russian left against the river. Pressing their advantage, Dupont's infantry advanced on Friedland and the Russian bridges. Senarmont sent six guns to support Dupont, while the main battery supported other French infantry, which had joined the general advance after the destruction of the Russian main line of resistance.

Senarmont brought his companies forward again, so that the guns could sweep Friedland's streets with fire. Repeated Russian attempts to stand and reform were broken up by a combination of accurate artillery fire and infantry assault. Benningsen's army was losing its cohesion, many Russians drowning in the river rather than surrender. Many more died in an uncoordinated attempt to recross the badly sited pontoon bridges, which turned Friedland into a bottleneck and a deathtrap, an easy target for Senarmont's gunners.

Friedland marked the first time in military history that massed artillery had been used decisively on its own to seize a tactical initiative. Generals who knew their business had massed their artillery in the past; this time, though, the aggressive use of a mass of artillery to attack an enemy main line of resistance and shatter it, paving the way for an infantry assault, would revolutionize the employment of artillery and made it the equal of the other two major combat arms, the infantry and the cavalry:

> . . . Senarmont had introduced a new school of artillery tactics. Competent generals had massed their artillery for years; Senarmont had used these massed guns to seize the initiative, pushing them aggressively forward in advance of the French infantry to dominate the decisive point of the battlefield with their firepower.[10]

Senarmont, after asking for, and receiving, permission from his corps commander, Victor, to support Dupont's infantry division, formed his artillery in two large 15-gun batteries, plus a six-gun reserve battery, behind the village of Posthenen in the center of the French line. The right battery consisted of ten 6-pounders, two 3-pounders, and three howitzers. It was placed under the command of *Colonel* Forno, who was the Chief of Staff of the corps artillery; *chef de bataillon* Bernard was second in command of this battery. The units composing the battery were the 6th Company of the 1st Regiment of *Artillerie à Pied*, plus detachments from the 1st Company of the 2nd Regiment of *Artillerie à Cheval* and the 2nd Company of the 3rd Regiment of *Artillerie à Cheval*. The left battery was commanded by *Major* Raulot. The units comprising this battery were the 2nd and 6th Companies of the 8th Regiment of *Artillerie à Pied* and by 3rd Company of the 3rd Regiment of *Artillerie à Cheval*, plus a detachment of the 2nd Company from the same regiment. The reserve had six guns, together with the caissons supporting each of the batteries. Senarmont soon outpaced Dupont's infantry, and, because of the terrain, was in the end forced to form the two batteries into one large unit. He advanced his artillery by alternate bounds, one battery firing, the other advancing, covered by the fire of its twin. The guns moved rapidly to a range of 390 meters, fired five or six salvos, and then advanced again, halving the range and opening a very rapid fire on the Russian center. Judging this not to be close enough, Senarmont ordered the entire formation forward by bounds, closing the range to 117 meters, and again opened a rapid fire.

During the fight, four officers and 52 other ranks were killed or wounded: *Colonel* Forno was killed in action, and *Chef de Bataillon* Bernard and *Lieutenants* Ondard and Marcillac wounded. Fifty-three horses were put out of action. *Général* Senarmont had his horse shot out from under him. *Colonel* Forno and *Major* Raulot were singled out by Senarmont and commended for their gallantry and competence. The corps artillery expended 2,600 roundshot and 400 canister rounds during the action, which had lasted no longer than thirty minutes.[11]

As an interesting note, the flute-playing Guard artillery officer *Major* Boulart was present at Friedland and was an eyewitness. His short account verifies both the corps' after-action report and Senarmont's letter to his brother,[12] which was written on 26 June 1807, twelve days after the battle:

> The position of the enemy showed 4,000 dead on this spot alone. I lost the chief of my staff, Colonel Forno, killed by a ball at the end of the action. I have had three officers and sixty-two gunners hors de combat, and a charming horse wounded under me; I fear I shall not be able to save him.

Friedland ended the war that had begun in September 1806. Prussia's army had been destroyed in the most complete defeat suffered by any belligerent during the war. Russia had lost another major war to the French, the second in less than two years. The participants met at Tilsit in July, to sign the peace treaty, and Prussia was lucky to survive as an independent nation.

At the end of the fighting in June 1807, Major General Sievers, the commander of a Russian artillery brigade, wrote a final report on "tactics and equipment." He stated that the "French artillery equipment was not better than the Russians," but French commanders used their artillery more skillfully; they chose better positions for artillery batteries, and the actions of their whole army helped their artillery to be more effective." This was because they usually ouflanked the Russian Army, so that their artillery fire was concentrated at the Russian lines and the Russian reserves were under a crossfire (though, at the same time, Sievers noticed that the French liked to fire at long range and elevated the barrels of their pieces too high in order to do that, and so their fire was not very effective). Comparing the ways of selecting artillery positions, Sievers wrote that the Russians usually placed their weapons on every hill in their position, so that the enemy could count almost all Russian guns. In contrast, the French placed their batteries of howitzers in depressions or behind hillocks, so that their pieces could not be observed by the enemy. He also wrote that Russian artillerymen often fired at enemy batteries, and that senior commanders were partly responsible for that, because some of them liked to give orders to "silence the enemy battery." In order to perform this counterbattery fire, the Russian artillery expended too much ammunition and time.[13]

NOTES

1. Esposito and Elting, *A Military History and Atlas of the Napoleonic Wars*, Map 73
2. Denis Davidov, *In the Service of the Tsar against Napoleon*, p. 34.
3. Wilson, *The Campaigns in Poland in 1806 and 1807*, p. 101.
4. Information generously supplied by Greg Gorsuch.
5. Nafziger, *Imperial Bayonets*, p. 273.
6. Elting, *Swords Around a Throne*, pp. 60–1.
7. Downey, *Cannonade*, p. 171.
8. Advancing by "bounds" can be of two different types—successive, and alternate. When advancing in successive bounds, the entire unit goes forward at once; alternate bounds involves part of one unit (in Senarmont's case, half at a time—either the left or right 15-gun battery), the other battery covering the advance of the other by fire.
9. Esposito and Elting, *op. cit.*, Map 81.

10. *Ibid.*, Map 82.
11. The detailed information on Senarmont's action, such as casualties and ammunition expenditure, was taken from the 1st Corps' after-action report.
12. From a personal letter to the author by Jonathan Cooper. See also the memoirs of Bon Boulart, who was a Guard artillery officer and later became a general.
13. Zhmodikov and Zhmodikov, *Tactics of the Russian Army in the Napoleonic Wars*, p. 70-1.

Chapter 8

Smola

"The cannons have their bowels full of wrath,
And ready mounted are they to spit forth
Their iron indignation."
—Shakespeare, *King John*

"This habit of attempting anything, with the weakest of forces, this insistence that nothing was
impossible, this unlimited confidence in our success, which at first gave us one of our greatest
advantages, was fatal to us in the end."
—Fezensac

1400, 22 May 1809: Between the villages of Aspern and Essling
Lannes' assault had failed; so, too, had the Austrian infantry assaults that followed, held off
and defeated by the furious infantry of the II Corps. In the distance the infantry of the Old
Guard, in position in the open behind the II Corps, saw clouds of dust as battery after battery
of Austrian artillery was brought into position to bombard the French infantry. There must be
almost two hundred guns being brought in, replacing the defeated *Kaiserlich* infantry. The
French cavalry had withdrawn, a big, enticing target for the Austrian gunners. The infantry,
however, had to stay and take it, and this one was going to be really rough.

In front of the stately, impeccably drawn-up ranks of Guard infantry, their commander
Général Dorsenne sat his horse, perfect in attire and bearing, seemingly oblivious to it all. His
officers and men would stay there until ordered to move or die in the attempt. The Austrians
had shot their bolt and there would be no more infantry attacks against the French line, but
the almost overwhelming number of guns being brought into position by the Austrians pre-
saged only more death among the exhausted French.

On the Austrian side of the field, *Oberst* Josef Smola was supervising battery after battery of
artillery as it was brought into position. Party to a conference with the Archduke Charles,
Smola knew that some of the Austrian infantry had refused to advance after being repeatedly
repulsed by the unyielding French. Some of his batteries were already engaging in counterbattery
fire against the outnumbered French artillery, and it was his intention to overwhelm the French
artillery and then concentrate on their infantry; perhaps that would convince the Archduke to
order, once again, an attack against the French. There was a chance to drive them into the river
and win a decisive victory over the Grande Armée commanded by Napoleon himself. Smola was
assembling almost 200 guns for this bombardment, and if the Austrian command and staff didn't
recognize it for the golden opportunity that it was, then maybe they deserved to lose once again.

*   *   *

The general situation in early 1809 saw Napoleon and France deeply involved in Portugal and
Spain. To the east, Austria, humbled by repeated defeats in 1796, 1797, 1800, and 1805, was
stirring, motivated by revenge and the desire to be dominant in Germany. She was planning on
war—and what better time than while Napoleon and his Grande Armée were deeply involved
in the Spanish peninsula?

The Austrian Army had undergone a period of reform and reorganization under its best general, the Archduke Charles, brother of the Emperor Francis. Charles did not support war in 1809, as he believed the Austrians were not prepared—yet. Austria wanted to avenge her defeats of 1797, 1800, and 1805, hopefully reacquiring her lost territory. The Austrian government also believed that Germany was ready to rise up and "throw off the French yoke," and would support her attack on the French Empire. However, the decision was made and the die cast. On 9 April, the Austrians invaded Napoleon's ally Bavaria without declaring war, employing 209,400 men commanded by the Archduke Charles.

This unprovoked Austrian attack failed to catch Napoleon unawares. Davout had been left in central Europe after Tilsit in 1807 with 60,000 French veterans, including the heavy cavalry and his own redoubtable III Corps. There were also 60,000 new conscripts and 50,000 troops belonging to the Confederation of the Rhine. Davout, with his usual thoroughness, had also established an efficient intelligence network along the Empire's eastern marches, and when there were indications of Austrian troop concentrations above the normal peacetime level, he launched limited cavalry reconnaissances across the border.

Thus forewarned, Napoleon quietly prepared to fight with the forces available. All he could pull out of Spain were the Guard and some of the commanders, such as Lannes, that he needed in central Europe. He had left Spain on 17 January 1808, arriving in Paris a week later. Napoleon since then had prepared for what he knew was coming, and would fight with what he had available. For the first time, the contingents of the Confederation of the Rhine would provide a considerable portion of the Grande Armée's combat power.

After some confusion at the beginning of the campaign, which resulted from Napoleon's insistence on running operations by letter and telegraph from Paris instead of letting the commanders in theater run them, Napoleon arrived in Donauworth on 17 April. By the next day, he had begun to sort out the mess he had made with his contradictory instructions sent to Berthier, who was in theater ahead of the Emperor. Grasping the operational situation, Napoleon swiftly planned operations against Charles's slow-moving Austrians. In a campaign of maneuver and frequent battles—which Napoleon later stated were the best of his career—the Grande Armée outmarched and outfought the Austrians, sending them in retreat towards Vienna by 24 April, their offensive shattered and their army suffering heavy losses. By 12 May, the Archduke Maximilian had abandoned Vienna to the French, burning the Danube bridges behind him. He also left the well-stocked Vienna arsenal intact—a repeat performance, since the Austrians had done the same thing in 1805.[1]

After his defeats around Ratisbon, Charles had advised his brother Francis to sue for peace. Francis had refused, and Charles had rejoined the army, which was in a very sorry shape. The recent defeats had demonstrated that his corps commanders were neither ready nor competent enough to command at corps level. Worse, Austrian divisions did not have their own staffs, which threw the onus of all the Army's staff work onto the corps staffs, though some of it reverted to the Army staff. While the new staff system the Austrians employed in 1809 was an improvement on what had gone on before, it was still not up to the task of running a modern army.[2]

Charles occupied positions opposite Vienna on the eastern bank of the Danube. With the bridges destroyed, Napoleon had to execute an assault to come to grips with the Austrians. What he planned was a hasty river crossing to get as much of the army across in as short a space of time as possible, before the Austrians could mass against him. Napoleon mistakenly believed that Charles would fight somewhere north of Vienna.

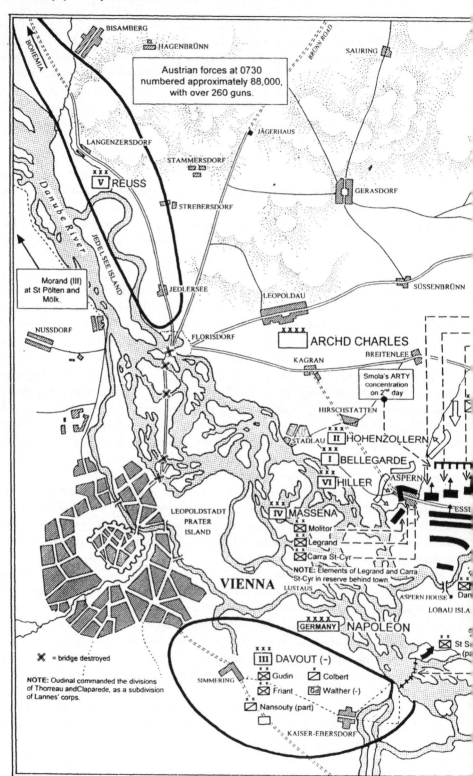

Austrian forces at 0730 numbered approximately 88,000, with over 260 guns.

BISAMBERG

HAGENBRÜNN

SAURING

BOHEMIA

BRÜNN ROAD

JÄGERHAUS

LANGENZERSDORF

STAMMERSDORF

GERASDORF

Danube River

JEDELSEE ISLAND

X X X
V REUSS

STREBERSDORF

Morand (III) at St Pölten and Mölk.

JEDLERSEE

LEOPOLDAU

SÜSSENBRÜNN

NUSSDORF

FLORISDORF

X X X X
ARCHD CHARLES

KAGRAN

BREITENLEE

Smola's ARTY concentration on 2nd day

HIRSCHSTATTEN

STADLAU

X X X
II HOHENZOLLERN

X X X
I BELLEGARDE

ASPERN

X X X
VI HILLER

LEOPOLDSTADT PRATER ISLAND

X X X X
IV MASSENA

ESSL

X X
Molitor

X X
Legrand

X X
Carra St-Cyr

NOTE: Elements of Legrand and Carra St-Cyr in reserve behind town.

VIENNA

LUSTAUS

ASPERN HOUSE　Dan

LOBAU ISLA

X X X X
GERMANY NAPOLEON

X X
St S
(pa

X = bridge destroyed

NOTE: Oudinal commanded the divisions of Thorreau and Claparede, as a subdivision of Lannes' corps.

X X X
III DAVOUT (-)

SIMMERING

X X
Gudin

X
Colbert

X X
Friant

Gd Walther (-)

X
Nansouty (part)

KAISER-EBERSDORF

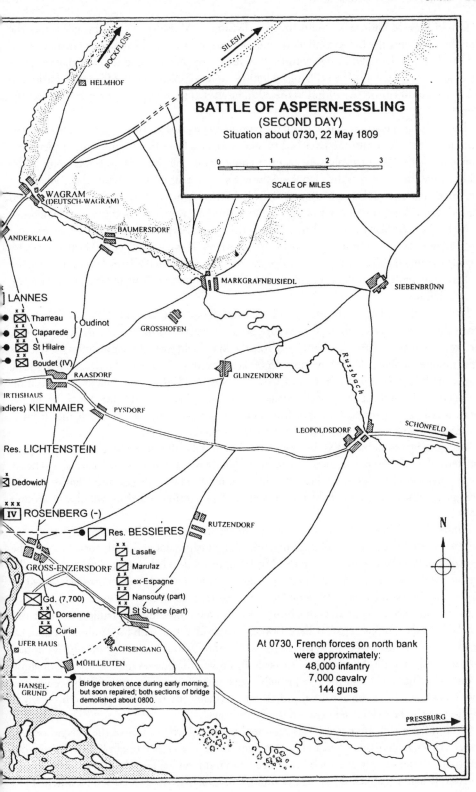

BATTLE OF ASPERN-ESSLING
(SECOND DAY)
Situation about 0730, 22 May 1809

0   1   2   3
SCALE OF MILES

HELMHOF

BOCKFLOSS

SILESIA

WAGRAM
(DEUTSCH-WAGRAM)

ANDERKLAA

BAUMERSDORF

MARKGRAFNEUSIEDL

SIEBENBRÜNN

LANNES

Tharreau
Claparede   Oudinot
St Hilaire
Boudet (IV)

GROSSHOFEN

RAASDORF

GLINZENDORF

Russbach

IRTHSHAUS
adiers) KIENMAIER   PYSDORF

Res. LICHTENSTEIN

LEOPOLDSDORF

SCHÖNFELD

Dedowich

ROSENBERG (-)

Res. BESSIERES

RUTZENDORF

N

Lasalle
Marulaz
ex-Espagne
Nansouty (part)
St Sulpice (part)

GROSS-ENZERSDORF

Gd. (7,700)

Dorsenne

Curial

UFER HAUS

SACHSENGANG

MÜHLLEUTEN

HANSEL-
GRUND

Bridge broken once during early morning,
but soon repaired; both sections of bridge
demolished about 0800.

At 0730, French forces on north bank
were approximately:
48,000 infantry
7,000 cavalry
144 guns

PRESSBURG

On 18 May, Molitor, who commanded a division in Massena's IV Corps, got across the Danube occupying the Lob-Grund along the southern portion of the island of Lobau close to the east bank of the river. Bridge construction began immediately and the Austrian outposts were cleared from Lobau. The bridging operations were completed by 20 May, and Charles was not alerted until late on the 19th. On the 20th, he started to concentrate his army to meet the French.

The bridging operations were without the customary precautions taken to protect the bridges. No piles were driven into the river bed to stop obstacles from floating into the bridges and damaging them. Naval patrols were also not employed in the river.[3] However, as soon as the bridges were thrown across the Danube, Massena's corps crossed and occupied the villages of Aspern to the west and Essling to the east of the French bridgehead. Massena put a division in and around each village, with one in reserve. Cavalry formed a screen between the two settlements.

At 1700 on 20 May the main bridge across the Danube was broken by a large, heavy boat that had been launched from upstream by the Austrians. This occurred when Marulaz's cavalry brigade was making its crossing. The bridge was not repaired until 0300 on 21 May. It would be broken again at 1000 and not repaired until 1430. This ultimately would be a cause for the French defeat.

By 1500 on 21 May, Napoleon had a little over 16,000 infantry and almost 7,000 cavalry across the Danube. Fewer than 90 guns supported this relatively small force. At around 1430, the French saw the Austrians advancing across the Marchfeld toward their positions. Charles's army numbered about 80,000 infantry, 15,000 cavalry and 264 guns. The desperate fighting that ensued centered around the two villages of Aspern and Essling. Massena took up position in Aspern to direct the defense of the village, Lannes, who had crossed before his corps, taking over in Essling. Aspern had a large church and cemetery, which greatly aided the defense. Essling had a large stone granary that the Austrians would never take.

The fighting was desperate as the French tried to stop the almost overwhelming numbers of Austrians. By 1800 French reinforcements arrived—a division of infantry and part of two heavy cavalry divisions. Somehow, the French held on to most of both villages, and Charles did not attempt to attack the weakly held French center. The fighting ended for the day at around 2000.

Lannes' II Corps, with the Guard infantry, crossed the rickety bridges overnight, which gave the French 48,000 infantry, 7,000 cavalry, and 144 guns present and ready for action on the east bank of the Danube by 0730 on the 22nd. Napoleon decided to seek a quick decision by having Lannes attack the Austrian center. Davout, whose was the next corps scheduled to arrive, would exploit Lannes' attack and split the Austrian center.

Lannes attacked as ordered, taking heavy losses from intense Austrian artillery fire that also knocked out most of his corps artillery. Bessières supported him with his cavalry, but Lannes' attack stalled against desperate Austrian resistance and Davout failed to show up. What had happened was that the Austrians had successfully broken the bridges once again by launching "a huge floating mill"[4] into the river, which struck the bridge, sweeping away the center section. It could not be readily repaired, and Napoleon finally ordered Lannes back to his original position, in the French center between the two villages.

Meanwhile, attack after attack was mounted by the Austrians against the villages on the French flanks. Aspern was taken and retaken four times. The French finally held it, halting the Austrians' attempt to get into their bridgehead and trapping the French on the wrong side of the river. Rosenberg attacked Essling five times, and took five bloody repulses. Finally, at 1330

Charles decided make a major effort to pierce the French center and pocket the two halves of Napoleon's troops against the Danube. The Austrian infantry failed to penetrate the French line, their assaults being fought into the ground by the desperate French, who knew that if the Austrian penetrated to the bridgehead they would be trapped.

Rosenberg tried once more to seize Essling. Bitter fighting ensued, no-quarter attrition reducing Boudet's division to nothing but a remnant. Boudet and some of his troops took refuge in the big granary, but the rest of the division was ejected from the village. Napoleon sent one of his generals' *aides-de-camp*, Mouton, with most of the Young Guard infantry to retake the village. Their rush cleared the village, but the French Guardsmen, in turn, were surrounded by the overwhelming numbers of Austrian infantry until another *aide*, Rapp, was ordered to attack with the remainder of the Young Guard to extricate Mouton. With Mouton rescued, the two of them, on their own initiative, decided to counterattack and retake the entire village. The Guard's move was both unexpected and vicious: the Austrians were surprised by this sudden counterstroke, and Rosenberg's exhausted infantry was once again ejected from the village that was choked with dead and wounded. This time, the French kept the village.

What happened on the battlefield now marked the largest single concentration of artillery to date in the period. Charles withdrew his shot-up and demoralized infantry from the French center, and *Oberst* Josef Smola, the Artillery Chief for Hohenzollern's Austrian II Corps, organized the artillery batteries assigned to him into one large, 200-odd-gun battery whose mission it would be to destroy the French center and open the way to the Bridgehead to Lobau island.

Josef *Freiherr* von Smola (1764–1820) entered the service in the 1st *Feldartillerieregiment*. In 1791 he was in the Netherlands with the *Artillerie Fusilier Bataillon*, and in 1792 he fought at Jemappes. Distinguished service at Neerwinden in 1793 while still a lieutenant in command of a cavalry battery reinforced to fourteen guns and howitzers brought him the Knight's Cross of the Order of Maria-Theresa. He was a *Kapitänleutnant* in 1796 and a *major* in 1800, and was serving in the *Bombardierkorps* as a lieutenant colonel in 1808. Promoted to colonel in 1809, he was the Artillery Chief for the II Corps under Hohenzollern in the campaign of 1809, serving throughout and particularly distinguishing himself at Essling/Aspern, massing and commanding the 200-gun battery that defeated the outnumbered French artillery.

He also distinguished himself at Wagram in 1809, that same year being named a commandant in the Order of Maria-Theresa on 24 May for his outstanding service at Essling. In April 1813 he was promoted to *Generalmajor* and was designated Hiller's Artillery Chief. His son was also a distinguished artillery officer. He was undoubtedly the foremost Austrian artilleryman of the period, but, unfortunately, is a relatively unknown officer. His exploit with his reinforced cavalry battery at Neerwinden in 1793 demonstrated that he both knew his business and that he was an aggressive and imaginative officer who deserved to be promoted. It also showed that he could think for himself in a pinch and understood the principle of massed artillery fire and infantry/artillery cooperation. Unfortunately, he was the exception and not the rule in the Austrian service. That he was only a colonel in 1809 was truly a shame. He looked like a cherub in uniform, but he had the heart of a lion and the head to be able to think quickly.

Coignet described the effect of massed artillery fire against formed troops in line at Essling:

A second cannon ball struck the drum sergeant. One of my comrades went immediately and took off his stripes and epaulets and brought them to me. I thanked him, and pressed his hand. This was only a prelude. To the left of Essling the enemy planted fifty guns in front of us. I felt an urgent call to relieve nature, but it was strictly against orders to move a step towards the rear. There was no alternative but to go forward in advance of the line, which I did; and, having put down my musket, I began operations with my behind to the enemy. All at once a cannon ball came along, ricocheted within a yard of me, and threw a hail of earth and stones all over my back. Luckily for me I still had my pack on, or I should have perished.

Picking up my musket with one hand and my trousers with the other, black and blue behind, I was on my way back to my post when the major, seeing the state I was in, came galloping up. "What's this?" said he; "Are you wounded?" "It's nothing major; they wanted to wipe my breech for me, but they didn't succeed." "Ah! Well, have a drink of rum to pull you together."

He took a flask in a wicker case from his pistol holster, and held it out in front of me. "After you, if you please." "Take a good pull! Can you get back alone?" "Yes," I answered. He galloped away, and I moved off again, with my musket in one hand and my trousers in the other, bringing up the rear, and was soon back in my place in the ranks. "Well, Coignet," said Captain Renard, "that was a near thing." "It was, sir; their paper's too hard, and I couldn't use it. They're a lot of swine." And then followed hand-shakes all round with my officers and comrades.

The fifty guns of the Austrians thundered upon us without our being able to advance a step, or fire a shot. Imagine the agony we endured in such a position, for I can never describe it. We had only four of our own guns in front of us, and two in front of the chasseurs, with which to answer fifty. The balls fell among our ranks, and cut down our men three at a time; the shells knocked the bearskin caps twenty feet in the air. As each file was cut down, I called out, "Right dress, close up the ranks!" And the brave grenadiers closed up without a frown, saying to one another as they saw the enemy making ready to fire, "The next one's for me." "Good, I'm behind you; that's the best place; keep cool."

A ball struck a whole file, and knocked them all three head over heels on top of me. I fell to the ground. "Keep cool," I called out; "close up at once." "But, sergeant, the hilt of your saber is gone, your cartridge pouch is half cut off." "That's nothing; the battle is not over yet."

. . . A shell fell and burst near out good general, covering him with dirt, but he rose up like the brave soldier that he was, saying, "Your general is not hurt. You may depend upon him, he will know how to die at his post." He had no horse any longer; two had been killed under him. How grateful the country ought to be for such men! The awful thunder continued. A cannon ball cut down a file of soldiers next to me. Something struck me on the arm, and I dropped my musket. I thought my arm was cut off. I had no feeling in it. I looked, and saw a bit of flesh sticking to my wrist. I thought I had broken my arm, but I had not; it was a piece of the flesh of one of my brave comrades, which had been dashed against me with such violence that it had stuck to my arm. The lieutenant came up to me, took hold of my arm, shook it, and the piece of flesh fell off. I saw the cloth of my coat. He shook my arm, and said to me, "It is only numbed." Imagine my joy when I found I could move my fingers! The commander said to me, "Leave your musket and take your saber." "I have none; the cannon ball cut off the hilt of it." I took my musket in my left hand.

The losses became very heavy. We had to place the Guard all in one rank so as to keep up the line in front of the enemy. As soon as this movement had been made, a stretcher was brought up on our left, borne by grenadiers, who deposited their precious burden in our center. The Emperor, from the top of his pine tree, recognized his favorite, left his post of observation, and hurried to receive the last words of Marshal Lannes, who had been mortally wounded at the head of his corps. The Emperor knelt upon one knee, took him in his arms, and had him carried over to the island; but he did not survive the amputation. This ended the career of that great general. We were all filled with dismay at our great loss.[5]

Elzear Blaze added his comments on the sheer terror of being hit by artillery fire:

There are men, however, who, gifted with an extraordinary strength of spirit, can cold-bloodily face the greatest dangers. Murat, bravest of the brave, always charged at the head of his cavalry, and never returned without blood on his saber. That can easily be understood, but what I have seen General Dorsenne do—and [have] never have seen it done by anyone else—was to stand motionless, his back to the enemy, facing his bullet-riddled regiment, and say, "Close up your ranks," without once looking behind him. On other occasions I have tried to emulate him. I tried to turn my back to the enemy, but I could never remain in that position—curiosity always made me look to see where all those bullets were coming from.[6]

Smola's expertly handled artillery silenced the outnumbered French artillery. Then, the artillerymen "lifted and shifted" their fire onto the now helpless, and largely defenseless, French infantry, that had to stand and take it—or the army would have been driven into the Danube. General Pouzet, a longtime friend of Marshal Lannes, was killed, and St Hilaire was mortally wounded, having a foot blown off by artillery fire. Lannes saw his friend being taken to the rear in a blanket, and he was later hit by a roundshot which shattered both knees, mortally wounding him. Both he and St Hilaire would die in great agony after the battle was over and they had been evacuated. Lannes could not save them.

II Corps' casualty lists were growing from the almost overwhelming rain of roundshot coming down on them. There was a panic among some of the units, who attempted to go to the rear. They ran into *Général* Dorsenne at the head of the Old Guard infantry, who did not flinch from the heavy and destructive Austrian artillery fire, and whose example kept the conscripts of II Corps to their duty.

What the Austrians needed to do now, under the heavy artillery bombardment, was to launch an all-out coordinated attack on the French. Lannes' II Corps was almost being overwhelmed. The Old Guard infantry, Napoleon's last reserve, was in place, but suffering heavily from the Austrian fire. The French artillery was out of the game, having taken heavy losses that could not be immediately replaced. But no Austrian assault took place. Perhaps Charles could not get his infantry to go into the fire just one more time. There are indications by some historians that the Austrian infantry had refused to advance after their last repulse at the hands of Lannes' infantry. Whatever the case, the Austrian infantry had been repeatedly defeated or held in check by inferior numbers of French and Confederation of the Rhine troops, and their cavalry had been whipped by Bessières' hard-riding and hard-fighting horsemen. Only in artillery had the Austrians been superior, and the reason for that had been because not only numbers of guns, but also their expert employment by *Oberst* Smola.

Whatever the case, the fighting had flickered out by 1600 on 22 May, and the Grande Armée, which had suffered between 19,000 and 20,000 casualties—almost half of the troops engaged at Essling—began to withdraw to Lobau island. The withdrawal was orderly and well-executed, the wounded being shown every consideration. The Austrians refrained from interfering. Their own losses, though not of the same proportion to their engaged strength as those of the French, were heavier in actual numbers, at 23,400. This was Napoleon's first battlefield defeat since 1796. Smola had a lion's share in the Austrian victory, but four more years would elapse before he was promoted to major general. Charles was satisfied with an ordinary victory. Had he at least tried, he could have finished off the French Army on the east bank of the Danube. As it was, he allowed Napoleon to recover and eventually defeat him at Wagram in July.

Napoleon is usually heavily criticized for the hasty river crossing of a major waterway in the face of the enemy. The French did feel undefeated. The next time they would cross the Danube, it would be a major, well-planned, and well-executed, deliberate operation, with bridges that could be swung out into the waterway between Lobau and the east bank and emplaced in five minutes, and the main bridges across the Danube would be properly protected from waterborne objects launched against them. French naval units and armed landing craft would be employed, and the French would control the islands in the Danube and cross behind a well-planned artillery deployment.

As for the Grande Armée, it believed that the only thing that had beaten it was the river:

> ... had the bridge held an hour or so longer, [Napoleon] would have won a decisive victory—which would have been hailed as a masterpiece of daring initiative. The French had fought magnificently. The Danube, and not the Austrians, defeated us.[7]

Smola's concentration of a huge artillery battery—larger than any French concentration of the period—is noteworthy. Smola, one of the best artillerymen in any army, presented his commander with an opportunity to drive the units of the Grande Armée on the north bank of the Danube into the river, perhaps capturing or killing Napoleon in the process. That achievement could have ended the wars, and could certainly have put France in chaos. Had her army been decisively defeated and her Emperor killed or captured, the entire strategic position in Europe would have changed, and placed Austria and her army in an enviable position, especially from the point of view of prestige.

However, Charles's satisfaction with an "ordinary" victory left the issue undecided. The explanation probably lies in his innate caution, the result of his experience and military education. Never one to bet everything on one throw of the die, he was satisfied with defeating the outnumbered French, forcing them to retire. He was, in the final outcome, an eighteenth-century general facing a commander, and an army, that went for the throat in every encounter.

As for *Oberst* Smola, soon to be promoted and decorated for his outstanding performance, one may wonder why he did not exploit the advantage he had created at Essling. There was no attempt to move the artillery into canister range to create a significant advantage, as Senarmont did in 1807 at Friedland or as Drouot did at Lützen in 1813. Neither was there an attempt at an "economy of force" move as Senarmont employed at Ocana in Spain, where he used his artillery aggressively on the Spanish left flank, completely "occupying" that part of the Spanish Army while the French massed against its right and center and drove it off the field, inflicting crippling losses.

The opportunity created by Smola with the silencing of the French artillery could have been exploited by maneuvering his own artillery forward into canister range, destroying part of the French line, allowing a decisive attack to crush the French center, and pocketing both flanks against the river. This was not done, and the French retired intact, albeit with heavy losses, to Lobau to cross again, this time decisively, in July. While Smola's artillery concentration was masterly and effective, it did not lead to a decisive Austrian victory, as French artillery employment frequently did: it merely added to the already long casualty list arising out of indecisive confrontations.

NOTES

1. For background material on the campaign see Esposito and Elting, *A Military History and Atlas of the Napoleonic Wars.* The Austrian viewpoint is given in the General Staff study "Krieg 1809:" Eugene's operations are covered in Epstein, *Prince Eugène at War.*

2. The shortcomings of the Austrian General Staff are duly noted in Rothenberg, *Napoleon's Great Adversary: Archduke Charles and the Austrian Army 1792–1814*, and *The Army of Francis Joseph.* See also Gordon Craig, "Command and Staff Problems in the Austrian Army" in Michael Howard, *The Theory and Practice of War*; for the "other side of the hill," see Elting, *Swords Around a Throne*; Martin van Creveld, *Command in War*; and Griffith, *The Art of War in Revolutionary France.*

3. For the bridging problems over the Danube, see Douglas, *An Essay on the Principles and Construction of Military Bridges &c.* The second crossing was one of the best planned and best executed operations of the period. Naval gunboats patrolled the river. Islands were held and fortified, batteries being constructed to support both an amphibious landing and crossing. Armed landing craft manned by sailors (who also manned the gunboats) were constructed, and a prefabricated pontoon bridge was built and swung into place for the crossing in early July.

4. Esposito and Elting, *op. cit.*, Map 102.
5. Coignet, *The Notebooks of Captain Coignet*, pp. 176-9.
6. Elzear Blaze, *Military Life Under Napoleon*, pp. 101-2.
7. Esposito and Elting, *op. cit.*, Map 102.

Chapter 9

Ramsay

Many a time it falleth out that most men employed for gunners are very negligent of the fear of God.

—Anonymous Puritan

The enemy came to us. They are beaten. God be praised! I have been a little tired all day. I bid you good-night and am going to bed.

—Turenne

1000, 5 May 1811: Near Fuentes d'Oñoro, Portugal

Captain Norman Ramsay, second in command of Bull's Troop, Royal Horse Artillery (RHA), stood behind his section of two 6-pounders, which were loaded, primed, and ready to fire. The troop were engaged in a delaying action against the French cavalry, and had been withdrawing and reemplacing for most of the morning. Sometimes they fired, sometimes not, but the constant movement, as well as having the battery deployed in sections and not as a single entity against what appeared to be a very large French force, was proving somewhat tiring– and very unnerving.

The French cavalry were rallying and getting ready for another go at them, and the infantry of the Light Division on either side of them was preparing to withdraw. Commands were being shouted by the company commanders, and the battalions' drums were rattling away, echoing those commands up and down the line. British cavalry thundered past them, going at the French one more time, and it was definitely time to go.

Ramsay didn't have a trumpeter, but as he commanded only his section, two guns, he didn't need one. He bellowed to his section to limber up, and the gun captains prepared the guns for withdrawal as the limbers came up, each drawn by six horse teams. As they trotted into position, raising the interminable, and unavoidable, cloud of dust, the infantry were rapidly displacing, and were soon out of sight in the dust and mess. Suddenly, cavalry roared past with a shout and a wave, and Ramsay's guns were just then limbered and ready to go.

Without warning, Ramsay's section was engulfed in a cloud of horsemen uniformed in dark green and shouting in French. Instantly he realized that he was surrounded by the enemy and was in grave danger of being captured, along with his guns and crews. Without hesitation, he turned to his shocked gunners, drew his saber, and shouted "Charge!" above the crash and din of combat. Leading off at the gallop, he took his section at and he hoped through, the engulfing French cavalry. They would either make their lines or die trying.

*   *   *

The British artillery, excellent in both personnel and equipment, was not employed in mass in the Peninsula. In 1809 there were only five batteries with the field army, and these included the batteries of the excellent King's German Legion. Fortunately for them, the Portuguese artillery arm fielded enough batteries to make up for the shortage to a degree, and to allow Wellington to attach at least one battery to each of his divisions and actually create a small artillery reserve.

While both branches of the Royal Artillery served well and ably, the Royal Horse Artillery (RHA) stood out as a true *corps d'élite* under such battery officers as Hew Ross and Norman Ramsay. No battle of the Peninsular War stands out as an example of how technically and tactically proficient the RHA actually was than that at Fuentes d'Oñoro in May 1811. It lasted over a three-day period, 3-5 May, an involved Wellington's Anglo-Portuguese Army and Marshal Massena's Army of Portugal. That it was finally won by the Allied army is a tribute to the steadfastness of the troops, and the skill of their commanders.

The strategic situation was somewhat grim for Massena and his long-suffering Army of Portugal in the spring of 1811. Blooded and defeated at Bussaco, and then starved and checkmated by the famous Lines of Torres Vedras, Massena was determined to give battle one more time to try to defeat the British and their Portuguese allies and to save his military reputation. Having been driven out of Portugal, Massena's army was in bad shape. It was hungry and hard-used, and Wellington had expected that it would be quite some time before Massena could refit and rebuild his shattered divisions and take the field again. Wellington badly underestimated his enemy in this respect.

Moving against the fortress of Almeida and investing it, Wellington wanted to advance into Spain and take the war to the French. Massena rapidly responded, ostensibly to relieve the Almeida garrison, which later broke out and escaped. More probably, Massena's objective was to fight again and attempt to destroy the Allied army. This was to be his last fight, but one which Wellington remarked upon, stating that, had Napoleon been present, the Allies would have been defeated.[1]

Most of the fighting centered around the village of Fuentes d'Oñoro, and it was bloody, bitter, and prolonged. The engagements on 3 May were indecisive, and the contest resumed on the 5th, both armies determined to drive their opponents from the field. The heaviest fighting took place on that day, though there had been hard fighting in the village on the 3rd. At the end of it, any French gains in the village had been taken back by the resolute action of the British infantry, and the two exhausted combatants were facing each other on opposite sides of the Dos Casas river, which ran in front of the village. The hours of 4 May were, interestingly, mostly hours of rest and maneuver for the two armies, Massena trying to jockey for position and Wellington trying to guess what Massena might try next.

Massena planned to renew his attack on the village on the 5th; this would be the main French effort. A supporting attack, intended to take Wellington's attention away from the village, was to be mounted against the British right flank, which included the weakest division in the army, the 7th, with only two battalions—and those were newly arrived in country. Most of the French cavalry under Montbrun, who was considered the most skillful of Napoleon's senior cavalry commanders, and two divisions of infantry from Loison's corps would make this attack.

The movement was initially successful, Montbrun sweeping the British cavalrymen of the 16th Light Dragoons, the 1st Hussars of the KGL, and the 14th Light Dragoons before them. It seemed to the Allies that the French cavalry filled the plain. Some of the 85th Foot and the 2nd Portuguese Cazadores were caught in the open and overrun, and the two French infantry divisions of Marchand and Mermet were following on the heels of the cavalry's success to consolidate what had been gained. The 7th Allied Division was mauled, but it was not cut off, and Wellington's quick-witted response to the French success was to issue orders to form a new line at right angles to the Allied left using the village of Fuentes d'Oñoro as a pivot.

The swirling cavalry action on the British right flank was a mask for the withdrawal of the Allied 7th Division. "Black Bob" Crauford's elite Light Division came up to relieve pressure on

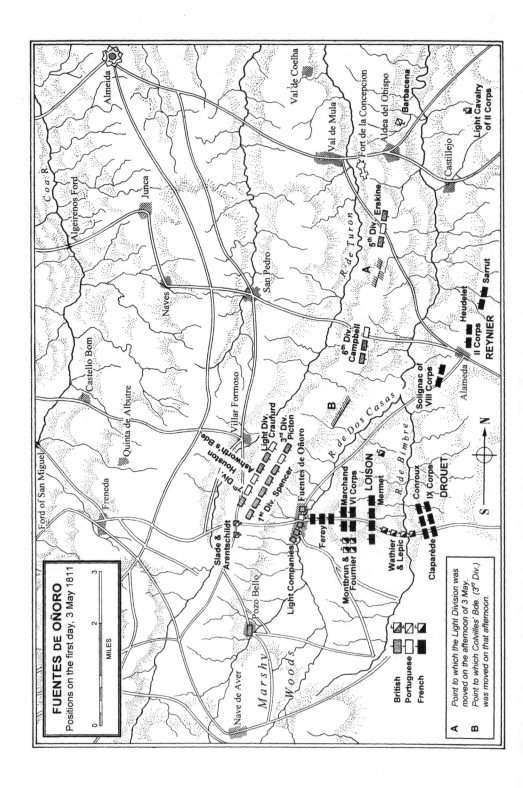

FUENTES DE OÑORO
Positions on the first day, 3 May 1811

MILES
0   1   2   3

British
Portuguese
French

A   *Point to which the Light Division was moved on the afternoon of 3 May.*

B   *Point to which Colvilles' Bde. (3rd Div.) was moved on that afternoon.*

N

Coa R.
Almeida
Algeirenos Ford
Junca
Castello Bom
Quinta de Albutre
Freneda
Ford of San Miguel
Pozo Bello
Nave de Aver
Marshy Woods
Villar Formoso
Naves
San Pedro
Val de Coelha
Val de Mula
Fort de la Concepcion
Aldea del Obispo
Barbacena
Light Cavalry of II Corps
Castillejo
R. de Turon
5th Div. Erskine
A
6th Div. Campbell
B
R. de Dos Casas
Light Companies
Slade & Arentschildt
Houston's Div.
Ashworth's Bde.
Light Div. Craufurd
3rd Div. Picton
1st Div. Spencer
Fuentes de Oñoro
Ferey
Montbrun & Fournier
Marchand VI Corps
Mermet
LOISON
Wathier & Lepic
Claparéde
Conroux IX Corps
DROUET
Solignac of VIII Corps
R. de Bimbre
Alameda
Heudelet
II Corps
REYNIER
Sarrut

Houston's 7th Division so that it could settle into its newly assigned positions and slide to the right, becoming the far right flank of Wellington's army. The tactical skill of the British infantry commanders made the sacrifice of the British and German light cavalry, who were gradually being overwhelmed by Montbrun, worthwhile. Artillery was brought up on both sides: a battery of horse artillery that had accompanied Montbrun's troopers went into action, as did some foot artillery with the infantry divisions, for a total of fifteen French guns on the field.

With Crauford's Light Division came Bull's Troop, RHA, the second-in-command of which was Captain Norman Ramsay. The light infantrymen and the horse artillerymen went to work with a will, covering the remnants of the British horsemen as they retreated, regrouped, and charged the French cavalry yet one more time. Bull's battery was broken up into two-gun sections, Ramsay commanding one of them. The sections were put between the squares of Allied light infantry with the cavalry in support. The division was now to withdraw into the space in the new line left by the 7th Division's move to the far right flank.

It was slow, nerve-racking work. The stately squares withdrew in perfect order, covered by the guns and light cavalry, only stopping to fire or show a bold front when the French cavalry got too close. The guns, in their turn, would fire a few rounds, limber up quickly and displace to the next position to cover the cavalry's and infantry's withdrawals. The cavalry would charge as the guns displaced. It was a careful and methodical maneuver: if there were the slightest error, the guns could be overrun and lost.

That is almost exactly what happened next. Ramsay may have stayed in position too long: perhaps his gunners and drivers were tired from the constant strain of a planned withdrawal; then again, maybe the French cavalry saw an advantage and went for the guns, sensing an opportunity to hurt their frustrating enemy. Whatever it was, as Ramsay's section was limbering up getting ready for one of their withdrawals, they were engulfed by French light cavalry, *chasseurs à cheval*, the French troopers sensing victory and trophies. The quick-witted Ramsay, staying cool in what was clearly a fluid situation, bellowed to his gunners and drivers and led them in a "charge" towards the Allied line. Startled at the British artilleryman's unexpected action, the French troopers were momentarily thrown off balance. Gathering their senses, they set off in pursuit, some of them neck and neck with the gun team horses.

The horse artillerymen fought off the French light cavalrymen with saber and boot, the mass in a billowing dust bowl, the British drivers bending low over their team horses so as not to make too big a target. The horses strained at their harnesses, pulling their guns and limbers with great effort, sweat pouring from them, their foam-flecked hides shimmering in the sunlight, and the foam from their mouths spraying the troopers of both sides who surrounded them.

The British line was visible, and it is not be too difficult to imagine what the British infantry thought of this once-in-a-lifetime spectacle. Two British cavalry squadrons, one each from the bloodied 14th Light Dragoons and from the 1st Royal Dragoons, dashed to Ramsay's rescue, fighting off the intrepid French cavalrymen who were still vainly trying to stop Ramsay from escaping.

As they reached the new British line amid cheering from the incredulous British troops, the artillerymen had to be both relieved and exhausted. Horses, stopping, undoubtedly were shivering in the letdown after such a mad dash. Gunners slid from saddles to collapse on the ground, or took well-deserved swigs from their canteens, some of which were not doubt filled with liquid other than water.

Ramsay and his gunners were immortalized by Sir William Napier, the soldier-historian who had served in the Peninsula, but was not always accurate in his recollection:

... a great commotion was observed amongst the French squadrons; men and officers closed in confusion towards one point where a thick dust was rising, and where loud cries and sparkling of blades and flashing of pistols indicated some extraordinary occurrence. Suddenly the multitude was violently agitated, an English shout arose, the mass was rent asunder, and Norman Ramsay burst forth at the head of his battery, his horses breathing fire and stretching like greyhounds along the plain, his guns bounding like things of no weight; and the mounted gunners in close and compact order protecting the rear.

Sir Charles Oman, in his epic *History of the Peninsular War*, states that

Captain Norman Ramsay, with two guns of Bull's troop, had halted, not for the first time, for a shot or two at the pursuing cavalry; lingering a moment too long, he found himself cut off, just as he had limbered up, by a swarm of chasseurs, who rode in from the flank. But he put his guns to the gallop, and, charging himself in front of them with the mounted gunners, was cutting his way through the French when he was brought off by friends. On one side a squadron of the 14th Light dragoons under Brotherton, on the other a squadron of the Royals, had turned back when they saw the artillery in danger. They fell upon the chasseurs before Ramsay had suffered any hurt, and saved him and his guns, which were brought into the lines of the 1st Division amid loud cheers from all who had seen the affair.[2]

As to the rest of the action, Fuentes d'Oñoro was not taken by the French, and the movement of Wellington's right flank was successful: he had won, but only just. Casualties for the Allies were 192 killed, 958 wounded, and 255 taken prisoner; the French had lost 267 killed in action, 1,878 wounded, and 47 captured. It was a hard-fought action on both sides, and Wellington's comment that he never slept well when opposing Massena was undoubtedly based on his experience at Fuentes d'Oñoro. Finally, as a result of this action the French were ejected from Portugal, and Massena was relieved by Marshal Auguste Marmont on 11 May.

Some of the British artillerymen who performed so superbly in the Peninsula and at Waterloo were in great measure responsible for making Wellington a conqueror. They were skilled professionals, and without them the success of the British in Spain and Portugal might have been far different, for they also trained and cadred the excellent raw material that became the Portuguese artillery arm that so strengthened Wellington's army.

Alexander Dickson (1777-1840) was commissioned into the Royal Artillery in 1794. The son of Admiral William Dickson, he was not only an outstanding artilleryman who worked his way up the command ladder by sheer competence, but a talented organizer, logistician, and combat leader. He ended up as Wellington's artillery commander in Spain, though to get him into that eventual position it was necessary to have him commissioned into the allied Portuguese artillery to overcome the somewhat archaic seniority rules of the service. It is interesting to note that, with all of his command and combat experience, his actual, or "regimental," rank in the Royal Artillery during the period was that of captain, though his brevet and Portuguese rank was lieutenant colonel.

After the Peninsular War, he served in North America at New Orleans, and because of that delay had to serve in the Waterloo campaign as the commander of the siege train, as Sir George Wood had already been appointed as the artillery commander of Wellington's polyglot organization. Before going to the Peninsula he served at Malta and Buenos Aires, and his skill, devotion, and courage earned him Wellington's trust. He was one of the few officers who can be seen wearing glasses in a portrait; even Davout did not do that. In 1822 he was appointed Inspector of Artillery, and eventually reached the rank of major general. He left a very interesting and accurate set of letters, *The Dickson Manuscript*, which is a treasure trove of information relating to the British Army, and to the artillery in Spain and Portugal in particular.

Wellington's horse artilleryman was Augustus Frazer (1776-1835). Born in France at Dunkirk, the son of a Royal Engineer, and junior to Dickson, Frazer rose to command the horse artillery

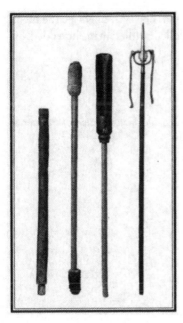

British artillery sidearms. From left to right: handspike, sponge, powder ladle, linstock.

in Spain in 1812 as well as in Belgium in 1815. His service record included the Netherlands in 1794-95 and 1799 as well as Buenos Aires. He knew Dickson, and, judging by the correspondence in Dickson's *Manuscript*, the two men got along very well. Apparently on his professional insistence, the British horse artillery troops were equipped with 9-pounders instead of the regulation 6-pounders for the Waterloo campaign. He was considered "a thorough soldier, a perfect gentleman, a delightful companion, and a modest and unassuming man." Frazer was knighted in 1814, and after Waterloo was promoted to colonel in 1825. He was Director of the Woolwich Laboratory from 1828 until his death in 1835.

The Royal Horse Artillery was consistently well trained and well led during the course of the wars, and three captains personify the dash, spirit, and skill of this elite branch of a distinguished fighting arm. Norman Ramsay (1782-1815), of Fuentes d'Oñoro fame, was the eldest of three sons of a retired Royal Navy officer. He entered the Army in 1798 and was subsequently sent to Egypt as an artilleryman. He went to the Peninsula, where he was second in command of Bull's Troop, RHA, and served throughout the Peninsular War. He was a highly skilled and aggressive officer who liked to use his own initiative. This trait could cause trouble with Wellington, and for Ramsay it did. He disobeyed one of Wellington's orders at Vittoria in 1813, moving his battery to a troublespot during the action—but contributing to the British victory by so doing. Nevertheless, Wellington placed him under arrest, and the brevet he was expecting was "withheld," as was the Mention in Despatches that he fully deserved. Wellington, however, for whatever reason, restored him to full duty after three weeks in the ducal doghouse, and he gained his brevet in November 1813. Wellington might have felt that he had been unjust. After Ramsay's restoration to full duty, Wellington saw him in the field as he one day galloped past his subordinate's artillery position, and raised his hand to wave with a shout. Ramsay did not return it. In 1815, Ramsay commanded H Troop, RHA, and was killed in action at Waterloo. Buried on the field, he was later disinterred and brought home for his final resting place.

Hew Ross (1779-1868) was commissioned as an artillery officer in 1798 and was the commander of A Troop, RHA, from 1806 until after Waterloo. An immensely skilled and experienced officer, he was assigned to the famous Light Division throughout the war in Spain and Portugal, being breveted twice in the Peninsula—to major in December 1811 and to lieutenant colonel after the Battle of Vittoria in 1813. Ross was wounded at the Siege of Badajoz but served with distinction at Waterloo, which he survived, later becoming a general and a field marshal. An outstanding artilleryman, he was much revered in the Light Division, and was one of the best small-unit commanders in the British Army.

Cavalie Mercer (1783-1868) had only one combat tour during his service—at Waterloo. The son of a general, he was commissioned into the artillery in 1799. He did serve in South America, but he missed the war in Spain and Portugal. He commanded G Troop, RHA, at Waterloo, where he performed with distinction. His greatest contribution, however, might be the memoir of 1815, *Journal of the Waterloo Campaign*. A dashing, skilled artilleryman, he ended his career as a major general.

NOTES

1.   Background information can be obtained in David Gates, *The Spanish Ulcer: A History of the Peninsular War*, as well as Oman, *A History of the Peninsular War*, vol. IV.
2.   Oman, *op. cit.*, p. 327.

Chapter 10

Eble

I've fooled the Admiral. He thinks I'm at the spot where I've ordered the feint attack.
He's hurrying off to Borisov.
—Napoleon

Our position's unheard of. If Napoleon gets away with it today he's the devil himself.
—Ney to Rapp at the Berezina

*All honor to the French. Honor to the nation that bred such men! And shame on the cowards who
would tarnish the glory they earned—a glory even more precious than the laurels coveted by their
descendants, and that of the Europeans who were never able to beat them . . .*
—Caulaincourt

0400, 26 November 1812: Studenka, the Ukraine

The distinctive sound of hammers striking iron rang through the snow-covered pine forests
and across the ice-choked river, undoubtedly within range of curious Muscovite ears. The
artilleryman stood near the eastern bank of the Berezina river at the fording place that had
been luckily found by General Corbineau's cavalry on the 17th. He gazed across the river into
the pine forests and swamps: they were the way home, but they could equally be filled with
Russians ready either to stop their attempted crossing or to throw them back into the river
when they tried.

Behind him, troops were still taking apart, plank by plank, the village of Studenka, throwing
the unfortunate inhabitants who still remained onto the mercy of the Russian winter. Some of
his *pontonniers* were assembling the trestles for the two bridges they had to construct across this
river, one for cavalry and artillery, the other for infantry, to get the army across and to the
relative safety of the western bank. French cavalry had reported Tshitshagov's army on the
other side of the river, but further to the south. They also knew that Wittgenstein was following Victor, who was to be the army's rearguard for the crossing. So, there would be a fight for
the Berezina crossing. It might have to be a fight to the finish.

Pontonniers carrying completed trestles were bringing them forward under cover of the river
bank in preparation for taking them into the water. Others were building rafts, in company
with the attached sailors who were going to be needed when the bridges were put together in
the middle of the river. It was going to be cold work for the *pontonniers*, the sailors, and the few
engineers that he and Chasseloup, the army engineer, had assembled for this undertaking. The
400 men of the 1st *Pontonnier* Battalion would have to bear the brunt of the work, as they were
the only men in the army who had the requisite tools for the job.

At Orsha, the Emperor had ordered all excess vehicles burnt, to lighten the army and give
more horses to the artillery. The artilleryman had bitterly protested at the burning of the
pontoon train, but the Emperor had been adamant. Reluctantly obeying, he had the pontoons
and their *hacquets* dutifully added to the resultant bonfire. He had, however, ordered his officers to keep two field forges and eight wagons filled with the necessary charcoal. Additionally,
each of the *pontonniers* was ordered to carry spikes and clamps, along with a tool. This decision

now bore fruit as the Emperor needed two bridges; the bridge over the Berezina that he had optimistically counted on at Borisov had been captured and later burned by the Russians.

The artillery of Oudinot's II Corps was going into position on the ridge behind him, ready to cover the bridge building and the crossing. Hammers still rang out from the field forges, all the ironwork needed for the bridges being forged on the bank. The *pontonniers* would soon be ready. The army was either waking up in the cold of a Russian winter or moving into position. Turning to an orderly to give the word that the bivouac fires were to be kept burning to warm those coming out of the river, Général Eble, commander of the pontoon units of the Grande Armée, turned and walked away from the freezing water to see to his men.

*   *   *

It may seem curious in a volume on field artillery to recount an fight wherein the decisive action was the construction of two trestle bridges—usually an engineer's specialty, which allowed an army which was apparently surrounded by enemies to escape. In actuality, it is not. The two bridges were constructed by French *pontonniers*, with some engineers and sailors attached to them. *Pontonniers* in the Grande Armée were artillerymen, as were most of the pontoon units in European armies of the period. The entire bridging enterprise was commanded by an artilleryman, Général Jean-Baptiste Eble, a legendary figure in the ranks of the Grande Armée even before the amazing feat at the Berezina.

There had been a long and bitter argument in the French Army over who should control the *pontonnier* units after they came into being during the Revolutionary Wars. They were initially composed of Rhine bargemen. The engineers believed they should control them, as they built bridges—which was an engineering mission, not a task for the artillery. However, the engineers had until quite recently been a corps composed entirely of officers, and had only lately been allowed to have battalions of engineer troops raised and trained specifically for engineer-type missions. Therefore, the argument was settled in favor of the artillery, at least for the time being, since that arm had the greater assets and the ability to support the Army's pontoon units and train.[1]

The crossing of the Berezina is usually depicted, and therefore seen, as a disaster, thousands of fugitives of the Grande Armée streaming across two rickety bridges built in desperation from the wood of a dismantled Russian village. The usual picture is of a defeated army, further ruined by cold, hunger, and deprivation, running from two Russian armies and lucky that its survivors actually get across the bridges to the dubious safety of the "friendly" side of the river. For some of the Grande Armée, that is an accurate picture; for the rest, it is not.

The Russian campaign saw the employment of the largest army Europe had ever seen. Napoleon had assembled a mass of nearly 600,000 men in ten *corps d'armée*, four cavalry corps, and the Imperial Guard. It was the most thoroughly prepared and provisioned force that Napoleon had ever commanded. Nearly every facet of what the army needed had been seen to. Besides the normal preparations, a siege train had been prepared to accompany the army, naval troops had been attached for the invasion, and a large pontoon train was also ready for action. It was also a polyglot army: a little over one-half of the infantry was foreign, as was one-third of his cavalry. His artillery also had many foreign elements, but that arm was also huge—over 1,100 guns were taken into Russia.

Supply train battalions were activated for the invasion, and depots were established in Poland and along the French line of communication as the Grande Armée advanced deeper into Russia. Davout's corps was the best-trained and best-equipped in the army, on a par with the

Imperial Guard. Napoleon's plan was to outmaneuver and trap the Russian Army close inside their own border, and then dictate peace to Tsar Alexander. The Russian armies were heavily outnumbered at the outset of the campaign. Their original plans failed, and they withdrew deeper into Russia. Napoleon's advance seemed overly cautious, and the decisive battle seemed to elude him.

The French advanced on a broad front, with subordinate forces on the northern flank under Macdonald and St Cyr in the north and Schwarzenberg and Reynier in the south. While there were clashes and minor fights, along with larger battles such as Smolensk, the Russians kept withdrawing into the interior. There is no evidence of any Russian plan to draw the French deeper into the interior of Russia, but it happened anyway. Finally, a new Russian commander of the main army, Kutusov, who had replaced the more competent Barclay de Tolly, stopped the retreat and offered battle to the French at Borodino, about 70 miles west of Moscow. It was a huge, sprawling, bloody fight, marked by over 70,000 casualties in total, but it was indecisive. The Russians bolted for Moscow early in the morning after the battle, and Napoleon entered Moscow during the afternoon of 14 September.

Peace, however, was not achieved. Alexander vowed not to make peace as long as the French were on Russian soil (this was probably wise, as his doing so might have prompted the Russian nobility to end his reign as abruptly as they had his father's), and after "a campaign unequaled since those of Genghis Khan,"[2] Napoleon was in a quandary. His army had lost heavily both in battle and through sickness and wastage. He occupied the traditional Russian capital (to which the Russian governor of the city, perhaps in collusion with Kutusov, promptly set fire, and most of the buildings going up in smoke and flames as a result), but the campaign was not over, and the Russians had not capitulated.

Napoleon left Moscow in October, planning an 1813 campaign after wintering in Smolensk. His projected route of withdrawal was blocked by the Russians at Maloyaroslavets. The subsequent action there convinced Napoleon to fall back along his invasion route, even though Kutusov had been thoroughly whipped. This led to a lack of supplies and forage, and with the onset of winter in November, and a decidedly lackluster performance by Napoleon as army commander, as well as many of his subordinates, indiscipline in the Grande Armée led to straggling, casualties, and a developing mob that followed those still with their units on the way out of Russia.

The general situation facing the Grande Armée in November 1812 was poor to grim. The retreat from Moscow had taken on the aspects of disaster early on. Instead of retreating along the easier southern route as initially planned, Napoleon launched the Grande Armée on the track that it took on its advance. Officers failed to shake down their troops to ensure that unnecessary articles and plunder were thrown away and only the necessities carried. As a result, nothing was abandoned and the retreat was slow. Exhausted horse teams, overloaded and not properly looked after, collapsed on the roads and died. The administrative officials ignored their responsibilities, and even when provisions were available and plentiful, these officials proved either cowardly or incompetent, or both. Many men left the ranks, out of exhaustion, in a search for food, or simply by giving up. Officers abrogated their responsibilities, and the columns grew longer, and more indisciplined. Stragglers almost overran Davout's rearguard, earning Napoleonic reprimands for moving too slowly. The Grande Armée was defeating itself.

On the positive side, the weather was initially excellent, and the Russians did not immediately pursue the French, probably for two reasons: first, they were as exhausted as their enemy; and secondly, Kutusov had a healthy respect for Napoleon and the Grande Armée. He had

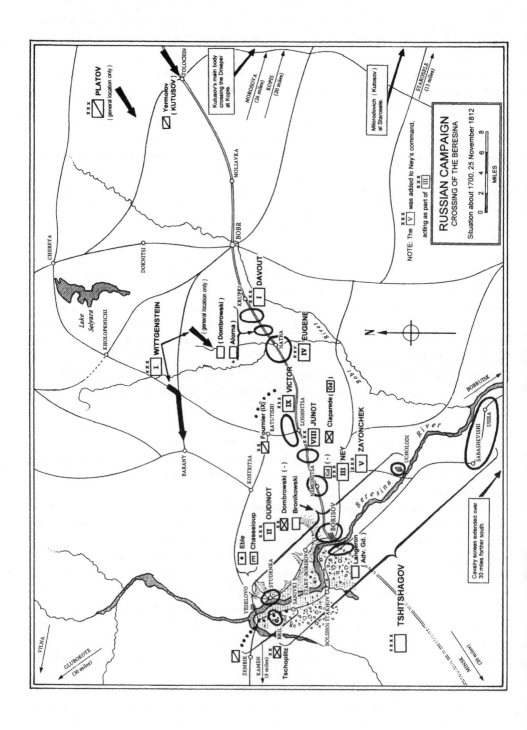

RUSSIAN CAMPAIGN
CROSSING OF THE BERESINA

Situation about 1700, 25 November 1812

0   2   4   6   8
MILES

NOTE: The xxx V was added to Ney's command,
acting as part of III

Kutusov's main body
crossing the Dnieper
at Kopis.

MOROSOVA
(26 miles)
KOPIS
(20 miles)

STAROSELE
(13 miles)

Miloradovich (Kutusov)
at Starosele.

PLATOV
xxx (general location only)

Yermolov
(KUTUSOV)

TOLOCHIN

MOLIAVKA

BOBR

CHEREYA

DOKNITSI

Lake
Selyara

KHOLOPENICHI

WITTGENSTEIN
xxx I
(general location only)

(Dombrowski)
Aloma)
DAVOUT
xxx I
KRUPKI

EUGENE
xxx IV

Bobr River

VICTOR
xxx IX

Fournier (IX)
xx

RATUTISHI

BARANY

KOSTRITSA

LOSHNITSA

JUNOT
xxx VIII

Ciaparede (Gd)

NEY
xxx III

Gd (-)

NEMONITSA

ZAYONCHEK
xxx V

Beresina River

Bobr River

ICHOLODI

SABASHEVISHI

USHA

BOBRUISK

Cavalry screen extended over
30 miles farther south.

MINSK
(30 miles)

OUDINOT
xxx II

Dombrowski (-)
Bronikowski

Eble
Chasseloup

STUDENKA

VESELOYO

BORISOV

Langeron
(Adv. Gd.)

STARY-BORISOV

BOLSHOI STAKHOV

TSHITSHAGOV
xxxx

ZEMBIN

KAMEN
(8 miles)
Tschoplitz
xx

BRIL

VILNA

GLUBOKOYE
(30 miles)

N

been beaten twice in this campaign already, and undoubtedly he had vivid memories of Austerlitz seven years earlier. He had no desire to tempt fate a fourth time. This gun-shy reluctance would have serious strategic consequences later in the campaign:

The largest problem, though, was the Emperor himself. He had become morose and depressed over the unsuccessful campaign, and he seemed to withdraw into himself. No longer riding with his advance guard, overseeing everything and completely in command, he was content to settle in the middle of his Guard on the march westward, leaving both routine and important matters to his staff and subordinate commanders. He failed, at this decisive time in the campaign, to draw on the devotion and skill of his army to withdraw intact and prepare for 1813. Fortunately for the French, Napoleon came to his military senses, and, on or around 15 November, realized the seriousness of the situation. Perhaps it was the desperate fighting at Krasny, where the Young Guard suffered heavy losses, that woke Napoleon out of his funk. Whatever it was, he would be at his best at the Berezina crossing—more than a match for the three Russian army commanders in theater.

The situation grew progressively worse with the main army, however, and outlying corps were called in its support. The corps were straggling on the march, and the army was not keeping together. Ney waited too long, despite a warning from Davout to hurry and catch up, and was cut off by Kutusov. Ney attacked, was repulsed, and had to be rescued by Eugene. Thus situated, the army straggled through Orsha between 17 and 21 November.

Orsha was the site of a large, well-organized depot, with a dedicated and efficient administrative staff. Units were quickly resupplied, and stragglers were rearmed and put back into ranks, and moved on. Napoleon ordered all surplus baggage burned, he himself setting the example. Orsha offered one of the two things the Grande Armée needed—resupply and rearming. The other was rest, which could not be given. Napoleon had to get the army out of Russia and into friendly territory as soon as possible, before it disintegrated through hardship, straggling, and sickness.

Napoleon also overconfidently ordered General Eble, commander of the Army's pontoon train, to burn it, as the Emperor believed it would not be needed: the French were holding the bridge at Borisov on the Berezina river, the last natural obstacle that had to be crossed before the Russia border. Eble protested, was overruled and finally obeyed—to a point. He duly ordered the pontoons and their *hacquets* burnt, but kept two field forges as well as eight supply wagons loaded with coal and tools. Every pontonnier in the command was told to carry a tool, along with spikes and clamps.[3]

Unfortunately for the French, Borisov and its bridge were lost to the Russians on 21 November. Oudinot's cavalry attempted to retake it, but the Russians just managed to burn it under assault from dismounted light cavalry. The Russians lost 350 wagons "loaded with supplies" and over 1,000 prisoners; the French lost the bridge that was their way home.

Oudinot quickly found out that there were two other fords across the river, both upstream. A Polish regiment had discovered one just upriver from Borisov, and Corbineau, the commander of Oudinot's cavalry (which included Marbot's 23rd and Amiel's 24th *Chasseurs à Cheval*), had found one at Studenka, which was more out-of-the-way and shallower than the ford nearer Borisov.

The resulting operations on the Berezina from 23 to 28 November resulted in one of the outstanding victories of the Grande Armée over seemingly insurmountable odds. Indeed, the operations in the vicinity of Studenka deserve to be called masterful. General Berthezène of the Imperial Guard referred to it in this manner as one who fought there:

It has been said that the bridges presented a hideous spectacle due to the crowding and confusion . . . In reality, the crossing of the Berezina in the face of the enemy was a very large military undertaking that reflects further glory on the army and its chief.[4]

Victor, covering the main army's rear, was withdrawing skillfully before Wittgenstein, who was following at a respectful distance. Oudinot, under Napoleon's expert eye, was in the process of both executing his feint and preparing to cross the river and hold the other bank so that the rest of the army could cross behind him. While it is true that there was a mass of stragglers with the army, it is also true that there were still-formed units ready and willing to fight, and commanders more than willing to lead them. One of those commanders was Jean-Baptiste Eble.

While in 1812 General Eble did not have an artillery command *per se*, he did command the pontoon train of the Grande Armée, and in the French service *pontonniers* were artilleryman, not engineers, just as Eble was an artilleryman (starting his commissioned life as a horse artilleryman)—not. as sometimes depicted and described, an engineer. It was because of his single-mindedness, devotion to duty, and farsightedness that the Grande Armée was able to execute an assault river crossing at the Berezina, the last water obstacle on the way out of Russia.

It should be remembered that a river crossing is one of the most complicated military operations to execute. An assault river crossing in the face of one Russian army while being pursued by two more, and defeating two out of the three while the commander of the third declines to participate, is more difficult yet.

Jean-Baptiste Eble (1756–1812), the son of an artillery sergeant, enlisted in the Auxonne Artillery Regiment (later to become the 6th Foot Artillery Regiment), in 1773. He was a sergeant by 1775, and became a sergeant-major in 1779. Commissioned in 1785, he was promoted to captain in 1792 in the 9th Horse Artillery Company. He served in the Armées du Ardennes and Nord from 1792 to 1795. Promoted *chef de bataillon* in 1793, he served at Hondschoote, and later that year he became general of brigade and made the commander of the artillery *parc* in the Army of the Ardennes. He was promoted to general of division also in 1793, becoming the artillery commander in the Armée du Nord. He served at the Sieges of Ypres and Nieuport in 1794, and was the Inspector of Artillery in the Army of Holland in 1795. The next year he was transferred to the Armée du Rhin et Moselle as its artillery commander, and fought at the defense of Kehl. Then transferred to Italy, he was the artillery commander of the Army of Rome, being present at the capture of Capua and Naples. He later transferred to the Armée des Alpes as the artillery commander, and was back in Germany in 1799 in the same capacity in the Armée du Rhin.

In 1801 he was made a member of the Artillery Council, and in 1803 he was sent to Holland to command the artillery troops there. The year 1804 saw Eble commanding the artillery of the Army of Hanover, and as the Grande Armée was activated and eventually was launched into Germany, he was assigned to I Corps as its Artillery Chief, serving at Halle and the storming and capture of Lübeck in 1806. He was assigned as military governor of Magdeburg from 1806 to 1808, and was briefly the commander of the 3rd Westphalian Division, becoming Jerome's Minister of War in Westphalia from 1808 until 1810. In that position he quelled the unrest among Jerome's hastily assembled army, sniffing out the minor and major conspiracies. He was the creator of the Westphalian Army.

Made a Grand Officer of the *Légion d'Honneur* in 1804, he was created a Baron of the Empire in 1808. He was again assigned to the artillery commission in 1810, later that year being sent to the Army of Portugal to command its artillery. He was present at the Sieges of Almeida and Ciudad Rodrigo, and returned to the Artillery Committee in 1811. Eble became the commander of artillery in the Army of Germany in 1811 and was made the commander of the *pontonnier* units for the invasion of Russia in 1812. He served at Smolensk, and he and his indomitable *pontonniers* are famous for their assault crossing of the Berezina in 1812. Because of his performance there, French *pontonnier* officers are authorized to wear golden spurs in full dress. Eble was made Commander of the Artillery of the Grande Armée in place of Lariboissière in December 1812 after the latter's death, but he died of exhaustion at Königsberg at the end of the retreat on 31 December 1812.

Eble was said to have had "the appearance of an ancient Roman;" Bernadotte remarked that he seemed to be a "man out of Plutarch." He was also described as

> . . . tall, taciturn, brusque, energetic, and persevering, he could make artillery units and bridges alike out of the most unpromising materials. Superior as a man, a commander, and a technician. Few friends, but those he had were devoted. Universally admired. Called his soldiers "my comrades," but kept strict discipline—with his fists if necessary.[5]

Pelet, Massena's *aide-de-camp*, knew him in Portugal in 1810 and was impressed by him, and the two men became good friends. He described Eble as "the best and most devoted man in the world and a devil of an artilleryman." Massena, whose Artillery Chief Eble was in Portugal, "treated the brave and dignified Eble with great distinction," and "told the general [Eble] in front of everyone that he was worth more than twenty thousand men to the army." Finally, Pelet described Eble as "the personification of integrity, refinement, and honor, whose firmness and rigor could almost become rudeness."[6]

The crossing of the Berezina is notable for three different operations that went on at the same time, under different commanders. The first was the feint accomplished by Oudinot, which not only masked the actual bridging operations and crossing site, but duped "the Admiral," the Russian commander Tshitshagov, who held the opposite bank of the Berezina and who had taken Borisov and burned its bridge—the bridge Napoleon was counting on using in order to cross the river and get out of Russia. The second was the bridging operation itself, commanded by the indefatigable Eble and accomplished by his redoubtable pontonniers, though at horrible cost to themselves. Lastly, there was Victor's skillful rearguard action against Wittgenstein, the commander of the second Russian army on the field. Victor's hard-held position and operations are noteworthy in that he used a rear-slope defense which defeated every Russian attempt to overrun his position and get to the bridges. This was done without one of the division's of his corps, Partennoux's, most of which was captured by the Russians in the confusion and mess of the withdrawal and cover operations. This constituted the only Russian success of the action.

It is noteworthy that Kutusov, ostensibly pursuing the Grande Armée from Moscow, kept his distance and did not press himself or his army to aid Tshitshagov and Wittgenstein. Possibly he was a victim of poor maps, which plagued the Russians throughout the campaign, even though that campaign was conducted in their own country. It is more likely, however, that Kutusov's tardiness was a reflection of his genuine reluctance to fight Napoleon again, having been beaten twice by the Grande Armée during the campaign, once at Borodino and the second time at Maloyaroslavets.

One of the problems facing the bridging operations was a thaw that had hit and softened the marshes on the west bank of the river. It also made the Berezina wider and somewhat deeper—"in midstream the flood has doubled its normal 3½ foot depth"—making the bridging operations more challenging. This would make operations after crossing, especially for the cavalry and artillery extremely difficult. However, during the night of 23/24 November, winter was back, both banks were frozen and French operations continued.

Oudinot's mission was to make the Russians believe that the French bridging operations would be made in the Borisov area, the site of the destroyed bridge. Told by Napoleon that "You'll be my locksmith," Oudinot successfully fooled the Russians so that they started to withdraw from the woods across from Studenka, moving south to rejoin the Russian main body around Borisov:

> . . . we saw the enemy march off. His masses had vanished. The fires were going out. All we saw were the tails of his columns losing themselves in the woods, and 500 or 600 Cossacks spread about the fields. We examined the matter more closely through our spyglasses, and became convinced he'd really broken camp.[7]

Tshitshagov had been warned by couriers from Kutusov bearing a message: "You have to do with a man as clever as he is cunning. Napoleon will make a demonstration that he is going to cross at one point, to draw your attention to it, while most likely doing it on the other side."[8] This was the last help that either Tshitshagov or Wittgenstein received from Kutusov until after the fighting and the French were across the river.

By 0430 on 25 November, Eble was with Chasseloup, the army engineer, at Borisov. Napoleon and his staff had actually gone out onto the destroyed bridge to be seen by the Russians. Oudinot's feint was very well done, and the Russians swallowed the bait, warning or no warning. Eble left a detachment of *pontonniers* at Borisov to add credence to the bridge repair work, and went north to Studenka to start work on the two trestle bridges that had been decided upon for the operation. To support the feint, Chasseloup left one of the valuable pioneer companies in Borisov as the rest of the command went north to the Studenka ford. Oudinot's main body followed after dark, quietly, at around 1800.

The engineers did not have enough equipment or tools to build a planned third bridge across the river. Chasseloup attached himself and his troops to Eble, and there was also a detachment of sailors to help. Eble's foresight at saving the equipment he did at Orsha was now going to pay off as the *pontonniers* "brought six wagons full of tools, nails, iron clamps, plus two campaign forges and all the iron needed for constructing one or more trestle bridges. Likewise two carts loaded with coal."[9]

Napoleon, urged by Murat to cross with a small escort and escape, categorically refused while the army was still in danger of being lost: he would never consider leaving his army when it was faced with such a critical situation and with a battle imminent. Napoleon was seen and described by many eyewitnesses during the crossing and ensuing fighting, always where he was needed most, heedless of exposing himself to enemy fire:

> The Emperor passed close by us to mount a small hillock that dominated the river on our side. All our eyes were fixed on him. Not a sigh, not a murmur arose from our ranks. The pontonneers throwing the bridge were up to their necks in water. They were wholly unopposed. It was exceedingly cold. The Emperor was generous with encouragement.[10]

The Emperor's calmness under fire was also noted as he sat

> . . . on a little white horse, surrounded by his whole staff. There he was, in the midst of a very well-nourished fire, as calm as at the Tuileries. He had, I remember, a singular habit. Each time musket balls or a roundshot whistled in his ears, he shouted: "Go past, rascals!"[11]

And while watching the intrepid *pontonniers* working on the bridges, waiting to get his army across and out of danger:

> I saw him at close quarters. His back was resting against some trestles, his arms were crossed inside his overcoat. Silent, having an air of not paying attention to what was going on, only fixing his glances from time to time on the pontonneers a few paces away, sometimes up to their necks amidst the ice floes, busy placing the trestles, which they seemed to have the greatest difficulty in fixing deeply, while others, as soon as they were in place, were laying the planks on them.[12]

At the point of the projected crossing at Studenka, the Berezina is about one hundred yards wide. The bottom is muddy and soft, and at its deepest point about six or seven feet deep. The current is not swift, but there were cakes of ice in the river, which would hit and tear at the *pontonniers* in the water during the construction of the bridge and in the subsequent repair operations that had to be undertaken until the army was across. The left bank was solid, but the right bank was covered with marshes. Normally, this would have greatly hampered any crossing operations, but as there had recently been a frost, the ground was frozen on that bank also.

On the morning of 26 November, before dawn, Oudinot's artillery was emplaced on the ridge behind Studenka—24 guns, divided into two batteries of twelve guns each. Eble's *pontonniers* had assembled the trestles that needed to be sunk in the river, and were under cover of the river bank so as not to be spotted by the Cossack patrols that lingered in the position that had been abandoned by the Russians across the river.

The *pontonniers*, sailors, and engineers constructed 23 trestles for each of the two bridges. One of the bridges was to be for infantry alone, the other for cavalry and artillery, as well as any ancillary vehicles that could be sent across. The trestles varied in height from three to nine feet, and the caps, or ridge beams, were fourteen feet long. That number of trestles made twenty-four bays, or intervals between them, each at thirteen feet long. Timber was obtained by tearing down Studenka and the neighboring village of Veselovo. Additionally, tall trees, usually sixteen to seventeen feet long, were cut down for the required beams, and were used as they were: time was critical and the wood could not be cut into timber. The roadway of the bridges was made of round trees fifteen to sixteen feet long. For the vehicle bridge, cut planking was used for the flooring, taken from the demolished houses in the village. Any ironwork needed for the bridges was forged on the spot, much of it taken from derelict vehicles and brought with the *pontonniers* by Eble's order.

Eble sent his men to work with the knowledge that the situation of the army was critical:

> Without delay we got busy demolishing the best-preserved houses to obtain materials needed to build a bridge . . . All the works were being done with timbers from the demolition, already carried out during the night of 25 November, of the houses of Weselovo . . . Hidden inside the houses, they were beginning to work on the construction of materials for trestle bridges . . . the pontonneers worked ceaselessly all day and night.[13]

At 0800 the advance guard was sent across the river. Polish lancers, each with a *voltigeur* carried behind him, went into the river to ford and sweep the opposite bank for Cossacks and any other hostile Muscovites:

> Soon, the pontonneers know, they'll have to go down into the icy water to plant them in the soft muddy bottom—something which will become progressively harder because of the "immense ice floes" swirling downstream from right to left.[14]

Then rafts were used to ferry 300 more infantrymen across the river:

Behind them, the pontonneers pick up their trestles, run to he water's edge and enter the river. Rafts had been built for them to work in the center of the river where the water was too deep to stand in. Oudinot's artillery is in support, but they remained silent by the Emperor's order so that Tschaplitz wouldn't be alerted. The bridges had just been started. It was 8 AM, and the first trestles were still being sunk.[15]

Two problems faced by the pontonniers were keeping the trestles steady, lessening the reverberations that would be caused by horses and vehicles crossing the fragile bridges. The trestles, because of the muddy bottom, were not steady until the planking was placed on them, and then straw was placed on the roadway to reduce the vibrating effect of the weight coming across. This was not always successful, as the bridges broke a number of times during the crossing, forcing the half-frozen pontonniers back into the water to repair them.

The Russians were not idle during all this activity, as a

... detachment of light troops sent upstream on observation and to try to establish contact with Wittgenstein . . . [and] to warn him that the French were preparing to throw a bridge at Studenka, had assumed—the place being so swampy and thus ill-suited to throwing a bridge—it was a feint; and that the French would profit by it to make the true crossing at some opposite point. At Beresino, for example. It appeared that Eble's bridge-building operations at Studenka, so far from alerting Tshitshagov to what was really going on, have caused him to give the whole army the immediate order to march for Beresino. However, Count Langeron was sent with 4,000 men and eight guns to a point facing Studenka, to observe the enemy's movements. Another detachment under that general's orders had been left to guard the [Borisov] bridgehead and prevent any attempt to reestablish the broken bridge.[16]

However, working in shoulder-deep water, and buffeted by floating cakes of ice, the *pontonniers*, engineers, and sailors of Eble's command finished the infantry/cavalry bridge at 1300. Baron Fain, an eyewitness, noted that the men in the water were "Braving the cold, fatigue, exhaustion, even death, they're working ceaselessly, water up to their shoulders. The death they must find under the ice floes is not less the death of brave men for that." Immediately, Oudinot's infantry and cavalry crossed, as did Dombrowski's Poles. Oudinot himself was preparing to cross, but was stopped by the Emperor: " 'Don't go over yet, Oudinot. You'll only get yourself captured!' But Oudinot points to his men: 'Amongst them, Sire,' he replied, 'I'm afraid of nothing.' "[17]

Merle's infantry division of Oudinot's corps begin to cross the bridge, the redoubtable Swiss regiments shouting "*Vive l'Empereur*" as they passed Napoleon, who seemed not to notice, preoccupied as he was with the bridging operation. As Oudinot's men reached the west bank of the river, and started to deploy off the roads, they came across Cossack dead, all of whom had been shot in the head. The Polish lancers and the "*kleinen Männer*" had done their work expertly, clearing the bank and the woods of the Russian pickets.

Napoleon was anxious to get across and get on with it: the more time spent on the east bank, the more time for the Russians who were pursuing them to catch them astride the river with only rickety trestle bridges as a lifeline. Père Roguet, who belonged to the Guard and was one of the toughest generals in the army, "watched him as he tested the planks, putting his foot on each plank as it was laid." Swiss Captain Louis Begos, of the 2nd Swiss Regiment, stated that Napoleon had dismounted near one of the bridges and said to Eble,

"It's taking a very long time, General. A very long time"; "You can see, Sire," replied Eble in a vivacious and self-assured manner, "that my men are up to their necks in the water, and the ice is holding up their work. I've no food or brandy to warm them with." "That'll do."[18]

That was all the Emperor said to him, as there was no food or liquid sustenance to be had.

The second, vehicular bridge was finished at 1600. Artillery was now pushed over to the west bank of the river for the attack that everyone knew would be coming from the south. At 2000 three trestles on the vehicular bridge collapsed into the river. Eble, whose men were around their campfires to dry out, get warm, and get some sleep, took half of his men back into the river to repair the bridge. By 2300 the bridge was repaired. Three hours later it again broke. Eble woke up the other half of his troops, took them into the water and repaired the bridge. At around 0200 the artillery bridge broke again in the middle of the river. Eble's pontonniers were reaching the end of their endurance—even the shift that had been asleep around the bivouac fires. Eble, revered by his men, went down to the river and into the water with them. He had not slept, but, although 50 years old, had the endurance of a much younger man. Through force of personal example, he encouraged his men to keep working: the whole army was depending on them. The exhausted, half-frozen bridgemen finished the repairs by 6 a.m. Straw and tow had been placed on the bridges to reduce the vibration from the horses and vehicles, but the bridges, not strong to begin with, were collapsing under the constant strain.

By 0600 on 27 November, Eble's exhausted men had again repaired the broken bridge. It held for ten hours this time, before breaking again at 1600. Once more the deeply "revered and respected" Eble led half of his men into the river. They repaired the bridge in two hours.

The following eyewitness accounts of the bridges' appearance and the indefatigable dedication to duty of the pontonniers speak for themselves:

> Both Grenadier Pils and Colonel Marbot admired the work of Eble's pontonneers. They continually threw "themselves completely naked into the Berezina's cold waters, though we didn't have a single drop of brandy to give them." The pontonneers continually worked, "placing their trestles at equal distances in the river, with its huge icefloes, and with rarely exampled courage going out into the water up to their shoulders. Some fell dead and disappeared, carried away by the current; yet their comrades' energy wasn't the less for seeing them come to this tragic end. The Emperor stands watching these heroes; [he] doesn't leave the river bank."
>
> The bridges themselves have "the structure of sloping saw horses, suspended like trestles on shallow, sunk piles; on these lay long stringers and across them only bridge ties, which were not fastened down. Straw was placed across both of the rickety, hastily built structures to lessen the impact of the thousands of men and hundreds of guns and vehicles that would soon be rumbling across the timber that used to be a Russian village."
>
> [The bridges] certainly wouldn't have found grace from an expert. But if one bears in mind that there'd been no materials at all, and that of the entire equipment only a few wagons filled with clamps and nails, two campaign forges and two coal carts had been saved, that the neighborhood's houses had to be demolished and trees felled to get the necessary timber, that the pontonneers were working with the water up to their necks while the cold formed crystals all over their bodies—then one will certainly regard this construction as one of the most glorious of all warlike actions in this campaign which counted so many.[19]

The ubiquitous artilleryman, Boulart, was present at the crossing, and was more than ready to cross. He

> ... was at the bridge taking his guns across among the press and general confusion, busy getting his teams methodically across one by one, is finding the bridges "not very solid" and having to be "incessantly repaired" by the indefatigable Eble's pontonniers, "who had the courage to put themselves into the water and work there despite the cold. They behaved admirably."[20]

One artillery battery was waiting for its turn to cross the bridges when Napoleon happened by. Napoleon asked the battery commander what he was doing, and he "replied that we were waiting our turn behind the other batteries. And as he turned to go back to the fire, a clumsy gunner trod on his foot. The Emperor gave him a gentle shove between the shoulders, saying calmly, "What a clumsy bugger he is."[21]

Rapp later remembered one French artillery battery in action that was commanded by the intrepid Captain Brechtel:

> . . . who did the whole campaign with a wooden leg, which didn't prevent him from mounting his horse. During the action a roundshot, (evidently from one of Arnoldi's guns), has carried it away and thrown him over. "Fetch me another leg out of wagon No. 5," he told one of his gunners. Strapped it on and went on firing.

Victor had arrived on 27 November after a hard cross country march. He left one division at Borisov as the army's rear guard (this was Partouneaux's, that would later be captured). With his other two divisions, he took up a position on the Studenka ridge and organized a reverse slope defense. His troops were in good physical shape, and were shocked at the appearance of the main army as well as the mass of stragglers that accompanied it. It was noted that his caissons were "drawn by fine horses, their harness in good condition."

Once the two divisions and their corps cavalry were in position,

> Napoleon ordered a battery of Imperial Guard to take up position on our left, near the river bank. By aiming its fire across it, it took the enemy battery on the other bank obliquely, thus forcing it to withdraw to a distance. At the same time, it turned back a column that was preparing to deploy from the wood on which IX Corps' right was resting. Then we saw infantry skirmishers, who'd just been driven out of the wood return with elan, throw out the enemy's, who in their turn emerged from it and thus under our eyes restored IX Corps' support. On the far left we could see repeated cavalry charges which didn't cease to maintain their superiority there.[22]

From his ridge, Victor waited for either Wittgenstein to show up or for the army to get across the river, whichever came first.

Tshitshagov finally realized by 26 November that he had been tricked, and that the French were going to cross in force at or near Studenka. He sent an advanced guard forward to Brili, which was directly across the river from Studenka. He halted at Borisov, as it looked from the numbers of French present that they were going to try and force a crossing. What he saw was a mass of stragglers and not formed troops. By the time he understood the situation, the French were across the river with enough troops to protect the bridgehead while the rest of the army crossed behind them. Wittgenstein was informed during the night of 26/27 November that the French were building bridges at Studenka, and hurried forward across country. He and Tshitshagov agreed to attack the French on both sides of the river against both ends of the bridges on 28 November. Nothing had been seen or heard from Kutusov.

There was fighting on the 27th between the French on the west bank and the Russian advance guard under Lambert and Tschaplitz. Ney finally defeated them, and drove them south to Bolshoi-Stakhov. Tshitshagov counterattacked furiously, but Oudinot and Ney held him off, away from the line of retreat behind them and from the bridges.

The four Swiss infantry regiments of Merle's division held the hard shoulder of the French line on the far left. They had taken 7,065 into Russia; now, at the Berezina, they were down to 1,500. They were attacked a total of seven times by the Russians, and seven times they hurled the Muscovites back, holding their ground, and keeping all their eagles, but losing eighty percent of their total strength. Before the Swiss had crossed the rickety infantry bridge, their division commander, Merle, had been questioned by the Emperor:

> "Are you pleased with the Swiss, General?"
> "Yes, Sire. If the Swiss attacked as sharply as they know how to defend themselves, Your Majesty would be content with them."
> "Yes . . . I know they're a good lot."[23]

After Merle and his stalwart Swiss infantry had crossed the bridges, they sent up a loud "*Vive l'Empereur*" that rang through the pine forests that would soon hear them singing their hymns after repulsing one Russian assault after another, saving the bridgehead for their exhausted comrades who crossed afterwards and moved on westward behind their positions.

The fighting on the west bank was vicious, no-quarter attrition:

> Outposts are driven in and the Swiss can see their enemies. An aide-de-camp rides towards them, shouting, "Our line's been attacked," and the chiefs shout "Forward!" Everywhere the charge is beaten. We're flung at the enemy, cross bayonets at point-blank range. Slowly the Russians retire, still firing.
>
> They come on again, regardless of losses against the defiant Swiss, who are singing hymns between attacks. "On both sides the firing was murderous. It wasn't long before General Amey and several staff officers had been wounded and several killed, among them our commandant Blattman. A bullet went through his brain. General of Brigade Canderas and his adjutant had fallen too; a roundshot had taken off the latter's head."[24]

One of the most admired officers, "the intrepid Vonderveid," was mortally wounded after giving his horse to his wounded adjutant. Vonderveid

> ... was fighting on foot at the head of his braves when a Russian musket ball went through his throat. He gave a cry, stifled by blood, and fell backwards into my arms. After the first moment had passed, he, without losing consciousness, said these simple words to his fellow citizen: "Bourmann, I've died here a Christian."[25]

Oudinot was shot out of his saddle, taking yet another wound, one of 34 in his career. Ney took over, but, as Colonel Fezensac remarked, losses were so heavy that

> Only three weak battalions [were] placed on the road—all that was left of I, III, and VIII Corps, served as their reserve. For a while the fight was sustained; under pressure from superior forces, II Corps was beginning to sag. Our reserves, hit by roundshot at ever closer range, were moving towards the rear. The movement put to flight all the isolated men who filled the wood, and in their terror they ran as far as the bridge. Even the Young Guard was wavering. Soon there was no more salvation except in the Old Guard. With it we were prepared to die or conquer.

Then, when it seemed as if all was lost, Doumerc's cuirassiers burst out of the snow-choked pine forests onto the Russian right flank. The Russians were taken completely by surprise:

> ... the brave cuirassiers of the 4th and 7th Regiments, who were standing only 1,000 paces away from us, had seen the enemy too. We clearly heard the word of command: "Squadrons, by the left flank, march!" As soon as the cuirassiers had crossed the road, they went into the attack.[26]

The Russians were overrun by the shock and violence of the cuirassiers, charge, and over 2,000 prisoners were scooped up. Many more were dead or wounded on the ground, those in front of the Swiss stacked like cord-wood.

On his ridge, Victor was fighting for the Grande Armée's life. Every Russian assault or penetration was driven back with casualties, but his own two divisions were steadily shrinking from heavy losses. Napoleon sent the Baden Brigade back across the river to help, and Victor's excellent corps cavalry, comprising the Baden Hussars and the Hesse-Darmstadt Cheveaux-Légers, sacrificed themselves in a gallant charge, forever after known as the "Death Ride," led by Colonel von Laroche, which broke a Russian infantry square and defeated a provisional cuirassier regiment. Victor and his battered troops held hard, allowing the bridges to remain intact and enabling the army to cross and escape the Russian trap.

The fighting virtually over, Victor withdrew across the bridges in perfect order between 2100 on 28 November and 0630 on 29 November. Eble, ordered to burn the bridges at 0700, waited until 0830 to see if any stragglers would cross from the immobile mass of them around their fires. Perhaps 10,000 remained when Eble finally fired the bridges. The Russians did not follow. They had had enough.

The final verdict on the performance of the Swiss during the Russian campaign, especially appropriate for their epic fight to keep the bridges open at the Berezina, was rendered by Gouvian St Cyr, who had been their commander: "They were, right to the end of the retreat, invincible, they outdid nature and they spread a radiance of heroism into this desert of snow."

In more senses than one, Napoleon had snatched an outstanding victory out of his worst defeat. The Grande Armee might be dying on its feet, but neither winter, hunger, rivers, nor overwhelming odds in men and guns could halt it. It trampled them underfoot and went on.[27]

Clausewitz should have the last word on the Berezina action, as not only was he one of Napoleon's opponents, he also participated in the campaign:

There was never a better opportunity to force the surrender of an army in the open field. Napoleon had to rely for the most part upon the reputation of his arms; and he made use here of an asset he had been accumulating for a long time . . . Because the enemy was afraid of him and his Guard, no one dared face him. Napoleon capitalized on this psychological effect, and with its assistance worked his way out of one of the worst situations in which a general was ever caught. Of course this psychological force was not all he had. He was still supported by his own brilliant strength of character and the peerless military virtues of his army, not yet destroyed by the greatest of trials. Once out of the trap, Napoleon said to his staff: "You see how one can slip away under the very nose of the enemy." Napoleon in this action not only preserved his military honor, he enhanced it.[28]

On a final note, one of the French Guardsmen commented, after the Guard had crossed the Berezina to make their presence felt on the west bank, that if the positions had been reversed, and the French had trapped a Russian army instead of the other way round, not one would have escaped. Eble and his men had performed one of the most epic feats in the history of the Napoleonic Wars. Their skill and devotion had saved an Emperor and an army. Eble died of exhaustion at Königsberg in late December, as did his comrade-in-arms, General Larriboissière, joining his son, who had been mortally wounded at Borodino in September. Of the gallant *pontonniers* who worked almost totally in the water during the critical operation of the battle, ninety percent died of exhaustion or hypothermia. "The escape of Napoleon was thus so much owing to the foresight, ability, and enterprise of General Eble, and to the intelligence and enterprise of the corps of pontonniers . . ."[29]

NOTES

1. See Elting, *Swords Around a Throne*, ch. XII, XIII.
2. Esposito and Elting, *A Military History and Atlas of the Napoleonic Wars*, Map 119
3. Douglas, *An Essay on the Principles and Construction of Military Bridges &c*, pp. 360-1.
4. For Eble, see George Six, *Dictionnaire Biographique des Généraux et Amiraux Français de la Révolution et de l'Empire (1792–1814)*, the biographical sketches in Esposito and Elting, and Pelet's memoirs of the campaign in Portugal, edited by Don Horward.
5. Lachouque, Henry, and Brown, Anne, *The Aanatomy of Glory*, p. 264
6. Esposito, Vincent J., and Elting, John R., *A Military History and Atlas of the Napoleonic Wars*, Biographical Sketches,
7. Britten-Austin, *1812: The Great Retreat*, p. 254.
8. *Ibid.*
9. *Ibid.*, p. 250.
10. *Ibid.*, p. 255.

11. *Ibid.*, p. 293.
12. *Ibid.*, p. 260.
13. *Ibid.*, pp. 249–50.
14. *Ibid..*, p. 251.
15. *Ibid.*, p. 257.
16. *Ibid.*, p. 254.
17. *Ibid.*, p. 261.
18. *Ibid.*, p. 260.
19. *Ibid.*, pp. 257, 258, 269.
20. *Ibid.*, p. 273.
21. *Ibid.*, p. 262
22. *Ibid.*, p. 301.
23. *Ibid.*, p. 263.
24. *Ibid.*, p. 290
25. *Ibid.*
26. *Ibid.*, p. 293.
27. Esposito and Elting, *op. cit.*, Map 125
28. Freytag-Loringhoven, Major General Baron Hugo von, in *The Roots of Strategy. Book 3: The Power of Personality in War*, p. 280.
28. Douglas, *op. cit.*, p. 366.

Chapter 11

Drouot

*Many a time it falleth out that most men employed for gunners
are very negligent of the fear of God.*

—Anonymous Puritan

*A numerous artillery is necessary for forming great enterprises, for attacking a foe with
advantage, and for facilitating the defence of an army.*

—Le Blond

*In most battles the Guard artillery is the deciding factor, since, having it always at
hand, I can take it wherever it is needed.*

—Napoleon 1813

1500, 22 April 1813: Lützen, Saxony

The fighting had been intense and savage all morning since Ney's III Corps had been surprised in their bivouacs by the jubilant Russians and Prussians. Furious counterattacks by the
survivors, some led in person by the enraged, cursing "Red Michael," had restored a fluid
situation, but the crisis was far from over.

Napoleon was determined to reach a swift, violent decision. Alerting the Guard infantry to
be prepared to attack the Allied center behind the Guard artillery, he sent his hard-riding *aides-
de-camp* to give his instructions to the units concerned. One mud- and blood-spattered *officier
du ordnance* galloped up to and halted before the commander of the Guard artillery, *Général*
Drouot. Without dismounting, he relayed the Emperor's intentions to the general, and galloped off to the next designated recipient. Drouot summoned his two immediate subordinates—*Généraux* Desvaux St Maurice and Dulauloy, the commanders of the Guard horse and
foot artillery, respectively. Imparting the Emperor's wishes, and his own instructions, Drouot
dismissed the two general officers, who saluted and galloped to their respective commands to
prepare a very unpleasant surprise for the unsuspecting Allies.

In one of the horse artillery companies of Desvaux St Maurice's command, the guns were
being checked and rechecked by the Chiefs of Section, the senior NCOs of the company, and
by the company officers. Harness leather and trace chains had been scrutinized carefully for
signs of stress and wear, unserviceable portions being rapidly replaced if worn too much from
the company supply wagon. The company farrier had personally checked the remounts that
had been issued the previous evening when the company had stopped at the end of another
horse-killing road march. An improperly shod mount was the last thing the company commander needed.

As troopers dozed and unemployed drivers slept in their saddles, the senior NCOs once
again went up and down the company column looking for something wrong. One grizzled
veteran gunner looking at some of the newer train drivers had been horribly wounded in the
right hand. He had been an infantryman, and could no longer load and fire a musket. How in
the *sacré nom de Dieu* was he supposed to control a galloping gun team with only one good
hand? At least he had a wheel pair, and not a swing or lead team.

Suddenly, there was a clatter of equipment as a dozing driver fell from his mount with a loud oath. Snorting horses came awake, seasoned cannoneers still amazed at the animals' innate ability to lock their knees and sleep standing up. Other men were roughly awakened by voice or fist—the more recalcitrant ones being knocked sprawling over a gun trail—to fix or repair some shortcoming with their horses' or weapon's equipment

The company commander watched the growing level of activity among his gunners and drivers. He had just received their orders, and they were about to launch an artillery attack, to be mounted against the Allied center, getting as close as possible before unlimbering and opening fire. This one ought to be interesting. *Monsieur le capitaine* was a veteran of Spain and Russia, and had entered the service as an enlisted man. He won entrance to the Guard at the Berezina the year before. He was a strict commander, but fair with his men, and he took excellent care of his horses. He wanted all six of his 6-pounders in action today, which was why his NCOs were endlessly inspecting. He stood with his two nervous *sous-lieutenants*, both young *blanc-becs*, one just out of school, and the other from the Navy. It would be interesting to watch them today. They were about to get a real education. Behind, but very near *monsieur le capitaine*, his trumpeter held both his and his commander's horses. It seemed that he never left the captain's side. *Monsieur le capitaine* was dressed very conspicuously today, in a brand new regulation uniform, topped by an immense nonregulation colpack, topped again with a huge red, cut-feather plume. They would be fighting under the Emperor's eye today, as well as Drouot's, and the captain wanted to look his best. At the very least, he would make a handsome corpse if his luck ran out.

Suddenly, to their front, there was a flurry of activity, as Drouot and his trumpeter took their place in front of the massed artillery companies. Giving the order, the gunners raced to their picketed horses, mounted, and took their place with their gun sections. Calmly, *monsieur le capitaine* swung into the saddle, took his place at the head of his company and nonchalantly drew his saber. His trumpeter, behind and to his right, spat into his trumpet and wiped the residue with his glove. All eyes were on *Général* Drouot as he raised his saber and bellowed, *"En avant!"*

*   *   *

French artillery tactics had evolved to the point that using large, massed batteries as close artillery support for assaulting infantry was becoming, if not a doctrinal (or system) procedure, at least common practice. It had been used to advantage at Wagram in 1809, and would be again at Hanau in 1813, and at Ligny and Waterloo in 1815. However, the most spectacular use of this innovative tactic was at the Battle of Lützen in 1813. Much like Senarmont's maneuver with 36 guns at Friedland in 1807, Drouot used 80 guns from the Guard and Marmont's VI Corps.

Antoine Drouot (1774-1847) was a product of the Metz artillery school from which he graduated in 1793. An excellent, intelligent artilleryman, he was assigned to the Armée du Nord as a *sous-lieutenant* in the 1st Foot Artillery Regiment and served at Hondschoote. Promoted to 1st lieutenant in 1794, he was with the Armée de Sambre et Meuse from 1794 to 1796 and served at Fleurus. Promoted to captain in 1796, he was successively in the armies of the Rhine (1797) and Naples (1798-99), serving on the Trebbia. He was on Eble's staff in 1800-01 and fought at Hohenlinden in 1800. He commanded the 14th Company of the 1st Foot Artillery Regiment from 1803 until 1804 and fought at Trafalgar in 1805. Promoted to *chef de bataillon* in late 1805, he was made inspector for the manufacture of arms at Mauberge while serving on the General Staff of the Grande Armée in November 1805.

Drouot was promoted to major in the 3rd Foot Artillery Regiment in 1807 and was the inspector of arms manufacture at Charleville late that same year. Named the director of the *parc* for the Army of Spain in early 1808, he was later chosen by Napoleon to organize and command the *Régiment d'Artillerie à Pied* of the Imperial Guard that same year. This he did with great competence, leading it in Austria with distinction in 1809. Wounded at Wagram, he later procured the famous visored bearskin headdress for his beloved Guard gunners. He was promoted to colonel in July 1809, and was made a Baron of the Empire the next year.

Drouot served throughout the Russian campaign in 1812 and again in 1813. Promoted to general of brigade in early 1813, he served at the Battles of Lützen, Bautzen, Leipzig, and Hanau. He distinguished himself at Lützen by leading an artillery assault that destroyed the Allied center and led the way for the final decisive assault by the Guard. At Hanau, his expertly emplaced guns shattered Wrede and again paved the way for a victory. Serving throughout 1814, he accompanied Napoleon to Elba, and was appointed the island's governor. He served ably in Belgium, remaining loyal both before and after Waterloo. He was refused permission to accompany Napoleon to St Helena, and he rejected a pension from the Bourbons until well after Napoleon's death.

Drouot was a deeply religious man and read his Bible every day. He was also so deeply intelligent that he was dubbed "The Sage of the Grande Armée." He was such an expert, deadly artilleryman that his artillery assault at Lützen shattered the Allied center, paving the way for the Young Guard's decisive assault that saved the day and turned possible defeat into victory.

As a relatively junior officer, he had expertly organized the *Artillerie à Pied* of the Guard in 1808, and led it into the cauldron of combat at Wagram in 1809, losing so heavily that his regiment had to be augmented by volunteers from the Old Guard infantry. He was also the artilleryman who led his 12-pounders into line at Hanau, bombarding the Austro-Bavarian Army that attempted to stop the Grande Armée from leaving Germany after Leipzig, standing his ground against an Allied cavalry assault, and decimating the attacking cavalrymen so that, by the time the survivors reached Drouot's gunline, they had to fight hand-to-hand with the Guardsmen, and were routed when the *Grenadiers à Cheval* rode to the rescue.

The Grande Armée's losses in Russia included over 1,300 guns and more than 175,000 horses. Replacements had to be found, and the artillery establishment had to be reconstructed as the war would continue in the spring of 1813. Eugène's newly christened Army of the Elbe, made up of freshly inducted conscripts, hastily assembled replacements, and sullen veterans from Russia, could hardly be expected to defend and hold the Empire's eastern marches indefinitely.

Napoleon's tremendous capacity for work had never been given such a test before. These days were even more desperate than those of 1800, but the Emperor went to work with a will to build another army that would march east and face the Russians and their newly acquired allies, the resurgent Prussians. Napoleon raised another army for the campaign of 1813 in Saxony. There were already 120,000 conscripts in training, called up the year before, but he activated 80,000 men from the National Guard, and also set out to screen the conscription, which added 100,000 men who had missed the previous call-ups between 1809 and 1812.[1] Troops were drawn from the veterans in Spain. Cadres for new units had been sent back before the Grande Armée had taken Moscow the previous September, and these valuable men were used to stiffen and train new conscripts. Men who had survived the Retreat and who were not needed with Eugene's Army of the Elbe were also used as cadres. Naval troops were sent to the

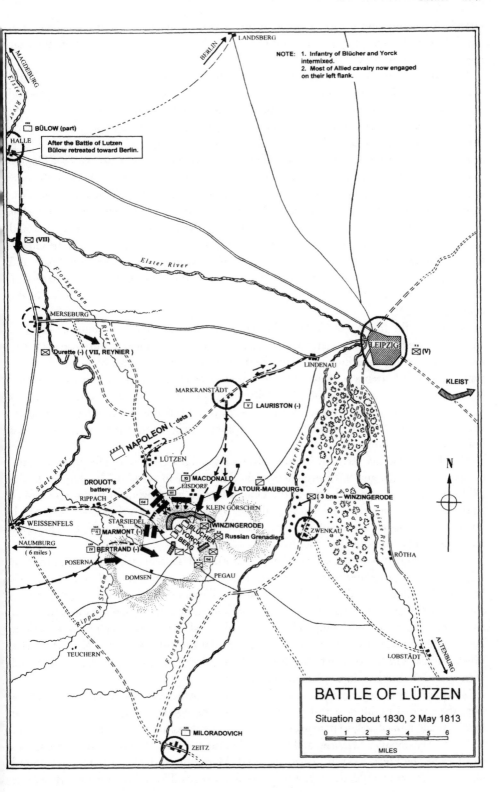

NOTE: 1. Infantry of Blücher and Yorck intermixed.
2. Most of Allied cavalry now engaged on their left flank.

After the Battle of Lutzen Bülow retreated toward Berlin.

BATTLE OF LÜTZEN

Situation about 1830, 2 May 1813

0 1 2 3 4 5 6

MILES

Grande Armée for land service, assigned as infantry—for example, the four big regiments of naval infantry that ended up in Marmont's VI Corps. Naval troops were also sent to the engineers and to the artillery.

The two most important parts of the Army that had to be rebuilt carefully were the Guard and the artillery. Most of the artillery's equipment had been lost. There were the older 4- and 8-pounders of the Gribeauval System in the armories, placed there when the new 6-pounders of the Système AN XI started to be fielded in 1805. They were still excellent pieces, and serviceable. Work on new gun carriages, limbers, caissons, and field forges went on at a frantic pace. Both the cavalry and artillery were hobbled by the huge losses of horses in Russia—over 175,000 of the creatures had been lost, and the cavalry did not start to recover as an effective offensive arm until August. However, the priority was to get horses to the artillery. When the men of the new Grande Armée put on their packs and hit the road for Saxony in April, there were guns enough to support them, and gunners enough to serve the guns: by August, Napoleon would have 1,300 serviceable weapons available for his purposes.[2] The other priority was the Guard. It was reformed by veterans for the senior regiments, recalling picked men from Spain and from the retired list. The best of the conscripts went into the Young Guard. The Guard artillery was carefully rebuilt. Naval artillerymen were drafted into it, ensuring its quality in the coming campaign.

Lützen was the first major battle of the campaign of 1813 in Saxony. Minor clashes had already occurred, Marshal Bessiéres having been hit by a chance artillery round in one of them, and killed. Napoleon and Eugène had united their two armies, that of the Main and the Elbe, respectively, and Lützen was essentially a meeting engagement: both armies were hunting each other. The Allies, consisting of 73,000 Russians and Prussians, were commanded by Wittgenstein, who had been chosen more or less by consensus after Kutusov had died earlier in the year. However, trying to command an Allied army with both interfering sovereigns present was no without its problems.

Napoleon's objective was, as usual, the Allied army and its destruction. The Allies, with the exception of Blücher and Wittgenstein, thought that Napoleon would not be able to take the field before June, and the advance of the Grande Armée into Saxony in the second half of April must have given them mental convulsions. They only had two choices—retreat, which might mean giving up Berlin and stopping at some point east of that city, or fight. They were outnumbered by Napoleon, but they boldly chose to fight.

The Grande Armée was moving on Leipzig by 30 April. Lack of efficient cavalry hindered Napoleon's ability to gather deep intelligence or obtain an accurate picture of the Allied army's location. The numerous Allied cavalry, well mounted, generally well trained, and numbering about 25,000 men, found the Grande Armée en route to Leipzig and reported it as such, but also reported that the French only had "a weak flank guard" southwest of Leipzig, at Kaja, near Lützen. The Allies prepared to attack, and found the flank guard at Kaja to be Ney's III Corps, which was just a little too large to brush aside. Both sides were surprised at the meeting, and both started shooting at once, at about 1145 on 2 May.

What developed was an eight-hour slugging match, in which Ney's troops were driven back from their initial positions with heavy losses. Ney, who was with Napoleon at the time at Markranstadt, immediately went to rejoin his corps, while Napoleon issued orders for Marmont's VI Corps, Macdonald's XI Corps, and the Guard to support Ney. Most of Lauriston's V Corps and Latour-Maubourg's cavalry corps followed. Marmont reached the field at 1300 and Macdonald at about 1500, the rest of the units following and being committed as they came up. The initial Allied assault had carried almost all the small villages to their front. Ney coun-terattacked viciously, retaking what had been lost, and then losing it again to repeated Allied counterattacks.

Napoleon reached the battlefield at 1430, helped to rally Ney's shaken corps and was under constant enemy fire for most of the afternoon. The fighting in the center of the battlefield turned into no-quarter attrition. Ney's conscripts were worn out and wavering, though Marmont and Macdonald were taking off some of the pressure. The rapid French concentration had given Napoleon a numerical advantage. There was hard fighting all along the line, and most of the Allied troops were committed. The only reserve they had left by 1800 were the Prussian Guard infantry and Russian grenadier units.

At this critical juncture, Napoleon ordered General Drouot to assemble the artillery of the Guard into a large battery, along with the reserve artillery of Marmont's corps: sixteen battal-ions of fresh infantry from the Middle and Young Guard would attack the Allied center—or what had been the Allied center. Drouot massed 58 guns from the Guard artillery, both horse and foot, along with Marmont's 22 guns, between the villages of Starseidel and Kaja.[3] To his left rear, the Guard infantry massed in four columns, commanded by Marshal Mortier. What followed was a quick decision and one of the most decisive artillery actions of the period.

Drouot advanced his artillery, limbering up and galloping forward, horse artillerymen fol-lowing their guns individually mounted and panting foot artillerymen running behind their galloping gun teams, trying to stay as close to them as possible so as to take the least time catching up when they went into position. Drouot, stopping to unlimber his companies amidst enemy fire and watched by both the Emperor and the waiting Young Guard, eventually man-handled his guns within "canister range of the enemy,"[4] and opened a deadly fire into the Allied center, destroying company after company of infantry and ignoring incoming fire and the rest of the vulgar uproar that was raging around him and his gunners. He saw "the deadly blasts from out guns cut down the enemy by the thousands."[5]

Opening fire from his initial position on the ridge between the two villages, Drouot judged the distance too great, limbered up, and led his gunners in a charge at the Allied center. Unlim-bering at half the distance, the French again opened fire, causing heavy casualties in the Allied center. Advancing by successive bounds, the French artillery companies swept forward by lim-ber, by *prolonge*, and finally by *bricole*, the gun crews in man-teams, pushing and pulling their pieces into point-blank canister range. As the batteries were laid, commanders gave the order to load with canister and open fire. It was Friedland all over again: the massed artillery blew the center out of the Allied line. Yorck's and Blücher's troops attempted to stand, but were shot down or blown away by the massed canister fire. Attacking through the smoke and the mess, the Guard infantry broke what remained of the Allied center, the remainder retreating for the rear in front of them.

Drouot's action lasted between 20 and 30 minutes. General Flahaut, who had led part of the Guard's assault, stated that

> The Emperor ordered four Imperial aides to accompany the troops of the Guard selected for the attack. I accompanied General Berthezène at the head of the Fusiliers of the Guard. This brave general and his fine troops had earlier attacked and routed the enemy from their positions around Kaja; the men com-prising the Fusiliers were all veteran soldiers, and their discipline and elan were no match for our adver-saries: the Fusiliers were supremely confident of victory.
>
> The signal to advance being given, our brigade moved out, and eventually passed by the left flank of the grand battery. The discharges of these pieces were deafening, and the smoke covered the field, ob-scuring our view. Our battalions were formed in attack column of two pelotons width and rapidly tra-

versed the ground already devastated by the day's fighting. We passed over the wreckage of entire regiments which had been cut down by our guns. At times, the enemy dead and wounded were so thick that our men's feet did not touch the ground. My horse hesitated often as it looked for firm footing.

The enemy could not withstand our advance. They fired a few, sporadic volleys, broke ranks, and fled before out bayonets. His Majesty can be pleased with the soldiers of the Guard who carried this attack into the heart of the enemy line.[6]

Ney's remnants, along with Marmont and Bertrand's IV Corps, had attacked with the Guard, the latter two corps supporting them on the right. They chased the Allies off the field, but had no effective pursuit, as the French cavalry was not up to the task. Losses on both sides were heavy—22,000 French and 20,000 Allied. The drain, though, on the Allies was greater, their having lost almost 30 percent of their effectives. In two and a half weeks, the Allies fell back to Bautzen, northeast of Dresden and about 70 miles east of Leipzig. There, they prepared to do battle with the Emperor one more time.

Drouot's performance at Lützen verified Senarmont's new artillery tactics first used at Friedland. Raw as the rebuilt French artillery arm was, it was more than capable of performing any mission it could be given.

NOTES

1. Esposito and Elting, *Introduction to the Leipzig Campaign.*
2. *Ibid.*
3. The numbers quoted as making up Drouot's large battery usually vary between 72 and 80. The latter seems the most likely.
4. Bowden, *Napoleon's Grande Armee of 1813*, p. 81.
5. *Ibid.*
6. *Ibid.*, p. 82.

Chapter 12
Auld Lang Syne

. . . never had so grand and awful an idea of the resurrection as . . .
[when] I saw . . . more than five hundred Britons emerging from the heaps of their dead
comrades, all over the plain rising up, and . . . coming forward . . . as prisoners.
—Major General Andrew Jackson,
Chalmette Plantation, 8 January 1815

It is not big armies that win battles, it is the good ones.
—Maurice de Saxe

. . . the nimble gunner
With linstock now the devilish cannon touches,
And down goes all before them.
—Shakespeare, *Henry V*

0745, 1 January 1815: The Chalmette Plantation outside of New Orleans

There was bustling activity along the entrenchment. Troops of all types, militia, volunteers, Regulars, Marines, and even a party of Baratarian pirates, manned the breastwork, or worked steadily behind the main line of resistance. The artillery was also manned, portfires already alight, ammunition for ready use, caissons close by to replenish when needed. There were fifteen pieces in all, well mounted on wooden platforms to keep them out of the muck and the ammunition as dry as possible.

The had been enemy activity in the distance all night long. The Americans had stood to arms at 0500, just in case. Jackson wasn't taking any chances on a nasty British surprise before dawn: the British had a reputation for surprise attacks with the bayonet in the dark, and it paid to be careful. The troops were being relieved in shifts for breakfast, but they all carried their weapons with them.

Out in the predawn gloom, the voices of the enemy carried across the flat plain of the fields. Orders were being given, men were swearing repeatedly, and there was constant hammering in at least three directions. It had subsided some in the last hour, but there was something ominous going on. There would be a fight today, no doubt about it. But when and from where would the British come? When they did come, they would have to cross the fields that would be under artillery fire the entire way across: -there was no cover for them at all. There was a ditch in front of the American position, and then a breastwork that could not be scaled without ladders. On the far right, there was a small redoubt that could sweep the entire ditch with cannon fire if the British got that far. The line of the canal—and hence the defensive line—was as straight as an arrow. Easy to hold and defend, it was refused on the far left flank where it went into the swamp. Across the river there were further entrenchments and artillery if the British tried from that side.

As the visibility cleared, the Americans saw in the distance, about seven hundred yards out, that the British had constructed three batteries of artillery overnight, and they looked as if they were ready for action. They had, upon closer inspection, at least twenty guns mounted and protected—and they also had those damned rockets. The Regulars and Marines weren't concerned about them, but the thought of them made the Louisiana militiamen nervous. They could be terrifying.

Suddenly, from each of the British batteries one gun fired—ranging shots. One projectile went over the breastworks and two were short, one bounding into the ditch, rolling harmlessly to a stop. A moment later, three more shots were incoming, one short, and two slapping harmlessly against the breastwork. Well, it looked as if the British wanted a gun fight this fine New Year's morning, and the American gun crews manned their pieces as the drummers beat the long roll.

*   *   *

There had been artillery in the New World since the time of the explorers and Conquistadors. What they had been familiar with in Europe, they had brought with them, and that included military systems. Artillery had been used since the early days in fortresses and stockades, protecting settlements against marauding bands of French and Indians, as well is in the larger fortresses against assault from the sea. In the War of the American Revolution, artillery had made itself felt on battlefields the length and breadth of the thirteen original states. After the Battle of Monmouth in 1778 ,Washington had made the comment about the artillery of the Continental Army that no artillery had been "served better than ours."[1] However, until the Battle of New Orleans in January 1815, no battle in North America had been decided by artillery. It was a harbinger of what was to come.

American artillery had come into being in the midst of revolution, though it had been used by the American colonists with authority prior to the establishment of their own army to fight the British. Its parentage was mixed, as mixed as the peoples who came to settle in North America. The main foundation was British, as was, at least initially, most of the guns that were employed against the British in the War of the Revolution. There was also a large Spanish impact in North America, as well as a French influence, both of which groups of settlers brought some of their native artillery with them across the Atlantic. For the young United States Army, facing the threat of a vengeful Great Britain at the beginning of the nineteenth century, the singular influence for the period was undoubtedly the Gribeauval System, which the United States partly adopted in 1809.

Gribeauval guns and equipment had been in the United States since before 1809, however: the French Expeditionary Force under the Comte de Rochambeau had brought some with them when they had landed at Newport, Rhode Island in 1780. Down the long road to Virginia and the Siege of Yorktown the next year, the French took their excellent artillery train, and American soldiers had noticed its *matériel* and organization, as well as its efficiency in the siege. Later, when the United States Army was activated, thoughtful officers remembered what had been seen and done with the French artillery train, and, eventually, French model gun carriages were manufactured in the United States for its fledgling army and put into service. Gun tubes may or may not have been used, but as iron was plentiful in the United States, both iron and brass/bronze tubes were cast and employed. Additionally, since there were plenty of artillery pieces available, the Gribeauval gun tubes may never have been used, nor the standard calibers adopted, regardless of the material in the manuals of the period. As far as practicable, however, the Gribeauval System was adopted, along with an excellent three-volume manual in published in 1809, and put into service with the American artillery arm.[2] This happened none too soon, as the United States, tired of British interference with its merchant shipping and its support of the Indian tribes in the Old Northwest, declared war on Great Britain in June 1812. A more mismatched pair of belligerents never took the field against each other.

The story of the War of 1812 is a long and sorrowful one of a nation going to war with arguably the strongest nation on earth completely unprepared to fight. The US Army was small and ill-trained. The efficient navy that had repeatedly defeated the French in the quasi-war had been neglected by both the Jefferson and Madison administrations, being effectively gutted and left with only thirteen men-of-war, few of which were ready for sea in June 1812. If it were not for a dedicated handful of soldiers and sailors who fought their way out of the concocted mess, generally at the abandoned end of some forgotten line of communication, the very existence of the United States as a sovereign nation would have been in doubt. Luckily for the United States, Great Britain was in a death struggle with Napoleonic France, and until the summer of 1814 most of her military resources were engaged in that titanic tussle.

The United States Army had two artillery regiments in existence prior to 1812—the Regiment of Artillerists and the Light Artillery Regiment. The former consisted of thirteen companies, one of which was always recruiting, and the regiment was scattered in posts along the frontier. The Light Artillery Regiment consisted of ten companies and was meant to be horse artillery. The only mounted company before the war, though, was Captain Peter's, an excellent, show-horse outfit that was later disbanded for reasons of economy, even though the trials it conducted were very successful. Captain Peter resigned in disgust, but did serve in the War of 1812.

With hostilities imminent with Great Britain, two more artillery regiments were raised and formed, the 2nd and 3rd. The Regiment of Artillerists became the new 1st Artillery Regiment, and the Light Artillery Regiment remained as organized. The two new regiments were of two battalions of ten companies each. All of the artillery regiments, with the exception of the 1st, served with distinction throughout the war. The 2nd Regiment was undoubtedly the best unit in the United States Army for the period, and units belonging to that regiment served with distinction wherever they fought.

In May 1814, the three numbered regiments were consolidated into the Corps of Artillery of twelve battalions, each of four companies. The Light Artillery Regiment remained independent, as it would until 1821.[3] Distinguished service was rendered by Major Jacob Hindman's battalion (consisting of the companies of Captains Towson, Barker, Ritchie, and Williams) in the Niagara campaign of 1814, where it served with Major General Jacob Brown's famous Left Division, which had, through hard service and excellent training, become the best field unit in the United States Army. Under commanders such as Winfield Scott (who had been the executive officer and commander of the 2nd Artillery Regiment), the units distinguished themselves in the Battles of Chippawa and Lundy's Lane, and at the Siege of Fort Erie. The artillery companies had performed so splendidly during that "long and bloody summer," and had so impressed their enemies, that one of their opponents, Captain James Maclachlane of the Royal Artillery, remarked—giving them the "supreme compliment"—"We thought you were French."[4]

The main fighting was conducted on the northern frontier with Canada in the first two years of the war, neither side gaining a decisive advantage. British successes in 1813 at Chrysler's Farm and elsewhere were negated by Jacob Brown, Winfield Scott and their famous "Left Division" at Chippawa, Lundy's Lane, and Fort Erie the next year. It appeared that the war was going into a stalemate, but then, from across the Atlantic, dreaded news arrived—Napoleon had abdicated and almost twenty-five years of constant war was over. The British could now concentrate their considerable military power on the United States to end the nuisance in

North America. Thousands of British veterans—"Wellington's Invincibles"—were sent across the Atlantic into Canada and the West Indies for operations in North America. Fortunately for the United States, combat-proven officers, especially general officers, were now commanding American troops in the field. One of these was Andrew Jackson.

Andrew Jackson (1767-1845) was not an artilleryman. However, at New Orleans in 1814-15 he proved at least one thing: he knew how to use it, especially from an entrenched position. This demonstrates that he had either an ingrained talent for using his guns, or, more probably, he listened to those who did.

Jackson, the son of Irish immigrants, became a lawyer and then became interested and involved in politics. Having a hot temper and an inflated sense of personal honor, and being naturally quarrelsome, he fought a number of duels. In one of these his opponent shot first, seriously wounding Jackson in the chest. Straightening up toughly, Jackson took careful aim and shot and killed his somewhat shocked opponent. He was a volunteer general of militia, winning the decisive victory of Horseshoe Bend against the Creek Indians in early 1814, and thereafter being named a regular brigadier general. He was a frontier soldier, self-taught and growing up hating the British, a scar inflicted by a British officer during the Revolution when he was a boy, thence forward forever fostering a hatred for his opponents. He certainly took his revenge in January 1815—with interest. Earning his general's stars for leading successful and ruthless campaigns against the Creek Indians in the south, he was without formal military training but was a born leader, who had a knack for getting his orders obeyed, and a no-nonsense commander who usually got what he wanted. A competent tactician, he was not a strategist, but his "won't-be-whipped" attitude carried him through to his final victory.

The overall strategic situation for the United States was grim at the end of 1814. Along the Niagara frontier there was stalemate. Generals Jacob Brown and Winfield Scott had won a spectacular little victory at Chippawa, (Scott's brigade was actually the only one engaged in the division, so he won the fight on his own), only to be fought to a standstill at Lundy's Lane. Later, besieged in Fort Erie, Brown successfully defended his post, and ruined the British army that opposed him. Still, the works were destroyed and the American "Left Division" withdrew from Canadian territory after the siege had been broken and the British army had left with its tail between its legs.

Washington DC, the American national capital, had been captured and burned, the largely militia army sent to stop the British invader had been routed at Bladensburg, and the only American unit that really stood and fought being Commodore Joshua Barney's flotillamen and Marines. Barney himself was wounded and captured. There were American successes to report, however. At Plattsburg, a sizeable British invasion force had been held and turned away by Alexander Macomb, largely the result of Thomas MacDonough's spectacular naval victory on Lake Champlain, in which the entire British flotilla was taken in the victory—akin to Oliver Perry's equally spectacular victory on Lake Erie in 1813. Only on Lake Ontario did the Royal Navy have any success, largely because of the most gun-shy American naval commander, Chauncey, who maintained a naval arms race with his Royal Navy opponent, James Yeo, but would not risk his beloved ships unless he had a definite superiority on the lake.

Flushed with victory at Bladensburg and Washington, the British reembarked, and marked their next target as Baltimore. Maryland militia turned out in large, disciplined numbers, and fought an excellent delaying action at North Point, killing the British ground commander, Robert Ross, and inflicting more losses than they incurred. The naval side of the battle also met with determined resistance, and Baltimore harbor could not be forced, ably defended as it

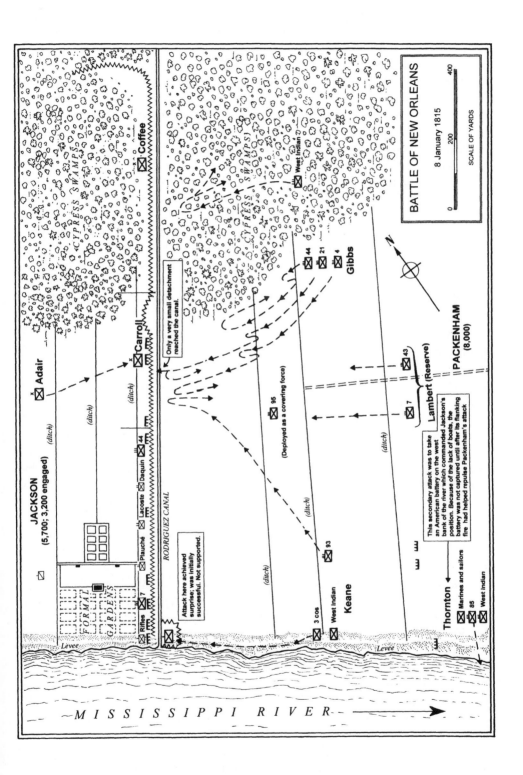

BATTLE OF NEW ORLEANS

8 January 1815

0   200   400

SCALE OF YARDS

MISSISSIPPI RIVER

CYPRESS SWAMPS

CYPRESS SWAMPS

JACKSON
(5,700; 3,200 engaged)

FORMAL GARDENS

Levee

Rifles ☒ 7

☒ Plauché

☒ Lacoste

☒ Daquin ☒ 44

RODRIGUEZ CANAL

(ditch)

(ditch)

(ditch)

Coffee ☒

Adair ☒

Carroll ☒

Only a very small detachment reached the canal.

Attack here achieved surprise; was initially successful. Not supported.

West Indian ☒

☒ 44
☒ 21
☒ 4
Gibbs

☒ 95
(Deployed as a covering force)

☒ 93

West Indian
Keane

3 cos ☒

☒ 43

☒ 7

Lambert (Reserve)

PACKENHAM
(8,000)

N

(ditch)

(ditch)

Levee

Thornton ☒

Marines and sailors ☒ 85

West Indian

This secondary attack was to take an American battery on the west bank of the river which commanded Jackson's position. Because of the lack of boats, the battery was not captured until after its flanking fire had helped repulse Packenham's attack.

was by Major Armistead at Fort McHenry. The "rockets' red glare" gave a good backdrop for what would become the American National Anthem, but the fort, and Baltimore, held. The British force limped off, looking for easier prey.

One theater had been completely left alone by the British—the newly acquired Louisiana Territory, purchased from Napoleon in 1803, with the bustling commercial center of New Orleans near the Gulf of Mexico just up the Mississippi River from the Mississippi Delta that emptied into the Gulf. That multilingual city became the next target for the reinforced British invasion force that had been frustrated off Baltimore. North from the Atlantic sailed disaster in the form of a British fleet and a large, veteran army commanded by one of the Duke of Wellington's trusted generals, and his brother-in-law, Sir Edward Packenham.

The area in and around New Orleans, and the Mississippi Delta in general, is some of the worst terrain in which to campaign, especially from the point of view of the attacker. The Mississippi Delta and surrounding area is a hodgepodge of lakes, bayous (swamps) and generally waterlogged terrain that is difficult to navigate. Additionally, along much of the Mississippi, the closer the approach to the city, the higher the river becomes compared to the surrounding countryside. To control this situation, huge *levées* (which are still used) had been built along the banks of the river to keep the water out and give the population more arable land. Cutting the *levées* would make movement almost impossible and could trap the unwary commander.

Thus, moving an army overland would be a herculean undertaking. That the British actually did get an army over that nightmare and into the field speaks volumes for their tenacity and skill, especially moving guns and ammunition by water in small boats and then overland by pure manpower. The effort was accomplished using the Royal Navy and the fleet's boats. The task was accomplished with the skill and dedication of the seamen of the Royal Navy in a much overlooked feat of endurance: without them, the British army would never have come ashore. The terrain they crossed was described by one British officer as nothing but "a collection of mud."

The terrain was a collection of bayous, cypress swamps, thick forest, execrable roads, and open, flat plantation land that was below the level of the very wide Mississippi river, which itself was controlled by a *levée* on both sides (another obstacle). While the British expeditionary force had the "teeth" for a fight, its logistical tail was short and tenuous. The transportation of the available artillery was particularly difficult, the terrain being much rougher than even that of Spain, causing Packenham's artillery commander, Alexander Dickson (a capable and reliable officer) no end of head- and heartache. That the mission was successful is a tribute to the skill and determination of Dickson and his men.

New Orleans is ninety miles, as the crow flies, northwest up the Mississippi from the tip of the Delta—and the Royal Navy were not crows. The Mississippi is usually straight-line distance from South Pass at the tip of the Delta to Point à la Hache—about 60 miles all told—but for the last 30 miles the river degenerates into twists and turns that could be somewhat chancy for warships in the age of sail. To the north and east of the city are three lakes—Lake Maurepas, the smallest; Lake Pontchartrain, in the centre; and Lake Borgne, which opens on the eastern side to the Gulf of Mexico. The British decided to launch their offensive across the lakes, completely avoiding the hazards of the Delta.

Jackson, was never a strategist, and not an overly inspired tactician, but he was a stubborn, aggressive fighter and not one to be frightened off. He reached New Orleans on 2 December 1814. Short of everything, from flints to long arms, but especially Regulars, he set to work with a will, to ensure that New Orleans was properly defended. If it were a nightmare for the attacker, New Orleans was also a difficult place to defend, especially if the enemy had strategic mobility, as did the British. Suffice it to say that the British surprised Jackson in coming across Lake Borgne, a straight line to New Orleans.

The Americans had a gunboat squadron on Lake Borgne, commanded by Lieutenant Catesby Jones. On 14 December, in a sharp action, he was attacked and defeated by the British, who attacked in boats across the lake. All of the American gunboats were taken. Jackson found out about the American naval defeat the next day. Undoubtedly he had some unofficial, and quite colorful remarks on the *débâcle* which robbed the Americans of over half of their naval strength.

The British advance guard—the light brigade under Colonel Thornton, who had led the British advance at Bladensburg earlier in the year—disembarked in broad daylight after coming across Lake Borgne overnight. They landed, gobbled up the American pickets, advanced through the bayou, and emerged in the open near the Villare Plantation. There they found Major Villare and his militia company, and scooped them up as well. No warning was given, and no picket or patrol reported the British presence so close to New Orleans. It was the low point of Jackson's generalship in the campaign. The irony was that the British route was one of the avenues of approach identified by Jackson that had to be vigilantly watched:

> The record of American generalship offered many examples of misfortune but none so complete as this. Neither Hull nor Harrison, neither Winder nor Samuel Smith, had allowed a large British army, heralded long in advance, to arrive within seven miles unseen and unsuspected, and without so much as an earthwork, a man, or a gun between them and their object. The disaster was unprecedented, and could only be repaired by desperate measures.[5]

Jackson, however, was not Hull, Winder, Smith nor any other American general who could be stampeded into panic. He immediately ordered a counter to the British arrival and planned a raid that night on the British encampment. He rose to the occasion, whereas the others in the moment of greatest crisis gave in to panic and despair. New Orleans would not be lost without a fight.

There were three major actions during the campaign. The first was a raid against the British camp during the night of 23/24 December. The second was the artillery duel on 1 January, which proved to be the main battle—the British assault on the American line and on the fortifications at Chalmette. The first was a draw or perhaps a British victory, as the raiders were either driven off or withdrew (depending upon one's point of view). The last two were definite defeats for the British, and the common denominator in those two defeats was the professional performance of the American artillery.

The American raid hit the British camp from two directions, though unfortunately not quite simultaneously. The main attack down the *levée* along the river was carried out by Regulars and militia with two field pieces, supported by fire from the river by the schooner *Carolina*. The British were surprised, especially by the *Carolina*'s fire, but their rocket company opened fire on the ship with a lively firework display. There was confused fighting in the camp, the fury of the American attack making the British believe there were more Americans than there actually were. The Americans finally withdrew upriver, losses about equal. Then, as the British thought it over as Jackson was disengaging, Coffee's brigade of riflemen infiltrated the British camp from the north in an attack in loose order. Combat with the riflemen was confused—the confusion heightened by a fog that had rolled in unexpectedly. Finally, the riflemen drew off and got back to the American position, meeting Jackson on the *levée* on the way out. It was the first American offensive of the campaign, and the first action that was anywhere near a success. The Americans suffered 24 killed, 115 wounded, and 74 missing; British losses were 46 killed, 167 wounded, and 64 missing.

For the planned offensive against the main American position at Chalmette, the British started to emplace their artillery, and first they dug holes for gun emplacements in the *levée* so that they could deal with the American schooners on the river: no offensive against Jackson could be undertaken until the threat of naval flanking fire could be dealt with. The emplacements were constructed and camouflaged, and at 0745 on the morning of 27 December, Dickson saw his chance. The *Carolina* was in range, and the British opened an accurate, deadly fire on her at 800 yards, and the vessel "soon caught fire and blew up." Seeing her consort in trouble, the crew of the *Louisiana*, the other American schooner, was being warped upriver as the British guns lifted and shifted to her. However, the range was too long and she got away.

The flank on the river now secured, the British moved ahead for a scheduled assault on New Year's Day. The American position was along the dry Rodriquez Canal on the Chalmette plain:

> A British engineer officer who inspected the American defenses after the war reported that the canal was about 8 feet deep and 15 feet wide for some 650 yards in from the Mississippi. The remaining 350 yards measured only 4 and 10 feet, respectively. The Americans had made no effort to deepen or widen it, and had left it full of brambles. Their breastwork had been made by scraping up earth on the far side of the canal; the inner side was revetted with planks, held in place by posts.[6]

During the night of 31 December, the artillery moved into position and emplaced its batteries for a bombardment of the American fortifications the next morning. Major Forrest, the British Assistant Quartermaster-General saw that

> Four 18-pounders were placed in a battery formed of hogsheads of sugar, on the main road, to fire upon the ship if she dropped down. Preparations were also made to establish batteries—one of six eighteen pounders, and one of four 24-pounders; also batteries for the field pieces and howitzers, the latter to keep the fire of the enemy under, while the troops were to be moved forward in readiness to storm the works as soon as a practicable breach was effected.[7]

Colonel Dickson, the British Chief of Artillery, was somewhat concerned about the construction of, and the amount of protection afforded by, the British batteries. There was insufficient ammunition for a sustained bombardment, let alone for supporting a major attack against a well-sited and well-fortified position. The battery positions themselves were jury-rigged in the flat terrain that would become a quagmire in anything worse than a heavy mist. Finally, they would be in range of the excellent American field artillery—that could hardly be expected to do nothing as the British prepared their positions and got ready to open fire.

The gunfight on 1 January was quick and deadly. The British opened fire at around 0800, and the Americans slowly replied, building their volume of fire carefully as they got the range of the British guns. Soon, their accurate fire became overwhelming. British firing platforms had been hastily built in the mud and muck. Ammunition was short, and the American artillery, though starting out by firing slowly, gradually picked up momentum and was deadly accurate. Their expertly handled guns were "worked partly by regular artillerists, partly by sailors, partly by New Orleans militia, and partly by the 'hellish banditti' of Barataria, who to the number of twenty or thirty were received by General Jackson into the service and given the care of two 24-pounders." The American artillerymen outnumbered by the British artillery, both in numbers of guns and in the total weight of shot that they could "throw." The difference was that the American guns were mounted on well-built, solid gun platforms behind excellent defenses. They were well commanded and well served, and the gunners went to work with a will.

After two hours of fighting, a ceasefire was called in the British positions. They had come off a very poor second best, to the chagrin of Dickson, who knew his business. The center

British battery was wrecked, and the unsteady platforms constructed in the mud could not support the heavier guns. The British had been plainly outshot, the skill of the Americans, and the superiority of their artillery, dominating the two-hour duel. They were almost out of ammunition, several pieces had been dismounted, and the battery positions were a shambles. There was not enough left to support a major offensive, and ammunition replenishment was a long way off. Hence, the planned infantry assault was called off. Packenham decided to wait a week, and preparations went rapidly ahead in the most primitive conditions for fresh assault on 8 January.

It started to rain that afternoon, which multiplied the problems facing the British, who withdrew their guns after darkness fell, the ground soaked. Both the fields and roads had turned into one continuous bog and, the British sailors and artillerymen were working in mud up to their knees:

> The enemy having made no attempt to carry off our heavy guns, which we abandoned to their fate, it was judged advisable to bring them into the camp as soon as circumstances would allow; and for this purpose working parties were again sent out as soon as the darkness screened them. It was my fortune to accompany them. The labor of dragging a number of huge ship's guns out of the soft sand into which they had sunk, crippled too as most of them were in their carriages, was more extreme by far than any one expected to find it. Indeed, it was not until four o'clock in the morning that our task came to the conclusion, and even then it had been very imperfectly performed. Five guns were eventually left behind. These were rendered useless, it is true, by breaking their trunnions; but it cannot be said that in the course of the late operations the British army came off without the loss of some of its artillery.[8]

TABLE 18: US AND BRITISH ARTILLERY DEPLOYMENT, 1 JANUARY 1815[9]	
American	
32-pounder	1
24-pounder	3
18-pounder	1
12-pounder	3
24-pounder	1
long 12-pounder	2
British	
18-pounders (against the gunboats	2
on the river)	
18-pounders	2
5½-inch mortars	3
Rocket batteries	2
6-pounders	3
9-pounders	2
5½-inch howitzers	2
18-pounders	6
24-pounder carronades	4

Artillery present and emplaced on 1 January was as indicated in Table 18.

The British reaction to the defeat was as mortifying as it was unexpected. Admiral Codrington bitterly remarked upon it in typical Royal Navy fashion by damning the artillery for failing to silence the American artillery. His attitude towards the army, and the artillery in particular, tended to blame them even for the weather and mud that was present.

The other comments from British eyewitnesses was equally as damning, not the least of which was Dickson's own, more reasoned critique. Dickson took responsibility for the action, but the outcome was not entirely his fault. He had been given inadequate resources for this type of campaign, though apparently the senior British officers expected the level of resistance to be comparable to that during the raid that burned the American capitol in Washington. In fact, the British army sent to take New Orleans was better suited to launching raids than to conducting a sustained land campaign against a determined enemy. With Jackson, that is what they had run into: the

Americans were ready to stand and fight, and they had clearly demonstrated that they possessed adequate artillery and knew how to use it.

Major Latour, the senior American senior engineer, and a very competent officer (and a veteran of Napoleon's Grande Armée), gave due credit to the British. He stated that their artillery fire had been sustained and accurate. At least two guns had been damaged by British artillery fire, the rockets had blown up two ammunition caissons, and some of the fieldworks had been damaged. Dickson's gunners had not disgraced themselves as a disgruntled admiral had implied.

The British planned to attack the American defenses on both sides of the Mississippi on 8 January. The main thrust would be directed against the American left by the British 2nd Brigade, reinforced by most of the 95th Foot, which, commanded by Major General Samuel Gibbs, was to advance under supporting fire from Dickson's artillery, its leading regiment carrying fascines and ladders to handle the ditch and parapet of the American position. On Gibbs' right flank, as cover, would be another light infantry detachment and 100 men of the 1st West India Regiment. Gibbs' strength was about 2,200 all ranks. Captain Robert Renny was to lead an assault along the river bank on the American right to seize the redoubt against the river; he had a forlorn hope of three light infantry companies as well as a detachment of the 1st West India Regiment. Colonel William Thornton would lead an assault against the American positions across the river in a coordinated supporting attack, and Major General John Keane's 3rd Brigade, about 1,200 all-ranks positioned to the left of the 2nd Brigade, would stand by, awaiting the results of Gibbs' attack. The newly arrived (4 January) 1st Brigade of Major General John Lambert would be the army reserve.

Dickson's artillerymen had some difficulties in setting up their positions. He was ordered to emplace his guns between the staging areas of the 2nd and 3rd Brigades, but not only was the work to be done again at night, the weather was foggy to boot. By 0600 he was in position and ready to fire. Packenham ordered the assault, and Dickson opened fire. Rockets were launched with a terrific noise, arcing high into the early morning sky and signalling Gibbs to advance:

> . . . the advance guards on both flanks ran forward toward Jackson's line and the American guns opened fire. They were answered at once by Dickson's batteries, and from across the river, Patterson's guns took up the challenge. Amid the roar of cannonfire could be heard the steady beat of drums form the advancing British columns and, from Keane's brigade on the left, the skirl of bagpipes of the 93rd Regiment. For the brief moment before men began to die Packenham's army paraded in proud, colorful, and stirring display. Within five minutes the image was shattered; within ten the parade ground had become a churned field of mud heaped with tangled and bloodied masses of scarlet, tartan, and green.[10]

There was a mist hanging over the battlefield, shrouding most of it. Gibbs' leading regiment had forgotten to pick up their fascines and scaling ladders when they had moved into position. They had been sent back to get them, but had not managed to regain the head of the assault column when the rockets signaling the advance had gone up, and Gibbs' brigade lurched forward, the attack almost launching itself. Moving forward, Gibbs was headed towards his objective, the delinquent 44th Foot trying to catch up with the ladders and fascines on his left. Just as the brigade got into motion, the fog lifted; and then "the guns began to tear at them."[11]

The American artillery went swiftly into action, and Gibbs' brigade was torn apart, as if it had walked into a buzz saw. The American guns, rapidly served, ate up the British battalions, and the light infantry on Gibbs' right ceased to exist as a cohesive force. Gamely coming on and getting into musket range, the British infantry were again hit with a mailed fist as the American works exploded in one huge volley of musketry. Men went down in heaps. Riding to the head of the column, Gibbs tried to rally his men, and was shot out of the saddle with a mortal wound. Some infantrymen under a Major Wilkinson made it to the ditch, crossed it, and went up the parapet, only to be shot down in their turn. Wilkinson died inside the American position. Renny attacked up the levée and actually broke into the American works between the redoubt and the main parapet. His supporting regiment, however, the 93rd Highlanders, had been diverted by Packenham at the last minute to reinforce Gibbs' depleted regiments. Reinforcing failure usually does not work: Renny was killed, and his command all but annihilated, his momentary success for nothing.

Keane led the 93rd in their attack on the American line. He was shot down, dying from a neck wound. The Highlanders were decimated as they crossed the fields, suffering 75 percent casualties and the loss of their commander. Packenham, seeing his two brigades wrecked and some of the survivors starting to go to the rear, went galloping to the 2nd Brigade, or what was left of it, trying to rally its remnants. Almost immediately he was wounded and his horse killed under him. His faithful *aide-de-camp* dismounted and gave the general his horse, but Packenham was almost immediately blown out of the saddle with a mortal wound.

As he had gone forward, Packenham had ordered Lambert to commit the 1st Brigade to the assault. On hearing of Packenham's wounding, and now with three generals dead or dying, Lambert, as the senior unscathed officer on the field, called a halt to the slaughter. Nothing had been gained but the ruination of an excellent British army, and the Americans had not been appreciably hurt. There was no word from Thornton. It was now about 0830, and it was all over. Putting his brigade in a defensive position, Lambert tried to salvage what he could as best he could.

Thornton's crossing was flawed from the start. The river was flowing fast; the embarkation took too long. Therefore, he went with what he had, was understrength, landed in the wrong place, and attacked late. Still, his was the only British success that terrible day, driving the Americans from their entrenchments. However, Thornton's skillful attack ended up accomplishing nothing because of the bloody failure of the main attack. He was ordered to withdraw by Lambert, now the army commander.

British losses were very heavy—291 killed, 1,262 wounded, and 484 missing or taken prisoner. American losses were light, most taken on the west bank—13 killed, 39 wounded, and 19 missing. The battle had been decided by the much superior American artillery and conventional musketry, and, contrary to legend, the famed Kentucky or Pennsylvania rifle had little or nothing to do with the victory. Packenham had not coordinated his infantry assault well, and had allowed it to go in with poor artillery preparation. He paid for that mistake with his life, and the lives of his excellent infantry. There was good reason why Wellington had refused the American command and had urged his political masters to end the war which was a drain on the British war effort in Europe as well as on their prestige internationally.

So ended the last battle and campaign of the War of 1812—a war that could and should have been avoided, and the battle that was fought after the peace treaty had been signed on 24 December 1814 in Ghent, Belgium, by the representatives of both nations. The British attitude towards their opponents can be summed up by Michael Scott, a contemporary British observer of the wars, as well as a participant from time to time:

> I don't like Americans. I never did and I never shall. I have seldom met an American gentleman, in the large and complete sense of the term. I have no wish to eat with them, drink with them, deal or consort with them in any way. But let me tell the whole truth—nor to fight with them, were it not for the laurels to be acquired by overcoming an enemy so brave, determined, alert and in every way so worthy of one's

steel as they have always proved. In the field, or grappling in mortal combat on the blood-slippery quarter deck of an enemy's vessel, a British soldier or sailor is the bravest of the brave. No soldier or sailor of any country, saving and excepting always those damned Yankees, can stand against them.[12]

Since that time, Briton and American have not fought against each other, but have since been, especially in the twentieth and early twenty-first centuries friends and allies, and have fought side by side in five major wars. The "cousins" are now steadfast allies—though of course, they do not always agree. Families do have their differences.

NOTES

1. The full quotation is: "No artillery could be better served than ours." It was published by General Washington in a General Order to the Continental Army at Freehold, New Jersey on 29 June 1779 after the Battle of Monmouth, where the Continental Artillery particularly distinguished itself.
2. See Graves, "American Ordnance of the War of 1812."
3. See Chartrand and Graves, "The United States Army and the War of 1812: A Handbook."
4. Graves, "For Want of this Precaution so Many Men Lose Their Arms: Official, Semi-Official, and Unofficial American Artillery Texts, 1775-1845," p. 13.
5. Adams, *The War of 1812*, p. 301.
6. Elting, *Amateurs, To Arms! A Military History of the War of 1812*, p. 300.
7. Adams, *op. cit.*, p. 311.
8. *Ibid.*, p. 314.
9. For further information on the campaign and Battle of New Orleans, see Reilly, *The British at the Gates: The New Orleans Campaign in the War of 1812*, which is probably the best reference available in print. Additionally, Adams, *op. cit.*, and Elting, *op. cit.*, both have excellent accounts of the fighting as well as good insights into the events surrounding the campaign.
10. Reilly, *op. cit.*, p. 317.
11. This quotation is borrowed from Bruce Catton, *Glory Road*, the second volume of his trilogy on the Army of the Potomac during the American Civil War. While referring to the Federal artillery opening up on Picketts Charge on 3 July during the Battle of Gettysburg in 1863, and not to the Battle of New Orleans, I thought the use of the quotation particularly apt, as virtually the same thing happened to the assaulting infantry in both actions.
12. King, Dean, and Hattendorf, John B., (eds), *Every Man Will Do His Duty: An Anthology of First-Hand Accounts from the Age of Nelson, 1793–1815*, p. 293.

Epilogue
"*La Garde à Feu!*"

Then shook the hills with thunder riven,
Then rushed the steed, to battle driven,
And louder than the bolts of Heaven,
   Far flashed the red artillery.
                    —Thomas Campbell, *Hohenlinden*

The cannon's breath
Wings far the hissing globe of death.
                    —Byron, *The Siege of Corinth*

No one accuses the Gunner of maudlin affection for anything except his beasts and his weapons . . . He serves at least three jealous gods-his horse and all its saddlery and harness; his gun, whose least detail of efficiency is more important than men's lives; and, when these have been attended to, the never-ending mystery of his art commands him.
                    —Rudyard Kipling

Thus terminated the war, and with it remembrance of the veteran's services.
                    —General Sir William Napier

2030, 18 June 1815: The east side of the Brussels highway, near La Belle Alliance
The two Old Guard battalions on the other side of the highway were starting to withdraw. Streaming past them in rout was the rest of the Armée du Nord. *Monsieur le capitaine* sat on his horse in disgust and resignation, his gunners by their pieces ready to fire their last rounds. He calmly nodded to his sergeant-major, and the grizzled Grognard bellowed through cupped hands, "*Feu!*" Gun captains echoed the command to their gun crews, portfires touched vents, and the guns exploded in smoke and fire, almost in unison, one of the flank pieces being a little slow, causing both *Monsieur le Capitaine* and the sergeant-major to wince and shake their heads. The offending gun captain turned to look at them, and with a typical Gallic shrug, communicated his frustration to his commanding officer.

Quickly putting his glass to his eye, the battery commander watched the fall of shot land amongst enemy cavalry, both horses and men going down from the well-sighted last rounds. Ready boxes and caissons now stood empty. With a shout from the left flank gun, both men turned and noticed that both of the Old Guard infantry battalions, which had stood among the growing flood of fugitives and ever-bolder enemy like two rocks in a mountain torrent, were starting to withdraw. Both battalions were from the 1st Regiment of Grenadiers à Pied, the oldest of the old, three-fourths of whose men held the *Légion d'Honneur*. They were retiring in perfect order, ignoring the vulgar uproar around them.

Gun captains and gunners, as well as the company drummer now watched *Monsieur le Capitaine* and waited for the command for "March." It was time to limber up and save what they could. The veteran NCO, however, knew his commander wouldn't give that order. He had been with him for a long time, and he wasn't surprised when the captain calmly turned to him and gave the order to load.

Turning towards the gunline, the faithful NCO echoed the captain's command to the company, most of whom stood motionless and looked at him, slack-jawed, as if he were crazy. Then training and experience kicked in. Gun captains dutifully, if albeit a little less than enthusiastically, echoed the command to their gun crews, who went through the intricate gun-drill with now-imaginary rounds. Tubes were rammed and the crews stood by, portfires smoldering, ready to fire.

The Allied cavalry, just starting their charge, came to an abrupt, teeth-jarring halt, some of the cavalrymen falling from their horses to the grim satisfaction of the exhausted Guard artillerymen. At the bellowed command "*Feu!*", portfires went dutifully to the vents, and, as expected, nothing happened. The startled, shocked, and now furiously embarrassed Allied cavalry gathered themselves, trumpets blew the charge, and the horsemen thundered down on the artillery company, who, after suitably jeering their fooled enemies were frantically grabbing muskets, handspikes, and rammers to defend themselves. *Monsieur le Capitaine*, grimly glancing once more at his faithful sergeant-major, drew his saber and prepared to defend his battery position to the last.

*   *   *

The guns had at last fallen silent. For the first time in almost twenty-five years, Europe was at peace. Armies, and the men who had made them up, were on winding roads going home, to India, or on occupation duty in France. Prisoners were being released and sent home, and the lessons of war, as well as their causes, were once again being put aside and forgotten in the euphoria of victory or the bitterness of defeat.

There had been an eleven-month respite in Europe with the first abdication of Napoleon. The hated Bourbons had returned to rule a restless France. At first they did well, abolishing conscription and attempting, on the surface at least, to placate the senior officers of the Army, who remembered nothing but war.

Then, ignoring the Treaty of Fontainebleu, they refused to pay Napoleon his pension, and the heads of state of the major powers, or their representatives, met in Vienna to "divide the loot." They openly talked of moving Napoleon to a more remote location, to keep him out of Europe. In conjunction with this, the Bourbons gradually treated the French Army, its leaders, and those who had served long and loyally, indifferently at best. That indifference also saw many of Napoleon's veterans replaced with recently returned Royalists, many of whom had served against France. Those who no longer had a place in the Army were retired and put out on half-pay, many times not receiving that. Marshal's wives were insulted, duels were fought, and Royalists learned to stay off the streets at night and never go into dark alleys.

Napoleon returned to regain his throne and fight his last campaign. For a while, the guns thundered once again and the drums beat the long roll. However, it was a desperate, lost campaign, and the Bourbons, and the Allies, came back full of righteous wrath and vengeance, running down Napoleon's veteran officers, forcing some into exile, imprisoning others, judicially murdering some of those remaining.

The War of 1812 having been concluded, and the boundaries of the United States and Canada remaining as they were prewar, the guns were finally, permanently silent. The world, though, would never be the same. Too much had happened socially, politically, and militarily. Warfare and nations, as well as peoples, had changed.

So it was with the artillery, which was now a respected, and equal, third combat arm. Maimed Prussian General von Holtzendorf, nursing his Ligny wound, would insist on improvements in

Prussian artillery. The Prussian artillery system of 1812 was firmly, completely, and finally instituted, and, for the first time in its history, the Prussian Army had a unified artillery system, the last of the great powers of Europe to accept it. The French, impressed with the British Congreve block carriage, instituted a new artillery system in 1827 which introduced the block trail, and the old Gribeauval System was phased out by 1829. Russians, Austrians, and other peoples, including the French, enthusiastically continued to experiment with rockets, which were used increasingly in later campaigns and wars, but would not really see fruition and implementation until the twentieth century and more costly, and bitter, wars.

Though no one realized it at the time, the real up-and-coming power in the world was the United States. Based on the experience of the War of 1812, and the good fortune that the Madison administration finally left power in 1817, the US Army was left in the hands of the generals who had won their stars on the battlefields of the War of 1812. Winfield Scott, Alexander Macomb, and Edmund Gaines, as well as John Wool, molded the army into their own image of it—a professional fighting force that came of age in the war with Mexico in 1846-47. Both it and the US Navy were first-rate organizations by then, and one of the elite arms of the service was the artillery—as it was to prove on the battlefields of that foreign war, and in more bitter, longer, and bloodier wars to come.

The American Civil War of 1861-65 would see the last large-scale use of muzzle-loading field artillery, and rifled muzzle-loaders took their place alongside the old bronze smoothbores on the battlefields of North America that were the harbinger of things to come in warfare. Though many European professional soldiers would scoff at the early scramblings as being fought by nothing more than "armed mobs," there were indisputably lessons to be learned. The United States learned them, though they would not bear fruit until the twentieth century.

One of the lessons concerned the employment of field artillery, which in the United States Army was considered a *corps d'élite*, and which had in its lineage the hard-hitting batteries that fought with Winfield Scott and Jacob Brown on the Niagara frontier in 1814. These batteries, and the artillerymen who served in them, were influenced by a man and his artillery system— Jean Baptiste de Gribeauval.

Appendices

These appendices are intended to help the reader follow the intricacies of late eighteenth- and early nineteenth-century artillery. They contain information the author believes to be very useful, but not entirely appropriate to place in the text.

The information contained in the appendices was taken from the *Dickson Manuscripts*, Adye's *Bombardier and Pocket Gunner* (as codified in Don Graves' excellent booklet *The Rockets' Red Glare*, on Congreve and his invention), Alexander and Yurii Zhmodikov's comprehensive *Tactics of the Russian Army in the Napoleonic Wars*, DeScheel's *A Treatise on Artillery*, and the monumental Louis de Tousard's *The American Artillerist's Companion*. Some information has been extracted, but most has been taken from the references *verbatim* in order to keep the "flavor" of the original.

During the period of the French Revolutionary and Napoleonic Wars, the Industrial Revolution was blossoming. This was one of the reasons that the large armies could be supplied and equipped more or less efficiently during the period. Though mass manufacturing, the interchangibility of parts, and other innovative production techniques were in their infancy, they were used by the belligerents, the British and French most notably, to produce weapons on a scale never dreamed of during the last great European conflict, the Seven Years' War (1756–63).

Not only could armies be swiftly equipped and supplied, they could also be resupplied with an efficiency unknown in Europe before—witness the huge effort iinvolved in equipping the new Grande Armée of 1813, especially in artillery, after the disastrous losses in Russia in 1812. This was done by a "horse-powered" economy, and took place before the widespread use of the steam engine (though that, too, was just "puffing over the horizon").

Cannon were now mass-produced and bored out on huge horizontal boring apparatuses, thanks to Maritz, and gun locks for muskets were mass-produced, and if their interchangeability was limited, so it was also being thought about and attempted. Casting cannon, improved ammunition, using pre-determined powder charges, attaching the separate pieces of the artillery round into single, compact pieces of equipment for ease of loading, storing, and firing, and the invention of newer, more sophisticated tooling—all this contributed to the ability of armies to take the field repeatedly, year after year, until a final "decision" had been reached. Looking back on it from the technology-heavy early twenty-first century, one can only be amazed at what the mind of man can achieve, but it is also a misfortune that these accomplishments usually take place only in time of war. That is our burden, and man's unending tragedy. The study of war is fascinating, but all should heed Robert E. Lee's sage advice: "It is good that war is so terrible, else we should grow too fond of it."

Appendix I: The Strasbourg Experiments

The first object of these experiments, and the most interesting one, was, to determine to what point it was possible to lighten pieces proper to be used in the field, so as to compose an Artillery as moveable as that with which the other Powers of Europe made war and at the same time to leave as much strength and solidity as was necessary to produced the effects expected from it. As those who attended these operations were judicious men, they will readily concur in the following positions.

1. That the destination of pieces of Artillery being generally to destroy troops, and rarely to batter walls, the size of caliber is not the principal object. It is sufficient if it be capable of destroying villages, and opening breeches in entrenchments; and the caliber of twelve being sufficient for these operations, it was not necessary to use a greater one, and thereby uselessly to embarrass the marching of an army.

2. That in consequence of these principles, the sixteen pound cannon, which was formerly drawn after an army, should be placed in the magazine of the nearest neighboring army, to be always ready for use, to be drawn by the horse of the cavalry to batter any post which might be too considerable to be attacked by twelve pounders.

3. That it would be directly contrary to the end proposed, to employ sixteen pounders at the same time in sieges and in battle; because the least length given to pieces employed in the Park Artillery is 9 feet 7 inches, and at the greatest reduction the weight 8903 lbs. That then they would scarcely bear the service of small sieges for which they were principally designed, without being of any real use in the line; since two pieces of this caliber would require as much tackle as three pieces of twelve, or four of eight, when made light; that they would discharge only two balls, whilst the three pieces of twelve would fire four, and the four pieces of eight, would discharge six or seven.

   It may be farther observed, that the disadvantages attending the use of these pieces would be still greater when the proximity of the enemy permitted the firing of cartouches and that in all cases of cannon being dismounted, which is frequent in battle, these disadvantages would be considerably increased, on account of the embarrassment which so much appendage would occasion in the line, from the impossibility of moving them by hand; and, above all, for the loss of them in battle, in consequence of their size and weight.

   For these reasons, the experiments are confined to the calibers of twelve, eight, and four, which are the pieces proposed to be reduced.

4. Those who attend to these experiments will readily agree, that to send a ball beyond its object, is not only unnecessary, but occasions an useless consumption of ammunition which is always precious in war, since an army can carry with it only a determinate quantity; besides that the ammunition thus uselessly expended, might be wanted in a decisive moment when by its failure you give your enemy an advantage, and teach him to brave your fire. Neither ought guns to have the power of carrying farther than they can be accurately directed. In sieges, where cannon may be served with greater precision than in battle, experience has proved that they ought not to be farther distant than three hundred toises [a little over 300 fathoms—i.e., 600 yards] from the batteries attacked. It was going beyond all the advocates for firing at a great distance could require, to allow five hundred toises in firing upon a line of Infantry five feet ten inches high, or upon Cavalry eight feet and a half high. In fixing it at four hundred toises, it is believed, would be determining upon as great a distance as any Field Artillery can carry with effect. We may, therefore, confine the power of carrying within these limits, even if, by the proposed diminution of the length and weight of these pieces, it should appear that any of this power is lost, which the greater part of those who attended the experiments believed, but which the general officer, who required them to be made, did not acknowledge and which, in fact, had been disproved by the experiment.

This distance of five hundred toises being the base of all the experiments, it was only necessary that all the new pieces should be proved capable of carrying to that distance.

But, to conform ourselves to the essential results, verified by the officers who directed the experiments, and the greater part of them, as hath already been observed, entertained opinions unfavorable to the enquiry, it appears.

1. That the old has no advantage over the new caliber, neither with respect to the correctness of carrying, nor to the accuracy of direction (which are essential objects) supposing each to be charged with their appropriate quantity of powder and ball, and pointed at the same elevation.

2. That none of the new pieces, even of the caliber of four, carry to a less distance than 500 toises, although fired in an angle of three degrees—a distance far exceeding (as hath already been shown) that at which troops can be fired at with certainty.

3. That if the old pieces had any advantage over the new, in these experiments, the superiority, as it respected the distance of carrying, is not worthy of consideration; since when the object fired at is so far removed, no accuracy of direction can be expected. This superiority was principally owing to an equality which was attempted to be established in the service of different pieces, in which the carrying power was to be compared. They generally used for both one and the other, balls which left about the twelfth of an inch windage, instead of one-sixth, as directed by the ordinance of 1732, and according to which the ball was still proportioned, until these experiments were made. Gribeauval, when he proposed light pieces, proposed also to reduce windage to one-twelfth of an inch.

These changes are calculated to produce three things; first, more accuracy in the direction, the ball being so much the more disposed to depart from its true line of direction, as it strikes the mouth of the gun on leaving it under more obtuse angles: 2dly, it occasions less injury to the pieces; for what ruins the guns long before they are apparently worn, from any external sign, are the dents produced in the barrel by the rattling of the ball in its passage through the bore, which is most dangerous when the piece becomes heated in action; and the less windage there is allowed, the less the gun will be exposed to injuries of this kind. The 3d effect which this reduction of the windage of the ball produces, is an augmentation of the distance to which the piece will carry; for the ball having less play within the piece, there remains less space for the escape of an elastic fluid which propels the ball forward. Besides its center of gravity applying nearer to the axis of the gun, its impulse will be made in a more direct line, and with greater force.

Gribeauval, in proposing the reduction of the windage of the ball to one-half, had only in view the accuracy of direction, and the preservation of the guns, and did not suppose it would also have communicated the power of carrying to a greater distance than the gun before possessed, as appears from what has already been said.

Remarks on the Experiments at Strasbourg

Those who think they have sufficient reason to censure the use of the new pieces, lose sight of the principle of lightness given to them, and which have directed the late improvements: for it is vastly advantageous for a general to be at the head of an army which can, with all possible celerity, execute any maneuver which he thinks proper to order.

Admitting that the range of these new guns be inferior to that of the old guns at great distances; or even that their duration be less on account of their lesser thickness, ought not something to have been sacrificed to the advantage which is to be obtained from their lightness? There are besides, very few circumstances in war where long ranges may be really useful, as almost all firings beyond eight or ten hundred yards are without effect, owing to the difficulty of pointing with any justness or accuracy at this distance. This is so positive a fact, that, although twenty-four pounders have very long ranges, yet in sieges, where cannon can be served with greater precision than in the field, experience has proved that they ought not to be farther distant than six hundred yards from the place it is intended the shot should batter.

Besides, an army can carry with it only a determinate quantity of ammunition (say about two hundred rounds to each gun) on account of the great number of horses that a larger quantity would require; it would betray an ignorance of the service which may be obtained from artillery, to employ it beyond the distance at which it may be fired with at least any justness of direction: it would occasion a useless consumption of ammunition, which is always precious in war, and which might be wanted at a decisive moment (as has happened in many cases) when, instead of destroying, or even annoying, your enemy, by its failure you give him the advantage of profiting by your error.

Lastly . . . it may be seen that when fired at three, or three and two thirds, degrees of elevation, the new guns carry their shot nearly as far as the old ones: they are, besides, capable of much longer ranges when at greater degrees of elevation; though this ought never to be done, on account of the useless consumption of ammunition. On this subject we will remark that it is very easy to be mistaken in the estimation of distances, especially from one hill to another. Complaints have often been made of the deficiency of range of the French cannon, because their shot was not perceived to reach the enemy, whilst his fell into their camp; no one paid any attention to the principle of the French artillery, which is always to point directly at the object which it wished to strike, and, in this case, the range of cannon has no extensive limits, especially when the shot meets a high ground, which stops it at its first fall. Other belligerent nations, on the contrary, point their guns much above the horizon; it is not, therefore, surprising that they should range much farther. But let us remark the effect of their shot: they fall from a great height, make only a hole, where they bury themselves, and are very seldom dangerous, because shot fired above fifteen or eighteen degrees of elevation, can never rise after the first fall, and consequently lose the advantage of ricochet. They are to be numbered among those useless cannonades which we have mentioned; they can produce uneasiness, but cannot perform a decisive part in an action.

There exist many circumstances in war where it may be necessary to attack an army [in the flank] from a great distance, as was done at the battles of Dettingen and Fontenoy, in which a battery was placed on the left bank of the Rhine at the former, and of the Scheldt at the latter. The position is always advantageous, becomes often decisive, and should be taken whenever it can be done without risking the loss of the artillery. These are uncommon occasions; but the foresight of a prudent general should prepare such a resource, by keeping a few sixteen pounders at the nearest deposit in the neighborhood of his army to be always ready for use, which could be easily drawn by country horses, and follow the progress of his maneuvers. These pieces will be, principally, useful and sufficient for the attack of small fortified towns, which, although unable and unwilling to stand a siege in form, keep their gates shut as long as they can, and which might be too considerable to be forced by twelve pounders.

It is not, however, practicable to carry these guns when an army is marching at a great rate; they can be employed only in countries where the ground is gained and disputed *pied à pied*, foot by foot; otherwise the inconvenience would recur, which it was wished to obviate by adopting the light artillery.

A general, who would choose to change a part of the light cannon necessary to his army for some of these heavy pieces, and who should be limited to a certain number of horses, ought to be informed that two sixteen pounders require as much appendage, and as many horses, as three twelve or four eight pounders: on a calculation of their usefulness in battle, he may perceive that he has but two shot of each sixteen pounder for three shot of the twelve and four of the eight pounders, and that at four hundred yards distance he certainly will lose much more: for the light guns would have a greater effect than the larger ones for which he exchanged them; since for the single sixteen pound shot he would have two twelve and three eight pound shot: the field twelve and eight pounders may be also removed with facility, whilst the sixteen pounders require a great number of horses, and occasion a great loss of time, which is extremely precious in action. Finally, twelve sixteen pounders would deprive him of twenty-four twelve, or thirty-six eight pounders, which, if judiciously disposed, are capable of determining the success of an action. These heavy guns are, besides, destructive of horses and roads, which are material considerations, especially in the fall of the year.

One of the chief advantages of the light field pieces is the possibility of being maneuvered *à bras*, with the hands, in any circumstances. There is no necessity of employing horses to withdraw them from the line, as was formerly the case with the sixteen pounders, and even smaller calibers of the old model; nor to have the whole team make a full conversion before the enemy, giving him, by that maneuver, the opportunity of throwing disorder both among the horses and drivers. Troops are also made very uneasy from such a number of horses going thus to and fro, and breaking through their line at moments when it would be important they should keep close order. At the battle of Rossbach a striking instance occurred of the disorder into which a line of infantry may be thrown, while marching before the enemy, when, from the direction given, the artillery is obliged to cross it to reach its ground.

Appendix II: Construction of French Brass Guns

There being but five calibers in the French artillery, and every part of its service being reduced to a complete system, it was thought proper to determine, irrevocably, the dimensions of cannon, whether battering, siege, or field pieces; and the precautions which were to be observed in the proof, and for the reception of the same.

This was regulated on March 31, 1766, when is was ordered as follows:

Henceforth, brass pieces, of the different calibers, cast in any of the foundries established in the kingdom, shall be visited by an officer of the Royal Corps of Artillery, chosen and ordered to that effect. It shall be his duty to attend to all the operations of the foundry, and to examine the pieces in all the situations they pass successively; from the moment they are raised from the pit, until they are brought to the proof field.

The dimensions and weights of the several pieces; the dimensions of the platebands and moldings; the position of the handles, trunnions and ornaments of the said pieces are, and will remain fixed agreeable to the tables, sketches, plans, and sections which are herein annexed, and under any pretense whatsoever, no alterations shall be made to them.

In order to verify the exactness and precision of these measures, each pieces shall be laid by itself, on two pieces of timber, one under the first reinforce, the other under the chase. The length, from the quick of the mouth to the rear of the plateband of the breech, shall be verified with a rule, laid parallel to the axis of the piece, and perpendicular to another placed flat on the mouth; the allowance for this measure is .044, more or less than the tables prescribe.

The length of the bore shall be measured with a rule, the extremity of which is made round so as to fit exactly the bottom of it. The same allowance is made as above.

The length of reinforces, moldings, and their position, should be taken with an iron rule, cut into a pattern exactly profiled. Salient marks are made on the said rule, to determine the position of the handles, and to measure their forepart towards the chase only. The allowance is also the same as above. The projection, width, and rounding of the moldings are of no material consequence; therefore no difficulty is made upon them.

The trunnions should be square with the bore of the piece; their axis should be perpendicular to a vertical place, which, passing through the vent, divides the piece into two equal parts. This will be verified with an instrument. No deviation is allowed on this part. The axis of the trunnions should be placed one half of the diameter of the shot below the axis of the piece, which is also verified with an instrument. On this, and on the proportions, dimensions, and breadth of the rimbases, which are prescribed by the table, an allowance of .044, above or below is made.

The thickness of the rimbases should be measured next to the trunnions towards the chase, and their projection should be perfectly equal; the distance between them is measured in the same place, and comprehends the thickness of the rimbases and the diameter of the piece a the same point: the allowance is only .002 deviation.

The separation of the rimbases being ascertained, their trench ought to answer exactly along a thread or a rule, one end of which touches the extremity of the plateband of the breech, the other end that of the rimbases towards the chase: no allowance is made on this measure.

A ring, or lunette, if the exact diameter of the shot is passed on and along the trunnions to the rimbase: only .022 is allowed on this measure.

The trunnion should be measured above its center, its length be a full diameter of the shot, and its end cut square to its axis: .044 variation is allowed.

The diameters of the several parts of the pieces should be conformable to the tables: .044 is the allowance; .088 may be allowed on the length and thickness of the button.

The bouch, or grain, in which the vent is to be drilled, should be fixed cold, *à froid*, and always in presence of the artillery officer attached to each foundry. His duty should be to see that the vent is drilled exactly in the center of the grain; that the grain be well turned and screwed exactly; that the male and female screw fit each other, so as to leave no vacuum between them; that the butt-end be forced into its place; and that the extremity of the said butt-end bears exactly on the place, which is forcibly made by the difference of its diameter with that of the screw.

The grain screw should make its way easily into the female screw until it comes within four turns of the bottom, then four men should apply a sufficient force, with a key or fly, five feet long on each side of its center, to force these last four turns: .088 may be allowed on the exterior position of the vent, and .132 on its position inside, but this last only towards the chase and never towards the bottom of the bore.

To ascertain the inner position of the vent, a wooden rammer is introduced into the bore, the end of which is made round, so as to fit exactly the bottom of the bore; when rammed home, a priming wire of .177 diameter, the end of which is made flat, and stamped with ink, is introduced into the vent, to mark its corresponding point on the rammer; then with a rule placed on the rammer, and a pair of dividers, the distance from the rule to the mark shall be measured.

The bore of the piece shall be concentric, without any undulation or apparent cut of the knives: the piece shall be discarded for any chamber above .132 deep, in whatever part of the bore, and when turned, for any chamber of more than .177 deep.

The diameter of the bore shall be of the prescribed caliber, .022 variation shall be allowed over, and nothing less than the exact dimension. It shall be measured with a star, the branches of which directed so that two of the points may be vertical. In this position any difference of diameter in the bore, however small, will be distinctly shown by the shaking of the horizontal points, in the moving of the instrument, along the bore. If any variation be perceptible, use shall be made of the mobile star to determine the depth of the widening, and if it shows that in some parts the diameter of the bore be larger than .044, the piece shall be rejected. This provisory inspection shall be made at the foundries; after which such of the pieces as are found to be sound, having the prescribed proportions, no deeper chambers than are allowed by this regulation, and none covered with screws or otherwise concealed, shall be mounted on old carriages of their caliber, and proved in the following manner.

Siege and garrison pieces shall be fired at a butt, five successive times; with a charge of powder of two-thirds the weight of the shot, and three with a charge half the same weight.

Field pieces, two rounds, point blank shot, with the following charges:

Pounder	Powder
12	5 lbs.
8	3¼ lbs.
4	2 lbs.

In order to ascertain whether the widenings which these first charges may have produced, would occasion any shakings of the shot, they shall be fired three times with the war charge, viz.

Pounders	Powder
12	4 lbs.
8	3½ lbs.
4	1½ lbs.

The charges to be made as usual with paper cartridges, and a wad of dry hay on them, which shall be rammed three strokes.

The balls are to be chosen among the smoothest and most exact calibers, a wad put on them, and rammed three strokes; the pieces are to be loaded in the presence of the commissary of the foundries.

The five discharges finished as ordered above, the piece shall be raised at the chase; the vent stopped, and filled with water. It shall then be carefully inspected on the exterior to observe if any water transpires, especially round the handles and the vent, in order to ascertain that the grain is forced into the metal and fits it exactly.

The first and second reinforce shall be carefully examined to ascertain that the metal has received no commotion, and that no flaw or crack is made on the outside, which, if any should appear, will be a sufficient cause for rejecting the piece. If the piece has none of the above faults, and now water appears, a sponge, covered with a sand bag, shall be pressed on to the bottom of the bore; after which the piece is scoured until it be right clean.

In the above operations, should water be apparent in any part of the length of the bore, pieces shall be discarded; except such where humidity might ooze only between the grain and the metal. But should so much water penetrate that part as to occasion it to run off, the founder shall be obliged to put another grain, and the piece shall undergo a second proof.

The bore shall be visited again with the caliber star, and carefully examined, to observe if it has not been strained at the end of its first reinforce; if the last firings have not occasioned bouncing of the ball, which is an indication of the widening of the bore at the place where the charge is placed; on the least suspicion of this king, the mobile star shall be introduced again, and if it shows that the powder has occasioned at any part between the breech and the place of the shot, a widening more than .044 in the diameter of the piece, it shall be rejected.

If it be found that the balls have made an impression more than .022 deep, or if any fault in the interior or at the exterior is remarked, the piece shall be rejected.

Whenever a piece is discarded, either at the foundry or at the proof field, the handles should be broken off.

If the pieces have none of the above imperfections, the cat's-foot searcher shall be introduced, and if no chamber be discovered, they shall be retained.

Reports shall be made of each proof, detailing the operations, as prescribed by the present regulations, and forwarded to the Secretary of War.

(Signed) LOUIS
Le duc de Choiseul

A great proof that this system has attained a sufficient degree of perfection is, that although, since that epoch, many experiments have been ordered and performed, very few alterations have taken place in the above regulations.

Proceedings in the Casting of Brass Cannon

The charge of the furnace consists commonly of old pieces of cannon unfit for service, of metals remaining from preceding castings, and of new copper. The size of this charge is proportioned to the molds which are to be filled. The founder ought to know how much is necessary for the casting, including the waste.

The metals should be so placed in an air furnace, that the most easy to melt may be least exposed to the fire, and so that none may fall in a lump before the furnace is sufficiently heated to receive them without their hardening: otherwise the whole will form a cake in such a manner that it will be impossible to discover the bricks of the furnace to place them better; it then forms a thick crust which no fire can penetrate; the casting then fails. This accident should be more particularly avoided, as, besides the loss of the molds, that of the furnace is also a consequence, of which there are many examples. But the founder ought to be acquainted with every part of this profession, and should also be able to construct his furnace with proper refractory earth for this purpose.

Everything being thus prepared, the furnace is lighted, the fire of which should be carefully attended; for too much activity in this element would produce the bad effects just mentioned.

The large pieces being in fusion, the new copper is put in. The founder attends to the proper time of putting in the fresh charges, and, when the whole is melted, the fire is increased to such a degree that all the heterogeneous particles are evaporated, which can only take place after an entire fusion.

A short time before the tin is put in, the fused metal is scummed to clear it of the vitrified earth which floats on the top. The proportion is eleven pounds of tin to one hundred of copper; this completes the purification of the metal.

The floating vitrified particles are nothing but a metalic calx, which occasions loss by the particles of copper which it carries with it, and which are afterwards detached from it.

In order to give a clearer idea of a casting, we will give an account of the operation.

Forty-four or forty-five thousand pounds of metal were put into an air furnace: of this about forty thousand pounds were old castings, and the rest new rosettes. The metal remained twenty or twenty-one hours in the furnace to acquire the quality proper for the casting. Half an hour before casting the pure tin of Cornwall was put in, and stirred with a long stick the better to mix it with the copper. Borings of brass guns were also used, and put in about three-quarters of an hour before casting.

The quantity of metal put into the furnace ought to be double the weight of the guns when completed. For example, these forty-four or forty-five thousand pounds were to make five sixteen and two eight pounders, which, when completed, were to weigh from twenty to twenty-three thousand: but it is necessary to consider the waste and the heavy spruces which are afterwards melted again in other castings.

When the metals were sufficiently melted, the casting was begun. For this purpose was suspended by its center a large wooden pole, with a long piece of iron at the end, which was made of red hot; this end entered a canal made at the bottom of the furnace. With this pole they drove in an iron stopper which closed the furnace at this place; the metal then ran through brick canals to the molds. These canals were kept as hot as possible with coals till the moment of casting.

When several pieces are to be cast, all these canals communicate with each other; but the metal runs into but two molds at a time. When the molds are full, an iron plate, moved with a hook, is lowered. The metal then runs into new canals to fill other molds, into which it falls as soon as two iron rods are raised, at the end of which an iron stopper closes the orifice by which the metal enters. The molds are generally filled in four or five minutes.

The earth is removed from about the casting the day following. The mold is raised, the cannon and spruce cut off, and the cannon prepared for boring.

Of Boring Cannon

Cannon were formerly cast hollow by means of a core covered with clay, which was placed in the middle of the mold, and kept in the center of the gun, at the bottom, by means of three iron rods which remained in the metal of the breech, so that when the core was taken off, there was nothing further necessary than to cleanse the bore of the gun with the allezer. For this operation the gun was fixed vertically in a grooved frame, with its mouth downwards; the allezer's rod served as an axis to the machinery, which was made to turn by means of two horses, or other power, and the weight of the gun forced it down as fast as the allezer worked itself into the bore. The pressure occasioned by the weight of heavy pieces was modified by a counterpoise, as it would have been too powerful.

But the core, which formed the bore of the piece, was liable to become eccentric, and would frequently occasion fissures, *soufflures*, by restraining the arrangement of the metal, so as to render the gun defective; cannon is, therefore, now generally cast solid, afterwards bored, and molds are made without a core.

Maritz, an eminent founder at Strasbourg, is the first who thought of boring guns horizontally, and to give them a circular motion, instead of causing the cutters, *forêts*, to turn. By this method cannon are easily bored to their axis, and you can ascertain that the bore is central when the rod of the cutter does not participate in the motion of the piece: whereas, if the cutter was made to turn, and its direction not to coincide exactly with the axis of the piece, the gun might be bored off its center.

Formerly, and even now, in the ancient foundries, the operation was performed by using several cutters in succession until the gun was bored to its caliber; each cutter increasing the diameter of six or eight lines, after which the bore was cleansed and completed with the allezer. In the new foundries only one cutter is used. The bore is cut at first to its caliber, and then cleansed with the allezer.

. . . their explanations are sufficient to indicate all the proceedings which are made use of in the new horizontal boring machine which is established at Chaillot, near Paris. It is put in motion by means of a steam engine; but there is nothing in the composition of the machine but what will also answer with any other mover, provided it is sufficiently powerful.

Appendix III

Maneuvering à la Prolonge

The prolonge is a long tight rope which is used to drag the pieces, and should be from thirty-eight to forty-two feet in its whole length, in order that twenty-seven may remain after it is tied and the loops made. It is fastened to rings placed, for this purpose, behind the bolster, and serves for the firing in retreat; it is an inch in diameter, and made of four strands. The prolonge for the horse artillery is 1.60 inches in diameter.

Method of fixing the Prolonge

Measure thirty-eight feet from the billet, envelop the left guide of the limber with the end exceeding the thirty feet; pass this end through the rings which are fixed behind the bolster: with the same end envelop the right guide, bringing it underneath the middle of the great sweep-tree, and fasten it below by a knot, called the prolonge knot (noeud de prolonge); then make two loops in the prolonge (ganse de prolonge) the first as near as possible to the sweep-tree, and the second nine feet from the first. Iron rings which are fixed in the strands of the rope are often used in the place of loops. The prolonge at full length is twenty-seven feet: when the billet is passed through the loop or ring, it is eighteen feet, and when doubled, that is to say, when the billet is passed through the loop or ring, it is thirteen or fourteen feet: when the prolonge is not used, it is interwoven with the guides, where it is kept by hooks, placed at the end to prevent it from slipping.

Prolonge Knot

To make it, the end of the prolonge being passed through the ring on the left of the limber, and then through that of the right, it furnishes two lengths; form with each a buckle so that the end of the prolonge of the left part, for example, passes above, and that of the right crosses also above, enter the buckle of the left into that of the right; pass through this last the end of the right part of the prolonge, always crossing upon it, and draw it tight; the knot is then made.

If you have begun by entering the buckle of the right into that of the left, then the end of the left part of the prolonge must be entered into the buckle of the right.

Prolonge Loop

Make with the prolonge a buckle with each hand crossing contrary ways, but leaving a certain distance between them; enter the buckle of the left hand into that of the right, pass the end of the buckle of the right hand through the buckle of the left hand, in such a manner that this end of the prolonge comes directly towards you: in this position keep the parts of the knot close together, holding them with the left hand, and taking with the right the length of rope necessary for the loop, which will be in the interval left between the buckles when the knot was begun. In this situation, the whole being drawn tight, the loop will be made, and will not slip.

When the prolonge is to be used, the word of caution is given, "Advance- prolonge!" then the drivers, or the men when there are no horses, bring up the limber, marching obliquely to the right, so that, having arrived as far as the breech, and having turned it by the left, it may be opposite to the trail transom; then the cannoneer on the right takes the billet and passes it through the lashing ring; during this time one of the assistants clears the prolonge: the cannoneer on the right commands "March!" . . . [and] the prolonge may be stretched to its full length. When it is intended to fire in retreat, the command is made "Advance prolonge to fire in retreat." In this case the cannoneer on the right, who has passed the billet through the lashing ring, draws it immediately to the loop, and, when ordered "Double-prolonge," places it through the loops under the guides. If the prolonge is at full length, the officer commands "Shorten" or "Double prolonge to fire in retreat:" this command is only a caution. "To action." The fire is executed *de pied fermé* until the word "March;" the piece then retires briskly, the cannoneers and assistants following the motions of their piece, and marching opposite their respective posts, each carrying the implements which he is to make use of; the second assistant on the right hooks the bucket before putting himself in motion, and unhooks it as soon as it is commanded "Halt: to- action!" At the word "halt," they all take their posts, and continue to charge, standing fast, *de pied fermé*, as long as it is necessary.

The cannoneers who have the care of the horses of those who execute the pieces, follow the movements either with and in front of the horses of the limbers, or with the surest or ammunition wagons; likewise for the following maneuvers.

Advance Prolonge for Flank Firing

The prolonge is disengaged, the same cannoneer passes the billet through he lashing ring, and in the loop, or ring, which is made nine feet from the sweep-tree; the prolonge is then seventeen feet long. For the execution of this fire, the piece is carried *à bras* about ten feet from the column, the chase turned to the enemy, the artillery officer commands "To action;" the piece fires *de pied fermé*, until the command "March." The piece follows the squadron, or column, until the word "Halt" is given; the piece is again removed three or four paces, and the chase turned towards the enemy, until the trail be in the direction of the limber: this motion is executed by the cannoneers and servants as in the command "Advance limber in front."

When the commanding officer thinks proper to occupy a position at a distance, and wishes that the artillery should reach the ground speedily to protect the arrival and formation of his troops, he gives the caution. If the maneuver is to be performed with the prolonge, the officer has only to give the direction, and to command "March!" If it be to follow cavalry for a great distance, and it be thought proper to execute the movement with more rapidity, the horse artillery officer commands "Take off prolonge," or "To your posts! Advance-limber! Limber the piece! Cannoneers and matrosses to your horses . . . march!" directing at the same time either "Forward or oblique, to the right or to the left." The pieces precede or follow the squad-

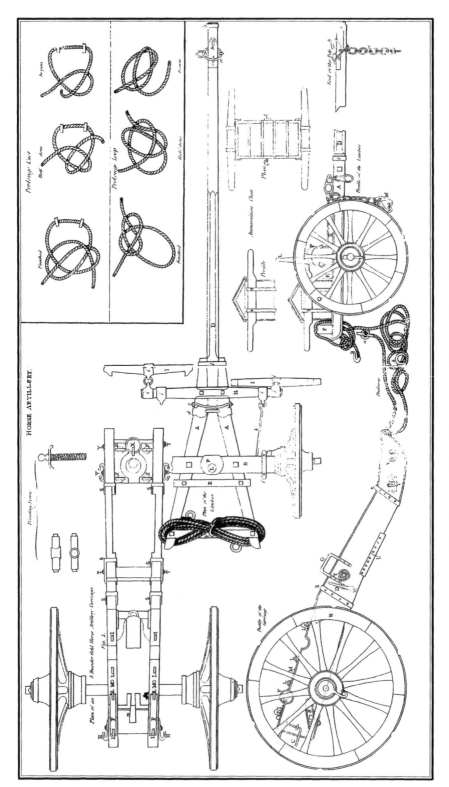

Rope knots used by artillerymen; and the use of the prolonge.

ron, or the battalion, as they are directed, either at full speed, or along the platoon, beginning the maneuver without paying attention to the cannoneers, who gallop to overtake and to arrive in time with them: as soon as the officer arrives at the position, he commands "Halt! Unlimber the piece! To battery! At the first command, cannoneers and matrosses dismount!" The horse cannoneers hand the bridles of their horses to those who are designed to take care of them, and those mounted on wursts dismount likewise; all repair speedily to their pieces.

When the prolonge is doubled, or at the length of the second loop, at the word "Lengthen prolonge," the cannoneer on the right clears the billet, fastens it to the lashing ring, and the second cannoneer draws the prolonge out to is full length. This command is made when a ditch is to be crossed, as in the following maneuver, which is performed with horses, or if intended either to retreat to a great distance, or to cover a column which may fear an attack from the enemy in flank; finally, to cross over ravines, creeks, declivities, &c. with field pieces. If the carriage be on its limber, the following words are given: "Unlimber the piece! Fasten prolonge!" The trail then rests on the ground; one end of the prolonge is fastened, as we have said, to the guides of the limbers, and its other end to the lashing ring. The length of the prolonge is twenty-seven feet between the carriage and the limber, to which the horses are tackled. At this distance the horses can easily draw the pieces over ditches and ravines, the trail of the carriage being cut in the form of a sleight runner. The cannoneers secure the pointing handspikes, and such of the implements which otherwise might run the risk of being broke in the crossing. The limber is drawn gently down the descent, and when the piece is on the border of the ditch or ravine, the horses pull with force and speed. If the trail stick in the ground, the men must disengage it with their handspikes.

When ascending the side of a ditch, or any steep hill, the cannoneers and matrosses unite their efforts to assist the horses. They must pay great attention not to entangle themselves in their traces, and to support the piece in places where it is liable to overset. This is a maneuver as difficult as it is dangerous; but in many instances it has been performed with twenty-four and eighteen pounders; with how much more ease may it then be attempted with light field pieces!

At the word "To your posts; take away—prolonge," the second assistant on the right unhooks the bucket, and all resume their positions for action. The cannoneer on the right displaces the billet, throws it a little in the rear, and gives the word "March," at which the limber resumes its post. If the maneuver is performed with horses, the third assistant on the right winds the prolonge round the guides; the third on the left does this duty when the maneuver is performed by men.

We are indebted to General Gribeauval for this maneuver, the facility of which has been proved by repeated experiments, and by its uniform success in the present contest.

Hitherto there has been but one opinion as to this manner of serving artillery. It has been judged by all who have witnessed the experiments respecting it as very advantageous for the purpose of covering the flanks of columns, in the field, against the oblique attack of an enemy in sight; and, above all, for retreating, since the guns can be fired marching as fast as infantry can retreat by quick step.

It is certain that if, out of respect to prejudice, Gribeauval reduced the French field pieces to eighteen calibers only, instead of sixteen, which is the length of the Austrian and Prussian field artillery, he gained the advantage of facility of movement by lightening the carriages and limbers, by the good arrangement of the men, and by performing his maneuvers with the dragrope or prolonge.

Trunnions

Trunnions are of such great importance to cannon, and their idea is so simple and natural, that their invention must have been coeval with that of cannon; for no other invention could be more convenient to give the necessary degrees of elevation to point the piece, and no other could be less fatiguing to the carriage when they communicate to it the impression of the charge.

However, their position has not been constantly the same, for, in order to derive the greatest advantage of them, they were first placed so that their axis formed a square angle with the axis of the piece, and was placed somewhat beyond the center of gravity, towards the breech of the piece: that is to say, that center was, as it still is, between the breech and the trunnions: they were placed thus in the year 1587, when Errard de Bar le Duc, an artillerist and engineer, published his work entitled *Fortifications Reduced to Art and Demonstration*, in which the only cannon he mentions has the axis of its trunnions placed on the same level with the axis of the piece. From that position of the axis of the trunnions relatively to the center of gravity of the piece, the breech has a superiority of 1-60 of the whole weight, which keeps steady the pointing quoin on which it rests, prevents its sliding in the firing, and preserves the direction given to the piece.

Probably an apprehension was entertained that the axis of the trunnions, being on a level with that of the piece, they were too much exposed to the recoil; it was then thought proper to place them below, so that their axis should be tangent to the inferior part of the bore, preserving to them the same distance beyond the center of gravity. It is the position which is fixed by the regulation of 1732.

From that position it results actually that the trunnions are not so strongly exposed to the effect of the recoil; as the inflamed powder exerts its action in every way as much on the breech as on the shot. This pressure, being parallel to the axis of the piece, may be considered entirely directed along every part of it; then, since the axis of the trunnions is perpendicular to that of the piece, the *point d'appuy* is chiefly the axis of the turnings, which is in the direction of the force which occasions the recoil, and thus the trunnions alone support the effort. But their axis not being in the direction of that effort as when it is placed below; in that case, the pressure of the inflamed powder on the breech, meeting with no resistance along that direction, tend to give the piece a motion round the axis of the trunnions, which are secured in their plates; then the pointing quoin, on the breech transom, forming a resistance to that motion, by supporting the breech, this last part becomes the point of resistance against the recoil, and helps the trunnions thus far.

It appears, however, that the preservation of the trunnions was not the only object which was contemplated in placing them thus. They had also other motives in view: such as to lessen the recoil of the pieces. This last position answered so far the purpose, that, as we have before remarked, the action of the trunnions against their plates not being so strong, it happens that the pressure of the breech on its transom increases the friction of the trail on the platform, and destroys a part of the wheel's motion. To these two real advantages another may be confidently added, which is the sheltering so much of the carriage from the enemy's shot, as the piece is raised above it. However, this position of the trunnions is not exempt from fault, as, from the pressure of the breech on the transom, which supports it, the carriage suffers the more for it in the firing, and, consequently, it cannot be of so long a duration.

In order to give the trunnions such dimensions as to render them capable of resisting the effort, the regulation prescribes to them a diameter equal to that of the shot, and a length equal to the same diameters; for they communicate to the carriage the efforts of the recoil, by their action on their plates, and then that effort is divided on the whole thickness of the cheeks, which has the same dimension.

Windage

The diameter of the shot must be smaller than that of the bore of the piece: first, because the containing is larger than the contained, and then to facilitate the introduction of the mobile, which, without that precaution, might be impeded from several circumstances, such as the dilatation of the metal, the alteration which is often occasioned in its form, by being exposed to frequent shocks in the ammunition wagon; finally by degradation, or encrustation of rust. The difference between the two diameters is called windage, and expresses the vacancy between the shot and the sides of the bore.

Shot for larger calibers are exposed in the transports to a greater alteration; the shocks they receive are greater than those of small calibers; and the dilatation of the metal is in ratio to their diameters. In consequence, it is necessary that the windage should be increased in ratio of their calibers. It was fixed to one twenty-seventh of the diameter of the shot by the regulation of 1732. That of 1765, in order to increase the range of field artillery, reduced their windage as follows. This reduction has that excellent advantage of preventing the danger and frequency of the balls' bouncing against the sides of the bore, by considerably lessening the angle of percussion.

Caliber	Bore Diameter (in.)	Shot Diameter (in.)	Windage (in.)
12-pdr	4.77	4.64	.13
8-pdr	4.18	4.05	.13
4-pdr	3.31	3.18	.13

Appendix V

Memoir extracted from a Treatise on Military Fireworks
As taught at Strasbourg, July 15, 1764

Of Cannon Cartouches

The cannon cartouches, as they were then made, were composed of a bag of serge, and a shot [sabot] or base, in which the ball was fixed by means of a tin cross, nailed to the shoe or base. The bag should be as large as the shoe, and long enough to contain the requisite quantity of powder. The shoe is a little less in diameter than the ball, so that the tin and the bag put upon it, do not increase its size beyond that of the ball. The shoe is flat on one side, and hollow on the other. The hollow part should be a spherical concavity, about one-third of the diameter of the ball. At a small distance from the bottom of the shoe, a groove is made sufficiently deep to contain the pack-thread, which is fastened to the bag.

In the construction of cannon cartouches, the ball must first be fixed to the base by means of two tin bands in the form of a cross, and nailed with two small nails at the bottom and sides of the base. These bands for sixteen and twelve pounders, are at least .44 decimal parts of an inch in width, and 15 inches long. Those for eight and four pounders, are .355 decimal parts of an inch in width, and 11.72 inches in length.

The ball being fixed on this base, it is put into a bag filled with powder, and the bag tied above to the base. Then a bit of parchment slaked in water, of from two to four inches in width, and of sufficient length to go round the cartouche, is placed round the bag, half on the shoe and half on the powder. Then tie it with a string passing in the groove, at about .27 parts of an inch below the base; so that the cartouch is tied in three different places—The two first above in the groove of the shoe, serves to hold the bag and it strongly together; the third below, is to prevent the powder from rising and slipping between the bag and the shoe. The band is placed on the part where the greatest friction is, to preserve the bag from being torn.

The cartouche thus being made, is to be calibered by trying it with the piece for which it is intended, into which it must enter with ease. This cannot be too strongly recommended. It is of all things the most essential, and the only way of ascertaining the goodness of ammunition.

Of Grape Shot

To make grape shot, you must have a bag of ticking, in which the small balls are arranged; also a shoe, to which not only the bag which contains the ball is attached, but also the serge filled with powder.

The shoe is made of the same wood with the ball cartridges, and of the following dimensions, viz. The sixteen pounder should have 4.97 inches diameter; the twelve pounders, 4.35; the eight pounders, 3.82; and the four pounder, 3.1 inch diameter. Those of the caliber of sixteen and twelve, should be 1.6 inches in thickness, with a groove in the middle of .44 parts of an inch in depth, and the same in width; the eight and four pounders have but 1.07 inches in thickness, with a groove in the middle of .36 parts of an inch in depth and width. Every shoe, or base, has a pin in its center, the size of which is in proportion to the vacancy left by the small balls of iron arranged about it. The height is in proportion to the different layers of ball.— In general thirty-six balls are put into one grape shot, of whatever caliber it be; that is to say, six heights of six each. The balls should be proportioned to the caliber, so that the six balls on the base should exactly fill the circumference of it. The pin in the middle of the base is exactly the size of the ball and seven times its diameter in height. At the top of the pin the groove is made to tie the threads, the width of which is one-third, and the depth, one-fourth of its diameter.

The bag in which the small balls are arranged, layer upon layer, should be of good strong ticking closely woven. It is of the size of the shot, and 2.13 inches in length above the top of the pin. It is strongly fastened at the bottom in the groove of the base with strong pack-thread. There must be 3½ fathom of strong pack-thread trebled, to tie the grape of the caliber of sixteen and twelve pounders, and three fathom only for one of eight and four.

Grape shot may be corded in the same manner as the carcasse is corded, with this difference, instead of eight turns, taking only six. The best and strongest method of tying the thread in grape shot, is in the network form-one person holding, and another tying it.

The grape shot composed of 36 iron balls, weigh without their charge of powder as follows:

For a caliber of 16	21 lbs.	10 oz.
For a caliber of 12	16	3⅕
For a caliber of 8	10	12⅘
For a caliber of 4	6	3⅓

The diameters of the small balls for grape shot, of which six exactly fill the circumference, are as follows: For 16-pounders, 1.66 inches; for 8-pounders, 1.31 inches; for 12-pounders, 1.5 inches; for 4-pounders, .16 inches.

Appendix VI

Casting of Cannon Balls

Cannon balls are cast of iron, the metal running in iron molds divided into two parts, which are denominated *coquilles*, shells, fitting each other exactly. The superior part sets on the other which is laying on its flat side; it should be sufficiently heavy to prevent the liquid metal from raising it. The vent or aperture of the set, through which the liquid metal is to be introduced, to fill up the mold, is made in this superior part: when the cast ball is refrigerated, the upper coquille is taken out of the joint, together with the ball which is held in it by the jet, and is broken from it with a single stroke of the hammer.

The liquid metal should be conveyed into the mold in a small stream, *filet*, as soon as it is up to the junction of the two coquilles; in order to prevent external or internal flaws, souflures, which might result from the ebullitions and the interception of air, which would not have time to escape, should the jet which is made perpendicular to the bottom of the coquille, be filled up with the metalic liquid falling through it. This inconvenience would be greater in casting cannon balls of small calibers, as they refrigerate much sooner.

The coquilles are molded in sand as well as the bombs, and their molding is likewise made in a frame with a wooden pattern.

When taken from the molds the balls are imperfect, and their surfaces seldom smooth: let the coquilles be ever so closely joined, the balls have almost always a circular seam formed by the metal running out through the juncture, and tearings at the fracture of the jet.

In order to smooth these unevennesses, which might scratch the bore of cannon, the balls are heated somewhat more than cherry red in air furnaces; out of which they are withdrawn with a strong pair of iron tongs, and placed on an anvil hollowed concave, one quarter of the shot's diameter deep; on this anvil they are hammered with heavy hammers of the same concave depth. These hammers are put in motion by means of water, or other machinery, and in the interval of the strokes, a workman holding the balls with the iron tongs, turns it on all sides until it becomes perfectly smooth: from one hundred to one hundred and thirty strokes are commonly sufficient for this operation.

Hammers for 24 pound shot weigh about 120 pounds.

16	80
12	60
8	40 or 50
4	30 or 40

The weight of these hammers, however, may vary according to the tenacity of the metal. We have seen that the diameter of the shot must be smaller than that of the bore of the piece, to facilitate the introduction of the mobile: this windage is also necessary, in case that notwithstanding all the precautions which are taken to smooth the balls under these hammers, some unevenness might have remained on their surfaces.

Great are the precautions which ought to be taken to have cannon balls of the prescribed diameter, on account of the danger and inconvenience which may result from their being either too large or too small. Should unluckily balls too large be carried in war, a gun would soon be rendered useless in presence of the enemy, as has happened many a time; because the cannoneer is always in hopes that a ball which at first enters the gun with difficulty, will make its way when employing his strength in ramming it; he, therefore, tries to force it home, but seldom succeeds, the ball, together with the cartridge to which it is fastened, remains some way up the bore, and the cannon is rendered useless until the charge can be fired off. This operation is long, difficult, and occasions much injury to the metal, because, from the inflammation of the charge at that place, there results a violent contest between the action of powder and the resistance which the shot, thus forced into the gun, opposes to it: this effort, besides, is made in a part of the gun, which is not as much susceptible of resistance as the breech, which is reinforced for the purpose. This inconvenience is not felt so sensibly in a cannon as it is in a musket, because the thickness of the bore of the latter is not so well proportioned to its charge as the former. A musket will often burst when the ball is too distant from the charge, whilst a cannon thus loaded will not; although, from the violence of the recoil, it is easy to perceive the violence of the effort which it has suffered.

A ball too small cannot have all the range of which it is capable, because a great part of the inflammation of the powder will escape through the excess of windage; and we have seen that balls which have the least windage, *cœteris paribus*, have also the longest ranges.

Appendix VII

List of Artillery Units with the British Army in the Peninsula, 1809–13

Year	Troop/company	Division attached to
1809	No 6, 7th Bn	1st
	No 2, Foot Arty KGL	2nd
	No 2, 1st Bn	3rd
	No 7, 8th Bn	4th
	No 4, Foot Arty KGL	Reserve
1810	"I" RHA	Cavalry
	"A" RHA	Light
	No 6, 7th Bn	1st
	No 2, Foot Arty KGL	2nd
	No 7, 8th Bn	3rd
	No 4, Foot Arty KGL	4th
1811	"A" RHA	Light
	"D" RHA	2nd Cavalry
	"E" RHA	7th
	"I" RHA	1st Cavalry
	1st Co., 4th Bn	2nd
	6th Co., 7th Bn	5th
	1st Co., 8th Bn	5th
	7th Co., 8th Bn	1st
	10th Co., 8th Bn	6th

Year	Troop/company	Division attached to
1812	"A" RHA	Light
	"D" RHA	2nd Cavalry
	"E" RHA	7th
	"I" RHA	1st Cavalry
	1st Co., 4th Bn	2nd
	7th Co., 8th Bn	5th
	9th Co., 8th Bn	1st
	10th Co., 8th Bn	6th
	10th Co., 9th Bn	3rd
	10th Co., 5th Bn	Reserve
	2nd Co., 1st Bn	Reserve

Year	Troop/company	Location
1813	"A" RHA	On the Nivelle
	"D" RHA	Oyarzun, Spain
	"E" RHA	On the Nive
	"F" RHA	
	"I" RHA	Bidart
	May's, 1st Bn	San Sebastien
	Campbell's, 2nd Bn	Cartegena
	Campbell's, 3rd Bn	Eastern Spain
	Hutchinson's, 3rd Bn	Oyarzun
	Maxwell's, 4th Bn	Villefranque, France

Morrison's, 4th Bn	Astigarraga, Spain
Lacy's, 5th Bn	Eastern Spain
Ilbert's, 5th Bn	Urrugne, France
Owen's, 5th Bn	Arcangues, France
Trelawney's, 5th Bn	Astigarraga
Holcombe's, 6th Bn	Lisbon
Thompson's, 7th Bn	Eastern Spain
Bredin's, 8th Bn	Lisbon
Williamson's, 8th Bn	Easten Spain
Lawson's, 8th Bn	Guethary, France
Carmichael's, 8th Bn	Guethary
Brandreth's, 8th Bn	Echallar, Spain
Michell's, 9th Bn	Villefranque
Hughes', 9th Bn	Cadiz
Douglas', 9th Bn	Fuenterrabia, Spain
Dickson's, 10th Bn	Fuenterrabia
Vacant (formerly Shenley's, 10th Bn)	Cadiz
Roberts', 10th Bn	Cadiz

Appendix VIII

List of Artillery Units not with the Army, 1810–12

Year	Troop/Company	Station
1810	"D" RHA	Lisbon
	1st Co., 8th Bn	Alhandra
	2nd Co., 1st Bn	Alverca
	10th Co., 5th Bn	Torres Vedras
	8th Co., 5th Bn	Cadiz
	6th Co., 9th Bn	Isla de Leon, Cadiz
	6th Co., 10th Bn	Isla de Leon, Cadiz
	4th Co., 10th Bn	Isla de Leon, Cadiz
	5th Co., 10th Bn	Cadiz
	1st Co., 4th Bn	Cabeca de Montachique
	10th Co., 8th Bn	Lisbon
1811	2nd Co., 1st Bn	Sabugal
	10th Co., 5th Bn	Villa de Ponte
	6th Co., 7th Bn	Lisbon
	8th Co., 5th Bn	Cadiz
	6th Co., 9th Bn	Isla de Leon, Cadiz
	6th Co., 10th Bn	Isla de Leon, Cadiz
	4th Co., 10th Bn	Isla de Leon, Cadiz
	5th Co., 10th Bn	Cadiz
	3rd Co., 6th Bn	Almeida
	9th Co., 8th Bn	Lisbon
1812	1st Co., 8th Bn	Ft St Julian
	6th Co., 7th Bn	Alicante
	8th Co., 5th Bn	Coimbra
	6th Co., 9th Bn	Isla de Leon, Cadiz
	6th Co, 10th Bn	Isla de Leon, Cadiz
	4th Co., 10th Bn	Valle de la Mula
	5th Co., 10th Bn	Cadiz
	3rd Co., 6th Bn	Alicante
	5th Co., 9th Bn	Covilha
	6th Co., 4th Bn	Lisbon
	6th Co., 8th Bn	Alicante
	4th Co., 5th Bn	Alicante

Examples of French Firing Tables

Tables of the Firings

The following tables are extracted from the very learned and extensive tables calculated by M. Lombard, professor of mathematics in the artillery school of Auxonne. Recurrence may be had to the publication made by this learned author, when necessary, for other than the common cases for which we present these.

As the strength of the powder has a great influence on the ranges, and as, since several years, the proof powder has crried the globe of the provet 213 yards, and sometimes as far as 299 yards, the following are calculated on the supposition that three ounces of powder will carry the provet globe 213 yards.

When we speak of velocities, it is always understood that the unit of time is equal to one second: thus, for instance, when we say, that, to produce such or such and effect, the shot should have 1386 feet 3.84 inches velocity, we understand, that, in one second, the shot must range 1386 feet 3.84 inches.

Table of firings for field pieces with round shot
(fixed shot require .18 of the elevator)

Calibers of	12	8	4	howitzer
Charges (pounds)	4	2/8	1/1	1/1
Initial velocity	1375' 3.08"	1356' 2.69"	1381' 6.53"	559' 10.34"
Point Blank	300 yds	290 yds	270 yds	

Distances				
		In.	in.	in.
At 1068 yds	2.13	2.04	1.96	
964	1.69	1.60	1.43	
855	1.24	1.15	1.07	
748	.79	.79	.79	in.
640	.44	.44	.44	4.09
534	.09	.09	.09	3.20
427				2.49
	3' 2.36"	3' 2.36"	3' 2.36"	
320	6' 11.3	6' 11.3"	6' 11.3"	1.78
213	6' 4.19"	6' 4.91"	6' 4.91"	1.15

The figures of the columns, which are on the same line with the distances, indicate the height to which the elevator ought to be raised to point-blank.

The figures underneath the lines indicate the quantity whichh the gun ought to be pointed beow the mark.

Table of firings for field pieces with canister shot
(This table is not extracted from Lombard)

Calibers of	12	8	4
Charges (pounds)	4/4	2/12	1/12
Distance for large canister (yds)	855	748	640
Distance for small canister (yds)	641	534	427

Elevation (inches)			
Large canister shot			
855 yds	1.78	2.13	
748 yds	1.07	1.34	2.66
640 yds	.53	.80	1.60
534 yds		.44	
Small canister shot			
640 yds	1.60		
534 yds	.53	.53	1.07
427 yds	.27	.27	.53

A Comparative Table of the ranges of two four pounders, one conformable to the Regulation of 1732 (Vallière System), the other to that of 1765 (Gribeauval System)

Charge	1.5lbs		2.0lbs		2.5lbs	
Degrees	Short	Long	Short	Long	Short	Long
	(Toises)		(Toises)		(Toises)	
0	197	224	215	235	179	258
3	635	622	554	593	584	597
6	845	941	818	941	843	949
10	1094	1058	1034	1129	1142	1139
15	1319	1406	1379	1328	1385	1334

Table of the angles of elevation of the field pieces corresponding to the different raisings of the elevator divided into parts of an inch.

Calibers	12-pdrs		8-pdrs		4-pdrs	
Height of Elevator	Angles of Elevation					
Inch	deg	min	deg	min	deg	min
0.00	0	58	0	58	0	58
0.18	1	5	1	6	1	8
0.27	1	9	1	11	1	13
0.36	1	13	1	15	1	18
0.45	1	16	1	19	1	24
0.53	1	20	1	23	1	29

0.62	1	23	1	28	1	35
0.71	1	27	1	32	1	40
0.80	1	30	1	36	1	46
0.89	1	34	1	40	1	51
0.98	1	38	1	45	1	56
1.07	1	42	1	49	2	1
1.16	1	46	1	54	2	7
1.24	1	50	1	58	2	12
1.33	1	53	2	2	2	17
1.42	1	57	2	6	2	23
1.51	2	1	2	11	2	29
1.60	2	5	2	15	2	34

A table of experiments made at Douai in 1778 and 1779 on the charges, distances, and degrees of the elevator of field pieces, loaded with fixed shot

Calibers	Distance	Height *French Measure*		*English Measure*		Charge
Pounders	*Yards*	*inches*	*Lines*	*inches*	*dec*	*lbs.*
12	639	0	0	2	0	Point Blank 4.0
	745	0	2	0	18	
	852	0	10	0	89	
	958	1	2	1	24	
	1000	1	4	1	42	
8	639	0	0	0	0	Point Blank 2.5
	745	0	6	0	53	
	852	1	0	1	7	
	958	1	4	1	42	
	1000	1	8	1	78	
4	532	0	0	0	0	Point Blank 1.5
	639	0	4	0	36	
	745	0	8	0	71	
	852	1	0	1	7	
	958	1	4	1	42	
	1000	1	6	1	60	

Six-inch Howitzers				*ounces*
	1623	3 degrees		17
	1733	3 degrees		

It is to be observed that when unfixed shot are used, two lines or 0.18 inches are to be added to the elevator for every distance: this observation accounts for the difference which appears to be in the result of the above experiments, and those made by M. Lombard. In these tables, the distance of a 12-pounder point-blank is three hundred toises; the range of the same is three hundred fifty with two lines of elevation, loaded with fixed shot. Let the fifty toises of that difference be added to the two hundred and forty-one toises which M. Lombard finds for the point-blank of a 12-pounder loaded with unfixed shot; and the two results will be as near as can be expected from experiments made in different places, temperature of the air, powder, etc.

In the above table French toises are reduced to yards: counting two hundred thirteen English yards for one hundred toises which is very near the truth; the fractions are neglected.

A table of experiments to ascertain the ranges of field pieces loaded with wrought iron canister shot

Caliber	Charge	Number of Balls In Cartridge	Distance	Elevator Height Fr. Meas.		Eng. Meas.	
Pounder	lbs		Yards	in.	lines	in.	dec.
12	4.5	112	426	0	0	0	0
		112	532	0	6	0	53
		112	639	1	0	1	7
		112	745	1	6	1	60
		41	639	0	6	0	53
		41	745	1	0	1	7
		41	852	1	6	1	60
8	2.75	112	426	0	0	0	0
		112	532	0	6	0	53
		41	639	1	0	1	7
		41	852	2	0	2	13
4	1.75	63	320	0	0	0	0
		63	426	0	6	0	53
		63	532	0	10	0	89
		41	426	0	0	0	0
		41	532	0	6	0	53
		41	639	1	6	1	60
		41	745	2	6	2	66

Without affecting the credit which is due to fixed canister shot of the new invention, we are not afraid to say, that those only who deceive themselves can insist, that, on all occasions, and at all distances, related in the table of experiments made at Strasbourg, each shot, with wrought iron balls, will be as effectual against a battalion, as the experiment shot against the large target.

That table shows that the balls struck constantly within an horizontal length of eighty-four or one hundred and eight yards upon an height of eight feet. It is then evident that, the cone of projection having one of the dimensions of its basis of such breadth, a great number of the shot struck above and many more below the object, and that the greatest number of those which pierced or struck the one inch sap-board, did it by ricochet, and many perhaps at the second bound. The ground, which was chosen for the experiments, being dry, smooth and visibly horizontal, must have contributed much to that effect which made such impressions on the spectators.

The inference which may be drawn from it, is, that in circumstances nearly similar to those of the experiments at Strasbourg, distances well ascertained, a proper time allowed for maneuvering, the same ground, new made cartridges, etc., the effect of the shot may be similar to those of the tables: but if a hollow is between the enemy and the battery; if the enemy stands on higher ground, or the battery is higher than the enemy; if the interval be soft and marshy, filled with bushes, planted with vine or hops, or covered with heaps of corn or deeply ploughed; if the enemy has secured himself behind a low parapet of earth; if he keeps under cover of abattis, hedges and palisados, the major part of the balls will be intercepted, and the effect produced by the canister shot be much less than that of a ball of the caliber of the piece. It is questionable that most of the fields of battle have one or more of the irregularities which I have here but feebly sketched.

In order to form a correct idea of the range and effect of these canister shots, would it not be proper to place the object upon an eminence, and the battery opposite upon another? The experiments might not be so showy, but the result of the good shots would be nearly the same in all cases. Should the ground be more unfavorable it would add to the result, and, instead of falling short in the calculation, the advantages would certainly be multiplied.

The uncertainty of the estimation, joined with the irregularities of the ground, will always render the small shot less injurious to an enemy than caliber shot.

At middling distances a half pound shot will only kill a man; a five ounce ball will kill him likewise.

Nearer, two and a half or two ounces will not do much more harm than a ball of one ounce and a half.

On the other side, the canister shot for the three field calibers contain each the same number of wrought iron balls; they will produce the same effect relative to the number of the enemy, which they may strike.

Appendix X

Weights and Measures

There has been some carelessness when using French measurement of the period. The French had an inch, foot, and pound, just as the English did, but they were not of the same length or weight, the French foot being longer than the English foot, and the French, or Paris, pound being a little heavier than the English pound. This also occurs when using Austrian measurements, the Nuremberg and Vienna pounds being both lighter than the French equivalent. Even careful historians have occasionally made this error. For example, Napoleon has always been considered in most histories as being "short." His height in French feet was five feet, two inches. This converts in English feet to a little over five feet, six inches, which was average height for the day.

The following conversion tables from Tousard are added in order to help the reader and historian, and hopefully the data contained can help to bring order from disorder.

Table I

The Paris pound . . . contains 9216 Paris grains; it is divided into 16 ounces, each ounce into 8 gros, and each gros into 72 grains; it is equal to 7561 English troy grains.

The English troy pound of 12 ounces contains 5760 English troy grains, and is equal to 7021 Paris grains.

The English avoir dupois pound of 16 ounces contains 7000 English troy grains, and is equal to 8588 Paris grains.

To reduce Paris grains to English troy grains divide by 1.2189
To reduce English troy grains to Paris grains multiply by 1.2189
To reduce Paris ounces to English troy, divide by 1.015733
To reduce English troy ounces to Paris, multiply by 1.015733
Or the conversion may be made by means of the following tables:

To reduce French to English troy weight

Paris pound	7561
Ounce	472.5625
Gros	59.0703
Grain	8204

To reduce English troy to Paris weight

English troy pound of 12 ounces	7020
Troy ounce	585.0833
Dram of 60 grains	73.1354
Penny weight, or denier, of 24 grains	29.2462
Scruple of 20 grains	24.3784
Grain	1.2189

To reduce English avoir dupuis to Paris weight

Avoir du pois pound of 16 ounces or 7000 troy grains	8538
Ounce	533.6250

Table II
Long and Cubical Measure

To reduce Paris running feet or inches into English multiply by 1.065977
English running feet or inches into Paris, divide by 1.065977
To reduce Paris cubic feet or inches to English multiply by 1.211278
English cubic feet or inches to Paris, divide by 1.211278
Or by means of the following tables:

To reduce Paris Long Measure to English

Paris royal foot of 12 inches	12.7977
Inch	1.0659
Line, or one twelfth of an inch	.0888
12th, or point	.0074

To reduce English Long Measure to French

English foot	11.2596
Inch	.9383
Eighth of an inch	.1173
Tenth of an inch	.0938
Line or one twelfth	.0782

To reduce French Cube Measure to English

Paris cube foot	1.211278
Cubic inch	.0007

To reduce English Cube Measure to French

English cube foot or 1728 cubical inches	1427.4864	
Cubic inch	.8260	
	Cube-tenth	.0008

Table III
Long Measure

The English standard long measure, or that whereby the quantities of things are ordinarily estimated, is the yard, containing three English feet, equal to three Paris feet, and one inch, and three twelfths of an inch, or seven ninths of a Paris ell. Its subdivisions are the foot, span, palm, inch, and barleycorn; its multipliers are the pace, fathom, pole, furlong, and mile.

The English foot to the French royal is as 107 to 114, and the French toise is equal to six English feet, two inches and a half.

Proportions of the long measures of several nations to the English foot

The English standard foot being divided into one thousand equal parts, the other measures will have proportioins to it which follow:

English foot	1000
Paris royal foot	1068
Rhineland foot	1033
Venetian foot	1162
Amsterdam foot	942
Foot of Antwerp	946
Spanish foot	1001
Toledo foot	889
Dort foot in Holland	1184
Middleburg foot	991
Strasbourt foot	920
Bremen foot	920
Cologne foot	954
Foot of Frankfurt am Main	948
Danzig foot	944

Foot of Copenhagen	965
Foot of Prague	1026
Riga	1831
Mantua	1585
Stockholm	1204
Lisbon	919
Ell of Amsterdam	2268
Antwerp	2283
Leyden, in Holland	2260

Appendix XI

The Congreve Rocket System, 1814

Rocket types	*Employment*
Heavy	
1. 8 in. carcass or explosion 50 lbs. Of combustible mixture	Bombardment by Royal Navy and Royal Marine Artillery
2. 7 in. carcass or explosion	
3. 6 in. carcass or explosion 25 lbs. Of combustible mixture	
Medium	
1. 42-pdr carcass; either 12 or 18 lbs of explosive	same as above
2. 42-pdr shell; either a 5½ in howitzer or 12-pdr spherical shell	same as above
3. 32-pdr carcass; 12–18 pounds of explosive	Bombardment by RN and RMA Field service by RHA and RMA
4. 32-pdr shell; 9-pdr spherical shell	same as above
5. 32-pdr shot; 18- or 24-pdr shot	same as above
6. 32-pdr case; 100 or 200 carbine balls	same as above

7. 32-pdr explosion; topped by a strong
   iron cone containing between 5–12 lbs
   of powder ignited by a fuse.
	same as above

8. 24-pdr shell; 5½ in shell	Field service-RHA, RMA
9. 24-pdr shot; 12-pdr shot	same as above
10. 24-pdr case	same as above
Light	
1. 18-pdr shell; 9-pdr spherical shell	Field Service, RHA, RMA
2. 18-pdr shot; 9-pdr shot	same as above

3. 18-pdr case   same as above
4. 12-pdr shell; 6-pdr spherical shell   same as above
5. 12-pdr shot; 6-pdr spherical shot   same as above
6. 12-pdr case; case shot containing either   same as above
    48 or 72 carbine balls
7. 9-pdr shell; grenade   same as above
8. 9-pdr case   same as above
9. 6-pdr shell; 3-pdr shell   same as above
10. 6-pdr shot; 3-pdr shot   same as above
11. 6-pdr case   same as above

Range and elevation (Adye)

Caliber and type	Elevation (degrees)	Maximum range (yards)
42-pdr Carcass and Shell	60+	3500
32-pdr Carcass	55-60	2000–3000
32-pdr Shell	50	3000
32-pdr Case (large)	55	2500
32-pdr Case (small)	50	3000
32-pdr Explosion	55	2500–3000
12-pdr Case (large)	45	2000
12-pdr Case (small)	45	2500

Appendix XII

Vents

The vent is a cylindrical opening through which the fire is communicated to the powder that composes the charge. In order to make sure the effect of the [pricker/priming wire], this opening is drilled obliquely to the axis of the piece, forming with this axis an angle of near one hundred degrees, its lower orifice nearly 0.65 inch from the bottom of the bore; besides, by this obliquity, the vent is rendered stronger, as it is less exposed to the natural direction of the flame.

Experiments have been made to discover to what point of the charge it would be most advantageous that the vent should correspond. The inflammation being spherical, it would appear best (the charge once determined) to have the vent drilled in such a manner, that the lower orifice should correspond to the extremity of the charge which is near the ball; for then the charge being always contained in its place, the flame would have less space to go through to penetrate it entirely. By the usual method of communicating the fire to the other extremity of the charge, that part which is not inflamed in the first instant, follows the motion of the ball in the bore, and, by this motion, refuses itself in some degree to the impresion of the flame, so that its velocity, in the estimation of the velocity of inflammation of the charge, ought to be deducted from that of the inflammation of the powder.

But if this manner of placing the vent were advantageous to the velocity of the inflammation of the charge, we must grant that it would be the cause of many dangerous inconveniences in practice; for then it would be impossible to blast and clear the pieces of the dirt, that commonly gathers at the bottom of the bore, and which would happen more frequently with this method; it would also be almost impossible to extract the balls which might have been lodged in the bore, without powder, either through mistake or on purpose, as it sometimes happens in war.

It was thought also, that by making it enter at the center of the length of the charge, the inflammation communicating to the two halves of the charge at the same time, would be more rapid, but experience has constantly proved that the effect of the explosion of powder is not as great in this case as when the vent is at the bottom of the charge. Thus one of the conditions in the position of the vent is, that it should enter the interior of the piece as nearly as possible to the end of the bore, in such a manner, however, that it may not be liable to be stopped by the bottom of the cartridges. Its direction is a little inclined towards the breech, generally making an angle of twenty-five degrees with a perpendicular to the axis.

We may say with truth that the vent is the weakest part of the gun, since however good may be the alloy of the piece, its vent by dint of firing, widens, and absorbs at last a part of the effect of the charge.

To prevent damage, the vent is drilled in the middle of a mass of copper, pure rozette, because this metal is less susceptible to the impressions of fire than brass metal.

The form that is given to this mass, which we call grain, is that of a truncated cone, which is exceeded on the side of its smallest basis, by a cylinder of the same axis and height as the grain; and it is by this cylindrical part that the grain holds to the mold; by this disposition the great basis of the truncated cone which is not cut quick, but turned in a convex form, is placed on the side of the bore, which prevents the action of the powder from forcing the grain back. In order that the copper may hold faster in the casting, the surface of the grain is carved with three circles, at equal distances, and 0.32 inches deep.

Since the regulation of 1765, in the three field calibers, these grains are placed cold after the piece is cast. They are then made in the form of a male screw, and forcibly turned into the piece which has threads cut into it for the purpose of receiving it, and are called screw bouches. It were to be wished that this method was adopted for battering guns; as the lumps of metal which are placed in the molds of large pieces destined for attack and defense, happen sometimes to melt entirely in the casting, which is an indication that their form is always more or less impaired in proportion to the degree of heat of the metal at the moment of fusion, when it precipitates into the mold; now, in the first case, the founder is obliged to put in a cold screwbouch; and, in the second case, which is most common, he has to drill the vent in a mass of metal which has sometimes imperceptibly lost half of its volume, or may have been chopped by the heat of the metal in fusion; as we perceive sometimes in the proof of the pieces, when these chaps happen to meet in the vent.

Formerly damaged vents were repaired by filling up the touch hole with melted metal, having previously widened it by making irregular cuts or ramifications in the inside, in order to effect a stronger cohesion, and that the metal might assimilate and mix better together; but these repairs are made now, by screwing in a new grain as in the field pieces.

However good may appear the method of drilling the vent in a mass of pure copper, it seems, nevertheless, that it might be improved, that is to say, the opening of the vent could be made more solid and durable, if it were not drilled through the axis of the mass of metal, which composes the grain; since, according to this disposition, its whole extent is in the part of that mass which has the least density, as it is very easy to demonstrate.

Experience proves that melted metals consolidate by layers which are concentric to the axis of their mass; so that the nearest parts to that axis are the last to consolidate, and as the matter has not the same fluidity in the last, as it has in the first instants of fusion, the metal in this state being, as we may say, more clammy, is less free to settle, which must prevent the cohesion of the matter in this part, where it has a coarser and looser appearance, and can neither be of as great a density.

In order to avoid this inconvenience it would then be advantageous to melt larger masses of copper, and to take from these large masses of grains, of which the axis of the whole mass should not make a part.

The vents of brass field pieces of the three calibers (as directed by the French government on the 12th of January 1765) must be bored in a mass of red copper, and fixed when cold. They must be 22.20 inches in diameter, and equal in the three calibers. They must be perforated in such a manner that the inferior aperture will fall in a point of the angle of the bore, traced square to the outside of the gun; the entrance of the vent should be two-twelfths in the rear of a perpendicular line from the end of the bore, and the priming wire being pushed down to the bottom of the bore, should point 0.53 inch in advance.

The vent bouches should be 2.31 inches in diameter, for the calibers of twelve and eight, and that of a four pounder should be 1.42 inches, including the filets. They must be of red copper, cast and not wrought, turned and passed through a cutting screw plate.

The excavation to receive the vent piece is to be bored out by a maachine for that purpose, and the borer must have its projecting threads so exactly conformable to those of the screw on the vent piece, that it may cut the receding threads of the female screw in the metal. The grain should enter without the smallest difficulty, and so accurately as not to require more than one turn, with a lever ten feet long, and the strength of four men, to fix it in the gun.

From experiments a difference is established between cannon and mortars. These two species of artillery were indistinctly furnished with vents in mass; that is to say, the mass of wrought copper was so introduced into the mold at the vent, that after the casting, it became fixed, forming a part of the body of the piece, and facilitated the boring of the vent in a mass which presented a greater resistance than cast metal.

But it has been observed, in practice, that this mass of metal bends, and sometimes melts in whole or in part, so that in many pieces the vent would be bored in the mass of wrought copper, but to a small thickness, the remainder of the vent would be found bored in the cannon metal, which would afford but a very weak resistance.

It has been proposed to replace these masses of metal by pieces of wrought metal screwed in when cold. This proposition, made long since, having been verified by experiments on guns, was finally adopted.

It was to be presumed, for the same reasons, that this would answer in mortars, which, however, the experiments at Strasbourg disproved, at a time when reason seemed to present the most certain conclusions. After these experiments, it was concluded that mortars should have masses of metal as before, but that guns should have their vent pieces screwed in when cold.

This variation in the vents of ordnance seems to present a revolting contradiction in spite of experience; reasoning, however, justifies this authority.

This difference arises from mortars being cast with a hollow nut, the mass of metal is less considerable than in guns which continue to be cast full; whence it follows, that the vent pieces enduring a less degree of heat, and being exposed to it a shorter time, are less liable to melt. Besides, reasoning ought always to go hand in hand with experiment; and in all objects of physics, the result of experiment, where it has been repeated and uniform, ought to be adopted, however difficult it may be to reconcile the fact with our ideas of theory.

The operation of taking out and replacing the bouches takes up but a few minutes; it may be performed upon the batteries without dismounting the guns.

Appendix XIII

Pontoons I

Over rivers which have little course, and are not above eighty toises broad, instead of these heavy boats, bridges are made with pontoons which can support a weight of 5000 lbs.

Pontoons are a kind of flat bottomed boats, and the bottoms are composed of compartments six inches broad, so that if the pontoons should spring a leak in the bottom, they cannot sink.

Pontoons are either made of copper, iron, plate, tin, leather, or sailcloth; the first two are of most general use; those of tin are confined to the British army; and the last two sorts, namely of leather and sail cloth, are neither so durable nor portable as the former.

The French troops, as well as the armies of several powers have copper pontoons, which are conveyed on hacquet wagons, but the Prussian and Dutch pontoons are made of iron plate, and the latter are transported in carts. In the Prussian service they were also formerly carried in carts, but at present they are conveyed like those of the French.

Pontoons of double iron plates were first introduced by the Dutch, and afterwards adopted by the Prussians. They are censured and rejected by many military men, not only on account of the defects resulting from the materials of which they are composed, but also, from the manner in which they are transported, and which is attended with numerous difficulties and inconveniences.

It was objected to pontoons made of iron plate, first, that this metal is not so durable as copper, and is liable to be corroded by rust. Second, if a pontoon of this kind is damaged, it becomes completely useless, which is not the case with copper pontoons, where the expense for workmanship only and soldering is lost. Third, white smiths must be kept on purpose to keep them in order. Fourth, pontoons made of iron plate, being generally conveyed in carts which are more easily overset than wagons, are for this reason more liable to be damaged than copper ones.

To these objections it was answered that, first, the iron plate pontoons are far less expensive than copper pontoons. Second, being less weighty and ponderous than those of copper, they can sustain a greater burden than the latter. Third, if they are lost, they may be more easily replaced than copper pontoons.

On maturely weighing these advantages, and taking into consideration that iron plate pontoons, from their being fitter to sustain great burdens than copper ones, answer the main purpose of pontoons better, and that iron is more abundant in the United States than copper, it must be obvious, that, in general, they are preferable to copper pontoons and ought to be adopted in the military establishments of this country.

Pontoons are carried in hacquet wagons with their bottoms upwards, that they may not be filled with rain water, and that the people who attend them may be able to take shelter under

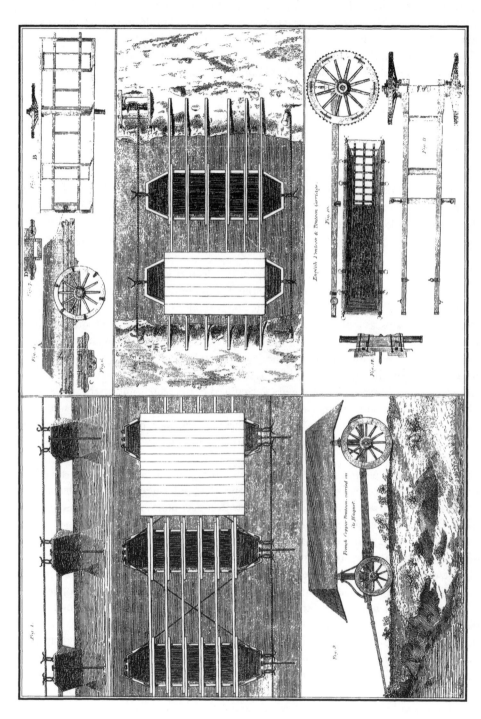

them from the inclemency of the weather: They may also be made use of for covering ammunition and other things: the planks, baulks, anchors, and ropes, which are necessary for the construction of the bridge, are also carried upon hacquet wqagons.

On account of the configuration of the pontoons, which presents a broad surface to the rapidity of the current, and of the thin copper that covers them, which renders them liable to be damaged, they are totally unfit for navigation and cannot be formed into trains, which might expose them in rapid rivers to be run against rocks or against one another; therefore their conveyance is practicable by water only when the river is perfectly smooth: in that case even the copper pontoon can never carry its hacquet wagon. Great precautions ought to be taken when loading them with their proportion of baulks, planks, etc., which on account of their length might easily break through the copper.

The unfitness of pontoons for navigation renders the addition of a few skiffs or batteaux, such as we have already mentioned for boats, necessary. These boats are 27 feet 8.4 inches long in the whole, with a mast 12 feet 9.42 inches high. They are also conveyed upon hacquets, particularly adapted to the purpose.

Appendix XIV

Pontoons II

Boats or pontoons being collected for throwing a bridge across a river, four large poles or stakes, when there are no trees to which the bridge can be fastened, must be driven into the ground, on both banks of the river which is to be crossed, inclining towards the water, and distant from each other, from 20 to 21 feet, according to the length of the pontoons: to these poles or stakes the two ropes which reach from one bank to the other, and to which the pontoons are fastened, are tied.

This being done, the pontoons are taken from their wagons, slipped into the water one after another, between the above two ropes, placed at the necessary distance, parallel to each other, and by means of the two iron rings, which every pontoon is furnished with, tied with thin, yet strong cords, to the ropes. These ropes are generally made to run through the above iron rings, instead of being tied to them, but the latter way appears preferable, inasmuch, as in the case of one of the pontoons being damaged, it may thus be easily withdrawn, without the whole bridge being loosened, and replaced by a fitter one; it is moreover attended with this advantage, that the pontoons, when shaken by a great weight, or moved by the stream, cannot draw nearer to each other.

The distance of the pontoons varies, partly according to the nature of the water which is to be crossed, and which may either increase or diminish the steadiness of the bridge; and partly according as the river is intended to be crossed by infantry, cavalry, artillery, or baggage. When they are too far asunder, the bridge may not be sufficiently strong, because the while burden would bear at one time on a single boad or pontoon, and cause it to sink; being placed nearer to each other, the burden is more equally divided on the collateral boats. The usual distance is eighteen or twenty feet from the center of the boats, and the bridge may be made stronger by placing them nearer. In general, a boat bridge is made two-thirds full and one-third empty, and a pontoon bridge equally full and empty.

The pontoons being thus placed at a proper distance and fastened with cords to the beforementioned ropes, by means of the iron rings, the anchors are to be grounded in the following manner. Take a skiff or a pontoon, which is either not wanted for the construction of the bridge, or is destined to form the extremity thereof; put anchors and cables on board, proceed within a proper distance ahead of the pontoons to which the cable is to be fastened, drop the anchor, make up to the pontoon, fasten the cable, and proceed in the same manner with regard to the rest of the pontoons, observing to drop the anchors according to the rules which we have laid down in the first section.

If the rivers are not very deep or not very rapid, one anchor will do for two pontoons, in which case it must be fastened to the middle of the cable, and the two ends of the latter to the two pontoons, taking care that this be done on both sides of the bridge, in order to keep it more steady. The pontoons on being fastened to the cables, may, at the same time, be placed in a straight line, if they are dressed by someone standing on shore.

Baulks or cross beams 4.80 inches square, and eighteen feet long, are thereupon put upon the pontoons and fastened with iron bolts; each baulk reaches across two pontoons and the end touches the grunnel of the third. Baulks for boat bridges are five or six inches square, and about twenty-two feet long, because boats are placed at a greater distance than pontoons. The number of these baulks must be proportioned to the weight which the bridge is to support; sometimes eight, six, or less are placed near each other.

The baulks or cross beams, being properly placed and fastened with iron bolts, boards or chests three inches thick are laid on them, pinned and sometimes nailed down with three or four nails, lest they should be moved from their places by the horses and wagons which pass over them. This nailing is, however, done but very seldom, as it occasions great trouble and difficulty when the bridge is broken down.

The length of the chests, or planks, determines the breadth of the bridge: those for boat bridges are seventeen or eighteen feet long; those for pontoon bridges are only twelve or thirteen feet. The first are made wider because being intended to be thrown across wide rivers, horses might be frightened in crossing a long and too narrow bridge.

Formerly bridges were made nineteen or twenty-one feet wide, under the opinion that infantry and wagons might cross at the same time: but it was found by experience that although the bridge might be sufficiently wide, the practice was dangerous for the infantry, as the weight of the wagons occasions a kind of undulation in the length of the bridge, and horses constantly derange the chests: infantry besides are always reluctant to cross by the side of wagons which seldom can keep the middle of the bridge.

Bridges intended to continue for a length of time are sometimes built with large boats, such as are often met with on rivers; these a prudent general, who enters a country, ought always to collect by means of small parties detached for the purpose, either to serve for throwing bridges or for transporting provisions or forage. These bridges may be built so broad as to enable two columns to cross at a time; but in this case a partition ought to be made in the middle, one side of which serves for wagons, artillery, and cavalry, the other for infantry, and in no instance ought the two former to be suffered to cross together.

Wagons ought to keep a proper distance between each other when crossing pontoon bridges, for fear of overloading or deranging the pontoons; horsemen should dismount, and lead their horses by the bridle. Cattle ought to be prevented from crossing in herds, as their weight would infallibly sink the pontoon bridge.

At the entrance and exit of these bridges, and to render the crossing more easy, butments, *culées de pont*, are constructed which connect the extremities of the bridge with both banks of the river.

When the army is marching, the projects of the general and local circumstances, which the nature of the country may present, determine the position of the pontoon equipage, which must always be in readiness to execute with celerity any orders they may receive. In camps their usual place is near the small park.

Appendix XV

General Rules for Artillery in a Field Battle
by Major General A. I. Kutaisov

Without speaking about the quality of our pieces and without getting into their details, which is already known by any conscientious artillerist, I will speak about actions of artillery in battle in general, and in this sense, it must be used according to the following rules:

1. In a field battle, fire at a range of more than 500 sazhen is ineffective; at 300 it is effective enough; at 200 and 100 it is murderous; at the three latter ranges our new canister can be used. Consequently, when an enemy is at the first range, one should fire slowly, to have enough time to aim the piece more accurately, and to make his movements difficult; at the second range, one is to fire faster, to stop or, at least, to slow down his approach, and towards this end, to hit as fast as possible, to overthrow or to destroy him.

2. At the beginning of a battle, one is to conceal the strength of his artillery, but to reinforce it during the action; thus the point of your attack will be concealed, and if he is attacking, he would meet the artillery there, where he might not expect it.

3. When the real intention of the enemy is not yet observed, then batteries must consist of a small number of pieces, and having been scattered at various places, you present a small target, have more means to do harm to him by oblique fire and crossfire, and to make his actions difficult.

4. Batteries of larger numbers of pieces should be formed, in cases when it is necessary to make a breach in the enemy line, or to stop his strong assault at some point, or when it is necessary to dislodge him from some position.

5. One should avoid placing batteries on very high and steep hills; to the contrary, batteries of unicorns can be placed with great advantage behind low hills, which would cover them, because their fire is an indirect one, excluding canister.

6. It may be taken, as a rule almost without exception, that, when we intend to attack, most of our artillery must fire at the enemy artillery; when we are attacked, most of our artillery must fire at enemy cavalry and infantry.

7. In addition to that, it is necessary to fire at batteries, when they prevent to taking some position or cause harm in defiles.

8. [When firing on] enemy columns, one is to fire cannonballs with full charge, and grenades, sometimes with decreased powder charges, in order to get them to ricochet and to explode in the column itself; canister is to be fired at columns only when he is at a very close range, because the effect of cannonballs is less murderous then.

9. [When firing at an enemy's] line, which is at an advantageous range from you, canister is principally to be fired; if one fires cannonballs and explosive shell, one is to place his batteries so as to fire along the line or obliquely, at least.

10. During a strong enemy [assault], when one intends to retreat, artillery covering the retreat must be deployed in two lines, so that the first line can go through the second one, which is to be ready to meet the enemy.

11. In any case, artillery must cover the movemetns of troops, and mutually the troops cover it; therefore, its commander, having reconnoitered terrain and having been informed about the intentions, places it, in accordance with the terrain, so as to support the actions [of the troops] with its fire.

12. Its main placement must be on the flanks of the lines, in the intervals [between infantry formations], and in reserve; this placement cannot prevent it from moving according to terrain and movements of enemy troops, because it is very dangerous to stay at the same position for a ong time during an attack.

13. The artillery reserve, being placed behind the second or third line, must be formed principally of horse artillery, which can rush to various places with great speed because of its swiftness and lightness, and heavy companies can position some part of thei men at horses and limbers for faster movement.

14. The commander of the reserve artillery, seeing the necessity to send reinforcements somewhere, sends batteries with the maximum speed possible according to the order from higher commanders or at his discretion, because his activity may turn the course of a battle.

15. If terrain permits, one is to place batteries so that the axle of one piece is not closer than 15 paces from the axle of another one; thus, movements and servicing will be easier, and enemy fire will not be so dangerous.

16. During an action, foot artillery need not keep at the battery more than one caisson per piece. All other [caissons] are to be left behind the lines. Horse artillery may keep even fewer caissons with it, observing only that the limbers are always filled with ammunition.

17. Men must be trained to shift barrels quickly and neatly from one carriage to another.

18. At outposts during night, pieces must be always loaded with short range canister, with a string fastened to it in order to be able to unload the piece when day comes, and there is no need [for the defensive measure].

19. Each battery commander will take care to have spare horses and spare harness for an action; one is to have usual simple breech-hands.

20. When a march over muddy or marshy terrain is expected, artillerists must have fascines, which can be fastened to the sides of caissons and pieces, trying to keep them dry.

21. In conclusion, I say that there is nothing more shameful to an army, than unnecessary waste of ammunition, which one must try to use so that each shot would cause the maximum damage to an enemy, keeping in mind how its production and transportation is difficult.

Bibliography

Reading and discourse are requisite to make a soldier perfect in the art military,
how great soever his practical knowledge may be.

—George Monck

The warrior who cultivates his mind polishes his arms.

—Chevalier de Boufflers

Anon., "Compendious Exercise for the Garrison and Field Ordnance as Practiced in the United States," Washington, 1810.

——, "Exercier-Borschrift mit dem Kaiserlich-Königlich Ordinären Feld-und Cavallerie Geschusse forvuhl einzeln als in Batterien," Wien, Austria, 1809.

——, *Exerzir-Reglement für die Artillerie*, Berlin, 1812.

——, "Extrait du Reglement Provisoire pour le Service des Troupes en Campagne," n.d.

——, *German Military Dictionary*, War Department, Washington, 1944.

——, *Maneuvres des Batteries de Campagne pour L'Artillerie de la Garde Imperiale*, Thionville, France, 1812.

——, *Petit Manuel de Canonier*, Paris, 1810.

——, "Titre Troisième École Artillerie," n.d.

——, *Zur Ausbildung und Taktik der Artillerie*, Biblio Verlag, Osnabrück, Germany, 1982.

Adams, Henry, *The War of 1812*, edited by H. A. De Weerd, Infantry Journal Press, Washington, 1944. Reprinted, with a new Introduction, by John R. Elting, Cooper Square Press, New York, 1999.)

Adkin, Mark, *The Waterloo Companion*, Aurum, London, 2001.

Adye, Ralph Willett, *The Bombardier and Pocket Gunner*, Nash, London, 1813

Alder, Ken, *Engineering the Revolution: Arms and Enlightenment in France, 1763–1815*, Princeton University Press, Princeton, NJ, 1997.

Barrere, Albert, *A Dictionary of English and French Military Terms*, Hachette, London, 1942.

Becke, A. F., *The Battle of Waterloo*, Kegan Paul, London, 1936. Reprinted by Greenhill Books, London, 1995.)

Bezotocnii, V. M., Vasilii, A. A., Gorshman, A. M., Parkaev, O. K., and Smirnoff, A. A., *The Russian Army, 1812–1814*, Moscow, 1999.

Boudou, Pierre, "France et Allies Artillerie 1804–1815," n.d.

Boulart, Bon, *Mémoires Militaire du Général Bon Boulart sur les guerres de La République et de l'Empire*, A La Librarie Illustrée, Paris, c. 1890

Bowden, Scott, *Armies at Waterloo*, Empire Press, Arlington, Texas, 1983.

——, *Napoleon and Austerlitz: The Glory Years, 1805–1807*, Vol. 1, The Emperor's Press, Chicago, 1997

——, *Napoleon's Grande Armée of 1813*, The Emperor's Press, Chicago, 1990.

Bowden, Scott, and Tarbox, Charles, *Armies on the Danube, 1809*, The Emperor's Press, Chicago, 1989.

Brack, Antoine de, *Light Cavalry Outpost Duties*, Mitchell, London, 1976. Reprinted by Demisolde Press, San Diego, 2000.

Britten-Austin, Paul, *1812: Napoleon in Moscow*, Greenhill Books, London, 1995.

——, *1812: The Great Retreat*, Greenhill Books, London, 1996.

——, *1812: The March on Moscow*, Greenhill Books, London, 1993.

Camon, H., *Napoleon's System of War*, translated and annotated by George F. Nafziger, The Nafziger Collection, Westchester, 2002.

Carnet de la Sabretache, "Bataille d'Eylau," p. 81.

——, "Bataille de Friedland (Journal d'opérations du 1ème corps de la Grande Armée," p. 325

——, "Deux lettres du général comte Druout," p. 717.

——, Deuxième Série, Vol. 7, Paris, 1908, "Le passage du grand Saint-Bernard," p. 413.

——, Deuxième Série, Vol. 8, Paris, 1909, "Le centenaire d'Essling et de Wagram," p. 321, 515.

——, Deuxième Série, Vol. 10, Paris, 1911, "Gribeauval, lieutenant général, premier inspecteur d'artillerie," p. 251.

——, "Lettre du général Druout," p. 509.

——, "Napoléon de Buonaparte, officier d'artillerie 1784-1785," p. 133

——, "Nouvelles lettres du général Druout, 1801-1814," p. 380

——, "Quelques lettres de Druout au capitaine d'habillement du régiment d'artillerie de la Garde, 1809-1810, pp. 128, 205, 245.

——, "Souvenirs militaires d'un officier du premier empire" (Colonel Noel), p. 433.

——, Troisième Série, Vol. 1, Paris, 1913, "Le colonel d'artillerie Chauveau, p. 385, 449, 513.

——, Troisième Série, Vol. 2, Paris, 1914-19, "Le chef d'escadron d'artillerie de Lassus-Marcilly," p. 369.

——, Troisième Série, Vol. 7, Paris, 1924, "Canonnier de l'artillerie légère de la Garde des Consuls," p. 225.

——, "Un péterinage du bord de la Beresina," p. 200

——, Vol. 3, Paris, 1895, "Le 7e Corps à Eylau," p. 3.

——, Vol. 4, Paris, 1896, "Le sage de la Grande Armée," p. 72.

——, Vol. 5, Paris, 1897, "Napoléon Bonaparte et les généraux du Teil," p. 54

——, Vol. 7, Paris, 1899, "Nouveautes touchant l'artillerie," p. 89.

——, Vol. 8, Paris, 1900, "Lettres inédites du général comte Druout," p. 408.

——, Vol. 9, Paris, 1901, "Un Épisode de la retraite de Russie: lettre d'un officier d'artillerie," p. 279.

——, Vol. 10, Paris, 1902, "Une lettre du général Druout," p. 310.

——, Vol. 14, Paris, 1906, "Officier d'artillerie à cheval de la Garde des Consuls," p. 449.

——, Vol. 15, Paris, 1907, "Le Centenaire de Friedland," p. 321.

Caruana, Adrian B., *British Artillery Ammunition, 1780*, Museum Restoration Service, Ottawa, 1979.

——, "British Artillery Drill of the 18th Century," Arms Collecting, Ottawa, 1977.

Caulaincourt, A. L. A., *With Napoleon in Russia*, William Morrow & Co., New York, 1935.

Chandler, David, *On the Napoleonic Wars*, Greenhill Books, London, 1994.

——, *The Art of War in the Age of Marlborough*, Batsford, London, 1976.

——, *The Dictionary of the Napoleonic Wars*, Macmillan, New York, 1979.

Chandler, David, (ed.), *Napoleon's Marshals*, Macmillan, New York, 1987.

Chappell, Mike, *The King's German Legion: (1) 1803-1812*, Osprey Publishing, Oxford, 2000.

——, *The King's German Legion: (2) 1812-1816*, Osprey Publishing, Oxford, England, 2000

Chartrand, René, *Fuentes d'Oñoro: Wellington's Liberation of Portugal*, Osprey Publishing, Oxford, 2002.

——, *Napoleon's Guns 1792-1815 (1)*, Osprey Publishing, Oxford, 2003

——, *Napoleon's Guns 1792-1815 (2)*, Osprey Publishing, Oxford, 2003

——, *The Portuguese Army of the Napoleonic Wars (3)*, Osprey Publishing, Oxford, 2001.

——, *The Spanish Army of the Napoleonic Wars 1812-1815 (3)*, Osprey Publishing, Oxford, 1999.

Chartrand, René, and Graves, Donald E., "The United States Army of the War of 1812: A Handbook," 1985. Unpublished manuscript.

Chlapowski, Desirée, *Memoirs of a Polish Lancer*, The Emperor's Press, 1992.

Coignet, Jean-Roche, *The Notebooks of Captain Coignet 1799-1816*, Chatto & Windus, London, 1897. Reprinted by Greenhill Books, London, 1989.

Congreve, William, *Details of the Rocket System*, Museum Restoration Service, Ottawa, 1970.

Corvisier, André, (ed.), *A Dictionary of Military History and the Art of War*, Blackwell Press, Oxford, 1994.

Craig, Gordon A., *The Politics of the Prussian Army 1640-1945*, Oxford University Press, Oxford, 1955.

Davis, Robert P., *Where a Man Can Go: Major General William Phillips, British Royal Artillery, 1731-1781*, Greenwood Press, Westport, 1999.

Denoeu, François, *Military French*, D. C. Heath, Boston, 1943

Detaille, Eduard, *L'Armée Française: An Illustrated History of the French Army, 1790–1885*, translated by Maureen Carlson Reinartsen, Waxtel & Hasenhauer, New York 1992.

Dickson, Alexander, *The Dickson Manuscripts*, 5 vols, Royal Artillery Institution, Woolwich, 1905-8. Reprinted by Ken Trotman, Cambridge, 1987.

Dodge, Theodore A., *Gustavus Adolphus*, De Capo Press, New York, 1998.

Dogureau, J.-P., *Guns in the Desert: General Jean-Pierre Dogureau's Journal of Napoleon's Egyptian Expedition*, translated by Rosemary Brindle, Praeger, Westport, 2002.

Dolleczek, Anton, *Geschichte der Österreichischen Artillerie*, Graz, 1973

Douglas, Howard, Major General Sir, *An Essay on the Principles and Construction* of Military Bridges and the Passage of Rivers in Military Operations, Thomas and William Boone, London, 1832.

Downey, Fairfax, *Cannonade*, Doubleday, New York, 1966.

——, *Sound of the Guns*, David McKay, New York, 1956.

Duffy, Christopher, *Instrument of War*, Vol. 1, The Emperor's Press, Chicago, 2000.

——, *The Army of Frederick the Great*, The Emperor's Press, Chicago, 1996.

——, *The Military Experience in the Age of Reason*, Atheneum, New York, 1988.

Du Teil, Jean, *The New Use of Artillery in Field Wars: Necessary Knowledge*, The Nafziger Collection, 2003.

D'Urturbie, Theodore, Manuel de L'Artilleur, Paris 1794.

Elting, John R., *Amateurs, To Arms! A Military History of the War of 1812*, Alqonquin Books, New York, 1991.

——, *Napoleonic Uniforms*, Vols 1 and 2, Macmillan, New York 1993.

——, *Napoleonic Uniforms*, Vols 3 and 4, The Emperor's Press, Chicago, 2000.

——, *Swords Around a Throne*, The Free Press, New York, 1988.

——, *The Superstrategists*, Scribner's, New York, 1985.

Elting, John R., (ed.), *Military Uniforms in America. Vol. 2: Years of Growth 1796–1851*, Presidio Press, California, 1977.

Epstein, Robert M., *Prince Eugène at War*, Empire Press, Arlington, Texas, 1984.

Esdaile, Charles, *The Peninsular War: A New History*, Penguin Books, London, 2003.

Esposito, Vincent J., and Elting, John R., *A Military History and Atlas of the Napoleonic Wars*, Praeger, New York, 1968. Reprinted by Greenhill Books, London, 1999.

Faber du Faur, Christian W., and North, Jonathan, *With Napoleon in Russia*, Greenhill Books, London, 2000.

Fave, Ildephonse, *The Emperor Napoleon's New System of Field Artillery, as Submitted to the French Service*, Parker, Furnival & Parker, London, 1854.

Fezensac, Raymond de, *A Journal of the Russian Campaign*, Parker, Furnival & Parker, London, 1852. Reprinted by Ken Trotman, Cambridge, 1988.

Franklin, Carl E., *Congreve Rockets of the War of 1812*, Arms Collecting, Ottawa, 2001.

Freytag-Loringhoven, Major General Baron Hugo von, *et al.*, *The Roots of Strategy*, Stackpole Books, Harrisburg, 1991.

Gates, David, *The Spanish Ulcer: A History of the Peninsular War*, Norton, New York, 1986.

Gill, John H., *With Eagles to Glory*, Greenhill Books, London, 1992.

Gooding, James, *An Introduction to British Artillery in North America*, Museum Restoration Service, Ottawa, 1988.

Goosef, E., *Russian Artillery of the Napoleonic Period*, Moscow, Minsk, 2001.

Graves, Don, "American Ordnance of the War of 1812," Arms Collecting, Ottawa, 1993.

——, "Field Artillery of the War of 1812: Equipment, Organization, Tactics and Effectiveness," Arms Collecting, Ottawa, 1992.

——, "For Want of this Precaution so Many Men Lose Their Arms: Official, Semi-Official and Unofficial American Artillery Texts, 1775-1845." Unpublished manuscript, n.d.

——, "Louis de Tousard and his Artillerist's Companion: An Investigation of Source Material for Napoleonic Period Ordnance," Arms Collecting, Ottawa, 1983.

——, *The Rocket's Red Glare*, Museum Restoration Service, Ottawa, 1985.

Graves, Don, (ed.), *DeScheel's Treatise of Artillery*, Museum Restoration Service, Ottawa, 1984.

Griffith, Paddy, *The Art of War of Revolutionary France*, Greenhill Books, London, 1998.

Hausmann, Franz, *A Soldier for Napoleon*, edited by John H. Gill, Greenhill Books, London, 1998.

Haythornewaite, Philip, *Austrian Specialist Troops of the Napoleonic Wars*, Osprey Publishing, Oxford, 1990.

——, *The Armies of Wellington*, Arms and Armour Press, 1994.

——, *The Austrian Army 1740–80. 3: Specialist Troops*, Osprey Publishing, Oxford, 1995.

——, *Weapons and Equipment of the Napoleonic Wars*, Arms and Armour Press, London, 1979.

——, *Wellington's Army: The Uniforms of the British Soldier, 1812–1815*, Greenhill Books, London, 2002.

——, *Wellington's Specialist Troops*, Osprey Publishing, Oxford, 1988.

——, *Who Was Who in the Napoleonic Wars*, Arms and Armor Press, London, 1998.

Heinl, Robert D., Jr., *Dictionary of Military and Naval Quotations*, United States Naval Institute Press, Annapolis, 1966.

Henry, Chris, *British Napoleonic Artillery, 1793–1815 (1)*, Osprey Publishing, Oxford, 2003.

——, *British Napoleonic Artillery 1793–1815 (2)*, Osprey Publishing, Oxford, 2003.

Hertenberger, H., and Wiltschek, F., *Erzherzog Karl der Sieger von Aspern*, Styria, Austria 1983.

Hicks, James, E., *French Military Weapons 1717–1938*, Flayderman , New Milford, 1964.

Hoen, M. von; Kerchnawe, Hugo; and Veltze, Alois, *Krieg 1809*, Vol. 4, Appendices, Vienna, Austria.

Hughes, B. P., *Firepower: Weapons Effectiveness on the Battlefield, 1630–1850*, Armour and Armour Press, London, 1974.

——, *Open Fire: Artillery Tactics from Marlborough to Wellington*, Antony Bird Publications, Chichester, 1983.

——, *Smooth-Bore Artillery: The Muzzle Loading Artillery of the 18th and 19th Centuries*, Arms and Armour Press, London, 1969.

Hulot, M., *Instruction sur le Service de L'Artillerie*, Magimel, Paris 1813.

Jany, C., *Die Preussische Armee von 1763 bis 1807*, Vols 3 and 4, Biblio Verlag, Osnabrück, Germany, 1967.

Jenkins, Michael, *Arakcheev: Grand Vizier of the Russian Empire*, Faber, London, and Dial Press, New York, 1969.

King, Dean, and Hattendorf, John B., (eds), *Every Man Will Do His Duty: An Anthology of First-Hand Accounts from the Age of Nelson, 1793–1815*, Henry Holt & Co., New York, 1993.

Kochan, James, *The United States Army 1783–1811*, Osprey Publishing, Oxford, 2001.

——, *The United States Army 1812–1815*, Osprey Publishing, Oxford, 2000.

Kosciusko, Tadeuz, *Maneuvers of Horse Artillery*, New York, 1808.

Lachouque, Henry, and Brown, Anne, *The Anatomy of Glory*, Brown University Press, Providence, and Lund Humphries, London, 1961. Reprinted by Greenhill Books, London, 1997.

Lauerma, Matti, *L'Artillerie de Campagne Française Pendant les Guerres de la Revolution: Évolution de l'Organization et de la Tactique*, Helsinki, 1956.

Laws, M. E. S., *Battery Records of the Royal Artillery 1716–1859*, Royal Artillery Institute, Woolwich, 1952.

LeBlond, Guillaume, *Treatise of Artillery, 1746*, Museum Restoration Service, Ottawa, 1970.

Le Diberder, Georges, *Les Armées Françaises a L'Époque Revolutionnaire 1789–1804*, Collections du Musée de l'Armée, 1989.

Leggiere, Michael, *Napoleon and Berlin*, University of Oklahoma Press, Norman, 2002.

Linck, Tony, *Napoleon's Generals: The Waterloo Campaign*, The Emperor's Press, Chicago, 1993

Litre, Emile François, *Les Régiments d'Artillerie à Pied de la Garde*, Paris, Toulouse, 1895.

Lossing, Benson J., *Lossing's Pictorial Field Book of the War of 1812*, Vol. 2, Harper & Bros, New York, 1868.

Luvaas, Jay, *Frederick the Great on the Art of War*, The Free Press, New York, 1996.

——, *Napoleon on the Art of War*, The Free Press, New York, 1999.

Lynn, John, *Giant of the Grand Siècle: The French Army 1610–1715*, Cambridge University Press, Cambridge, 1997.

——, *The Bayonets of the Republic: Motivation and Tactics in the Army of Revolutionary France, 1791–1794*, Westview Press, Boulder, 1996.

Lynn, John, (ed.), *Tools of War: Instruments, Ideas, and Institutions of Warfare, 1445–1871*, University of Illinois Press, Urbana and Chicago, 1990.

MacLannan, Ken, "Lichtenstein and Gribeauval: 'Artillery Revolution' in Political and Cultural Context," *War and History*, vol. 10, Issue 3, 1 July 2003.

Malinowsky, Louis, and Bonin, Robert, *Geschichte der Brandenburgish-Preussischen Artillerie*, Wiesbaden, 1982.

Manucy, Albert, *Artillery Through the Ages*, Government Printing Office, Washington, 1949.

Marbot, Marcellin, *The Memoirs of Baron de Marbot*, 2 vols, Longmans, Green, London and New York, 1892. Reprinted by Greenhill Books, London, 1988.

Maude, F. N., *The Jena Campaign, 1806*, Sonnerschein, London, 1809. Reprinted by Greenhill Books, London, 1998.

Mercer, Cavalie, *A Journal of the Waterloo Campaign*, Blackwood, Edinburgh, 1870. Reprinted by Greenhill Books, London, 1985.

Monhaupt, *Ueber den gebrauch der Reitenden Artillerie*, Berlin 1836.

Morla, T. de, *Tratado de Artillerie Para el Uso de la Academia de Caballeros Cadetes del Real Cuerpo de Artilleria en Tres Tomos y Otro de Laminas, Que tartan de la Principales functiones de los Officiales de este Cuerpo en pas y en ruerra*, Segovia, 1816

Muir, Rory, *Tactics and the Experience of Battle in the Age of Napoleon*, Yale University Press, 1998.

Muller, John, *A Treatise of Artillery, 1780*, Museum Restoration Service, Ottawa, 1977.

Nafziger, George, *Imperial Bayonets*, Greenhill Books, London, 1996.

——, *The Poles and Saxons of the Napoleonic Wars*, The Emperor's Press, Chicago, 1991.

——, *The Prussian Army of the Napoleonic Wars (1792–1815). Volume III: Cavalry, Artillery, Technical Troops, and Train*, The Nafziger Collection, Westchester, 1996.

Nafziger, George, and Worley, Warren, *The Imperial Russian Army (1763–1815). Vol. 2: Cavalry, Cossacks, Guard and Artillery*, The Nafziger Collection, Westchester, 1996.

Naulet, Frederic, *L'Artillerie Française (1665–1765): Naissance d'une Arme*, Economica, Paris, 2002.

Oman, Charles, *A History of the Peninsular War*, Vol. 4, Oxford University Press, Oxford, 1911. Reprinted by Greenhill Books, London, 1996.

——, *Wellington's Army*, Edward Arnold, London, 1913. Reprinted Greenhill Books, London, 1986.

Paret, Peter, *Yorck and the Era of Prussian Reform*, Princeton University Press, Princeton, NJ, 1966.

Parker, Harold T., *Three Napoleonic Battles*, Duke University Press, Durham, North Carolina, 1983.

Pelet, Jean Jacques, and Horward, Donald D., (ed.), *The French Campaign in Portugal 1810–1811*, University of Minnesota Press, Minneapolis, 1973.

Persy, N., *Elementary treatise on the Forms of Cannon & Various Systems of Artillery: Translated for the use of the Cadets of the US Military Academy from the French of Professor N. Persy of Metz, 1832*, Museum Restoration Service, Ottawa, 1979.

Peterson, Harold, *Roundshot and Rammers: An Introduction to Muzzle-loading Land Artillery in the United States*, Stackpole, Harrisburg, 1969.

Petre, F. Lorraine, *Napoleon and the Archduke Charles*, John Lane, London, 1909. Reprinted by Greenhill Books, London, 1991.

——, *Napoleon's Campaign in Poland, 1806–1807*, Samson, Low, London, 1901. Reprinted by Greenhill Books, London, 1989.

——, *Napoleon's Conquest of Prussia, 1806*, John Lane, London, 1907. Reprinted by Greenhill Books, London, 1993.

Pietsch, Paul, *Formations- und Uniformierungsgeschichte des Preussischen Heerres, 1808 bis 1914*, Band II, Helmut Gerhard Schulz, Hamburg, 1966.

Pigeard, Alain, *Dictionnaire de la Grande Armée*, Tallandier, Paris, 2002.

——, "L'Artillerie Napoléonienne et le Genie," *Tradition Magazine*, Hors Série No 23, Paris, 2002.

Pivka, Otto von, *Armies of the Napoleonic Era*, David & Charles, Newton Abbot, 1979.

Quimby, Robert, *The Background of Napoleonic Warfare*, Columbia University Press, New York, 1957.

——, *The U.S. Army in the War of 1812: An Operational and Command Study*, 2 vols., Michigan State University Press, East Lansing, 1997

Reilly, Robin, *The British at the Gates: The New Orleans Campaign in the War of 1812*, Robin Brass Studio, Toronto, 2002.

Rothenberg, Günther, *Napoleon's Great Adversary: Archduke Charles and the Austrian Army 1792–1814*, Batsford, London, 1982.

Roquerol, G., *L'Artillerie au Début des Guerres de la Révolution*, Paris, Nancy, 1898.

Ruty, Charles-Étienne-François, "Observations on the Part of the System Year XI Related to the Subdivision Scale of the Calibers of the Pieces of Ordnance for the Field and Siege Equipment Companies," translated by Scott Bowden, Carton 2w84, Archives du Service Historique de l'État-Major de l'Armée de Terre, Vincennes.

Sauzey, C., *Les Allemands sous les Aigles Françaises: Essai sur les Troupes de la Confédération du Rhin 1806–1813. II: Le Contingent Badois*, Chapelot, Paris, 1902.

Savory, Sir Reginald, *His Britannic Majesty's Army in Germany during the Seven Years' War*, Clarendon Press, Oxford, 1966.

Schafer, Klaus; Gartner, Markus; Umhey, Alfred; Wacher, Peter; and Wagner, Edmund, *Die Achenbach: Bilderhandschrift 1813/1814*, Darmstadt, Germany, 1994.

Scharnhorst, Gerhard, *Handbuch der Artillerie*, Hannover, Germany, 1806.

Scott, Samuel F., *From Yorktown to Valmy: The Transformation of the French Army in an Age of Revolution*, University Press of Colorado, Niwot, 1998.

Shanahan, William O., *Prussian Military Reforms 1786–1813*, Columbia University Press, New York, 1945

Six, Georges, *Dictionnaire Biographique des Généraux & Amiraux Français de la Révolution et de l'Empire (1792–1814)*, Bordas, Paris, 1947.

Smirnoff, Alexander, *Arachkeev's Artillery: The Russian Artillery System of 1805*, Moscow, 1998.

Smith, Digby, *Armies of 1812: The Grande Armée and the Armies of Austria, Prussia, Russia and Turkey*, Spellmount, Staplehurst, 2002.

——, *Napoleon's Regiments*, Greenhill Books, London, 2000.

Smola, Joseph Freiherr von, *Handbuch fur Kaiserlich-Königliche Österreichische Artillerie-Offiziere*, Vienna, Austria, 1839.

Tousard, Louis de, *The American Artillerist's Companion*, 2 vols, C and C Conrad, Philadelphia, 1809. Reprinted by Greenwood Press, Westport, 1969.

Tranie, J., and Carmigniani, J. C., *La Patrie en Danger 1792–1793: Les Campagnes de la Révolution*, Tome 1, Charles Lavauzelle, 1987.

Troiani, Don, *Soldiers in America 1754–1865*, Stackpole Books, Mechanicsburg, 1998.

Tsouras, Peter G., (ed.), *The Greenhill Dictionary of Military Quotations*, Greenhill Books, London, 2000.

Tulard, Jean, *Dictionnaire Napoléon*, 2 vols, Librarie Fayard, Paris, 1999.

Ward, S. P. G., *Wellington's Headquarters: A Study of the Administrative Problems in the Peninsula 1809–1814*, Oxford University Press, Oxford, 1957.

Wartenberg, Count Yorck von, *Napoleon as a General*, Kegan Paul, London, 1902.

Webber, William, and Wollocombe, Richard Henry, (eds), *With the Guns in the Peninsula*, Greenhill Books, London, 1991.

Wenge, August, *Die Schlacht von Aspern*, Berlin, 1900.

Werth, Albert, *Erinnerungen an den Kaiserlich Österreicheschen Generalmajor in der Artillerie Josef Freiherrn von Smola*, Vienna, Austria, 1905.

White, Charles, *The Enlightened Soldier*, Greenwood Press, Westport, 1990.

Willcox, Cornelis de Witt, *French English Military Technical Dictionary*, Harper, New York, 1917.

Willing, Paul, *Napoléon et ses Soldats. Tome 1: L'Apogée de la Gloire (1804–1809)*, Collections du Musée de l'Armée, Paris, 1986.

——, *Napoléon et ses Soldats. Tome 2: De Wagram à Waterloo (1809–1815)*, Collections du Musée de l'Armée, Paris, 1987.

Wilson, Sir Robert, *Brief Remarks on the Character and Composition of the Russian Army and a Sketch of the Campaigns in Poland in 1806 and 1807*, Egerton, London, 1810. Reprinted by Worley, Newcastle, 2000.

Winter, Frank H., *The First Golden Age of Rocketry*, Smithsonian Institution Press, Washington and London, 1990.

Wise, Terence, *Artillery Equipments of the Napoleonic Wars*, Osprey Publishing, Oxford, 1979.

Zhmodikov, Alexander and Yurii , *Tactics of the Russian Army in the Napoleonic Wars*, 2 vols, The Nafziger Collection, Westchester, Ohio, 2003.

Glossary

Absolute gravity   The force by which any body, including artillery ammunition, is impelled toward its center

Acceleration   The increased velocity of any body.

Accoutrements   Arms and implements, both personal and for crew-served weapons.

Action   A word of command in both the exercise of field pieces and in action, for example "Action, front," in which the guns would be emplaced to the immediate front of the position where there was either a target or imminent danger to the battery.

Advantage   Anything which gives one either a superiority or an opportunity in either offense or defense.

Affut   Gun carriage.

Aim   The pointing of guns in the direction desired to fire.

Alarm   The call to arms, especially in an emergency.

Alert   Ready, on watch, on call, or on guard.

Allezer   To clean the bore of a gun tube after casting (in the older method).

Allezures   The metal that is drilled out of a cast cannon after the tube has been bored.

Altitude   The vertical distance from the ground.

Ammunition   Military stores that include infantry cartridges, powder, artillery rounds (which, in turn, included artillery cartridges, cartouches, etc.), rockets, and other types of artillery ammunition.

Amorce   Fine-grained powder used for priming, as in a priming fuse.

Amplitude   The range from the piece to its intended target of any projectile.

Ange/angel shot   The French term for chain shot.

Appuy   As in *point d'appuy*, the fulcrum or decisive point.

Artificer   In French, *ouvrier*. A workman who made and repaired artillery vehicles and gun carriages.

Artillery   Pieces of ordnance larger than long arms and that are crew-served, such as cannon, howitzers, etc. Artillery includes field artillery (horse and foot), siege artillery, and coastal defense artillery.

Artillery volante   Horse artillery.

Astragal   A raised ring or section at three places on the outside of the gun tube at the breech, at the vent, cascabel and in front of the vent.

Axle, axletree   The bar which runs at right angles to the length of the gun carriage, limber, and other artillery vehicle to which the wheels are attached. Before the Gribeauval reforms, axles were made of wood; Gribeauval introduced one of iron, which was infinitely superior.

Ball   Round, cast projectile fired from a cannon. Also called roundshot or solid shot. The caliber was judged by the weight, for example a ball for a 6-pounder artillery piece.

Base ring   The raised portion at the rear of the tube just before the cascabel.

Batter, battering   A cannonade or barrage of siege pieces or other heavy artillery.

Battery   A term used during this period for any assemblage of guns in a position (as few as one would count as a "battery.") The French did not use the term "battery" to denote a company-sized artillery unit until 1829, referring to such a unit as a "company." The British used either "brigade" or "troop."

Continental armies, though, such as those of the Prussians and Austrians did use the term "battery" interchangeably for either.

Bear   A piece brought to point directly at an object or target.

Blast   The "wind" caused by the firing of the cannon or an explosion.

Block trail   The trail of a piece being a solid piece of wood. The only nation's artillery that used block trails during this period was Britain's.

Boîte à mitraille   A general French term for canister or grape shot.

Bomb   Another term for an exploding shell.

Bombardier   An artillery crewman always employed with mortars and howitzers.

Bore   The drilled-out inner tube of the gun barrel into which the round was inserted and rammed for firing.

Bouche à feu   The French general term for cannon (literally, "mouth of fire").

Boulet   Solid shot.

Boutefeu   See "Linstock."

Bracket   A gun carriage made out of two separate pieces of wood attached to each other by transoms. All of the artillery of this period used the bracket trail—with the exception of the British. Sometimes also referred to as a "split trail."

Breech   The rear of the gun tube from the platebande of the breech to the neck of the cascabel, or between the vent and the base ring, but not including the cascabel.

Bricole   A leather crossbelt worn by artillerymen to which is attached a length of rope with a metal hook on the end. With this tool the gun crew could fasten themselves to the gun by the various ring-bolts on the carriage and manhandle it into position or around the battlefield if need be. It was very helpful in muddy or rough terrain. This essential piece of equipment was invented by Gribeauval.

Brigade   A battery of British foot artillery. One of the confusing things about studying the Napoleonic period is that the same term can mean different things—*viz.* the two definitions for "battery." A brigade can also be used with infantry, meaning a tactical organization of two or more regiments. Division can be two companies in an infantry battalion, a permanent tactical formation of two or more brigades, or the number of guns served by a French artillery company.

Bucket   Guns were usually, if not always, equipped with a water bucket to help in swabbing out the tube after firing, to make sure that there were no pieces of burning wadding or powder left in the bore. The French Gribeauval water bucket was especially well made as it was wide at the bottom and narrow at the top: it was therefore hard to tip over, and the design also kept the water from spilling.

Button   The rounded end of the cascabel.

Caboche   An artillery wheel.

Caisson   An ammunition wagon.

Caliber   A determination of length in artillery, usually being the size or diameter of the muzzle of the piece.

Canister   A tin can packed with either musket balls or balls of a slightly larger caliber. Packed in sawdust and made into a cartridge by attaching a bagged powder charge (a sabot was not used), it made a very efficient antipersonnel round, and at close range it was murderous.

Cannon   A weapon having a long metal tube in which is placed gunpowder and some type of launchable projectile that can be fired on command.

Cannoneer   An enlisted artilleryman; one who serves the guns; a member of a gun crew.

Cap   A piece of sheepskin or leather placed over the mouth of a mortar when in action, to prevent the inside of the tube from getting wet in inclement weather.

Capsquare   The metal clasp that was placed and locked over the trunnion plates when the gun was in the carriage, to hold the gun in place when traveling and firing.

Carcass   A fire ball; or in modern artillery parlance, an illumination shell. French illumination rounds were filled with tar, turpentine, or rosin and were very effectively used in sieges to find enemy troops and positions.

Carriage   The wooden, iron-reinforced two-wheeled vehicle to which the gun tube was attached by the trunnions and capsquares for firing.

Cartouche   See "Cartridge."

Cartridge   A serge, flannel, parchment, or paper "bag" which contained the powder charge for a round of ammunition. Also the term used for the powder bag, round, and sabot that made up a single "fixed" round of ammunition.

Cascabel   The rear ring assembly at the breech of a piece to which the sight was attached. It was immediately behind the vent. It ran from the band of the breech to the end of the button. The parts it included were the breech, the listel, the neck, and the button (also called a "knob").

Case shot   Another term for canister.

Chamber   The rear area of the bore into which the powder charge was rammed. Field guns had no chamber as such, though the rear of the bore could be referred to as the chamber of the piece. Chambers were in howitzers and mortars, and in guns of large caliber. French guns were all without chambers during this period. By this time, guns that had chambers were inefficient weapons: Frederick the Great's artillerymen discovered this salient fact when they were issued with chambered guns at Frederick's insistence.

Chain shot   Artillery ammunition that is attached by a link of chain. It was used mostly at sea to cut up the rigging of an enemy ship.

Charge   The measure of powder for one round of artillery ammunition.

Charging cylinder   The space between the chase astragal and the muzzle astragal.

Chase   The space from the trunnions to the muzzle of a cannon tube.

Cheeks   The sides of a bracket trail carriage were referred to as the "cheeks." Sometimes this applied to the sides where the gun was mounted, especially in a block carriage.

Coffret   The trail ammunition box that contained ready ammunition for immediate use when going into action. When it was removed from the trails it was placed on the limber.

Coin   See "Quoin."

Collet   The muzzle.

Company   The French term ("*compagnie*") for the main tactical unit of artillery of the period. A French company served a "division" of guns and had a train company attached to it to pull the guns and vehicles such as the caissons and field forge.

Counterbattery   Firing at the artillery unit that is firing at you. Generally speaking, it was a waste of time and ammunition, and the French and British discouraged it in their training and doctrine. The only time it was encouraged was when the enemy's artillery was hurting your infantry more than you were hurting theirs. Then, it was best to use lighter guns, usually 4-, 6-, or 8-pounders, as they had a higher rate of fire. The trick was to concentrate your fire on one gun at a time, and putting the enemy piece out of action.

Coup d'oeil   To aim. Also used to describe the ability to see what you were looking at, tactically speaking. Literally, "at a glance."

Cravate   Tying off the reed primers.

Culot   The heavy part of a howitzer.

Cylinder   The bore of the cannon.

Dead ground   Ground in front of a battery that cannot be observed by the gunners and/or struck by their fire.

Depot   (1) A military base which is the home of a unit, where the unit inducts new recruits, gives them their first issue of clothing and equipment, and rudimentary training, before sending them to the unit in the field. (2) A military installation where the workshops for an artillery unit are based and where cannon, artillery vehicles and equipment are repaired and reissued.

Depress   To lower the gun tube with the elevating screw.

Discharge   To fire a piece.

Division   In the French Army, a company of artillery served a division of guns, which would be eight for the foot artillery (six guns and two howitzers) and either six guns or four guns and two howitzers in the horse artillery.

Dolphins   The handles on top of the gun tube that were used to lift the tube from the carriage. Originally quite ornate, and shaped like dolphins (hence the name), by this period they were quite plain and functional. Also referred to as "handles." If a newly cast cannon was found to be deficient after being proven, the handles were broken off to indicate a substandard piece. Cannon for light troops lacked handles.

Drivers   Members of the train battalions who drove the limbers and other artillery vehicles, as well as managing the horse teams.

Drought hooks   Hooks attached to the cheeks of the piece, located near the trail and trunnion holes.

Drag rope   A length of rope that attached to the gun by the crew by which they could pull it around the battlefield. It was replaced by the more efficient *bricole*. Sometimes mistaken for, and consequently misidentified as, the *prolonge*; the two are not the same thing.

Elevating screw   The mechanism—in reality, a very large screw assembly—for raising and lowering (elevating and depressing) the gun tube. For this period it was a rather new and very innovative development.

Elevation   Raising the gun tube.

Encastrement   The practice of having two sets of trunnion plates in the gun carriage which were used for the piece when traveling and for firing. This was found mainly in the French service with the 8- and 12-pounder guns and sometimes for the new 6-pounder of the Système AN XI. It was kept for the new 12-pounder.

Enfilade   Firing at the advantage of the enemy's flank, where you can hit him and he cannot hit you.

Equipage   Ordnance in artillery.

Equipment   The act of being supplied or becoming completely equipped.

Explode   The action in which a piece is discharged or a charge is detonated.

Felloes   Artillery wheels.

Fire   The command to launch the round of ammunition from the gun tube.

Fixed   Non-moving, or attached. Fixed ammunition had all of the components—charge, round, and sabot—attached as a single entity for ease and quickness of loading.

Flanks   The end of a line of the far extremes to the right and to the left of an army. Artillery achieves enfilade fire by getting on the flanks of the enemy unit or army.

Flying artillery   Horse artillery.

Foot artillery   Companies of artillery in which the individual gunners walk. This was also where the heaviest of the field guns, the 12-pounders, were assigned. Some artillery organizations, such as the British, had limbers with ammunition boxes attached, upon which the gunners could sit and ride—a considerable advantage when the speed of the foot artillery increased beyond that of a walk.

Forge   A two-wheeled vehicle for with equipment for making ironwork in the field. In French service, it was attached at the front to the ubiquitous artillery limber.

Formers   Round cylinders of wood that fit the diameter of the bore and around which cartridge paper is rolled before it is glued or closed.

Founder   A person who casts cannon.

Foundry   A place when cannon are cast and bored out.

Fuse   (1) The primer made of tin, copper, or reed that was inserted into the vent, penetrated the powder bag in the chamber of the piece, and completed the powder train and made the piece ready for firing. (2) The wooden assembly that was placed in common shell and shrapnel to ignite the round after it had been fired, causing it to explode down range.

Fusée d'amorce   Primer.

Galloper   A very light field piece, usually a 1- or 3-pounder, whose split trails were also the poles for the one horse that pulled it to fit into its harness.

Gangues   Brass-handled rings which fit the diameter of shot. Used to determine the diameter of roundshot.

Gargoussier   See "Pouch."

Gerbe   The shotgun effect of grapeshot after it is fired; the spread pattern of the round.

Gin   A large tripod assembly with attached block and tackle used in the depots for, among other things, lifting gun tubes on and off carriages.

Grain   A term used in the vent repair.

Grapeshot   An antipersonnel round, using much larger, and fewer, balls than either size of canister. While still a staple type of ammunition for the navies of the period, it was being used less on land, replaced by the more efficient canister round. Grapeshot was manufactured with a wooden tree base and with the balls grouped around it, the entire round being covered with a small net or encased in a bag—hence the resemblance to a bunch of grapes, and the name.

Graze   A round hitting the ground after being fired. A round that grazed was still very dangerous, as it had a tendency to ricochet, and bound or bounce towards its target. This method of firing became very common and was deadly to formed troops.

Grosses balles   Grapeshot.

Gun   See "Cannon."

Gun metal   Another term for brass.

Gunnery   The art and science of the study of projectiles in flight.

Gunner's quadrant   A graduated tool that was used to check and fix the elevation of the piece before firing.

Gunpowder   The propellant charge for artillery projectiles, composed of sulphur, charcoal, and saltpetre.

Hacquet   The long, two-wheeled wagon which, attached to the all-purpose French limber, was used to haul pontoons.

Handles   See "Dolphins."

Hand mallet   A hammer used to drive fuses into shells.

Handspike   A lever-like instrument used for traversing the gun and, in French service, for aiming as well as changing the 8- and 12-pounder gun tubes from traveling to firing position. Mountain artillerymen were sometimes issued folding handspikes.

Hausse   An adjustable sight invented by Gribeauval that could be attached to the breech of the piece, resulting in greatly enhanced aiming and accuracy.

Havresac   See "Pouch."

Head   The fore part of the cheeks of an artillery piece.

Hooks   Pieces of iron bent into a hook shape and attached to the transom plates of a field artillery carriage.

Honeycombs   Flaws in the casting of cannon that render the gun tube dangerous to fire and cause it to be discarded if found during the proofing process.

Horse artillery   Artillery companies or batteries in which all of the gunners are separately mounted on horses, in order to keep up with cavalry. The British mounted two of their horse artillerymen per gun section on their well-designed limbers. The Austrian cavalry batteries, not true horse artillery in the strictest sense, mounted their gunners on modified caissons, called wurst wagons (q.v.), which were padded and could not travel as fast as horse-mounted artillerymen. In the Wars of the Revolution, the French sometimes used wurst wagons, but found them to be unsatisfactory, and by 1800 had mounted all their horse artillerymen on horses.

Hot shot   Round shot heated in a furnace and immediately loaded into the gun tube for firing. Hotshot was the most effective incendiary round in use during the period, with the possible exception of Congreve's rockets. Wads were used, the last one being dampened, to prevent the round from prematurely "cooking off."

Howitz   An earlier term for howitzer.

Howitzer   A short-barreled gun that fired common shell and canister, usually at high angles. It was mounted on a field carriage and was usually found in artillery batteries.

Jetter   Pouring metal into the mold for casting cannon.

Knob   The button or rounded, protruding end on the gun tube which was attached to the end of the cascabel.

Ladle   The long pole used to put powder down the gun tube before the development of the powder cartridge. It was still used during the period for emergencies.

Laid over metal   A term used when the muzzle is higher than the breech.

Laffette   Gun carriage.

Lanterne   Any case or other type of container made of wood in which artillery rounds were carried from the powder magazine to serve the guns.

Lay   To emplace the gun for firing.

Lead   The pair of horses in the front of an artillery gun team.

Level   The line of firing or direction in which artillery pieces are aimed for firing.

Limber   A two-wheeled cart with a pintle for attaching the guns when traveling or moving. Some armies had ammunition boxes on the limbers.

Linchpin   A part of the wheel assembly that passes through the arms of the axletree both to give strength to and lessen the friction on the wheels.

Linstock   A three-foot section of wood, pointed at one end, to stick in the ground, the other end being split and having a slow match wrapped around it. If the supply of portfires ran out, the linstock could be used to fire the gun. Also known as a boutefeu.

Lissoir   To smooth out coarse-grained powder.

Load   The command and process of putting the ammunition (round) into the gun tube for firing.

Locking-plates   Iron plates nailed to the sides of the field carriage to prevent the limber wheels from rubbing against the bare wood of the carriage when the vehicle performs a tight turn.

Lock   To stop one or more wheels of a vehicle from rotating when going down an incline.

Magazine   A storage place for powder, shot, and other ammunition items.

Mark   To shoot at a target.

Masselotte   Surplus metal from the casting of cannon.

Massif   A short piece of wood used when making cartridges.

Match   Rope impregnated with chemicals to retain a lighted fire and act as a slow fuse. There were two types, slow match, used on the linstock and portfire, and quick match, used with primers. The names are self-explanatory..

Matross   An assistant cannoneer (an American and British term).

Merkin   A mop used to clean cannon.

Metal   See "Laid over metal."

Mitraille   To fire grape shot, canister, or miniature projectiles that come to hand, such as nails and stones.

Mount   As in to "mount cannon"–generally used when placing the gun tube on the carriage.

Mountain artillery   Light artillery, usually 3- or 4-pounders, that can be broken down into their component parts and loaded on mules with their ammunition.

Mouth   The entrance to the bore, where the cartridge is put in the gun tube. An English term.

Mouton   A rammer made out of cast iron.

Muzzle The "business end" of an artillery piece of the period. This was the end of the gun tube into which the round was loaded, and from which it exited at great velocity when fired. It was between the muzzle astragal and the quick of the mouth.

Muzzle swell A projection behind the muzzle moldings. Another English term: the French called it the "tulip."

Neck The piece of metal joining the button to the breech.

Nuremberg pound A measure of weight equal to 0.477 kilograms, was used to measure Austrian rounds for the appropriate caliber gun. It was a little less heavy than the French pound, so a French gun rated at the same caliber as an Austrian piece would have more throw weight. This was relatively insignificant per piece, but when guns were used in mass it could give the French an advantage, along with the longer range the French enjoyed. From the German *Nürnberg Pfund*.

Ogie See "Ogive."

Ogive An ornamental molding on the surface of artillery pieces.

Ordnance A general term governing any weapon that fires a gunpowder charge and the ammunition that goes with it.

Paille Any flaw in metal.

Park, *parc* An ancient artillery term that originally meant the artillery attached to the army. The *parc* in the Grande Armée was where the spare vehicles, guns, and carriages were kept and maintained, and where the *ouvriers* and armorers were usually stationed. Generally speaking, it was a movable depot where ammunition resupply would be obtained and vehicles and guns repaired.

Petites Balles Canister.

Picker A long, needlelike tool that was placed in the vent of the artillery piece in order to clear it after firing, and to then pierce the powder bag after loading in order to put the primer in the bag.

Piece A general term for a cannon, howitzer, or other item of artillery ordnance.

Pintle The spike-like apparatus on the limber to which the trail of the gun was attached when moving.

Pintlehole The hole in the trail transom of the piece through which the pintle was placed when the gun was "limbered up" for movement.

Pinons Iron pins used to keep the ironwork on carriages intact and tight.

Pointing Placing the business end of a piece on a sight line; pointing the tube at a target.

Point-blank The distance from the gun tube where the line of fire crosses the line of sight for the second time. It should be noted that the line of fire and the line of sight of the gun tube are not parallel, but form an angle beyond the muzzle of the gun tube.

Pontoon A boat-like piece of equipment used to make floating bridges across rivers. Usually, but not always, it was copper-bottomed, and either square-ended or rounded. Pontoons were also useful for ferrying troops across rivers or large lakes.

Portfire The instrument used to ignite the primer and fire the piece—essentially, a short stick wrapped with slow match.

Prime To prepare a piece for firing after being loaded, i.e., to put in the primer.

Primer Another name for the fuse inserted into the vent.

Projectile A round of ammunition, usually, but not always, referring to round shot.

Prolonge A long, strong rope that was run from the trail of the piece to the limber and allowed the gun to be displaced rapidly without "limbering up." It had a strong metal hook at one end and was generally between 35 and 40 feet in length . It was mostly used in rough terrain or under fire. Some authorities state that when French guns unlimbered and went into action, the *prolonge* was always attached to the guns in case of emergency. On reflection, this would seem an odd procedure to perform regularly, as it might hamper the gun crew and perhaps limit the traversing ability of the gun if they had to chance aiming points, as did Senarmont's crews at Friedland when attacked by Russian cavalry on the left flank. This was another tool invented by Gribeauval, and it greatly enhanced the battlefield mobility of the guns.

Proof   Testing the gun tube to see if it is serviceable by firing the amount of powder at which a piece is rated.

Pouch   A case made of brown "stout" leather, with a flap, in which the round was carried from the caisson to the piece, the pouch being slung over one shoulder and carried at the side of the designated cannoneer. Also known as a *havresac* or *gargoussier*.

Prime   To prime a piece was the process of clearing the vent, piercing the powder bag, and inserting the primer into the vent and powder bag. The piece was then "primed" and ready for firing.

Projectile   A round of ammunition of any type, though usually referred to as "roundshot."

Quadrant   See "Gunner's quadrant."

Quadrate   To ensure that a gun tube is seated properly and evenly on its carriage. Today this is called "leveling the trunnions."

Quoil   A rope laid and stored in a ring.

Quoin   A wooden, wedge-shaped lever that was placed under the breech of the gun tube to raise or lower it. A modification of this simple tool was used by the Austrian, Russian, and Prussian artillery of the period: the quoin was made much thinner, and it was combined with a screw apparatus which moved it along a wooden track on the carriage under the gun tube to raise or lower the tube. It was an improvement on the simple quoin, but it was not as advanced or as accurate as the elevating screw used by either the French or the British.

Ram   The process of pushing the round down the bore of the piece to the chamber, in preparation for firing. This was down with a rammer (q.v.) or rammer staff, and the motion was quick and usually carried out by two men.

Rammer   A long pole-like tool with a wooden, flat head at the end used to ram the round down the gun tube. Some had a sponge on the other end of the rammer staff, though, notably, that for the Gribeauval 4-pounder did not.

Range   The distance from the piece or battery to the position where the round first touches the ground. Also referred to as the "first graze."

Recoil   The sudden and very violent movement rearward that a piece performs when fired. As there was no recoil mechanism on smoothbore artillery, the entire piece recoiled when fired, requiring it to be manhandled back into position after each shot and relaid.

Red Bullet   Hot shot (q.v.).

Reeds   Probably the best primer material for the period. Usually swamp reeds, and cut to length specifics for the vents of the pieces, they could be stored for up to ten years before use. They were cut flat at one end and pointed at the other, the pointed end being that which was inserted into the pierced powder bag.

Reinforce   A raised ridge on the outside of the gun tube, supposedly strengthening the gun. In later models, such as the 6- and 12-pounder of the Système AN XI, they were abolished, except for one near the muzzle, it being found that they were unnecessary. The first reinforce—*le premier renfort*—was near the breech, and was intended to make the piece stronger there in order to resist the force of the powder explosion when a round was fired. The second reinforce—*le second renfort*—started where the first ended, was somewhat smaller, and was located in the area of the trunnions and handles.

Report   The loud noise made by a piece when fired.

Retardation   The opposite of acceleration (q.v.).

Rimbases   The base of the trunnions, where they meet the gun tube, intended to give extra strength to the trunnions. Interestingly, they were not evident on English cannon.

Rings   Round pieces of iron placed at different places on the gun carriage to which various tools, such as the *prolonge*, could be secured.

Ricochet Solid shot was sometimes used as bounding shot by firing along a trajectory that would cause the round to bounce along the ground on the way to the target. This actually increased the range of the piece by as much as 100 percent, and caused terrible damage to a target of troops in formation. It also unnerved its target, for though the enemy could see the round coming, he did not know where it would hit. Unnerving against the best troops, it could cause panic among green troops. The rounds never bounced or "ricocheted" along a straight path.

Round One piece of ammunition.

Sabot The wooden base attached to a round of ammunition that replaced wadding and also stabilized the round in the tube. This wooden shoe was fitted to the caliber of the ammunition.

Sachet A small bag of grapeshot.

Salute The firing of artillery in honor of a person of importance, real or otherwise.

Salvo A round fired from all the guns of a company or battery, ideally simultaneously and on command.

Searcher A long-handled tool used to find defects on the inside of a gun tube (bore), generally employed when proving a piece of ordnance. In the French service, this was replaced by a new tool, also called the cat, which was invented by Gribeauval.

Separate loading Ammunition loaded by first ramming the powder bag, and then the projectile, instead of having both parts made up into a single cartridge.

Serve To load and fire the piece "with promptitude and correctness." Good artillery was said to be "well served."

Shot A general term for all artillery ammunition.

Shell A hollow ball filled with explosive, and exploded by a wooden pre-cut fuse.

Shrapnel Spherical case shot. A British invention and "secret weapon," developed by Henry Shrapnel.

Side arms A general term for the accoutrements used to serve the gun, for example handspikes, rammers, and sponges.

Siflement The sound of a round of ammunition traveling through the air on its way to the target. The term's literal translation is "the noise of a whistle."

Sight In short, gunnery.

Solid shot Round shot.

Souffler As in *souffler les canons*, to scale a piece of ordnance. To accomplish this, a small charge of gunpowder is fired from the gun to clean it.

Spent A round is said to be "spent" when it has gone past the range at which it can penetrate a target—though it could still cause discomfort.

Spike To render a piece of ordnance unable to fire. This was usually done by hammering a spike, or large nail, down the vent.

Split trail See "Bracket," "Galloper."

Sponge (Also spunge.) The lambswool brush used to swab (clean) out the bore after a round was fired. It also cooled down the tube, so as not to ignite the next round of ammunition prematurely.

Surbande Capsquares (q.v.).

Swing The middle horse team in a six-horse arrangement, the animals harnessed in pairs.

Tampion A wooden muzzle-plug inserted in the bore when a gun was not in use.

Tertiate Judging the strength of a piece of artillery by the thickness of the metal of the gun tube.

Theodolite An engineer's or artilleryman's instrument for judging distance, usually set up on a tripod and looking like a small telescope. It was (and still is) also used in surveying. The modern equivalent is called an aiming circle.

Throw Forcing an object to go from one place to another. In artillery, "throwing" a shell is firing it from the piece. "Throw weight" is thus the weight of the round being fired from the piece.

Thumbstall A leather covering for the thumb used by a cannoneer for "thumbing the vent." It protected the thumb from the hot tube after it had been fired. Thumbing a hot vent without a thumbstall could sear a man's digit to the bone.

Thumbpiece   See "Thumbstall."

Tir   The explosion and firing of a piece in a certain direction.

Toise   A measurement of distance equal to a little over six feet.

Touchhole   See "vent."

Traces   Harness for the horse teams.

Trail   The end of the piece that was attached to the limber.

Train   The drivers of the battalions and companies specifically formed and trained to drive the horse teams that pull the artillery vehicles and guns; the artillery train. There were also supply trains, engineer trains, and pontoon trains.

Trajectory   The path of a projectile in flight.

Transom   Pieces of wood that held the brackets together. Generally speaking, there were three transoms on each gun carriage—one at the trail, which was pierced for the pintle, one roughly in the middle of the carriage, and one at the other end.

Traversing plates   The iron plates hammered to the trail of the piece from which the handspikes were used to traverse it.

Traverse   To move the gun tube from right to left (or vice-versa) by moving the trail of the piece. This was done with handspikes and manpower.

Troop   The British term for battery in a horse artillery outfit.

Trousseau   A piece of wood in the shape of a cone, used in the casting of cannon.

Trunnion   The cylindrical projections from the side of the tube that fit in the trunnion plates cut into the brackets, holding the gun tube in the carriage as well as allowing it to be elevated and depressed.

Trunnion plate   The cut sections in the brackets of the piece into which the trunnions were placed to hold the tube in the carriage. They were usually reinforced with iron.

Tulip   The muzzle swell at the end of the gun tube.

Tumbrels   Two-wheeled, covered ammunition carts.

Vent   The hole drilled at an angle to the muzzle in the top of the breech into which the primer was placed before the piece was fired.

Vent field   An English artillery term meaning the section of the vent that extended to the first reinforce astragal.

Ventre   In artillery, when a gun tube is not mounted on its carriage, but is lying flat on the ground. Literally, "belly."

Vienna pound   Measure of weight equivalent to 0.56 kilograms. Heavier than the Nuremberg pound, it was not, however, used as the artillery measure in Austrian service. From the German *Wiener Pfund*.

Volley   The act of firing all the pieces of a battery at once. Something akin to a salvo.

Wad   Rags, hay, or straw rammed in before and after the charge and round to hold the powder and ball in place in the chamber. Also "wadding." Replaced by the sabot, or "wooden shoe."

Wheel   The pair of horses closest to the caisson or limber that made up the gun team. These animals were usually the strongest and steadiest pair in the gun team.

Windage   The distance inside the gun tube between the round and the wall of the bore. The smaller the distance, the greater the accuracy.

Worm   A long-handled tool with a corkscrew-like tip, used to extract excess material out of the bore.

Wurst Wagon   A modified gun caisson, used by some horse artillery units and especially by the Austrian cavalry batteries, upon which gunners would sit when traveling or displacing. The French did not use them after the Revolutionary Wars, all their horse artillerymen being individually mounted. German *Wurst-Wagen*.

Index

Page references in **bold type** refer to illustrations

B

M

N

O

P

R